The Art of History

Trends in Classics – Supplementary Volumes

Edited by
Franco Montanari and Antonios Rengakos

Scientific Committee
Alberto Bernabé · Margarethe Billerbeck
Claude Calame · Philip R. Hardie · Stephen J. Harrison
Stephen Hinds · Richard Hunter · Christina Kraus
Giuseppe Mastromarco · Gregory Nagy
Theodore D. Papanghelis · Giusto Picone
Kurt Raaflaub · Bernhard Zimmermann

Volume 41

The Art of History

Literary Perspectives on Greek
and Roman Historiography

Edited by Vasileios Liotsakis and Scott Farrington

DE GRUYTER

ISBN 978-3-11-061173-1
e-ISBN (PDF) 978-3-11-049605-5
e-ISBN (EPUB) 978-3-11-049329-0
ISSN 1868-4785

Library of Congress Cataloging-in-Publication Data
A CIP catalog record for this book has been applied for at the Library of Congress.

Bibliographic Information published by the Deutsche Nationalbibliothek
The Deutsche Nationalbibliothek lists this publication in the Deutsche Nationalbibliografie;
detailed bibliographic data are available in the Internet at http://dnb.dnb.de.

© 2018 Walter de Gruyter GmbH, Berlin/Boston
This volume is text- and page-identical with the hardback published in 2016.
Logo: Christopher Schneider, Laufen
Printing: CPI books GmbH, Leck

♾ Printed on acid-free paper
Printed in Germany

www.degruyter.com

Foreword

The essays in this volume represent the proceedings of a conference entitled *Science/Fiction/History: The Literary in Classical Historiography* that convened in Athens on September 11–12, 2014 under the aegis of the Aristotle University of Thessaloniki. The conference took as its focus the stylistic and narrative qualities of Greek and Roman historiography and how ancient authors use those qualities to draw or blur the lines between literary and historical prose. The editors would like to thank all who participated in the conference, particularly our keynote speakers, Timothy Rood (St. Hugh's College, Oxford), and Kostas Vlassopoulos (University of Crete). We would also like to thank Craige Champion for providing the introduction to this volume and I.M. Konstantakos for offering his help in the indices. Furthermore, we thank Voula Nikolopoulou and Marina Korovessi for their help and hard work ensuring that the conference operated smoothly. We are grateful also for the financial support we received from Axia College, Athens. Finally, we would like to thank the editors of *Trends in Classics*, Antonios Rengakos and Franco Montanari and our anonymous readers. The volume was much improved by their guidance and advice.

Vasileios Liotsakis
Scott Farrington

Table of Contents

Craige B. Champion
Introduction —— 1

I Fifth-Century Greek Historiography

Giulia Donelli
Herodotus and Greek Lyric Poetry —— 11

Ioannis M. Konstantakos
Cambyses and the Sacred Bull (Hdt. 3.27–29 and 3.64): History and Legend —— 37

Vasileios Liotsakis
Narrative Defects in Thucydides and the Development of Ancient Greek Historiography —— 73

Vera Mariantonia Grossi
Thucydides and Poetry. Ancient Remarks on the Vocabulary and Structure of Thucydides' *History* —— 99

Stefan Feddern
Thucydides' *Methodenkapitel* in the Light of the Ancient Evidence —— 119

Edward M. Harris
Alcibiades, the Ancestors, Liturgies, and the Etiquette of Addressing the Athenian Assembly —— 145

II Greek Narrators of the Past Under Rome

Scott Farrington
The Tragic Phylarchus —— 159

Mario Baumann
"No One Can Look at Them Without Feeling Pity": συμπάθεια and the Reader in Diodorus' *Bibliotheke* —— 183

Eugénie Fournel
Dream Narratives in Plutarch's *Lives:* The Place of Fiction in Biography —— 199

III Roman Historiography

Suzanne Adema
Encouraging Troops, Persuading Narratees: Pre-Battle Exhortations in Caesar's *Bellum Gallicum* as a Narrative Device —— 219

Philip Waddell
Carthago Deleta: Alternate Realities and Meta-History in Appian's *Libyca* —— 241

Katie Low
Histories Repeated? The Mutinies in *Annals* 1 and Tacitean Self-Allusion —— 253

Pauline Duchêne
Suetonius' Construction of His Historiographical *auctoritas* —— 271

Contributors —— 289

Index nominum et rerum —— 293

Index locorum —— 307

Craige B. Champion
Introduction

On the long view, the study of ancient Greek and Roman historiography in the secular western tradition has undergone enormous transformation. Bewitched by the promise of the scientific revolution, early modern European thinkers vaunted the ancients, and above all the Greeks, in terms of their critical acumen and penetrating reasoning powers. Greek intellectuals, and by extension the ancient Greeks in general, were seen as objective and incisive rationalists to be imitated. The Presocratics were the Fathers of Science, and at least from the time of Winckelmann, Greek sculptors set the standard for beauty and perfection in the plastic arts with their severe classicizing style, an assessment leading to Neoclassicism and the credo of art as imitation (*Nachahmung*). With underlying presumptions such as these, the defenders of the "ancients" in the late-seventeenth and early-eighteenth century "Battle of the Books," or *querelle des Anciens et des Modernes*, and the so-called Founding Fathers of the American republic, steeped in classical learning and using Greek and Latin texts as models, could see ancient Greek and Roman elites as kindred spirits.[1] There were certainly some objections to that notion, going back at least as far as Giambattista Vico and Friedrich A. Wolf, but they did little to shake the idea for European and American intellectuals in the early modern period that ancient Greek and Roman elites were like themselves.[2] Subsequent scholarly trends have eroded that conviction, with E.R. Dodds' *The Greeks and the Irrational* being an important signpost along the way (at least in the Anglophone scholarly universe), and in the field of ancient Greek historiography F.M. Cornford's *Thucydides Mythistoricus* did much to unsettle the notion that ancient Greek historians approached their task with the conceptual underpinnings of a modern social scientist.[3]

Although seemingly moribund, such ideas have been in a long process of dying. R.G. Collingwood, for example, condemned Livy on positivistic grounds in his famous study, *The Idea of History*, posthumously published in 1946. Livy is passed over without much discussion in that book, but Collingwood

---

[1] On the "Battle of the Books," see Levine 1991, esp. 267–413; cf. Levine 1977; Levine 1999. On American political thinkers and the lessons from ancient Greece and Rome, see Bailyn 1967, 22–26; cf. Richard 1994.
[2] I have tried to counter such lingering scholarly presumptions regarding politics and religion in the Roman Republic in the book *The Peace of the Gods: Elite Religious Practices in the Middle Roman Republic*, forthcoming with the Princeton University Press.
[3] For the lofty goal of objectivity in the academic discipline of history, see Novick 1988.

did note that Livy "pitches the scientific claims of his work very low. He makes no claim to original research or original method. He writes as if his chance of standing out from the ruck of historical writers depended chiefly on his literary qualities." In Collingwood's mind, Livy lacked the intellectual and conceptual foundations for proper history writing. He observed, "[Livy] does his best to be critical; but the methodical criticism practiced by every modern historian was still not invented. Here was a mass of legends: all he could do with them was decide, as best he could, whether or not they were trustworthy." And he goes on, "There is here only the very crudest attempt at historical criticism. Presented with a great wealth of traditional material, the historian takes it all at its face value; he makes no attempt to discover how the tradition has grown up and through what various distorting media it has reached him; he therefore cannot reinterpret a tradition, that is, explain it as meaning something other than it explicitly says. He has to take it or leave it, and, on the whole, Livy's tendency is to accept his tradition and repeat it in good faith."[4]

The modern assessment of several of the historians treated in this volume – Herodotus, Diodorus, and Appian – frequently has run along similar lines as Collingwood's critique of Livy. In the case of Herodotus, Detlev Fehling's *Die Quellenangaben bei Herodot* (1971) – updated and revised in an English language edition in 1989 titled *Herodotus and His Sources: Citation, Invention, and Narrative Art* – revived the source-criticism skepticism of the earlier scholarship of A.H. Sayce and H. Panofsky. Fehling's book has come to be regarded as the foundational document for "The Liar School of Herodotus."[5] For many classicists today who are interested in historiography, the criticism of any such approach is that it is entirely wrong-footed, insofar as it fails to make the attempt to understand ancient Greek and Roman historiography on its own conceptual and methodological terms.

For Herodotus, the most influential counterpoint to the complaint that Herodotus fails as an historian by not being sufficiently objective, critical, scientific, and what have you, is F. Hartog's *Le miroir de Hérodote: Essai sur la représentation de l'autre* (1980), translated into English as *The Mirror of Herodotus: The Representation of the Other in the Writing of History* (1988). This sophisticated book is a penetrating study of Herodotus' representation of Scythians in Book 4. Hartog combined a structuralist approach to show how Herodotus constructs the "Other," with linguistic criticism and Reception Theory, which he uses to illumi-

---

[4] Quotations are from pp. 37–38 of the 1994 OUP paperback edition. For Livy and his use of Greek sources, see Champion 2014, 190–204.
[5] For a spirited reaction against Fehling's position, see Pritchett 1993.

nate Herodotus' technique for constructing a "rhetoric of otherness" for his ancient Greek readership.[6] The important point for this discussion is that Hartog's book is a highly theoretical literary analysis of Herodotus' text, and in contradistinction to Fehling, it is hardly concerned with the question as to whether Herodotus relayed historical events *wie es eigentlich gewesen ist*. Two of the essays directly concerning Herodotus in this volume nicely show the two orientations: Giulia Donelli's contribution is a literary study examining the interrelationship between Herodotean historiography and ancient Greek lyric poetry, and one of its main points is that both take independent stances vis-à-vis Homeric epic in order to establish their own authority and credibility.[7] Ioannis Konstantakos' chapter, on the other hand, engages with the question of the historicity of Herodotus' narrative in studying the historian's account of Cambyses and the Sacred Apis Bull (Hdt. 3.27–29 and 3.64), concluding that we have "historical legend" in this story, a "fictional narrative attached to a historical figure of the recent past."

Thucydides takes pride of place in any discussion of the ancient Greek and Roman historians as reliable guides for the historical reconstruction of past events. His analytical style and omniscient authorial stance impart to his work the impression of infallible accuracy and unimpeachable authority. Dionysius of Halicarnassus simply stated that Thucydides was "the greatest of all the historians" (*Th.* 2), and in more recent times Thucydides was hailed as the model *par excellence* for an objective, scientific historiography (and he is much in vogue with the Neorealist school of international relations theorists). But at least since Cornford's 1907 study, the picture has not been so simple. A.J. Woodman has called our attention to Thucydides' affinities with Homer, and W.R. Connor has argued that Thucydides' seemingly scientific, omniscient, and objective narrative style is an authorial posture, designed to establish the text's credibility at the same time as it evokes a profound emotional response from the reader.[8] Moreover, Thucydides apparently accepted the historicity of mythological figures such as Hellen, Minos, Itys, Procne, and Pandion (1.3–4; 2.29).

Like all ancient historians, Thucydides operates with a conceptual and methodological apparatus far different than that of any present-day historian. Nowhere is this more evident than in Thucydides' approach to reported speeches of his historical agents. In his famous methodological pronouncement (1.21–22), Thucydides essentially says that he will make his speakers say what the his-

---

[6] For push-back against "othering" in classical texts, emphasizing instead accommodation and assimilation, see Gruen 2011.
[7] On the question of authority and credibility in ancient Greek and Roman historiography, see above all Marincola 1997.
[8] Woodman 1988, ch. 1; Connor 1984.

torico-political situation demanded of them to say, in order to underscore the real issues at stake for the reader. Two of the essays in the present volume refine our understanding of this passage in particular and Thucydides' *History* generally. Vera Grossi shows how ancient commentators and scholiasts drew parallels between the poets, primarily Homer and Pindar, and Thucydides. The scholiasts worked hard to root out poetic, grand words in Thucydides borrowed from Homer. They did not criticize Thucydides for the use of elevated, poetic diction, but they rather approved or disapproved of the degree to which he did so. Moreover, both Thucydides and Herodotus (see Donelli's contribution to this volume), along with the Greek lyric poets, could take issue with Homeric epic in order to establish their authority and credibility. Stefan Feddern's paper looks at the programmatic statement at 1.21 from an ancient literary-critical perspective, and through painstaking philological analysis he offers two propositions: Thucydides' speeches are "speeches in character"; and these speeches, which broadly outline the character of the speaker in question, are motivated by the events of the war. Vasileios Liotsakis' wide-ranging study takes up Thucydides' narrative craft, and he shows how the historian emplots events with both informative and interpretative aims.

The conceptual underpinnings and methodological presumptions of ancient Greek and Roman historiography, then, were radically different from those of historians working today.[9] It has become a commonplace to say that ancient Greek and Roman historiography is best understood as a literary genre, with the closest of ties to rhetoric, rather than as a prototypical social science. In this connection mention has already been made of A.J. Woodman's *Rhetoric in Classical Historiography*, which provocatively makes the case for a large conceptual chasm between ancient and modern historiography. This is the "enormous transformation" with which this Introduction began. Other noteworthy books exemplifying this approach are T.P. Wiseman's *Clio's Cosmetics: Three Studies in Greco-Roman Literature* (1979), Christina Kraus' *The Limits of Historiography: Genre and Narrative in Ancient Historical Texts* (1999), and Jonas Grethlein's *Experience and Teleology in Ancient Historiography: "Futures Past" from Herodotus to Augustine* (2013).[10]

We may understand the literary-analytical approach to ancient Greek and Roman historiography as part and parcel of sweeping currents in academia generally, and in the historical profession particularly, that have challenged any

---

[9] For an overview, see Champion 2013, 3252–62.
[10] It would be remiss of me not to mention here Momigliano 1987, though its approach is more traditional.

form of positivism and the very notion that it is possible to *do history*. And here I am thinking of theorists such as Jacques Derrida and the post-structuralists, and critics of historical literature, such as Hayden White and Dominick LaCapra. In the historical profession per se, we can think of these developments in the large context of the "linguistic turn" generally. But when we regard ancient Greek and Roman historiography as a branch of literature, or even as akin to rhetoric, have we gone too far? It has become fashionable in some circles of the classics community to deny positivistic virtues of the Greek and Latin historians, or even to assert rather superciliously that questions about the reliability of ancient historical texts for historical reconstructions are misguided, and perhaps uninteresting. But is it wise to do so? Is there a chance that we are throwing the baby out with the bath water? J.E. Lendon, for one, thinks this is the case. He writes:

> This essay weeps at the intellectual motion this volume exemplifies: the triumph of what now masquerades as "Roman historiography," the academic study of the ancient Roman historians as a discipline sundered from Roman history, the study of what happened in ancient Rome and why. Its narrower target is the species of scholarship about the Latin historians arising in T.P. Wiseman's *Clio's Cosmetics* of 1979 and A.J. Woodman's *Rhetoric and Classical Historiography* of 1988. This writing, grown considerable in the late 1990s and the current decade as the founders' stars attracted satellites, studies the Latin historians as literature. In the hunt for the historian's artistry or ideas, his concern with historical material – that body of "what happened in the past" that the historian was trying to convey – is either argued away or passed over. The Latin historian is constrained to become – depending on modern whimsy – a rhetorician, a dramatist, a novelist, or, in the late-summer bloom of academic narcissism, a postmodern literary critic. What the Latin historian is not allowed to be is what he chiefly thought he was: a teller of true tales about the past.

In the course of his lament, Lendon calls for a corrective: "[T]o understand the writing of Roman history not as free creation but as a constrained art – where the author practiced his creativity within a tight box of acknowledged fact, of the tradition upon which he drew, and of the audience's expectations – offers an escape from some of the more anachronistic and solipsistic of today's analyses of the Latin historians."[11]

Such claims about the historical reliability of ancient Greek and Roman historians can most easily be made for Polybius of Megalopolis (as well as for Thucydides). Polybius' text first became known in the Renaissance in Western Europe in the early fifteenth century. Since then, Polybius has regularly been

---

[11] Lendon 2009, quotations from 41 and 43. Cf. Lendon 2009, 53: "So the theoretical distinction between history and oratory was preserved, and the ancient concept of historical truth…was not significantly different from our own." For perceptive comments of the nature of "truth" in ancient conceptions, see Luce 1989.

regarded as an exemplar of correct historiographical method. His no-nonsense and unadorned prose style, much like that of Thucydides, can appear to be a prototype or an anticipation for historiographical rigor in the quest for accurately reconstructing events in the human past. And so Arnold Toynbee wrote how Polybius was "superhumanly objective," and he compared him with the towering figure of ancient Roman historical studies in the late eighteenth century, Edward Gibbon. More recently, G.A. Lehmann has been a staunch defender of Polybius' impartiality and objectivity as an historian.[12] As with Thucydides, so with Polybius, scholars have now come to appreciate the historian's literary qualities and narrative techniques, despite the fact that Polybius himself proclaims that he is not overly concerned with prose style and literary embellishment.[13] We have also begun to attend increasingly to Polybius' moral universe, the politics of his didacticism, and his manipulations with cultural and ethnic constructs.[14] Scott Farrington's chapter on Polybius explores the interrelationship of history and tragedy as literary genres, taking up the old chestnut of "tragic history." In examining the fragments of Polybius' rival Phylarchus, Farrington concludes that Polybius attacks Phylarchus for confusing the ends of history and tragedy, disapproving of Phylarchus' combination of the elements of tragedy, as traditionally conceived, in crafting his "tragic style."

Even Polybius, as Farrington shows, arouses the emotions of his readership, as for example in his account of the Roman destruction of Carthage.[15] Philip Waddell discusses this catastrophic event as an historiographical phenomenon, as it is reflected in Appian's *Libyca*. He argues for an "alternate reality" in paired speeches in Appian's account, in which Carthage is destroyed after the Second Punic War. Mario Baumann also studies emotions in ancient historiography, this time in a study of *sympatheia* in Diodorus' *Bibliotheke*. K.A. Low considers the interplay between the accounts of two insurrections in Tacitus' *Historiae* (Book 1) and *Annales* (Book 2), suggesting that negative emotional responses and the potential for civil unrest were built into the Principate from the very beginning, at least in Tacitus' retelling of imperial history. In addition to the papers of Waddell, Baumann, and Low, which all make contributions to the burgeoning interest in depictions of the emotions in ancient Greek and Roman literature, Roman historiography, elastically defined, is well served by Adema's examina-

---

[12] Toynbee 1965, 472 n. 2, 411, 504; Lehmann 1967.
[13] See Sacks 1981; for an excellent narratological study of Polybius' narration, see J. Davidson 1991; and for more formal matters of style, see de Foucault 1972.
[14] See Eckstein 1995; Champion 2004.
[15] See Plb. 36.5–7, with Champion 2004, 164–65. On the emotions in ancient Greek and Roman literary texts, see Cairns/Fulkerson 2015.

tion of the role of hortatory speeches in Latin war narratives, with special focus on Caesar's *Bellum Gallicum*, Duchêne's paper on the literary devices by which Suetonius establishes authorial credibility in the *Lives*, and Fournel's exploration of the relationship of biography and history in Plutarch's *Caesar and Pompey*, with particular attention given to dream narratives.

In concluding, let us return to the broad theme with which we began: ancient Greek and Roman history writing as a guide for a positivist historical reconstruction of events as opposed to ancient Greek and Roman historiography as a literary genre. The good news, to my mind, is that there is no need for us to decide. These are complementary, and not mutually exclusive, approaches. We would go far wide of the mark were we to see classical historiography as a prototypical, putatively objective social science, of a sort that would have pleased the likes of Leopold von Ranke, just as we would grotesquely err in viewing it as nothing but historical fantasy, à la Jorge Luis Borges. That said, the present volume offers a fine collection of essays that on the whole emphasize the literary dimensions of the ancient Greek and Roman historians, broadly conceived.[16] Enjoy reading these papers; there is much to learn in them.

Bibliography

Bailyn, B. (1967), *The Ideological Origins of the American Revolution*, Cambridge / London.
Bagnall, R.S. et al. (eds.) (2013), *The Encyclopedia of Ancient History*, vol. VI, Oxford / Malden.
Cairns, D. / Fulkerson, L. (eds.) (2015), *Emotions Between Greece and Rome*, London.
Champion, C.B. (2004), *Cultural Politics in Polybius's Histories*, Berkeley.
Champion, C.B. (2013), "Historiography, Greek and Roman," in: R.S. Bagnall et al. 2013, 3252–62.
Champion, C.B. (2014), "Livy and the Greek Historians from Herodotus to Dionysius: Soundings and Reflections," in: B. Mineo 2014, 190–204.
Champion, C.B. (forthcoming), *The Peace of the Gods. Elite Religious Practices in the Middle Roman Republic*, Princeton.
Collingwood, R.G. (1946), *The Idea of History. Edited by T.M. Knox*, Oxford.
Connor, W.R. (1984), *Thucydides*, Princeton.
Cornford, F.M. (1907), *Thucydides Mythistoricus*, London.
Davidson, J. (1991), "The Gaze in Polybius' *Histories*", in: *JRS* 81, 10–24.
de Foucault, J.A. (1972), *Recherches sur la langue et le style de Polybe*, Paris.
Dodds, E.R. (1957), *The Greeks and the Irrational*, Boston.
Eckstein, A.M. (1995), *Moral Vision in the Histories of Polybius*, Berkeley.

---

16 Edward Harris' contribution is an exception: its orientation is as much historical as it is historiographical.

Fehling, D. (1971), *Die Quellenangaben bei Herodot*, Berlin / New York.
Fehling, D. (1990), *Herodotus and His Sources. Citation, Invention, and Narrative Art*, Francis Cairns, Leeds.
Feldherr, A. (ed.) (2009), *The Cambridge Companion to the Roman Historians*, Cambridge / New York.
Grethlein, J. (2013), *Experience and Teleology in Ancient Historiography. "Futures Past" from Herodotus to Augustine*, Cambridge / New York.
Gruen, E.S. (2011), *Rethinking the Other in Antiquity*, Princeton.
Hartog, F. (1980), *Le miroir de Hérodote. Essai sur la représentation de l'autre*, Gallimard.
Hartog, F. (1988), *The Mirror of Herodotus. The Representation of the Other in the Writing of History*, Janet Lloyd, Berkeley.
Kraus, C.S. (1999), *The Limits of Historiography. Genre and Narrative in Ancient Historical Texts*, Leiden.
Lehmann, G.A. (1967), *Untersuchungen zur historischen Glaubwürdigkeit des Polybios*, Münster.
Lendon, J.E. (2009), "Historians Without History: Against Roman Historiography," in: A. Feldherr 2009, 41–61.
Levine, J.M. (1977), *Dr. Woodward's Shield: History, Science, and Satire in Augustan England*, Berkeley.
Levine, J.M. (1991), *The Battle of the Books. History and Literature in the Augustan Age*, Ithaca.
Levine, J.M. (1999), *Between Ancients and Moderns. Baroque Culture in Restoration England*, New Haven / London.
Luce, T.J. (1989), "Ancient Views on the Causes of Bias in Historical Writing," in: *CPh* 84, 16–31.
Marincola, J. (1997), *Authority and Tradition in Ancient Historiography*, Cambridge.
Mineo, B. (ed.) (2014), *Blackwell's Companion to Livy*, Oxford / Malden.
Momigliano, A. (1987), *Essays in Ancient and Modern Historiography*, Oxford.
Novick, P. (1988), *That Noble Dream. The "Objectivity Question" and the American Historical Profession*, Cambridge.
Pritchett, W.K. (1993), *The Liar School of Herodotus*, Amsterdam.
Richard, C.J. (1994), *The Founders and the Classics. Greece, Rome, and the American*, Cambridge.
Sacks, K.S. (1981), *Polybius on the Writing of History*, Berkeley.
Toynbee, A.J. (1965), *Hannibal's Legacy*, vol. II, London / New York / Toronto.
Wiseman, T.P. (1979), *Clio's Cosmetics. Three Studies in Greco-Roman Literature*, Leicester.
Woodman, A.J. (1988), *Rhetoric in Classical Historiography. Four Studies*, London / Portland.

I Fifth-Century Greek Historiography

Giulia Donelli
Herodotus and Greek Lyric Poetry

Abstract: In this paper, I investigate some aspects of Herodotus' relationship with Greek lyric poetry. First, I address the historiographer's Homeric stance, interpreting it as possibly representing a 'lyric inheritance' in historiography. My focus on Homer's importance to the development of prose historiography resonates with V. M. Grossi's analysis of Thucydides' relation to poetry, and has implications for the study of the construction of historiographical authority, the subject of P. Duchêne's contribution to this volume. My article further refers to the issue of authority in surveying some Herodotean argumentative strategies that are usually regarded as betraying an influence from the Hippocratic Corpus, but appear to be already attested, *in nuce*, in Greek lyric poetry. Finally, I examine some Herodotean narratives that concern prominent historical figures and feature folktale motifs, and their interactions with extant lyric poems. Other contributions to this volume, particularly those of I. M. Konstantakos and V. Liotsakis, share an interest in the narrative patterns/models that Herodotus borrowed from other traditions and adapted for his own historiographical account.

Introduction

This paper[1] aims to address some issues of Herodotus' relationship with Greek lyric[2] poetry, a complex relationship that Herodotus articulates both explicitly and implicitly. The most obvious and evident examples accounting for the prominence of lyric poetry in the *Histories* are Herodotus' explicit references to lyric poets and poems. He names a total of nine lyric poets,[3] three of whom appear, significantly, within the first thirty chapters of book 1. Of these three, Solon is an especially prominent character even beyond the scope of the first book, not so much because he is mentioned again elsewhere, but because his speech to Croesus (Hdt. 1.30–2) programmatically introduces themes that will recur con-

---

[1] This paper represents an overview of themes, relevant to the relationship between Herodotus and Greek lyric poetry, that I discuss in greater detail in my PhD dissertation.
[2] The term lyric will be used, throughout this discussion, in its comprehensive sense, thus as including also elegy and iambus, cf. Budelmann 2009b, 2 f.
[3] Archilochus (Hdt. 1.12), Arion (Hdt. 1.23), Solon (Hdt. 1.29–34, 2.177, 5.113), Sappho (Hdt. 2.135), Pindar (Hdt. 3.38), Anacreon (Hdt. 3.121), Alcaeus (Hdt. 5.95), Simonides (Hdt. 5.102, 7.228), and Lasus (Hdt. 7.6).

sistently throughout the whole of Herodotus' oeuvre.⁴ There are explicit references to lyric poems too: after naming Pindar, Herodotus refers explicitly to the Pindaric poem preserved by fragment 169a S.-M. (Hdt. 3.38), and in book 7 we find three epigrams likely of Simonidean authorship.⁵

Besides these explicit cases, however, it is possible to think of further levels of engagement, on Herodotus' part, with the Greek lyric tradition: these will represent the main focus of the present discussion. In particular, in light of the fundamental role played by epic poetry as a genre *against* which other genres developed,⁶ I will first explore Herodotus' attitude towards Homer in order to propose that the historiographer's indebtedness to and engagement with Homer reflect his adoption of a 'lyric stance' towards the epic tradition. Secondly, I will consider some Herodotean argumentative strategies that are usually regarded as showing a sophistic influence of the kind attested in the Hippocratic Corpus, but could also be interpreted as having their roots in the Greek lyric tradition. Finally, I will examine three case studies that reveal suggestive parallels between some episodes of the *Histories* and lyric poetry in order to cast light on Herodotus' treatment of narratives presenting folktale motifs.

1 Herodotus and Homer: a 'lyric stance' towards epic poetry

Engagement with Homer appears to have been unavoidable for anyone setting out to claim authority on the past or to handle historical matters in antiquity. This can be inferred from a number of pieces of evidence,⁷ including poems and fragments of poems in the extant Greek lyric corpus. Within this corpus, some elegiac pieces of poetry that display 'epicizing features',⁸ at times com-

---

[4] On this story in Herodotus and its connections to Athenian greed in Thucydides see Liotsakis in this volume.
[5] For discussion, cf. e.g. Molyneux 1992, 175–9; Vannicelli 2007, 95–103.
[6] Graziosi/Haubold 2009, 95f.
[7] For evidence provided by sources other than the lyric corpus, cf. e.g. Hdt. 5.94 with Marcozzi/Sinatra/Vannicelli 1994, 167 and Cingano 1985; Hdt. 7.161; Arist. *Rh.* 1375b 29–30 with Kim 2010, 26. See Grossi in this volume for ancient scholarship on Thucydides' relation to poetry and his reputation as an emulator of Homer.
[8] Cf. e.g. the epic colouring in Mimn. frr. 13a and 14 W², with Grethlein 2010, 55. For epicizing features in Archilochus' 'Telephos Elegy' (*P. Oxy.* LXIX 4708) see D'Alessio 2006, 21 and Nobili 2009, 229f. For Simon. frr. 10–18 W² as a "mini epic in elegiacs", see West 1993, 5.

bined with others often described as forerunning prose historiography, offer an obvious example.⁹

·While this kind of engagement operates on an implicit level, some lyric poems account also for cases of *explicit* references to and criticism of a clearly identifiable source. For example, a tendency to take issue with Homer, selecting him as a particular rival, characterizes some poems by Xenophanes (e.g. frr. 2, 10–13 D.-K.), while Hipponax's frequent parody of Homeric epic (e.g. frr. 74, 77, 128 W²) has been interpreted as representing the poet's claim "to be the Homer of his trade".¹⁰

As will become clearer in the light of further relevant examples discussed below, the Homeric stance adopted by most lyric poets appears to be characterized by a high degree of ambiguity: if Homeric epic represents a fundamental intertext for many pieces of poetry, it is also a tradition against which lyric poets had to claim authority for themselves. It is in this sense that I consider Herodotus' Homeric stance to represent, in a way, a 'lyric inheritance' in historiography. In order to support this interpretation, I shall explore two out of the seven cases¹¹ where Herodotus engages openly with Homer.

The 'Helen Story' (Hdt. 2.113–20)

Hdt. 2.113: Ἔλεγον δέ μοι οἱ ἱρέες ἱστορέοντι τὰ περὶ Ἑλένην γενέσθαι ὧδε. Ἀλέξανδρον ἁρπάσαντα Ἑλένην ἐκ Σπάρτης ἀποπλέειν ἐς τὴν ἑωυτοῦ· καί μιν, ὡς ἐγένετο ἐν τῷ Αἰγαίῳ, ἐξῶσται ἄνεμοι ἐκβάλλουσι ἐς τὸ Αἰγύπτιον πέλαγος, ἐνθεῦτεν δέ (οὐ γὰρ ἀνίει τὰ πνεύματα) ἀπικνέεται ἐς Αἴγυπτον κτλ.

When I inquired of the priests, they told me that this was the story of Helen. After carrying off Helen from Sparta, Alexandrus sailed away for his own country; violent winds caught him into the Egyptian sea; and from there (as the wind did not let up) he came to Egypt [...].¹²

Hdt. 2.116: Ἑλένης μὲν ταύτην ἄπιξιν παρὰ Πρωτέα ἔλεγον οἱ ἱρέες γενέσθαι. δοκέει δέ μοι καὶ Ὅμηρος τὸν λόγον τοῦτον πυθέσθαι· ἀλλ' οὐ γὰρ ὁμοίως ἐς τὴν ἐποποιίην εὐπρεπὴς ἦν τῷ ἑτέρῳ τῷ περ ἐχρήσατο, [ἐς ὃ] μετῆκε αὐτόν, δηλώσας ὡς καὶ τοῦτον ἐπίσταιτο τὸν

---

9 These comprise e.g. the attention paid to the search for causes to historical events (e.g. Call. frr. 2–2a W², with Mazzarino 1966, 38; Mimn. fr. 9 W²) or to the chronology of events (e.g. Tyrt. 5 W²), the use of speech (e.g. Mimn. 13a.1 W²), the display of a moral slant (e.g. Mimn. fr. 9 W², with Mazzarino 1966, 40–1; see also Bowie 2001, 64) and so forth. Cf. above all Bowie 2001 and 2010; Lulli 2011.
10 Carey 2009, 164.
11 Hdt. 2.23; 2.53; 2.116; 2.117; 4.29; 4.32; 7.161.
12 All English translations of the Herodotean text quoted in this paper are by Godley 1920–24.

λόγον. δῆλον δέ, κατά περ ἐποίησε ἐν Ἰλιάδι [...] πλάνην τὴν Ἀλεξάνδρου [...]. ἐπιμέμνηται δὲ αὐτοῦ ἐν Διομήδεος ἀριστηίη· λέγει δὲ τὰ ἔπεα ὧδε· [Il. 6.289–92]. ἐπιμέμνηται δὲ καὶ αὐτοῦ ἐν Ὀδυσσείῃ ἐν τοῖσδε τοῖσι ἔπεσι· [Od. 4.227–30]. Καὶ τάδε ἕτερα πρὸς Τηλέμαχον Μενέλεως λέγει· [Od. 5.351–2].

This, the priests said, was how Helen came to Proteus. And, in my opinion, Homer knew this story, too; but seeing that it was not so well suited to epic poetry as the tale of which he made use, he rejected it, showing that he knew it. This is apparent from the passage in the *Iliad* [...] where he relates the wanderings of Alexander [...]. This is in the story of the Prowess of Diomedes, where the verses run as follows: [Il. 6.289–92]. He mentions it in the *Odyssey* also: [Od. 4.227–30]. And again Menelaus says to Telemachus: [Od. 5.351–2].

Hdt. 2.118: Εἰρομένου δέ μευ τοὺς ἱρέας εἰ μάταιον λόγον λέγουσι οἱ Ἕλληνες τὰ περὶ Ἴλιον γενέσθαι ἢ οὔ, ἔφασαν πρὸς ταῦτα τάδε, ἱστορίῃσι φάμενοι εἰδέναι παρ' αὐτοῦ Μενέλεω κτλ.

But, when I asked the priests whether the Greek account of what happened at Troy were idle or not, they gave me the following answer, saying that they had inquired and knew from Menelaus himself [...].

Hdt. 2.120: Ταῦτα μὲν Αἰγυπτίων οἱ ἱρέες ἔλεγον. ἐγὼ δὲ τῷ λόγῳ τῷ περὶ Ἑλένης λεχθέντι καὶ αὐτὸς προστίθεμαι, τάδε ἐπιλεγόμενος κτλ.

The Egyptians' priests said this, and I myself believe their story about Helen, for I reason thus [...].

These passages are part of the long excursus (Hdt. 2.113–20) on Helen's stay in Egypt during the Trojan War, where Herodotus reports a version of the story different from that of the *Iliad*. He presents it as the result of his personal interviews with the Egyptian priests, and as more authoritative and reliable than the Homeric version for two reasons. The first is the authority and the antiquity of the informants – who derive their information "from an eye-witness source (Menelaus)".[13] The second is the implausibility of the canonical Homeric narrative, which is questioned on the basis of an argument of probability.[14] The histor iographer's first move, therefore, appears to be aimed at criticizing Homer by putting forward the 'true' version of the events, thereby claiming authority for himself.

As far as this critical attitude is concerned, it is striking to notice how the 'Helen Story' similarly occurs in some lyric poems as the starting point for claims

---

13 Kim 2010, 32.
14 Kim 2010, 32; Nicolai 2012, 637–8.

of authority and as a means "to help define the speaker's persona"[15] and "the speaker's intent".[16] In his *Palinode* (*PMGF* 192 = 91 Finglass), Stesichorus famously declares that Helen 'of Troy' never in fact 'went on the well-benched ships, nor reached the citadel of Troy' (οὐδ' ἔβας ἐν νηυσὶν ἐϋσσέλμοις, / οὐδ' ἵκεο πέργαμα Τροίας). Alcaeus, in fr. 42 V, polemically contrasts Helen with Thetis. In Sappho's fr. 16 V, Helen is held up as proof in support of the speaker's professed value system – i.e. that 'the most beautiful', 'the best' (κάλλιστον, line 3), is defined by the 'desire' felt for it (κῆν' ὄττω τις ἔραται, lines 3–4)[17] – in polemical opposition (ἔγω δέ, line 3) to other value systems presented in the opening priamel.[18] Finally, Ibycus' re-telling (*PMGF* S151), in *praeteritio* of the story of Helen and the Trojan War, has been interpreted as a criticism of Homer's inadequacy and lack of historical accuracy[19] in a poem that "self-consciously differentiates itself from Homeric narrative".[20]

What these four lyric songs have in common is that the display of claims of authority is based – to different degrees and with different purposes – on an ambiguous distancing from Homeric epic. The starting point of these claims of authority is represented, in all four cases, by the 'Helen Story'; consequently, Herodotus' choice of the very same material as the starting point for his "sustained engagement with the question of Homer's historical reliability"[21] could be interpreted as suggesting his adoption of a 'lyric' stance towards epic.

Nevertheless, the historiographer's engagement with Homer in this same excursus is not limited to a destructive critique. He also undertakes the task of rehabilitating the poet by maintaining that Homer knew the true version of the story but remained faithful to his epic poetic purposes.[22] Herodotus supports this interpretation by means of three Homeric quotations (*Il.* 6.289–92; *Od.* 4.227–30; *Od.* 4.351–2). In the process, he re-establishes Homer as an authority aware of the 'historical truth' (Hdt. 2.116). This passage, therefore, reveals a high degree of ambiguity in Herodotus' attitude towards the epic poet, and this attitude can be compared to what we find in other crucially ambiguous lyric passages. A case in point is Simonides' Plataea poem (frr. 10–18 W²):

---

[15] Boedeker 2012a, 65.
[16] Boedeker 2012a, 82.
[17] Boedeker 2012a, 74. Cf. e.g. also Winkler 2002, 54.
[18] On the relationship between this poem and Herodotus' prologue, itself interpreted as a priamel, see Pelliccia 1992, 63–84, with further bibliography.
[19] Hutchinson 2001, 245–46.
[20] Boedeker 2012a, 81.
[21] Kim 2010, 30.
[22] Kim 2010, 33.

Simon. 11.15–21 W²
οἷσιν ἐπ' ἀθά]νατον κέχυται κλέος ἀγ[δρὸς] ἕκητι
ὃς παρ' ἰοπ]λοκάμων δέξατο Πιερίδ[ων
πᾶσαν ἀλη]θείην, καὶ ἐπώνυμον ὁπ̣[λοτέρ]οισιν
ποίησ' ἡμ] ιθέων ὠκύμορον γενεή̣[ν
ἀλλὰ σὺ μὲ]ν νῦν χαῖρε, θεᾶς ἐρικυ[δέος υἱὲ
κούρης εἰν]αλίου Νηρέος· αὐτὰρ ἐγώ
κικλῄσκω] σ' ἐπίκουρον ἐμοί, π̣[ολυώνυμ]ε Μοῦσα

On their heads is shed undying fame by the power of a man
who received from the violet-tressed Pierides
all truthfulness, who made a lasting name, among those to come
for the generation of demigods, swift to its doom.
But fare ye well now, brave son of goddess,
daughter of sea-deep Nereus. And I
implore you as my ally, O Muse of many names [...]. (transl. Obbink 2001)

In the process of comparing himself with Homer, Simonides indeed expresses admiration for him,[23] but at the same time, he contrasts the function of his own poetry and his relationship with the Muse to Homer's. Simonides invokes the Muse *only* as an ally (ἐπίκουρος, line 21), while Homer, in Simonides' words, 'received all the truth from the dark-tressed Muses'.[24] Simonides, therefore, distances himself and his poetry from Homer but at the same time he seems to feel the need to found his own authority to praise the heroes of Plataea right on Homer's. The glorifying function of epic poetry sets a precedent, provides a parallel, and legitimizes the function of Simonides' poetry even in a context in which he distances himself from that precedent.

Similarly, on several occasions Pindar displays a critical relationship with the epic tradition[25] so that he can criticize Homer as an unreliable predecessor, as is the case, for example, of *Nemean 7*, but he can also praise the epic poet either as a model, as in *Isthmian 4*, or as a source for wisdom, as in *Pythian 4*:[26]

---

23 West 2011, 55.
24 This is the conjectural reading of the text proposed by West. See e.g. Stehle 2001, 110; Aloni 1994, 16; Boedeker 2012b, 33.
25 Also see, e.g., West 2011, 51 f.
26 In addition to the cases mentioned, a further relevant Pindaric example could be provided by *Paean* 7b (fr. 52 h S.-M. = C2 Rutherford), whose lines 10–14 appear to represent a programmatic section concerning Pindar's adoption of a stance towards Homer, who is explicitly named at line 11. The nature of the Pindaric stance itself is debated in view of the lacunous state of the text in the crucial lines: for different interpretations of the poem, see D'Alessio 1992, 1995, 2004; Di Benedetto 1991, 2003; Rutherford 2001, 243 f.

Pi. *N.* 7.17–23
σοφοὶ δὲ μέλλοντα τριταῖον ἄνεμον
ἔμαθον, οὐδ' ὑπὸ κέρδει βλάβεν·
ἀφνεὸς πενιχρός τε θανάτου παρὰ
σᾶμα νέονται. ἐγὼ δὲ πλέον' ἔλπομαι
λόγον Ὀδυσσέος ἢ πάθαν
διὰ τὸν ἁδυεπῆ γενέσθ' Ὅμηρον·
ἐπεὶ ψεύδεσί οἱ ποτανᾷ ⟨τε⟩ μαχανᾷ
σεμνὸν ἔπεστί τι· σοφία
δὲ κλέπτει παράγοισα μύθοις κτλ.

Wise men know well the wind to come
on the third day and are not harmed by greed for gain,
for rich and poor travel to the tomb
of death. I believe that Odysseus' story
has become greater than his actual suffering
because of Homer's sweet verse,
for upon his fictions and soaring craft
rests great majesty, and his skill
deceives with misleading tales [...]. (transl. Race 1997a)

Pi. *I.* 4.37–9
ἀλλ' Ὅμηρός τοι τετίμακεν δι' ἀνθρώπων, ὃς αὐτοῦ
πᾶσαν ὀρθώσαις ἀρετὰν κατὰ ῥάβδον ἔφρασεν
θεσπεσίων ἐπέων λοιποῖς ἀθύρειν.

But Homer, to be sure, has made him honoured among mankind, who set
straight his entire achievement and declared it with his staff
of divine verses for future men to enjoy. (transl. Race 1997a)

Pi. *P.* 4.277–9
τῶν δ' Ὁμήρου καὶ τόδε συνθέμενος
ῥῆμα πόρσυν'· ἄγγελον ἐσλὸν ἔφα τι-
μὰν μεγίσταν πράγματι παντὶ φέρειν·
αὔξεται καὶ Μοῖσα δι' ἀγγελίας ὀρ-
θᾶς κτλ.

And among the sayings of Homer, take this one to heart
and heed it: he said that a good messenger
brings the greatest honour to every affair.
The Muse too gains distinction through true
reporting [...]. (transl. Race 1997a)

The perception of Homer as an inescapable source for the past and as an eminent predecessor appears to go hand in hand with challenges to his authority. Such an ambiguous Homeric stance is present in both the lyric corpus and in

Herodotus' *Histories*, and represents an important trait of continuity between the two traditions.

A further passage from the *Histories* where Herodotus engages openly with Homer follows in the next section of the paper, and it provides the opportunity to explore the matter of Herodotus' relationship with Greek lyric poetry on yet another level, that of methods of argument.

2 Homeric evidence and the language of proof (Hdt. 4.29)

Hdt. 4.29: Δοκέει δέ μοι καὶ τὸ γένος τῶν βοῶν τὸ κόλον διὰ ταῦτα οὐ φύειν κέρεα αὐτόθι. μαρτυρέει δέ μοι τῇ γνώμῃ καὶ Ὁμήρου ἔπος ἐν Ὀδυσσηίῃ ἔχον ὧδε· "καὶ Λιβύην, ὅθι τ' ἄρνες ἄφαρ κεραοὶ τελέθουσι" [*Od.* 4.85] ὀρθῶς εἰρημένον, ἐν τοῖσι θερμοῖσι ταχὺ παραγίνεσθαι τὰ κέρεα, ἐν δὲ τοῖσι ἰσχυροῖσι ψύχεσι ἢ οὐ φύει κέρεα τὰ κτήνεα ἀρχὴν ἢ φύοντα φύει μόγις.

And in my opinion it is for this reason that the hornless kind of cattle grow no horns in Scythia. A verse of Homer in the *Odyssey* attests to my opinion: 'Libya, the land where lambs are born with horns on their foreheads', in which it is correctly observed that in hot countries the horns grow quickly, whereas in very cold countries beasts hardly grow horns, or not at all.

In this passage, Herodotus supports a scientific argument of his own with a Homeric line (*Od.* 4.85), calling upon the epic poet as an authoritative source to confirm his own personal opinion. He does so without the faintest concern or reservation regarding the fact that the poet's intention was not to provide factual information on the matter under discussion.[27] The occurrence of the verb μαρτυρέω in this context is significant in that, as it pertains to the language of proof, it clearly attests Herodotus' perception of Homer as a source capable of providing proof.

The use of the language of proof in this passage provides the opportunity to shift the focus of this discussion to a further set of shared features between Herodotean historiography and Greek lyric poetry; namely, the use of comparable argumentative strategies.

Rosalind Thomas[28] has identified three points of connection between Herodotus and the scientific essays collected in the Hippocratic Corpus as far as the

---

[27] Verdin 1977, 63.
[28] Thomas 1993, 237 f.; Thomas 2000, 168–248; Thomas 2006, 60 f. See also Lateiner 1986.

use of methods of argument is concerned: (1) the use of the first person, (2) the sense of dialogue with opponents, (3) the use of the language of proof.

Leaving aside the use of the first person, which is prominent enough in lyric poetry,[29] the sense of dialogue with opponents, well represented in the Hippocratic Corpus, also characterizes several lyric poems and attests to the practice of establishing a dialogue with other poets within the poems themselves. Even in the case of 'anonymous' sympotic poetry, there is a drive towards correcting and improving the work of 'predecessors', creating an implicit 'argumentative strategy'.[30] Among the Attic *skolia*, for instance, *Carmina* 10 and 12 Fabbro (*PMG* 893 and 895) share the same first two lines (Ἐν μύρτου κλαδὶ τὸ ξίφος φορήσω, / ὥσπερ Ἁρμόδιος καὶ Ἀριστογείτων, "I shall carry my sword in a spray of myrtle, like Harmodius and Aristogeiton", transl. Campbell 1993), but then differ in the following ones (10.3–4: ὅτε τὸν τύραννον κτανέτην/ ἰσονόμους τ' Ἀθήνας ἐποιησάτην, "when they killed the tyrant and made Athens a city of equal rights", transl. Campbell 1993; 12.3–4: ὅτ' Ἀθηναίης ἐν θυσίαις / ἄνδρα τύραννον Ἵππαρχον ἐκαινέτην, "when at the festival of Athena they killed the tyrant Hipparchus", transl. Campbell 1993), as if the singers were competing to complete the song more appropriately than others.[31] The poetic exchange between Solon and Mimnermus (Sol. fr. 20 W² = Mimn. fr. 6 W²) shows the former quoting a line of the latter and correcting it:

Mimn. fr. 6 W²
αἴ γὰρ ἄτερ νούσων τε καὶ ἀργαλέων μελεδωνέων
ἑξηκονταέτη μοῖρα κίχοι θανάτου.

Would that my fated death might come at sixty, unattended by sickness and grievous cares. (transl. Gerber 1999)

Sol. fr. 20 W²
ἀλλ' εἴ μοι καὶ νῦν ἔτι πείσεαι, ἔξελε τοῦτο –
μηδὲ μέγαιρ', ὅτι σέο λῷον ἐπεφρασάμην –
καὶ μεταποίησον Λιγιαστάδη, ὧδε δ' ἄειδε·
"ὀγδωκονταέτη μοῖρα κίχοι θανάτου".

But even if now you will listen to me, remove
this – and do not be offended because my thoughts

---

[29] Indeed, features such as the use of the first person, the assertion of authority, the display of a different relationship with the Muse etc. are found in non-Homeric epic poetry too.
[30] On the sympotic practice of *metapoíēsis* see e.g. Vetta 1983b, esp. 30–3; for 'sympotic chains', see e.g. Ferrari 1987, 177–97; Rossi 1983, 41–50.
[31] See e.g. Griffith 1990, 193. For further examples from the Attic *skolia* see e.g. *Carmina* 15–6 Fabbro = 898–9 *PMG*; 17–8 Fabbro = 900–901 *PMG*.

are better than yours – and changing it, Ligyai-
stades, sing as follows: 'May my fated death come at eighty'. (transl. Gerber 1999)

Further cases in point are Solon's quotation from his enemies' accusations (Sol. fr. 33 W²), and the many mutual and often critical allusions between poets. Examples include those attested by Timocreon's fr. 10 W², which targets the 'Ceian non-sense' of, presumably, Simonides (Κηΐα με προσῆλθε φλυαρία οὐκ ἐθέλοντα· / οὐ θέλοντά με προσῆλθε Κηΐα φλυαρία, "Nonsense from Ceos came to me against my will. / Against my will there came to me nonsense from Ceos", transl. Campbell 1992), or by Pindar's O. 2, whose lines 86–88 attest a reference to 'a pair of crows crying in vain' (line 87 κόρακες...ἄκραντα γαρυέτων), that is to competitors, and a self-reference on Pindar's part, 'the divine bird of Zeus' (line 88: Διός...ὄρνιχα θεῖον).[32]

Competitive and polemical strategies of argument are also attested in the extant lyric corpus, as shown by the use of figures of speech like *praeteritio* (e.g. Stesich. *PMGF* 210; Sapph. 16 V; Mimn. 2 W²), or the practice of asserting the authority of a non-standard version of a myth (e.g. Stesich. *PMGF* 192; Pi. O. 1.52–53; Pi. O. 7.20–21; B. 19.37 f.):

Pi. O. 1.52–53
ἐμοὶ δ' ἄπορα γαστρίμαρ-
γον μακάρων τιν' εἰπεῖν· ἀφίσταμαι·
ἀκέρδεια λέλογχεν θαμινὰ κακαγόρους.

"But for my part, I cannot call any of the blessed gods
a glutton – I stand back;
impoverishment is often the lot of slanderers". (transl. Race 1997b)

Pi. O. 7.20–21
ἐθελήσω τοῖσιν ἐξ ἀρχᾶς ἀπὸ Τλαπολέμου
ξυνὸν ἀγγέλλων διορθῶσαι λόγον

"I intend, in proclaiming my message, to set forth truly
for them from its origin, beginning with Tlapolemos". (transl. Race 1997b)

---

[32] The bibliography on the interpretation of this debated passage and the relevant *scholia* (157–158 Drachmann) is endless: for discussion, see e.g. Gentili 1958, 24f.; Fränkel 1961; Carey 1981, 50–1; Lehnus 1981, 51–2; Molyneux 1992, 251–4; Cozzoli 1996, 7–36; Catenacci 2013, 50–53. What is relevant here is not the answer to the question whether the two crows are Bacchylides and Simonides, but that the passage attests a reference to competitors and a self-reference on Pindar's part; cf. e.g. Hornblower 2004, 288.

As far as the use of the language of proof is concerned, a few examples attest its employment in lyric poetry in references to historical events.[33] The verb μαρτυρέω occurs in fact in the output of both Pindar (*I.* 5.48) and Simonides (fr. 261 Poltera) in the context of references to, respectively, the battle of Salamis and the battle of Thermopylae. Moreover, in Simonides' elegiac fr. 16 W², the sun is said to be witness (μάρτυς) of the valour of Corinthian fighters at Plataea.

Pi. *I.* 5.46–50
πολλὰ μὲν ἀρτιεπής
γλῶσσά μοι τοξεύματ' ἔχει περὶ κείνων
κελαδέσαι· καὶ νῦν ἐν Ἄρει <u>μαρτυρῆσαι</u>
κεν πόλις Αἴαντος ὀρθωθεῖσα ναύταις
ἐν πολυφθόρῳ Σαλαμὶς Διὸς ὄμβρῳ
ἀναρίθμων ἀνδρῶν χαλαζάεντι φόνῳ.

My fluent tongue
has many arrows to ring out in praise
of them, and recently in war Salamis, the city of Aias,
could attest that it was preserved by her sailors
during Zeus' devastating rain,
that hailstorm of gore for countless men". (transl. Race 1997a)

Simon. fr. 261.5–9 Poltera
ἀνδρῶν ἀγαθῶν ὅδε σηκὸς οἰκέταν εὐδοξίαν
Ἑλλάδος εἵλετο·
<u>μαρτυρεῖ</u> δὲ καὶ Λεωνίδας,
ἀρετᾶς μέγαν λελοιπὼς
κόσμον ἀέναόν τε κλέος·

This precinct of noble men chose the glory of Greece as its inhabitant; witness to this is Leonidas himself, king of Sparta, who left behind a great adornment of valour and imperishable glory. (transl. Campbell 1991)

---

[33] There are indeed further examples accounting for the use of the language of proof in the lyric corpus, especially in connection with praise, therefore with truth, therefore with constructing authority. Cf. e.g. the use of τεκμαίρομαι, "to judge (by signs)" (Slater 1969, 492) in Pi. fr. 169a.4 S.-M., where Pindar relies on 'evidence' as a starting point for his own inferences. See also e.g. Pi. *O.* 6.21 (μαρτυρήσω) and 6.73 (τεκμαίρει); *O.* 13.8 (μαρτυρήσει); *N.* 6.8 (τεκμαίρει), etc. In this sense, these further instances from the lyric corpus could be interpreted as also bearing some comparison with Herodotus' use; if the historiographer's preference goes in fact to tangible evidence, he nevertheless does show a tendency to "claim to produce proofs [...] at precisely the point where he has to resort to complicated argument and deduction to make up for the lack of any clear empirical evidence" (Thomas 2006, 72). See also Hornblower 1987, 20.

Simon. fr. 16 W²
κάλλιστον μάρτυν ἔθεντο πόνων
χρυσοῦ τιμήεντος ἐ]ν αἰθέρ[ι· καί σφιν ἀέξει
αὐτῶν τ' εὐρεῖαν κλ]ηδόν[α καί πατέρων
           ] πολυ [

They established for themselves the finest witness of their struggle, a witness of precious gold in the sky, which increases the wide glory of both them and their fathers. (transl. Campbell 1991)

Finally, the lyric corpus also preserves examples of a concern to test statements and to provide evidence to support them, as suggested by the case of Mimnermus' fr. 14 W². This example attests to the poet's attention to the record of the source for the account of the episode narrated, along with the quoting of the eye-witnessing of that very source of information:[34]

Mimn. fr. 14.1–4 W²
οὐ μὲν δὴ κείνου γε μένος καὶ ἀγήνορα θυμὸν
τοῖον ἐμέο προτέρων πεύθομαι, οἵ μιν ἴδον
Λυδῶν ἱππομάχων πυκινὰς κλονέοντα φάλαγγας
Ἕρμιον ἂμ πεδίον, φῶτα φερεμμελίην·

That man's strength and heroic spirit were not such
(as yours), as I learn from my elders who saw him,
ash spear in his hand, routing the thick ranks of the
Lydian cavalry on the plain of Hermus". (transl. Gerber 1999)

3 Folktale motifs in the *Histories* and in Greek lyric poetry

One further feature of the *Histories* that suggests a complex relationship with the lyric tradition relates to Herodotus' attachment of folktale motifs to narratives

---

[34] Note that Grethlein 2010, 64–8 argues for a different reading of the passage based on the revival of a conjecture by Meineke consisting in the substitution of οἵ (line 2) with ὅς, so as to detect in the poem "a distancing of elegy from epic poetry, for the *Iliad*'s narrator claims to have heard his account from the Muses" (Grethlein 2010, 67). The text, however, already makes good sense in the *lectio tradita*, and the mention of eye-witnesses is relevant in itself as a feature foreshadowing the development of prose historiography: cf. e.g. Mazzarino 1947, 64–5 and 1966, 37 f.; Bowie 2001, 63.

concerning historical characters.[35] In recent scholarship, it has been proposed to regard the *Histories* as resulting, in a sense, from "a pre-existing story-telling tradition" of narratives,[36] at times employed by Herodotus without major changes, at times reworked. In some cases, we find suggestive similarities between the historiographer's treatment of narratives featuring folktale motifs and a piece of lyric poetry. The three case studies presented below concern a) the story of Croesus on the pyre (Hdt. 1.86–7), b) the story of Polycrates' ring (Hdt. 3.40–3) and c) the story of Alexander of Macedon at banquet (Hdt. 5.17–22).[37]

a. Croesus on the pyre (Hdt. 1.86–7)

Herodotus' treatment of Croesus has several implications for the relationship between the *Histories* and lyric poetry; we could think, in the first place, of his prominent association with a lyric poet, Solon (Hdt. 1.29–34).

As for the presence of a folktale pattern in the Herodotean story of Croesus of Lydia, Nino Luraghi[38] has pointed to a type known in the Aarne-Thompson classification system as 'Our lady's child' (AaTh. 710). This pattern – whose elements are distributed in Herodotus' narrative between the two characters of Croesus and Gyges – has the protagonist violating the prohibition to look into a room and refusing to acknowledge his fault. He is then deprived of his voice and condemned to be burnt on a pyre for some other crime for which he has been wrongly accused, but when the pyre is already burning, he regains his voice in order to acknowledge his fault and eventually be saved by a miraculous rain.

In lyric poetry, we find references to Croesus in a frustratingly fragmentary poem by Hipponax (fr. 104 W²) – arguably in the context of an allusion to the quasi-proverbial luxury of the Lydian king – and in an ode by Pindar (*P.* 1.94: οὐ φθίνει Κροίσου φιλόφρων ἀρετά, "the kindly excellence of Croesus does not perish", transl. Race 1997b). We also have indirect evidence concerning a poem by a later author, Licymnius of Chios, narrating the betrayal of the city of Sardis on the part of Croesus' daughter Nanis (*PMG* 772). Most importantly, Croesus plays a prominent role in the narrative section (lines 23–62) of Bacchylides' *Ode* 3. There are indeed differences between Herodotus' and Bacchylides'

---

[35] On other Herodotean anecdotal narratives that exploit fairytale motifs and storylines see Konstantakos in this volume.
[36] Luraghi 2013, 87. On Herodotus' employment of narrative patterns and models borrowed from different traditions see Konstantakos and Liotsakis in this volume.
[37] For Herodotus' narratives on powerful rulers, see Konstantakos and Liotsakis in this volume.
[38] Luraghi 2013, 101f.

versions of the story; for example, the responsibility for setting up the pyre, the depiction of Croesus, the divine source for the rain that quenches the fire, and the epilogue of the story.[39] These differences have led some scholars to deny a relationship between the lyric and the historiographical accounts, and to postulate in turn a relationship of each of the two accounts with two vase paintings portraying Croesus, namely the Myson amphora (ca. 490–480 B.C.),[40] and a hydria by the Leningrad painter (ca. 470–450 B.C.) that features also other men in oriental dress and a Greek auletes.[41] Since the presence of an auletes in Greek paintings usually implies a theatrical performance,[42] the hydria has been taken as evidence that Croesus was the subject of a tragedy, and thus connected to an extant papyrus fragment[43] apparently belonging to a lost 'Gyges tragedy' in a Lydian trilogy concerned with the Mermnad dynasty. In order to account for the differences between the two versions of the story, it has been argued that Bacchylides relied on the same source as Myson, while Herodotus looked to the 'Gyges Tragedy' that inspired the Leningrad painter.[44]

However, it has also been pointed out that this is not a necessary conclusion. In the first place, if the hydria represents a tragedy, we must allow for a good degree of artistic licence, since a burning pyre is more likely to have belonged to a reported speech rather than to an actual staging.[45] Secondly, the papyrus fragment has been interpreted as more likely dating to the Hellenistic period.[46] Rather than postulating two different sources for the two accounts, it is more economical to argue that each author adapted the story to satisfy their respective ends. In spite of the differences, the two versions display also some important similarities on the linguistic as well as the narrative level,[47] so that the divergences could have been triggered by the authors' differing aims.[48] Stephanie West has therefore convincingly proposed that we should interpret the Herodotean account as a rationalized version of Bacchylides' account,[49] since the divine element is still there in the *Histories*, mentioned as the third and thus most prominent possible reason why Cyrus should have put Croesus on a pyre (Hdt. 1.86:

---

[39] Maehler 2004, 80–2.
[40] Red figure. Louvre G 197; *ARV*² 238.
[41] *ARV*² 571; Beazley 1955, plate 85.
[42] E.g. West 2007, 120.
[43] *P.Oxy.* 2382 = *TrGF Adespota* 664.
[44] Cf. e.g. Maehler 2004, 81–82.
[45] West 2007, 121.
[46] E.g. West 2007, 120–1 with further bibliography. See also Asheri 2005⁷, 320–21.
[47] Cf. e.g. Segal 1971.
[48] Cairns 2010, 66.
[49] West 2007, 121.

βουλόμενος εἰδέναι εἴ τίς μιν δαιμόνων ῥύσεται τοῦ μὴ ζώοντα κατακαυθῆναι, "to find out if some divinity would deliver him from being burned alive"). Herodotus, however, combines this divine element with human action, in order to make his version acceptable to the "fifth-century Enlightenment".[50]

One further hint might suggest that a relationship occurs between the lyric and the historiographical versions of the story of Croesus, and that Herodotus might in fact have been acquainted with Bacchylides' competitive account, even though he never mentions the poet. This hint is represented by the explicit connection of the figures of Croesus and Polycrates in the *Histories*, which finds a parallel in Bacchylides' connection of *Ode* 3 and *Ode* 17 through a verbal echo. In order to clarify this point, it is necessary to address the next example, namely the tale of Polycrates and the ring.

b. Polycrates and the ring (Hdt. 3.40–3)

The folktale associations of this story have sometimes been called into question in scholarship, in favour of an interpretation of the thalassocrat's act of casting his σφρηγίς ('seal') into the waves as a symbolic wedding with the sea comparable to the practice of the Doge in Venice.[51] However, the use of a ring for marriage is unknown to Greek culture,[52] and the significance of the story seems to lie in its emphasis on ὕβρις and the mutability of fortune.[53] The episode illustrates these themes and explains the end of the political relationship between Egypt and Samos.[54] Moreover, the pattern of an object falling into the sea and returning to the place or to the person it belongs to in the belly of a fish (AaTh. N 211) – attested in Herodotus' narrative of the story – as well as the pattern of an object being cast into the sea by a character in a powerful position only to be retrieved by a character in a weaker position – found in Bacchylides' *Ode* 17 – are both known to folktale narratives. One could think of the story of *The Steadfast Tin Soldier*,[55] or of the medieval legend of *Colapesce*.[56]

---

50 West 2007, 121.
51 Cf. Reinach 1905, 9f.
52 Glotz 1925, 282 n. 153; Labarbe 1984, 21. For discussion of the different interpretations, see van Oeteghem 1940, 311f.
53 How/Wells 1928, 267; Labarbe 1984, 26.
54 Asheri/Medaglia 2005⁴, 260–61.
55 Cf. e.g. Andersen 1838.
56 Cataudella 1957, 44.

In the *Histories*, Polycrates throws his σφρηγίς into the sea to ward off the envy of the gods on the advice of Amasis (Hdt. 3.40). Nevertheless, he was destined to come to an evil end (Hdt. 3.43), and the act of putting a seal on the sea has obvious political implications when performed by a thalassocrat. Political implications play a part also in the episode recounted in Bacchylides' *Ode* 17,[57] a poem that similarly features a thalassocrat, Minos, who throws a ring into the sea and then challenges Theseus to retrieve it. The choice of a myth related to Theseus for a poem addressed to Delian Apollo and performed by a chorus from Ceos[58] has been interpreted as a homage to the growing power of Athens,[59] and as suggesting that Bacchylides was a supporter of Cimon,[60] who allegedly brought Theseus' bones back to Athens in 476/5 B.C. and was willing to present himself as a 'Theseus *redivivus*'.[61]

Like the story of Croesus on the pyre, the episode of Minos' challenge to Theseus was the subject of vase paintings; a cup by the potter Euphronios and the painter Onesimos (dated to 500–490 B.C.) features the scene of Amphitrite's greeting of Theseus,[62] and other Attic vases display Theseus' meeting with Amphitrite or with Amphitrite and Poseidon.[63] Moreover, Pausanias (1.17.3) reports that a wall painting by Mikon in the temple of Theseus in Athens depicted the scene.[64]

There are certainly differences between Herodotus' and Bacchylides' stories, most obviously that in Herodotus we have Polycrates and in Bacchylides Minos; however, it seems that Herodotus himself connects his and Bacchylides' narratives by explicitly pointing to Minos as Polycrates' mythical *alter ego* with his heart set on thalassocracy:

> Hdt. 3.122: Πολυκράτης γάρ ἐστι πρῶτος τῶν ἡμεῖς ἴδμεν Ἑλλήνων ὃς θαλασσοκρατέειν ἐπενοήθη, πάρεξ Μίνω τε τοῦ Κνωσσίου καὶ εἰ δή τις ἄλλος πρότερος τούτου ἦρξε τῆς θαλάσσης· τῆς δὲ ἀνθρωπηίης λεγομένης γενεῆς Πολυκράτης πρῶτος, κτλ.
>
> For Polycrates was the first of the Greeks whom we know to aim at the mastery of the sea, leaving out of account Minos of Cnossus and any others who before him may have ruled the sea; of what may be called the human race Polycrates was the first [...]

---

57 Cf. e.g. Fearn 2011, 207f.
58 Maehler 2004, 171; Palmisciano 2007, 52.
59 Palmisciano 2007, 52.
60 Vox 1984, 118.
61 E.g. Podlecki 1971, 141–3; Vox 1984, 117–20; Fearn 2011, 214 after Castriota 1992, 33–63.
62 Louvre G 104; Appendix 13. See Maehler 2004, 174.
63 Maehler 2004, 176.
64 Castriota 1992, 58f.

As mentioned above, there seems to be one further reason to regard the Herodotean tales of Croesus and Polycrates as possibly entertaining a relationship with the lyric corpus, namely the occurrence of an authorial connection between Croesus and Polycrates in the *Histories* that appears to mirror the connection between Croesus and Minos in Bacchylides' corpus.

To begin with Herodotus, Croesus and Polycrates are both associated with a lyric poet – Croesus with Solon (Hdt. 1.29 ff.) and Polycrates with Anacreon (Hdt. 3.121)[65] – but they are also meaningfully associated through verbal parallels internal to the *Histories*. Amasis' words to Polycrates (Hdt. 3.40) appear, in fact, to be strongly reminiscent of Solon's speech to Croesus (Hdt. 1.32–33):[66]

Hdt. 1.32: Ὦ Κροῖσε, ἐπιστάμενόν με[67] τὸ θεῖον πᾶν ἐὸν φθονερόν τε καὶ ταραχῶδες ἐπειρωτᾷς ἀνθρωπηίων πρηγμάτων πέρι κτλ.

Croesus, you ask me about human affairs, and I know that the divine is entirely grudging and troublesome to us […]

Hdt. 1.33: Σκοπέειν δὲ χρὴ παντὸς χρήματος τὴν τελευτὴν κῇ ἀποβήσεται· πολλοῖσι γὰρ δὴ ὑποδέξας ὄλβον ὁ θεὸς προρρίζους ἀνέτρεψε.

It is necessary to see how the end of every affair turns out, for the god promises fortune to many people and then utterly ruins them.

Hdt. 3.40: ἐμοὶ δὲ αἱ σαὶ μεγάλαι εὐτυχίαι οὐκ ἀρέσκουσι, τὸ θεῖον ἐπισταμένῳ ὡς ἔστι φθονερόν. καί κως βούλομαι καὶ αὐτὸς καὶ τῶν ἂν κήδωμαι τὸ μέν τι εὐτυχέειν τῶν πρηγμάτων, τὸ δὲ προσπταίειν, καὶ οὕτω διαφέρειν τὸν αἰῶνα ἐναλλὰξ πρήσσων ἢ εὐτυχέειν τὰ πάντα· οὐδένα γάρ κω λόγῳ οἶδα ἀκούσας ὅστις ἐς τέλος οὐ κακῶς ἐτελεύτησε πρόρριζος, εὐτυχέων τὰ πάντα.

But I do not like these great successes of yours; for I know the gods, how jealous they are, and I desire somehow that both I and those for whom I care succeed in some affairs, fail in others, and thus pass life faring differently by turns, rather than succeed at everything. For from all I have heard I know of no man whom continual good fortune did not bring in the end to evil, and utter destruction.

---

65 Compare also the cases of Arion of Methymna, associated with Periander of Corinth (Hdt. 1.23) and the case of Lasus of Hermione, associated with Hipparchus' entourage (Hdt. 7.6).
66 In terms of narrative consistency internal to the *Histories* this echo makes perfect sense: Herodotus in fact informs us 'in advance' (Hdt. 1.30) that Solon paid a visit to Amasis. On Solon's alleged trip to Egypt, cf. also Plu. *Sol.* 26.1, quoting Sol. fr. 28 W².
67 Solon's words are closely reminiscent of Herodotus' own words in the proem, cf. Hdt. 1.5. Solon's words and conceptions are then echoed by other characters in the narrative of the *Histories*, cf. e.g. Harrison 2000, 30–63.

Turning to Bacchylides, there is a verbal parallel in terms of γνῶμαι between *Ode* 3, which features Croesus as the main character, and *Ode* 17, which features a thalassocrat hubristically casting a ring into the sea:

B. 3.57–8 Maehler
Ἄπιστον οὐδὲν ὅ τι θ[εῶν μέ]ριμνα
  τεύχει· κτλ.

Nothing that the planning of the gods brings about is past belief. (transl. Campbell 1992)

B. 17.117–18 Maehler
Ἄπιστον ὅ τι δαίμονες
θέωσιν οὐδὲν φρενοάραις βροτοῖς·

Nothing that the gods wish is beyond the belief of sane mortals. (transl. Campbell 1992)

The concurrence of (1) the association of these two figures with narratives that present comparable folktale motifs and (2) the introduction of an explicit verbal echo that links Croesus and Polycrates in the *Histories* and Croesus and Minos in Bacchylides' corpus could be interpreted as suggestive of an intentional authorial connection between them, and thus of an interaction between the two traditions, all the more so in the light of Herodotus' explicit connection of Polycrates and Minos (Hdt. 3.122).

c. Alexander of Macedon at banquet (Hdt. 5.17–22)

Most scholarly interpretations of this episode focus on proving its historical inauthenticity, taking it as a product of Macedonian propaganda that emphasizes Alexander's "philhellenic purity"[68] in the face of his Medism, or as a story "invented by Herodotus that could be passed off, at least superficially, as plausible pro-Macedonian propaganda".[69] Herodotus, however, was not "engaged in a post-war cover up for Alexander's past",[70] as the ambiguity that characterizes Alexander in the rest of the narrative suggests.[71]

If a good deal of scholarly effort has been put into the attempt to prove the fictional character of the episode, the possibility of interpreting it as a folktale

---

[68] Badian 1994, 113. See also Fearn 2007a, 101.
[69] Fearn 2007a, 99. On Herodotus' depiction of Cambyses (Hdt. 3.27–9 and 3.64) as reflecting ancient propaganda, see Konstantakos in this volume.
[70] Scaife 1989, 130.
[71] On the complexity and ambiguity of this figure, see e.g. Vannicelli 2013, 68.

narrative⁷² has often been underemphasized, even though many of its elements of detail appear to point precisely in this direction. First, the number of the Persian envoys, seven, is a significant one for Persian traditions,⁷³ but also very common in folkloric and religious narratives.⁷⁴ Second, the setting of the tale, a banquet with a macabre outcome, has several parallels in both the mythological and folkloric traditions,⁷⁵ as do men and warriors disguised in women's clothes.⁷⁶

Alexander of Macedon, like Croesus and Polycrates, is another historical figure who 'interferes' with lyric poetry: he is in fact the addressee of two sympotic lyric poems, Bacchylides' fr. 20b and Pindar's frr. 120–1 S.-M. Bacchylides' poem may have provided the sympotic setting as a background to Herodotus' narrative, as some have suggested.⁷⁷

The Pindaric drinking song to Alexander might also have played a part in constructing the tradition attested in Herodotus. In the first line of the Pindaric poem, Alexander is addressed, with a reference to Alexander Paris, as "homonymous with the prosperous descendants of Dardanos"⁷⁸ (Ὀλβίων ὁμώνυμε Δαρδανιδᾶν). In light of the widely attested analogy between Persians and Trojans – and between the Trojan War and the Persian Wars⁷⁹ – the Persians' misbehaviour towards the Macedonian women could be interpreted as mirroring Alexander Paris' most famous abduction of Helen.⁸⁰ In the second line of the poem, Alexander is the "bold-counselling son of Amyntas"⁸¹ (παῖ θρασύμηδες Ἀμύντα); the term 'θρασυμήδης' is attested elsewhere in the Pindaric corpus only in the context of references to mythological characters,⁸² and if we are to seek a mythological episode concerning Alexander Paris and suitable to Alexander of Mace-

---

72 E.g. Maehler 2004, 244; Nenci 2006³, 177; Hornblower 2013, 109.
73 Errington 1981, 142; Hornblower 2013, 110.
74 Cf. AaTh. Z 71.5.
75 Compare e.g. the mythological instances of Thyestes and Pelops. Cf. also Charon of Lampsacus *ap*. Plu. *De virtutibus mulierum* 18.255a–e and Hdt. 1.73–4; 1.118–9; 9.111. For banquets in Herodotus, see A. Bowie 2003.
76 Cf. e.g. Paus. 4.4.2 f.; Plu. *Sol.* 8.5; Hdt. 4.146. See Brelich 1961, 80.
77 Fearn 2007b 28–86.
78 D'Alessio 2008.
79 Fearn 2007a, 106; Boedeker 2001, 124f; Boedeker 2011, 136; Hdt. 7.20.2; Th. 1.1; 1.10.3–4.
80 Fearn 2007a, 106f.
81 Translation by Race 1997a, 349.
82 Pi. *P*. 4.143 and Pi. *P*. 4.143 and *N*. 9.13, in reference to, respectively, Salmoneus and Amphiaraus.

don, indeed Helen's abduction seems to be most fitting in view of the tradition preserved by Herodotus.

If Pindar's play on the homonymy of the two princes is taken as a reference to their disregard of ξενία in episodes involving abuse of women, it might be tentatively suggested that Pindar may have alluded, perhaps in cursory fashion, to a tradition associating Alexander with an incident of the kind of the one attested in Herodotus. A verbal echo between Pindar's poem and Herodotus' narrative, which has already been pointed out by Pietro Vannicelli,[83] could support this speculative interpretation. Both texts – the last preserved line of the Pindaric fragment and the last Herodotean sentence on the Macedonian symposium–associate death, silence, and glorious deeds:

Pi. fr. 121.4 S.-M.
θνᾴσκει δὲ σιγαθὲν καλὸν ἔργον
but a noble deed dies when left in silence... (transl. Race 1997a)

Hdt. 5.21.2: Ὁ μέν νυν τῶν Περσέων τούτων θάνατος οὕτω καταλαμφθεὶς ἐσιγήθη.
It was in this way, then, that the death of these Persians was kept silent.

The Pindaric line is an instance of the *topos* of poetry's power to immortalize, and Herodotus may be playing on a verbal association (attested only here in the *Histories*) that occurred in a poem addressed to the same historical character.[84]

To conclude, I have argued that the *Histories* entertain a relationship of greater continuity with Greek lyric poetry than is usually acknowledged,[85] especially in terms of approach to tradition, strategies of argument, and use of narrative patterns. Of course, my conclusions do not discount the scientific and sophistic influences on Herodotus, the similarities between his work and those of Hecataeus of Miletus or the Hippocratic writers, and the impact of the rhetoric

---

[83] Vannicelli 2013, 72–3.
[84] The Pindaric and the Herodotean passages represent the first two extant occurrences of this form of the passive aorist of σιγάω (found also in Euripides, cf. *Supp.* 298; *Ph.* 349); if indeed this might be ascribed to the loss of much ancient literature, nevertheless the contextual occurrence of the form in the *Histories* and in the Pindaric corpus could be taken as an element strengthening the case for an interaction between the poetic and the historiographical text.
[85] But note the fundamental contributions of e.g. Bowie 2001 and 2010; Chiasson 2012; Grethlein 2010; Herington 1991; Hornblower 1987, 19–21; Mazzarino 1966, 37f.; Pelliccia 1992; Verdin 1977; West 2007.

of public debate and the courts.[86] However, the practice of placing emphasis on a source to make the author's statements reliable is present, in a way, already in lyric poetry, as a rhetorical device employed for the sake of enhancing the authority of the poets. Likewise, if Herodotus' interest in νόμοι may reflect the fact that νόμος and φύσις were 'hot topics' in his day among almost all the major sophists,[87] it is, nevertheless, a Pindaric line (fr. 169a S.-M.) that Herodotus uses to support his statements about νόμος (Hdt. 3.38). Moreover, we may recall that a subdivision of constitutional types into three categories occurs already in Pindar's *Pythian* 2.86–8, one generation before Herodotus' 'Constitutional Debate' (Hdt. 3.80–2).[88] Similarly, Herodotus' choice of the Helen story as the starting point for his claim of authority, though consistent with Gorgias' *Encomium of Helen*, is once again traceable back to lyric poetry, just as his ambiguous Homeric stance characterizes an attitude towards epic poetry already attested in the lyric tradition. Finally, the practice of drawing from a tradition of folktale narratives, and the 'competitive' engagement with lyric poems drawing from this same tradition, represent further important traces of continuity and suggest that Greek lyric poetry played a fundamental contributory role in shaping the cultural background and the intellectual milieu in which Herodotus' historiography developed.

List of Abbreviations

D.-K. = Diels, H.A. / Kranz, W. (1952⁶), *Die Fragmente der Vorsokratiker*, Berlin.
Finglass = Finglass, P. / Davies, M. (2014), *Stesichorus. The Poems*, Cambridge.
Maehler = Maehler, H. (1970), *Bacchylides. Carmina cum fragmentis*, Leipzig.
PMG = Page, D.L. (1962), *Poetae melici Graeci*, Oxford.
PMGF = Davies, M. (1991), *Poetarum melicorum Graecorum fragmenta*, Oxford.
Poltera = Poltera, O. (2008), *Simonides lyricus. Testimonia und Fragmente*, Basel.
S.-M. = Snell, B. / Maehler, H. (1980), *Pindari carmina cum fragmentis*, Leipzig.
V = Voigt, E.M. (1971), *Sappho et Alcaeus. Fragmenta*, Amsterdam.
W² = West, M.L. (1992), *Iambi et elegi Graeci ante Alexandrum cantati*, Oxford.

---

[86] Cf. e.g. Thomas 2000, 212.
[87] Thomas 2006, 69; Winton 2000, 98f.
[88] Asheri-Medaglia 2005⁴, 295; Hornblower 2006, 315.

Bibliography

Aloni, A. (1994), "L'elegia di Simonide dedicata alla battaglia di Platea (Sim. Frr. 10–18 W²) e l'occasione della sua performance", in: *ZPE* 102, 9–22.
Andersen, H.C. (1838), *Fairy Tales Told for Children. New Collection*, Copenhagen.
Asheri, D. (2005⁷), *Erodoto. Le Storie. Libro I. La Lidia e la Persia*, Milan.
Asheri, D. / Medaglia, S. M. (eds.) (2005⁴), *Erodoto. Le Storie. Libro III. La Persia*, Milan.
Athanassaki, L. / Bowie, E. (eds.) (2011), *Archaic and Classical Choral Song. Performance, Politics and Dissemination*, Berlin.
Badian, E. (1994), "Herodotus on Alexander I of Macedon: a Study in Some Subtle Silences", in: S. Hornblower 1994, 107–30.
Bastianini, G. / Lapini, W. / Tulli, M. (eds.) (2012), *Harmonia. Scritti di filologia classica in onore di Angelo Casanova*, II, Florence.
Boedeker, D. (2001), "Heroic Historiography: Simonides and Herodotus on Plataea", in: D. Boedeker / D. Sider 2001, 120–34.
Boedeker, D. (2011), "Early Greek Poetry as/and History", in: A. Feldherr / G. Hardy 2011, 122–47.
Boedeker, D. (2012a), "Helen and 'I' in Early Greek Lyric", in: J. Marincola / L. Llewellyn-Jones / C. Maciver 2012, 83–94.
Boedeker, D. (2012b), "Speaker's Past and Plupast. Herodotus in the Light of Elegy and Lyric", in: J. Grethlein / C. B. Krebs 2012, 17–34.
Boedeker, D. / Sider, D. (eds.) (2001), *The New Simonides. Contexts of Praise and Desire*, Oxford.
Bowie, A.M. (2003), "Fate May Harm Me, I Have Dined Today: Near-Eastern Royal Banquets and Greek Symposia in Herodotus", in: *Pallas* 61 (*Symposium, banquet et représentations en Grèce et à Rome*), 99–109.
Bowie, E. (2001), "Ancestors of Historiography in Early Greek Elegiac and Iambic Poetry?", in: N. Luraghi 2001, 45–66.
Bowie, E. (2010), "Historical Narrative in Archaic and Early Classical Greek Elegy", in: D. Konstan / K.A. Raaflaub 2010, 145–166.
Brelich, A. (1961), *Guerre, agoni e culti nella Grecia arcaica*, Bonn.
Budelmann, F. (ed.) (2009a), *The Cambridge Companion to Greek Lyric*, Cambridge.
Budelmann, F. (2009b), "Introducing Greek Lyric", in: F. Budelmann 2009a, 1–18.
Cairns, D.L. (2010), *Bacchylides. Five Epinician Odes (3, 5, 9, 11, 13)*, Cambridge.
Campbell, D.A. (1991), *Greek Lyric III. Stesichorus, Ibycus, Simonides and Others*, Cambridge / London.
Campbell, D.A. (1992), *Greek Lyric IV. Bacchylides, Corinna, and Others*, Cambridge / London.
Campbell, D.A. (1993), *Greek Lyric V. The New School of Poetry and Anonymous Songs and Hymns*, Cambridge / London.
Carey, C. (1981), *A Commentary on Five Odes of Pindar. Pythian 2, Pythian 9, Nemean 1, Nemean 7, Isthmian 8*, New York.
Carey, C. (2009), "Iambos", in: F. Budelmann 2009a, 149–67.
Castriota, D. (1992), *Myth, Ethos and Actuality. Official Art in Fifth Century B.C. Athens*, Madison.
Cataudella, Q. (1957), *La novella greca. Prolegomeni e testi in traduzioni originali*, Napoli.

Catenacci, C. (2013), "Olimpica II. Introduzione", in: C. Catenacci / P. Giannini / L. Lomiento 2013, 45–56.
Catenacci, C. / Giannini, P. / Lomiento, L. (eds.) (2013), *Pindaro. Le Olimpiche*, Milan.
Chiasson, C. (2012), "Herodotus' Prologue and the Greek Poetic Tradition", in: *Histos* 8, 114–43.
Cingano, E. (1985), "Clistene di Sicione, Erodoto e i poemi del ciclo tebano", in: *QUCC* 49, 31–40.
Cozzoli, A.T. (1996), "Aspetti intertestuali nelle polemiche letterarie degli antichi: da Pindaro a Persio", in: *QUCC* 54, 7–36.
D'Alessio, G.B. (1992), "Pindaro, *peana* VIIb (fr. 52 h Dn.M.)", in: A. H. S. El-Mosalamy 1992, 353–73.
D'Alessio, G.B. (1995), "Una via lontana dal cammino degli uomini (Parm. Frr. 1+6 D.-K.; Pind. *Ol.* VI 22–27; *Pae.* VIIb 10–20)", in: *SIFC* 88, 143–81.
D'Alessio, G.B. (2004), "Precisazioni su Pindaro, *Peana* 7b", in: *Prometheus* 30, 23–6.
D'Alessio, G.B. (2006), "Note al nuovo Archiloco (*POxy* LXIX 4708)", in: *ZPE* 156, 19–22.
D'Alessio, G.B. (2008), "David Fearn, Bacchylides. Politics, Performance, Poetic Tradition. Oxford Classical Monographs, Oxford 2007", in: *Bryn Mawr Classical Review*, 2008.11.14.
D'Alessio, G.B. (2009), "Defining Local Identities in Greek Lyric Poetry", in: R. Hunter / I. Rutherford 2009, 137–67.
Dell, H. (ed.) (1981), *Ancient Macedonian Studies in Honour of Charles F. Edson*, Thessaloniki.
Dewald, C. / Marincola, J. (eds.) (2006), *The Cambridge Companion to Herodotus*, Cambridge.
Di Benedetto, V. (1991), "Pindaro, *PAE.* 7b, 11–14", in: *RFIC* 119, 164–76.
Di Benedetto, V. (2003), "a Pindaro a Callimaco: peana 7b, vv. 11–14", in: *Prometheus* 29, 269–82.
Doglio, F. (ed.) (1983), *Spettacoli conviviali dall'antichità classica alle corti italiane del '400.* Atti del VII Convegno di studio, Viterbo 27–30 Maggio 1982, Rome.
El-Mosalamy, A.H.S. (ed.) (1992), *Proceedings of the XIX International Congress of Papyrology.* Cairo, 2–9 September 1989, vol. I, Cairo.
Errington, R.M. (1981), "Alexander the Philhellene and Persia", in: H. Dell 1981, 139–43.
Fearn, D. (2007a), "Narrating Ambiguity: Murder and Macedonian Allegiance (5.17–22)", in: E. Irwin / E. Greenwood 2007, 98–127.
Fearn, D. (2007b), *Bacchylides. Politics, Performance, Poetic Tradition*, Oxford.
Fearn, D. (2011), "The Ceians and their Choral Lyric: Athenian, Epichoric and Pan-Hellenic Perspectives", in: L. Athanassaki / E. Bowie 2011, 207–34.
Feldherr, A. / Hardy, G. (eds.) (2011), *The Oxford History of Historical Writing*, vol. I, Oxford.
Ferrari, F. (1987), "Sulla ricezione dell'elegia arcaica nella silloge teognidea: il problema delle variant", in: *Maia* 39, 177–97.
Fränkel, H.M. (1961), "Schrullen in den Scholien zu Pindars Nemeen 7 und Olympien 3", in: *Hermes* 89, 385–397.
Gerber, D.E. (1999), *Greek Elegiac Poetry. From the Seventh to the Fifth Centuries BC*, Cambridge / London.
Gentili, B. (1958), *Bacchilide. Studi*, Urbino.
Glotz, G. (1925), *Histoire Grecque* vol. I., Paris.
Godley, A.D. (1920–24), *Herodotus. The Histories*, Cambridge.
Graziosi, B. / Haubold, J. (2009), "Greek Lyric and Early Greek Literary History", in: F. Budelmann 2009a, 95–113.

Grethlein, J. (2010), *The Greeks and their Past. Poetry, Oratory and History in the Fifth Century BCE*, Cambridge.
Grethlein, J. / Krebs, C.B. (eds.) (2012), *Time and Narrative in Ancient Historiography. The 'Plupast' from Herodotus to Appian*, Cambridge.
Griffith, M. (1990), "Contest and Contradiction in Early Greek Poetry", in: M. Griffith / D.J. Mastronarde, 185–207.
Griffith, M. / Mastronarde, D.J. (eds.) (1990), *Cabinet of the Muses: Essays on Classical and Comparative Literature in honour of Thomas G. Rosenmeyer*, Atlanta.
Harrison, T. (2000), *Divinity and History. The Religion of Herodotus*, Oxford / New York.
Herington, J. (1991), "The Poem of Herodotus", in: *Arion* 1, 5–16.
Hornblower, S. (1987), *Thucydides*, London.
Hornblower, S. (ed.) (1994), *Greek Historiography*, New York / Oxford.
Hornblower, S. (2004), *Thucydides and Pindar*, Oxford / New York.
Hornblower, S. (2006), "Herodotus' Influence in Antiquity", in: C. Dewald / J. Marincola 2006, 306–18.
Hornblower, S. (2013), *Herodotus. Histories Book V*, Cambridge.
How, W. / Wells, J. (1928), *A Commentary on Herodotus*, vols. I-II, Oxford.
Hunter, R. / Rutherford, I. (eds.) (2009), *Wandering Poets in Ancient Greek Culture. Travel, Locality and Pan-Hellenism*, Cambridge.
Hutchinson, G.O. (2001), *Greek Lyric Poetry. A Commentary on Selected Larger Pieces*, Oxford.
Irwin, E. / Greenwood, E. (eds.) (2007), *Reading Herodotus. A Study of the* Logoi *in Book 5 of Herodotus'* Histories, Cambridge.
Kim, L. (2010), *Homer between History and Fiction in Imperial Greek Literature*, Cambridge.
Konstan, D. / Raaflaub, K.A. (eds.) (2010), *Epic and History*, Chichester / West Sussex / U.K. / Malden.
Kullmann, W. / Althoff, J. (eds.) (1993), *Vermittlung und Tradierung von Wissen in der griechischen Kultur*, Tübingen.
Labarbe, J. (1984), "Polycrate, Amasis et l'anneau", in: *L'Antiquité Classique* 53, 15–34.
Lateiner, D. (1986), "The Empirical Element in the Methods of Early Greek Medical Writers and Herodotus: a Shared Epistemological Response", in: *Antichthon* 20, 1–20.
Lehnus, L. (1981), *Pindaro. Olimpiche*, Milan.
Lulli, L. (2011), *Narrare in distici: l'elegia greca arcaica e classica di argomento storico-mitico*, Rome.
Luraghi, N. (ed.) (2001), *The Historian's Craft in the Age of Herodotus*, Oxford.
Luraghi, N. (2013), "The Stories Before the *Histories:* Folktale and Traditional Narrative", in: R. Vignolo-Munson 2013, 87–112.
Maehler, H. (2004), *Bacchylides. A selection*, Cambridge.
Marcozzi, D. / Sinatra, M. / Vannicelli, P. (1994), "Tra epica e storiografia: il "catalogo delle navi"", in: *SMEA* 33, 163–174.
Marincola, J. / Llewellyn-Jones, L. / Maciver, C. (eds.) (2012), *Greek Notions of the Past in the Archaic and Classical Eras. History Without Historians*, Edinburgh.
Mazzarino, S. (1947), *Fra Oriente e Occidente: ricerche di storia greca arcaica*, Florence.
Mazzarino, S. (1966), *Il pensiero storico classico*, vol. I, Bari.
McClure, L.K. (ed.) (2002), *Sexuality and Gender in the Classical World. Readings and Sources*, Oxford.
Molyneux, J.H. (1992), *Simonides. A Historical Study*, Wauconda.

Nenci, G. (2006³), *Erodoto. Le Storie. Libro V. La rivolta della Ionia*, Milan.
Nicolai, R. (2012), "Erodoto e la tragedia di Troia (2.112–120)", in: G. Bastianini / W. Lapini / M. Tulli 2012, 633–49.
Nobili, C. (2009), "Tra epos ed elegia: il nuovo Archiloco", in: *Maia* 61, 229–49.
Obbink, D. (2001), "The Genre of *Plataea*. Generic Unity in the New Simonides", in: D. Boedeker / D. Sider 2001, 65–85.
Obbink, D. / Rutherford, R. (eds.) (2011), *Culture in Pieces. Essays on Ancient Texts in Honour of Peter Parsons*, Oxford.
van Oeteghem, J. (1940), "L'anneau de Polycrate", in: *Les etudes des Classiques* 9, 311–4.
Palmisciano, R. (2007), "Elementi popolari nella poesia corale. Il modo narrativo del Ditirambo XVII di Bacchilide", in: *SemRom* 10, 41–67.
Pelliccia, H. (1992), "Sappho 16, Gorgias' *Helen*, and the Preface to Herodotus' *Histories*", in: *YCS* 29, 63–84.
Podlecki, A. (1974), "Archilochus and Apollo", in: *Phoenix* 28, 1–17.
Race, W.H. (1997a), *Pindar. Nemean Odes, Isthmian Odes, Fragments*, Cambridge / London.
Race, W.H. (1997b), *Pindar. Olympian Odes, Pythian Odes*, Cambridge (MA) / London.
Reinach, S. (1905), "Xerxès et l'Hellespont", in: *RA* 6, 1–4.
Rossi, L.E. (1983), "Il simposio greco arcaico e classico come spettacolo fine a se stesso", in: F. Doglio 1983, 41–50.
Rowe, C. / Schofield, M. (eds.) (2000), *The Cambridge History of Greek and Roman Political Thought*, Cambridge.
Rutherford, I. (2001), "The New Simonides: Toward a Commentary", in: D. Boedeker / D. Sider 2001, 33–54.
Scaife, R. (1989), "Alexander I in the Histories of Herodotos", in: *Hermes* 117, 129–37.
Segal, C. (1971), "Croesus on the Pyre: Herodotus and Bacchylides", in: *WS* 5, 39–51.
Slater, W.J. (1969), *Lexicon to Pindar*, Berlin.
Stehle, E. (2001), "A Bard of the Iron Age and His Auxiliary Muse", in: D. Boedeker / D. Sider 2001, 106–19.
Thomas, R. (1993), "Performance and Written Publication in Herodotus and the Sophistic Generation", in: W. Kullmann / J. Althoff 1993, 225–244.
Thomas, R. (2000), *Herodotus in Context*, Cambridge.
Thomas, R. (2006), "The Intellectual Milieu of Herodotus", in: C. Dewald / J. Marincola 2006, 60–75.
Vannicelli, P. (2007), "Simonide, Erodoto e le Termopile", in: *QUCC* 85, 95–103.
Vannicelli, P. (2013), *Resistenza e intesa. Studi sulle guerre persiane in Erodoto*, Bari.
Verdin, H. (1977), "Les remarques critiques d'Hérodote et de Thucydide sur la poésie en tant que source historique", in: *Symbolae* 6, 53–76.
Vetta, M. (ed.) (1983a), *Poesia e simposio nella Grecia antica*, Bari.
Vetta, M. (1983b), "Poesia simposiale nella Grecia arcaica e classica", in: M. Vetta 1983a, 13–60.
Vignolo-Munson, R. (ed.) (2013), *Herodotus. Volume 1. Herodotus and the Narrative of the Past*, Oxford.
Vox, O. (1984), "Bacchilide e Timocreonte contro Temistocle", in: *Prometheus* 10, 117–20.
West, M.L. (1993), "Simonides Redivivus", in: *ZPE* 98, 1–14.
West, M.L. (2011), "Pindar as a Man of Letters", in: D. Obbink / R. Rutherford 2011, 50–68.
West, S. (2007), "Herodotus Lyricorum Studiosus", in: *Palamedes* 2, 109–130.

Winkler, J. (2002), "Double Consciousness in Sappho's Lyrics", in: L. K. McClure 2002, 38–71.

Winton, R. (2000), "Herodotus, Thucydides and the Sophists", in: C. Rowe / M. Schofield 2000, 89–121.

Ioannis M. Konstantakos
Cambyses and the Sacred Bull (Hdt. 3.27– 29 and 3.64): History and Legend

Abstract: This article examines a pair of closely connected episodes in Herodotus' account of King Cambyses. The deranged Persian monarch kills the Apis, the sacred bull of Memphis, by striking the animal on its thigh with his sword; subsequently, he perishes after wounding himself on his own thigh with the same weapon. In fact, no Apis seems to have been slain during Cambyses' reign in Egypt. The Herodotean story is a historical legend, i.e., a fictional narrative attached to a historical figure of the recent past (cf. Donelli's and Liotsakis' papers in this volume). This fictitious creation presumably originated from elites in Egypt and Persia who were hostile to Cambyses and wished to slander him. Iranian religious and mythical motifs are especially prominent in the narrative. The ritual slaying of bulls, regularly connected with figures of Iranian legend and cult, such as Yima and Mithra, has been distorted into an act of madness, so as to denigrate the hateful king. The story of Cambyses also presents a series of parallels with the religious crimes and death of another impious monarch, Amar-Sin of Ur, as described in a Babylonian historical work, the *Weidner Chronicle*. Possibly, the Persian enemies of Cambyses used a religious legend akin to that of Amar-Sin as raw material for their defamatory storytelling. This case offers a good example of a piece of fiction that has infiltrated Greek historiography and has been absorbed into the largely legendary Herodotean portrait of an archetypical oriental autocrat.

1

Cambyses receives very bad press in Herodotus' History. He is depicted as a perverse, tyrannical ruler who slides into lunacy, commits atrocious acts, and meets an inglorious end. With his megalomaniacal insanity, he incarnates the mad king and stands in the rank of famous literary representatives of the same type, from Shakespeare's Richard III and Rabelais' Picrochole to Visconti's Ludwig and George R. R. Martin's Aerys Targaryen. As is usual with the important figures of Herodotus' oeuvre, this portrait of Cambyses is a composite construct, which amalgamates materials from various sources. All these materials have been extensively reworked and fused together into an integrated whole by Herodotus, who creatively shaped the historical narrative and the character of the

Persian king in accordance with his own intellectual preoccupations and the basic general themes of his work.¹

With regard to Greek sources, the influence of tragic models on the personality of the Herodotean Cambyses is conspicuous and has been often pointed out. Herodotus seems to have consciously assimilated patterns and motifs from Attic tragedy, especially from the characters and stories of great tragic transgressors, in order to turn his Cambyses into an exemplary personage, an archetype of the hubristic tyrant, similar to figures such as Pentheus, the Aeschylean Xerxes, or the Creon of the *Antigone*. Charged with rich tragic overtones, the Persian despot becomes in Herodotus' hands the paradigmatic autocrat who transgresses the limits of his power, violates all the religious norms and human customs, offends the divine order with his heinous crimes, and is severely punished by the gods as a result. At the very end, however, Cambyses regains his senses and recognizes his guilt in a moment of dramatic enlightenment (comparable to the self-discovery of an Oedipus, an Ajax, or a Heracles) which leads to a finale full of tragic ἔλεος.²

Most fruitfully, perhaps, the Herodotean "tragedy" of Cambyses can be read in comparison with Aeschylus' *Persians*, an important literary source for the entire oeuvre of Herodotus, especially with regard to the narrative of the Persian wars in the later books.³ In the text of the *Persians*, Cambyses is not named; his reign is rapidly passed over in Darius' overview of the Achaemenid history (A. *Pers.* 773) – possibly an indication of unease on the part of Darius' ghost, given that the negative aspects of Cambyses' rule were believed to far outweigh the positive ones.⁴ However, the Herodotean Cambyses presents a number of

---

1 On Herodotus' creative contribution to the shaping of the narrative see especially Köhnken 1980, 42–50; Brown 1982; Lloyd 1988, 57–62; Munson 1991; Erbse 1992, 45–55. On the Herodotean portrait of Cambyses see also the article of V. Liotsakis in this volume.
2 On the tragic elements in Cambyses' story see Legrand 1949, 12; Myres 1953, 52f., 77–79; Reinhardt 1966, 154; Aly 1969, 86; Friedrich 1979, 118f., 126; Chiasson 1979, 133–143, 214, 231; Brown 1982, 388; Gould 1989, 74–76; Erbse 1992, 49, 54f.; Nielsen 1997, 48, 53f., 66f., 77, 80f.; Saïd 2002, 120, 130f.; Griffin 2006, 48f., 52, 59; Asheri/Lloyd/Corcella 2007, 37–39, 389; Wesselmann 2011, 92–104, 109, 143–146; cf. Gammie 1986, 174f., 180–182, 185; Munson 1991, 45–47, 55f. I am indebted to one of the anonymous referees of the series for stimulating suggestions in this respect. On Herodotus' exploitation of Greek poetry generally, see the article of G. Donelli in this volume. On the relations between tragedy and Greek historiography, cf. the articles of S. Farrington and V.M. Grossi in this volume.
3 See e.g. Chiasson 1979, 4f., 13f., 31–49, 68–75, 235; Chiasson 1982, 156f.; Lazenby 1988; Nielsen 1997, 49–58; Pelling 1997b; Harrison 2000, especially 44–48, 53–55, 66–73, 132–135; Saïd 2002, 118, 137–145; Chiasson 2003, 31f.; Griffin 2006, 54–56; Wesselmann 2011, 41. All provide references to earlier bibliography.
4 See Belloni 1994, 239, 242f.; Garvie 2009, 300, 304; cf. also below, section 3.

similarities to Aeschylus' portrait of the hubristic Xerxes. Both these kings transgress the sanctioned limits of their empire, which have been ordained by nature or by the divine order; Xerxes crosses over to Europe and attempts to subdue mainland Greece, while Cambyses marches against the fabulous land of the Ethiopians at the very ends of the earth. Both expeditions prove to be disastrous and cause heavy losses to the Persian army, for which the senseless king is clearly responsible (A. *Pers.* 249–514, 550–557, 717–831; Hdt. 3.25). The Persian ruler himself returns from his foolhardy campaign in a sorry state (A. *Pers.* 834–851, 908 ff.; Hdt. 3.25.7, 3.27.1 f.).[5] Further, both Cambyses and Xerxes show impiety towards the religion of the lands they invade. In Aeschylus, Xerxes' army burns and demolishes the temples of the Greek gods, plunders their statues, and destroys the divine altars (*Pers.* 809–812); Xerxes himself is called "an offender against the gods" (θεοβλαβοῦνθ', *Pers.* 831). Similarly, Cambyses burns temples and divine statues in Egypt, derides the images of Egyptian deities, and desecrates old graves (Hdt. 3.16, 3.25.3, 3.37). In both cases, the Persian monarch pays dearly for his *hubris*.[6] As Cambyses lies dying, he bitterly wails for his catastrophic actions, and the Persian lords around him respond by tearing their clothes in despair and mourning loudly (Hdt. 3.65.7–66.1). This brings to mind the finale of the *Persians* (908 ff.) when King Xerxes and the Chorus of his noblemen similarly join in a long antiphonal lament for the Persian disaster.[7]

Without any intention of obfuscating or discounting these Greek components, the present paper will concentrate on a different aspect of the multifaceted Herodotean portrait of Cambyses. In what follows, the focus will be rather on oriental legends of Iranian (or more broadly Asiatic) and Egyptian provenance, which have been absorbed into Herodotus' complex narrative creation and have merged with the echoes from Greek tragedy and with the historian's paradigmatic worldview. In generic terms, the stories about Cambyses' transgressions, crimes, and punishment are indeed classifiable as historical legends, that is, fictitious narratives that revolve around historical personages and their deeds and are set in a more or less recent past. In traditional and pre-industrial societies, the narrator and his audience regularly regard legends as true, although in

---

[5] Cf. Nielsen 1997, 52–54, 80 f. Indeed, the ill-designed expedition against a faraway land, which is attempted by an arrogant and unwise king and ultimately leads to disaster and heavy losses, becomes a recurrent *topos* in Herodotus' Persian histories. Apart from Cambyses and Xerxes, the same pattern is applied to Cyrus' campaign against the Massagetae and Darius' Scythian expedition. Subsequently, the pattern was also taken over by Thucydides. See the article of V. Liotsakis in this volume.
[6] Cf. Griffin 2006, 48, 57.
[7] Cf. Saïd 2002, 131.

point of fact they are far from truthful historical accounts; usually, they contain a modicum of verifiable historical events, mixed with a generous amount of pure invention.[8] From our modern point of view, the legends of this kind represent perhaps the most elementary and primary form of "historical fiction".

In particular, Herodotus apparently based his dreary picture of King Cambyses on legends which were initially fabricated with a specific purpose: namely, to denigrate this Persian ruler and his memory by creating a distorted and negative image of his life and character and by propagating this creation among the populations of the Achaemenid Empire. As will become clear in the analysis below, elite groups, both in Iran and in Egypt, had reasons to be hostile to Cambyses and wished to defame him. Ultimately, their stories reached Herodotus' receptive ears and furnished the main material for his account.[9] In present-day terms, the narrative concoctions of these groups might be styled "propaganda", in the basic, "dictionary" sense: an organized attempt to circulate specially composed pieces of discourse in order to influence the audience in a particular way and serve a specific political agenda.[10] The following discussion will hopefully help to trace the methods and mechanisms through which the enemies of Cambyses created their defamatory tales and had them spread throughout the Near Eastern and the Hellenic world.

---

8 See Bascom 1965; Dégh 1996; Hansen 2002, 2, 13–16, 25f.; Röhrich/Uther/Brednich 2004. As demonstrated in the article of G. Donelli in this volume, Herodotus often reworks legendary narratives which largely consist of folktale or mythical motifs but have been attached to historical characters of the past, especially to great rulers, such as Croesus, Polycrates, Amasis, and Alexander I of Macedon. On legends about Persian kings in particular see West 2003.
9 On the defamatory and invented nature of the stories about Cambyses see Jacoby 1913, 427f.; Schwartz 1949, 65–70, 74–80; Atkinson 1956, 168–171; Aly 1969, 78, 86; Dandamaev 1976, 144–157; Hofmann/Vorbichler 1979, 9–15, 40–44, 60–74, 96–140, 172–178; Hofmann/Vorbichler 1980; Krauss 1980; Bresciani 1981, 218–221; Bianchi 1982, 943f., 948f.; Boyce 1982, 72–82; Lloyd 1982, 173; Walser 1983, 10–12; Cook 1985, 214f.; Bresciani 1985, 504–507; Gammie 1986, 180–182, 185; Balcer 1987, 50–53, 64–66, 69–72, 77–108; Briant 1988, 153f.; Cuyler Young 1988, 47–52; Lloyd 1988, 55–57, 62–66; Ray 1988, 255–261; Dandamaev 1989, 99–102; Griffiths 1989, 70f., 77f.; Erbse 1992, 47f.; Högemann 1992, 203–205; Balcer 1995, 103–114; Lenfant 1996, 369–371; Yamauchi 1996; Briant 2002, 50, 55–61, 97–106, 886–888, 896; Chimko 2003, 28, 31, 54; Cruz-Uribe 2003, 10, 37–39, 43–51; Dillery 2005; Asheri/Lloyd/Corcella 2007, 397, 414f., 423f., 431–434; Kuhrt 2007, 104–106; Minunno 2008, 130–143; Ruzicka 2012, 18, 235; Brosius 2013, 662; Lloyd 2014, 189.
10 See e.g. the definitions of the word "propaganda" in the *Oxford English Dictionary* or the *Concise Oxford Dictionary of Current English*. See also G. Donelli's article in this volume for another Herodotean episode (5.17–22) that probably reflects a propagandistic narrative – this time in favour of a king (Alexander I of Macedon).

2

In Herodotus' account, Cambyses' death forms the climax of his sensational course towards destruction. The king's fatal end is foreshadowed from earlier on in the narrative, in an episode recounting Cambyses' greatest sacrilege, for which he was eventually punished by the gods: the slaughter of the Apis, the sacred bull of Memphis, which was regarded as the manifestation of Ptah, the patron god of the city. The Apis was installed in special quarters within the southern court of the temple of Ptah at Memphis and received religious veneration and honours from the Egyptian priesthood and the faithful pilgrims. When it died, mourning was observed for seventy days, while its body was mummified and buried (formerly in a wooden coffin, from Amasis' reign onwards in a monumental granite sarcophagus) at the Serapeum, in the great necropolis of the Saqqara. After the death of the Apis, its successor was selected from among recently born oxen throughout the land of Egypt, on the basis of traditionally prescribed bodily marks.[11] Killing a holy Apis would have been one of the worst conceivable religious crimes for the ancient Egyptians, tantamount to deicide.

This was the abomination committed by Cambyses according to Herodotus (3.27–29). The Persian king had just returned from his disastrous Ethiopian expedition in a choleric mood, only to find the entire population of Memphis celebrating the epiphany of a new Apis bull. Cambyses was enraged, thinking that the Egyptians were delighted with his military catastrophe. He ordered the local priests to bring that strange Apis divinity before him. As soon as he beheld the sacred ox, he drew out his dagger and with deranged glee struck a blow at the animal, meaning to stab it in its belly; he missed, however, and wounded the Apis on its thigh. Seeing the spilled blood of the poor beast, Cambyses burst out laughing at what he considered to be the Egyptians' folly: "You silly people, is this the kind of gods you have, made of flesh and blood and susceptible to iron blows? Truly, this is the god the Egyptians deserve!"[12] The priests were sentenced to a flogging, while the religious festivities in honour of the Apis were forbidden. The injured bull eventually died of the wound, enclosed in its sanctuary. The priests then buried it in secret.

---

[11] On the cult of the sacred Apis and its burial customs see Vercoutter 1975; Lloyd 1975–1988, II 171f., III 135f.; Thompson 1988, 17f., 190–207; Jones 1990; Borgeaud/Volokhine 2000, 62–71.

[12] Hdt. 3.29.2 (in the edition of Hude 1927): Ὦ κακαὶ κεφαλαί, τοιοῦτοι θεοὶ γίνονται, ἔναιμοί τε καὶ σαρκώδεες καὶ ἐπαΐοντες σιδηρίων; ἄξιος μέν γε Αἰγυπτίων οὗτός γε ὁ θεός. All translations from ancient sources in this article are mine.

This entire episode seems to be a fictitious creation, as is widely acknowledged in modern research.[13] In the underground galleries of the Serapeum a number of sarcophagi and official burial stelae of the sacred bulls deposited there (from the time of the 26th Dynasty onwards) have been excavated. These findings, at least as interpreted by the majority of experts, indicate that no Apis was slain in the manner described above during Cambyses' domination in Egypt. Actually, only one of those holy animals is recorded to have expired within that particular period. According to the hieroglyphic stele commemorating its funeral, the Apis in question had been born in the 27th year of Pharaoh Amasis (543 B.C.) and was interred in the 6th regnal year of Cambyses, i.e. 524 B.C., more or less shortly after the Persian conquest of Egypt.[14] This bull was clearly a very old animal, about eighteen or nineteen years old at the time of its death – nothing like the newly born calf (μόσχος) which Cambyses injures in Herodotus' account (3.28.2f.). In addition, the inscription on the sumptuous sarcophagus of this Apis declares that King Cambyses dedicated the monument himself; in this respect, the Persian ruler followed a practice attested already

---

13 See Schwartz 1949, 68, 74f., 79f.; Atkinson 1956, 170f.; Hofmann/Vorbichler 1979, 176; Hofmann/Vorbichler 1980, 86f., 94f.; Krauss 1980, 303f.; Bresciani 1981, 218; Bianchi 1982, 943, 948; Boyce 1982, 73; Brown 1982, 397; Bresciani 1985, 504f.; Cook 1985, 215; Balcer 1987, 84–93, 102f.; Cuyler Young 1988, 51; Lloyd 1988, 64; Ray 1988, 259f.; Thompson 1988, 106; Dandamaev 1989, 82; Balcer 1995, 105–107, 109f.; Devauchelle 1995, 68–70; Lenfant 1996, 369; Yamauchi 1996, 381–387; Bichler 2001, 272f.; Briant 2002, 55–57, 887f.; Chimko 2003, 54; Cruz-Uribe 2003, 43–45; Dillery 2005, 394–400; Asheri/Lloyd/Corcella 2007, 397, 427f.; Minunno 2008, 130–133, 138; Van De Mieroop 2011, 310, 313f.; Ruzicka 2012, 18, 235.

14 As accepted by the majority of experts, the chronological indications of this and other Egyptian documents concerning Cambyses' reign take as point of reference the initial ascension of Cambyses to the Achaemenid throne (530/529 B.C.), not the actual date of his conquest of Egypt. See Parker 1941, 301; Atkinson 1956, 168–171; Ray 1988, 265; Dandamaev 1989, 76; Depuydt 1995b, 166, 169–173; Depuydt 1995c, 197f.; Depuydt 1996, 180–190; Kahn 2007, 103–106; Kuhrt 2007, 122; Quack 2011, 236–243. This dating system was not devoid of political significance. Cambyses presumably imposed it on the administration of the subdued Egyptian realm, presenting himself anachronistically as ruler of Egypt from the very time he acquired the kingship of the Persian Empire – as though the land he subsequently conquered were a rightful dominion of his from the start of his career. A radically different chronology has been proposed by Devauchelle 1998 and Cruz-Uribe 2003, 54–57: according to their theory, all Egyptian texts count Cambyses' years of reign starting from his occupation of Egypt (526 or 525 B.C.), not from his ascension to the Achaemenid throne. This interpretation would completely alter the dates recorded on the two Apis stelae. In practice, however, such a hypothesis is impossible to reconcile with the extant documents and testimonia and has been convincingly criticized by Kahn 2007, 103f.; Minunno 2008, 132; Quack 2011, 240–242; cf. Kuhrt 2007, 122; Van De Mieroop 2011, 314; Vittmann 2011, 414.

from the time of Pharaoh Amasis.[15] The texts on the epitaph stele and the sarcophagus also indicate that the sacred bull was solemnly buried, following the due customs and ceremonies. This clearly does not accord with Herodotus' statement that the Memphite priests interred the dead beast secretly (3.29.3). Finally, Cambyses himself is depicted on the stele in standard Egyptian pharaonic attire, kneeling before the Apis as a pious worshipper.[16] None of these elements suggests that the animal in question was violently slain or met an unnatural end.

As for the next Apis, which replaced the one Cambyses buried, it died peacefully quite some time later. Its burial stele in the Serapeum places its demise and interment in the fourth regnal year of Darius (518 B.C.), when Cambyses had been dead for four years.[17] There is no factual evidence, whether in the monuments of the Saqqara or anywhere else, that another sacred Apis intervened between these two. The most plausible conclusion is that Cambyses did not murder any sacred bull at Memphis. On the contrary, the available information shows that he fully respected the Egyptian religion; he took care of the divine creature's ritual burial, participated in the required ceremonies, personally dedicated an expensive sarcophagus, and generally behaved in such a manner that the Memphites could unambiguously present him as a devout venerator of the Apis.[18]

---

15 See Thompson 1988, 192; Borgeaud/Volokhine 2000, 65.
16 On the funeral stele and sarcophagus of this Apis bull see Posener 1936, 30–35; Atkinson 1956, 170f.; Porter/Moss 1974, 799; Boyce 1982, 73; Bresciani 1985, 504; Balcer 1987, 87–91; Depuydt 1995a, 121; Depuydt 1995c, 197f.; Devauchelle 1995, 68–70; Depuydt 1996, 185; Briant 2002, 57; Dillery 2005, 400; Kahn 2007, 105; Kuhrt 2007, 122–124; Minunno 2008, 131f. The bull may actually have died many months before his official burial, which could have been delayed because of the turmoil caused by Cambyses' invasion of Egypt or the initial reservations of the new Persian administration towards the Apis cult. See Posener 1936, 173; Depuydt 1995a, 121; Depuydt 1995c, 197f., 201f.; Devauchelle 1995, 69f.; Asheri/Lloyd/Corcella 2007, 427f.; Kuhrt 2007, 124; Minunno 2008, 132; Quack 2011, 231; Van De Mieroop 2011, 314. For a different explanation, which eliminates the long interval between the animal's death and its funeral, see Atkinson 1956, 169f.
17 See Posener 1936, 36–41; Parker 1941, 286f.; Atkinson 1956, 170; Porter/Moss 1974, 799f.; Bresciani 1985, 504f.; Balcer 1995, 108; Depuydt 1995a, 120f.; Depuydt 1995c, 197; Devauchelle 1995, 69; Depuydt 1996, 185; Cruz-Uribe 2003, 44; Dillery 2005, 400; Kahn 2007, 105; Vittmann 2011, 386, 392, 414.
18 See Briant 2002, 57, 887. On the historical Cambyses' respectful attitude towards Egyptian religious life and customs generally, cf. Posener 1936, 168–175; Atkinson 1956, 168, 176f.; Dandamaev 1976, 106; Bianchi 1982, 943f., 948; Boyce 1982, 71–74; Lloyd 1982, 169–173; Bresciani 1985, 503–507; Balcer 1987, 87–89; Cuyler Young 1988, 50; Dandamaev 1989, 76–79, 81f.; Balcer 1995, 103–107; Lenfant 1996, 370f.; Yamauchi 1996, 374f.; Briant 2002, 57–60; Chimko 2003, 28f.; Dillery 2005, 400–402; Asheri/Lloyd/Corcella 2007, 413f.; Kuhrt 2007, 105; Minunno 2008, 133–136; Ruzicka 2012, 18–20, 235; Lloyd 2014, 188f.

Of course, there have been attempts to salvage the credibility of Herodotus' narrative. Some scholars have postulated the existence of another Apis bull between the one which was buried in 524 B.C. and its successor which survived into Darius' reign. This hypothetical intermediary Apis is supposed to have never been officially installed; it was murdered by Cambyses at a very young age, soon after being discovered by the Egyptian priests, and was not properly enthroned. For this reason, its existence was recorded nowhere in archival documents. Further, because of the ignominious circumstances of its death, this Apis was not buried in the Serapeum; as Herodotus notes, the priests interred it secretly (λάθρη, 3.29.3), presumably at a now unidentifiable place.[19] However, the long chain of hypotheses involved in this line of argumentation does not seem persuasive.[20] The complete lack of any indication of such an intermediary Apis, either in the Serapeum or in other Egyptian documents, is a stumbling block for the Herodotean version of events.

In addition, the theory would presuppose another serious implausibility: that within a very short interval (practically a few months) Cambyses changed from a devout participant in the ritual funeral of one sacred bull to the sacrilegious killer of the next one.[21] A sudden onslaught of madness, like the one described in Herodotus' highly literary narrative, might account for such a mood swing. However, it is significant that Herodotus makes absolutely no mention of an earlier devout attitude of Cambyses towards the Apis or generally the cults of Egypt. There is no abrupt change or character contradiction in the Herodotean account, which consistently depicts Cambyses as impious and offensive against the Egyptian religion throughout his sojourn in the land of the Nile. In any case, a sudden loss of sanity seems a rather weak explanation in true historical terms. It would not be methodically sound to invoke such an extreme and rare psychological phenomenon in order to account for a purported historical anomaly, which is in essence an invention of a few modern researchers and finds no support in ancient documentary evidence.

Therefore, unless new data proving the existence of an interim Apis comes to light, the best solution is still to regard Herodotus' account of the slaughter of the

---

19 See Klasens 1945–1948, 346–348; Depuydt 1995a, 122–126. The theory has been favourably received, but without the support of new arguments, by Högemann 1992, 204; Devauchelle 1995, 70; Borgeaud/Volokhine 2000, 65 f.; Kahn 2007, 105–107, 112; Quack 2011, 231; Vittmann 2011, 374 f., 414; cf. Agut-Labordère 2005, 9 f.; Kuhrt 2007, 124.
20 Cf. the criticisms of many scholars who treat this theory with scepticism: Yamauchi 1996, 385–387; Devauchelle 1998, 17; Briant 2002, 887 f.; Cruz-Uribe 2003, 43–45; Dillery 2005, 400; Minunno 2008, 132 f.; Van De Mieroop 2011, 314.
21 Cf. Yamauchi 1996, 386; Dillery 2005, 400; Minunno 2008, 132.

holy bull as a defamatory invention, like so many other episodes concerning Cambyses' supposed madness. The lying tale was presumably fabricated with the intention of denigrating Cambyses as a sacrilegious lunatic. The inventors or disseminators of the story may have taken their cue from an actual event: one Apis did indeed perish (of old age) shortly before 524 B.C., approximately at the time when Cambyses was conquering Egypt and establishing himself as a ruler at Memphis. Inspired by that temporal coincidence, the enemies of Cambyses completely inverted the facts; they presented the Persian monarch killing the Apis, deriding and prohibiting its worship, while in reality Cambyses had shown reverence for the cult and duly played his religious role as the new Pharaoh.[22]

Nonetheless, the subsequent story of Cambyses' death, coming thirty-five chapters later in Herodotus 3.64, was evidently modelled on the episode of the Apis' murder. The cause and mechanics of the king's demise correspond exactly to the manner in which he fatally wounded the Apis, thus appearing to be retribution for the killing of the sacred beast. Cambyses learned about a revolt in Persia and hastened to return to his homeland in order to suppress the rebels and reclaim his throne. As he leaped up on his horse, the scabbard of his sword broke off and the naked blade hit and injured him on his thigh, at the very spot where he had himself stabbed the Apis bull. Herodotus expressly emphasizes that the location of both wounds was exactly the same, highlighting the parallelism between the two incidents (3.64.3). Afterwards, the king's gash festered, his bone putrefied, and he eventually died of gangrene (3.66.2). The sacrilegious ruler and his holy victim die in the same manner, from identical wounds on the same part of their body.

Furthermore, both injuries seem to have been inflicted by the same instrument. In the Apis episode Cambyses draws a dagger he is carrying and strikes the bull with it. In the death scene he is hurt by a sword that he similarly wears on himself. It is plausible to conclude that both cases involve the same weapon, even though this is termed ἐγχειρίδιον (hand-knife or poniard) in 3.29.1 and ξίφος (sword) in 3.64.3. In this latter passage Herodotus' description clearly indicates that Cambyses' sword is the characteristic Persian *akinakes*: a short sabre (ca. 35–45 cm in length) with a straight broad blade, which was used by various Iranian populations. Warriors would carry this weapon on their right side, in a scabbard suspended from their belts. The lower tip of the scabbard was shaped like a trefoil or a mushroom (for this reason it is called μύκης by Herodotus 3.64.3). Hanging down from the man's hip, the *akinakes* tilt-

---

[22] Cf. Cruz-Uribe 2003, 44 f.

ed forward and rested on the upper part of the thigh, to which it was fastened with a cord. Thus, as Cambyses jumped abruptly to mount his horse, the tip of the scabbard broke off and the entire sheath fell down, exposing the naked blade, which then cut into the king's flesh.[23] This short sabre was something between a proper sword and a large poniard; it could thus be called both ξίφος and ἐγχειρίδιον. Indeed, in other passages Herodotus uses both these words for this type of weapon (ξίφος in 7.54.2, ἐγχειρίδιον in 7.61.1).[24] It is admittedly odd that Herodotus does not explicitly draw attention to this particular coincidence with regard to the weapon, as he does with the identical locations of the two wounds. Perhaps the original report about Cambyses' death (the tendentious oral tale ultimately lying behind the Greek historian's narrative) pointed out more clearly that the same dagger had inflicted the fatal injuries both on the Apis and on the king. If so, then either Herodotus himself or his immediate informers must have missed that striking and ominous detail.[25]

As becomes evident, Cambyses' death fully conforms to the principle of retaliation; he suffers the same type of wound on the same bodily spot and by the same weapon as the creature he killed.[26] Like the sinners punished in the circles of Dante's Inferno, the dying Persian king could veritably exclaim: *Così s'osserva in me lo contrapasso* (*Inferno* XXVIII 142). The precise application of the *lex talionis* with regard to Cambyses' end can certainly be read as an exemplary *tisis*, the mark of the divine intervention for the punishment of a *hubristes*. This motif ech-

---

[23] See Walser 1983, 15–18 (and plates 1–5); Calmeyer 1987, 13; Asheri/Lloyd/Corcella 2007, 462. On the *akinakes* generally, see Stucky 1976; Kuhrt 2007, 533–535 (figures 11.26–11.28).
[24] Similarly Xenophon calls this weapon μάχαιραν ἢ κοπίδα (*Cyr.* 1.2.13). In Ctesias fr. 13.14 Lenfant, Cambyses wounds himself on the thigh with a μάχαιρα. Cf. Walser 1983, 12f., 16.
[25] It has repeatedly been argued that the coincidence of both wounds on the same bodily part was an invention of Herodotus himself. The historian was possibly informed that Cambyses had died from an injury on his thigh (cf. Ctesias fr. 13.14 Lenfant for a variant of this tradition). Consequently, he presented the Persian king striking the holy bull at the same spot, so as to emphasize the motif of retribution in Cambyses' punishment. See Köhnken 1980, 46, 49f.; Erbse 1992, 54f.; cf. Schwartz 1949, 68; Minunno 2008, 132f. If this were so, however, Herodotus would not have failed to stress that the weapon was also the same in both episodes; this fact is plainly discernible from the data provided in the Herodotean narrative, yet it is strangely overlooked by Herodotus. It thus seems that the retaliation theme was already a feature of earlier traditions, which Herodotus received and reworked.
[26] On the retaliation principle in Cambyses' death, cf. Schwartz 1949, 68f.; Reinhardt 1966, 156f.; Aly 1969, 86, 97f., 160, 250; Bresciani 1981, 218; Gammie 1986, 180; Balcer 1987, 94f., 99f., 106; Griffiths 1989, 61, 75; Yamauchi 1996, 387, 390; Gould 2003, 301; Asheri/Lloyd/Corcella 2007, 428f.; Minunno 2008, 131–133; Wesselmann 2011, 81, 120, 122–127.

oes tragic schemes of transgression and *nemesis*[27] and is so well integrated in Herodotus' peculiar view of the world order, that many scholars brand it as a typically Herodotean mannerism.[28] Nonetheless, the same principle of retaliatory punishment is evident in early Greek myths, as well as in some very ancient Near Eastern legends, which strongly recall Cambyses' fate and will be discussed below (section 4).[29] This case illustrates once again the composite nature of the Herodotean narrative, the fusion of ingredients and influences from diverse sources within Herodotus' historiographical construct.

3

Like the other defamatory tales concerning Cambyses' madness and tyranny, the Apis episode and the death story are regularly considered in modern scholarship to be products of Egyptian slander.[30] It is often thought that the priestly elites of Egypt had some grounds for disliking Cambyses. One of this king's decrees, fragmentarily preserved on a Demotic papyrus from the early Ptolemaic period, indicates that he introduced economic reforms that reduced the revenues of certain

---

[27] Cf. Reinhardt 1966, 156 f.; Saïd 2002, 130.

[28] See e.g. Köhnken 1980, 42 f., 46, 49 f.; Munson 1991, 51 f.; Erbse 1992, 54 f.; Asheri 1999, 110; Asheri/Lloyd/Corcella 2007, 462. On the pattern of *hubris* and divine punishment in Herodotus, cf. also the article of V. Liotsakis in this volume, concerning Croesus' story and its reception in Thucydides.

[29] Cf. Hofmann/Vorbichler 1980, 102. In Greek myth, the motif is inherent in the stories about the underworld punishments of great sinners, such as Tantalus, the Danaids, or the criminals of Polygnotus' *Nekyia*. Tantalus, for instance, has misbehaved at Zeus' table with regard to the food and drink of the gods; he is therefore tormented in the netherworld through perpetual loss of food and drink. The same pattern underlies the myth of Neoptolemus, who kills Priam on the sacred altar of Zeus and is himself slain beside another holy altar (the one of Apollo in Delphi). For discussion of these and further examples see Nilsson 1967, 690 f.; Nilsson 1972, 116–118; Friedrich 1979, 99 f.; Wesselmann 2011, 122–127.

[30] See Jacoby 1913, 427 f.; Posener 1936, 170–175; Schwartz 1949, 68, 74 f., 79 f.; Legrand 1949, 18–25; Aly 1969, 86, 97 f.; Bresciani 1981, 218–221; Lloyd 1982, 173; Bresciani 1985, 505 f.; Cook 1985, 215; Calmeyer 1987, 13; Cuyler Young 1988, 50 f.; Lloyd 1988, 62–66; Ray 1988, 260 f.; Griffiths 1989, 78; Högemann 1992, 204 f.; Lenfant 1996, 369 f.; Yamauchi 1996, 386 f.; Briant 2002, 59, 887 f.; Chimko 2003, 31, 54; Dillery 2005, 389–391, 394–400; Minunno 2008, 134–143; Van De Mieroop 2011, 314; Brosius 2013, 662; Lloyd 2014, 189. Cf. also Brown 1982, 394, 397; Walser 1983, 11 f.; Erbse 1992, 48, 50, 54; Devauchelle 1995, 67–70; Asheri 1999, 109; Cruz-Uribe 2003, 47–51; Asheri/Lloyd/Corcella 2007, 433 f.; Ruzicka 2012, 18, 235; and see the surveys of Hofmann/Vorbichler 1980, 86 f. and Agut-Labordère 2005, 9–11.

Egyptian temples. Various royal offerings in prime materials (wood, flax), edible commodities (bovines, birds, cereals), and valuable goods (silver), which had previously been donated to those sanctuaries ever since the time of Amasis, were curtailed or altogether abolished. It was further prescribed that thenceforward the temples would have to obtain the aforementioned goods through their own initiative. The priests themselves should acquire birds for their divine offerings; they should also procure wood (for construction or fuel) from specific properties awarded to their sanctuaries. Such measures were bound to cause financial harm to the hieratic personnel of the temples involved. Therefore, the priesthood would have been inclined to present Cambyses as a blasphemous enemy of Egyptian religion.[31] It is also conceivable that the Persian monarch expressed disdain for certain aspects of Egyptian worship, such as the animalistic representation of gods, which he might have regarded as too lowly or grotesque from his own Iranian point of view.[32]

Indeed, another Demotic legal text, from the same Ptolemaic papyrus, briefly refers to the Persian dynast's death in terms that might recall Herodotus' description. The relevant passage is damaged, but according to the restoration proposed by Edda Bresciani, it should read as follows: Cambyses "became himself the cause of his own death for punishment and did not succeed in returning to his homeland".[33] If such a reading is adopted, then the king is once again pre-

---

[31] See Spiegelberg 1914, 32f.; Posener 1936, 170f.; Bresciani 1958, 164–166; Hofmann/Vorbichler 1980, 86; Bresciani 1981, 218f., 221; Bresciani 1985, 505f., 508; Cook 1985, 215; Tuplin 1987, 151f.; Cuyler Young 1988, 50f.; Lloyd 1988, 64–66; Ray 1988, 260; Devauchelle 1995, 75f.; Balcer 1995, 104; Yamauchi 1996, 388f.; Briant 2002, 60f., 887f.; Cruz-Uribe 2003, 48; Dillery 2005, 402; Asheri/Lloyd/Corcella 2007, 434; Kuhrt 2007, 124–127; Minunno 2008, 134–139, 142; Vittmann 2011, 375; cf. also Dandamaev 1976, 106; Dandamaev 1989, 77, 79; Högemann 1992, 276; Lloyd 2014, 189, 195. A different interpretation has been proposed by Agut-Labordère 2005: the main purpose of the decree was to enhance the financial autonomy and self-sufficiency of the temples, as well as to stimulate the local economies developing around them. It was for this reason that local provisioning was promoted over the former royal subventions; cf. Minunno 2008, 135; Ruzicka 2012, 20, 236. It is also noteworthy that the preserved text of the decree only touches upon a limited group of (mostly) consumer goods; it imposes no restrictions concerning other royal gifts, especially in precious materials (gold and gems). Also, it has nothing to say about the large wealth of the temples in real and movable property. See Johnson 1994, 152; Agut-Labordère 2005, 12.

[32] So Minunno 2008, 138f., with further references.

[33] See Bresciani 1981, 217–222: tw-f mwt-f ḥr tb3 bw.ir tw-f pḥ p3e-f tš. Cf. Minunno 2008, 133, 137. The proposition is rejected by Kuhrt 2007, 125f. and Quack 2011, 234f. Cf. further Spiegelberg 1914, 30f.; Dandamaev 1976, 147; Dandamaev 1989, 100; Devauchelle 1995, 74. On the information of ancient sources concerning Cambyses' death and the historical problems

sented as dying of a self-inflicted injury far away from his country, and his end comes as a penalty, presumably for his impiety or his crimes. Stories of this kind might have circulated in the Egyptian tradition. Indeed, Herodotus cites Egyptian informants at various points of his biographical account about the mad Cambyses.[34] It would thus seem that the "Father of History" received most of his relevant material from Egyptian hearsay, possibly transmitted to him through interpreters or Greek residents of the Delta. The primary role of well-known Egyptian figures, locations, and institutions in various episodes also points to Egyptian storytelling.[35]

Nonetheless, there are also other identifiable strata within the complex Herodotean narrative about Cambyses. The adventures of the mad king teem with characteristically Iranian elements; interestingly, these are not restricted to the episodes that take place in the Persian court, but also frequently surface in the chapters concerning Cambyses' Egyptian campaign and sojourn. Inge Hofmann and Anton Vorbichler, in their seminal studies, have especially highlighted the role of distinctive patterns from ancient Iranian mythology, theology, and ritual.[36] Traditional motifs from Persian heroic legends or ceremonial customs of the Mazdaic religion are reflected within Cambyses' story in a distorted, perverted form, so as to appear as crimes and atrocities committed by the crazy monarch.

To cite some telling examples: in the Apis episode, Cambyses puts to death the prefects of Memphis for telling lies (Hdt. 3.27.3). The "Lie" and the "Truth" constitute a fundamental pair of concepts in ancient Iranian faith. The lie not only represents the capital moral crime, but also is identified with the principle

---

posed, see Dandamaev 1976, 146–151; Walser 1983, 8–15; Balcer 1987, 52–59, 93–100; Yamauchi 1996, 389f.; Gippert 2001; Asheri/Lloyd/Corcella 2007, 462; Minunno 2008, 133.
34 See Hdt. 3.16.5, 3.30.1, 3.32.3; cf. Jacoby 1913, 427f.; Lloyd 1988, 60, 62; Erbse 1992, 48, 51; Briant 2002, 59.
35 For instance, the holy Apis and the festival in its honour, Pharaoh Amasis and his tomb, the priests of Memphis, the temple of Hephaestus (i.e. Ptah) in this same city, the oracle of the Egyptian town Buto etc.: see Hdt. 3.16, 3.27–29, 3.37, 3.64.4; cf. Walser 1983, 11f.; Konstantakos 2008, 174–176.
36 See Hofmann/Vorbichler 1979 and Hofmann/Vorbichler 1980; cf. Bichler 2001, 277; Konstantakos 2008, 167–224; Konstantakos 2011, 101–151; and V. Liotsakis' article in this volume. Lloyd's criticism of this approach (Lloyd 1988), though highlighting valuable methodological issues, does not touch upon the distinctive Iranian mythical patterns and ritual motifs that are inherent in Cambyses' story. There is only one way to account for the presence of such elements: to assume that material of ultimately Iranian origin (i.e. Persian calumniatory discourses against Cambyses) has entered into the Herodotean narrative through suitable intermediary informers.

of cosmic evil. It is a demonic power of universal deception, which opposes harmony and distorts the truth about the cosmic order. The ideal Iranian monarch has a duty to combat the lie and uphold the truth.[37] In Herodotus' narrative, however, the Memphite officials are not lying. Their reports to their Persian overlord are entirely truthful. The Apis' epiphany is in fact the sole reason for the joyous celebrations at Memphis. Cambyses' death sentence, therefore, is not a battle against the lie, but simply the murder of innocent people.[38] Further, Cambyses weds his own sister (3.31). So did Yima, the archetypical first man and first king of Iranian myth. Indeed, Zoroastrian religious texts commend the practice of endogamy, including marriages within the close family circle (such as sister with brother).[39] In the Greek historical account, however, this primordial Iranian marriage archetype is perceived as common incest and perverted lust.[40] In other passages, Herodotus presents Cambyses as a heavy drinker of wine and implies that the king's alcoholism contributed to his insanity (3.34.2f., cf. 3.35). This brings to mind the ancient Iranian warriors who drank the sacred intoxicating *haoma*-potion, in order to fall into ecstatic frenzy and thus become fearless in battle.[41] Cambyses' drinking, however, leads not to heroism but to disaster; the resulting madness is no sacred warrior's mania against his enemies, but a catastrophic lunacy decimating the king's immediate environment. Instead of slaying his adversaries in war, the madly drunk Persian ruler murders or at-

---

[37] See Boyce 1975, 193, 200f.; Hofmann/Vorbichler 1979, 43f., 174f.; Hofmann/Vorbichler 1980, 101f.; Boyce 1982, 120–123; Malandra 1983, 12f., 19–24, 47; Schwartz 1985, 641, 685f.; Lecoq 1997, 163f.; Skjærvø 2005, 14, 18–20, 29; Kuhrt 2007, 152, 471; Skjærvø 2011, 19f.; Alberti 2013, 56f.; Skjærvø 2013, 552, 555, 561–563.
[38] See Hofmann/Vorbichler 1980, 94; cf. Asheri/Lloyd/Corcella 2007, 391–393.
[39] Yima's marriage to his sister is recorded in the Pahlavi religious books of medieval times; but the same act is attributed to the corresponding figure (Yama) already in the Sanskrit *Vedas*. The myth, therefore, presumably derives from the oldest Indo-Iranian background. See Boyce 1975, 96; De Jong 1997, 429, 431; Skjærvø 2007, 176, 210. For marriage between blood relatives in the Persian religious and royal tradition see Boyce 1982, 75–77; Schwartz 1985, 656; Herrenschmidt 1987; De Jong 1997, 217, 243f., 424–432; Asheri/Lloyd/Corcella 2007, 430f.; Kuhrt 2007, 578.
[40] See Hofmann/Vorbichler 1979, 175; Hofmann/Vorbichler 1980, 96; De Jong 1997, 426f. Cambyses' marriage to his own sister cannot be read as an attempt to conform to native Egyptian royal customs (for which see Allam 1975, 1164). The episode is said to have taken place in Persia, before the invasion of Egypt (Hdt. 3.31). It therefore belongs to the Iranian components of Herodotus' narrative. See Boyce 1982, 75; Dillery 2005, 395.
[41] On this practice see the following passages from the *Avesta*: *Yasna* 9.17f., 9.20, 9.27, 9.30f.; *Yašt* 14.57f. (Darmesteter 1883, 246; Mills 1887, 236–239; Malandra 1983, 153–155; Rachet 1996, 47–50, 248; Skjærvø 2007, 11–13; Skjærvø 2011, 176f.; Alberti 2013, 116–119, 366). See also Mills 1887, 231; Boyce 1975, 106, 158f.; Malandra 1983, 151; Skjærvø 2005, 24.

tempts to kill his closest relatives (his brother Smerdis and his sister, 3.30–32), as well as his most faithful courtiers (his young cupbearer, son of the nobleman Prexaspes; his counsellor Croesus; and his royal servants, 3.35f.).[42] In another instance, Cambyses punishes twelve top-ranking Persian aristocrats by burying them alive (3.35.5). This may reflect an Iranian ritual custom of great antiquity, a kind of sacrifice to underworld divinities, here transformed again into a brutal and unjustifiable atrocity.[43] There are many more such cases in the Herodotean narrative. Motifs of this kind betray the tendentious storytelling activity of Persian circles, which exploit their familiar mythological and ritual material in order to denigrate the hateful king.[44]

There were influential parties in Persia that must have detested Cambyses or could have expected tangible profits from his defamation. Firstly, the associates of Darius, the next occupant of the Achaemenid throne, had ample reason to calumniate the dead son of Cyrus, so as to exalt by contrast Darius' successive regime.[45] Darius' official inscription at Behistun, whose text was translated and diffused throughout the Achaemenid territories, displays a conspicuous tendency to blacken Cambyses' reputation; the latter is presented as the slayer of his brother, and emphasis is placed on the falsehood and evil that prevailed

---

[42] See Hofmann/Vorbichler 1980, 96f.; cf. Hofmann/Vorbichler 1979, 106f., 162f. Asheri/Lloyd/Corcella (2007, 432) doubt the connection. But Herodotus may simply have not understood the Iranian background: he thus turned *haoma* into wine (an evident instance of *interpretatio Graeca*) and assimilated Cambyses' addiction to other cases of alcoholic insanity, such as that of the Spartan king Cleomenes (Hdt. 6.84).

[43] For this Persian custom see Hdt. 7.114; Boyce 1975, 109–112; Hofmann/Vorbichler 1980, 98f.; Boyce 1982, 167; Schwartz 1985, 691f.; Briant 2002, 97, 896.

[44] These elements should not be mistaken for general themes that might occur in the exact same form within any cultural context or narrative tradition. As shown by the examples provided above, each one of these motifs can be linked to a very specific belief or ritual custom of the ancient Iranian cult and faith. Some motifs refer indeed to cardinal notions of the Iranian religious worldview (Truth and Lie) or lifestyle (endogamy). In other cases, the very fact that the incidents are attributed to a Persian ruler suggests an association with well-known corresponding elements of Persian culture. For example, the insanity that is caused by alcoholism, when ascribed to Cambyses the Persian warrior-king, is more plausibly correlated with the *haoma*-induced frenzy of ancient Iranian warriors than e.g. with Dionysian wine-drinking and *mania* or with Egyptian Hathoric inebriation and ecstasy (see also above, n. 42). Most importantly, such elements are not mere isolated cases; a large number of them are accumulated within the Herodotean biography of Cambyses and thus collectively point with some force to an Iranian background.

[45] See Dandamaev 1976, 145–152; Hofmann/Vorbichler 1980, 101f., 104; Boyce 1982, 74f., 78–82; Walser 1983, 10f.; Cook 1985, 215; Balcer 1987, 50–53, 64–66, 69, 89–93; Dandamaev 1989, 99f.; Erbse 1992, 47f., 54; Balcer 1995, 107f.; Briant 2002, 102f.; Kuhrt 2007, 106; Minunno 2008, 137f.; cf. Lenfant 1996, 369; Bichler 2001, 277; Cruz-Uribe 2003, 51.

in the country under his reign.⁴⁶ Significantly, even in Aeschylus' *Persians*, when the ghost of Darius surveys his predecessors on the Achaemenid throne, he devotes only a brief and hasty phrase to the rule of Cambyses, as though the latter were a source of embarrassment.⁴⁷ As the lawful heir of the great Cyrus, Cambyses could not be omitted from the catalogue of Persian monarchs. Yet Aeschylus' audience had presumably heard some of the defamatory tales about this king's supposed crimes; several Greeks may also have been aware of the historical Darius' inimical attitude and condemnatory official pronouncements against Cambyses. In the light of these circumstances, the Aeschylean Darius' hurried suppression of details sounds quite ominous.

Groups of the Iranian aristocracy may also have been hostile to Cambyses. At least Herodotus' account reveals considerable tensions between this king and the lords of his realm. On several occasions the deranged monarch inflicts a humiliating and torturous manner of death on Persian grandees or their families (Hdt. 3.35, 5.25). The noblemen themselves openly describe Cambyses as a hubristic and authoritarian despot (3.80.2, 3.89.3). Even when they assemble around the king's deathbed, they cannot bring themselves to trust his last words (3.66.3–67.1).⁴⁸ Various hypotheses have been advanced with regard to the causes of such hostility. Cambyses may have attempted to restrict the privileges of the tribal and feudal Iranian aristocracy for the benefit of centralized royal command. Or he might have pressed the Persian noble families too hard

---

46 DB I § 10 (1.26–35): "Darius the king says: This is what I did after I became king. A son of Cyrus, Cambyses by name, of our family – he was king here formerly. This Cambyses had one brother, Bardiya by name, of the same mother and the same father as Cambyses. Afterwards Cambyses killed this Bardiya. When Cambyses killed Bardiya, it did not become known to the people that Bardiya had been killed. After that, Cambyses went to Egypt. When Cambyses had gone off to Egypt, then the people became evil. The Lie grew greatly in the country, in Persia and in Media and in the other provinces" (Schmitt 2009, 40 f.: θāti Dārayava.uš xšāyaθiya: ima, taya manā kṛtam, pasāva yaθā xšāyaθiya abavam; Kambūjiya nāma, Kurau̯š puça, amāxam tau̯māyā – hau̯ paruvam idā xšāyaθiya āha; avahyā Kambūjiyahyā brātā Bṛdiya nāma āha, hamātā hamapitā Kambūjiyahyā; pasāva Kambūjiya avam Bṛdiyam avāja; yaθā Kambūjiya Bṛdiyam avāja, kārahyā nai azdā abava, taya Bṛdiya avajata; pasāva Kambūjiya Mudrāyam ašiyava; yaθā Kambūjiya Mudrāyam ašiyava, pasāva kāra arīka abava utā drau̯ga dahyau̯vā vasai abava, utā Pārsai utā Mādai utā aniyā.uvā dahyušuvā). See further Kent 1953, 117–119; Boyce 1982, 78 f.; Balcer 1987, 50–53, 64–66, 69, 89 f.; Lecoq 1997, 189 f.; Asheri/Lloyd/Corcella 2007, 392, 530; Kuhrt 2007, 136 f., 143; Skjærvø 2013, 555; cf. Dandamaev 1976, 145 f., 150, 244; Dandamaev 1989, 83, 88–92; Asheri 1999, 107–109; Minunno 2008, 137.

47 *Pers.* 773: Κύρου δὲ παῖς τέταρτος ηὔθυνε στρατόν, "the son of Cyrus was the fourth to direct the army". Cf. Belloni 1994, 239, 242 f.; Garvie 2009, 300, 304.

48 Cf. Legrand 1949, 21–23; Dandamaev 1976, 145, 150 f., 156; Cook 1985, 215; Balcer 1987, 105; Dandamaev 1989, 99–102, 106; Högemann 1992, 205 f., 336; Briant 2002, 97 f.

with his heavy taxation and fiscal measures.⁴⁹ For this reason, the gentlefolk execrated the king and willingly smeared his name.

Even with regard to its oriental components, therefore, Herodotus' overall narrative about Cambyses is a complex and multilayered construction, which merges together ingredients of varying provenance. The defamation of Cyrus' son and heir must have started from his own homeland, from Persian circles inimical to him. These circles fabricated calumniating stories about Cambyses' insanity and outrages, largely out of traditional Iranian mythical or religious stuff. Subsequently, this cycle of tales was transmitted to Egypt, which was of course under Persian rule and thus hosted a great number of Iranian officials, administrators, and military commanders⁵⁰ – all of them committed servants of Darius' new regime and potential conveyors of propagandistic storytelling. In the land of the Nile, these slanderous creations were gladly received by priestly groups that enriched and developed them further, doubtless adding characteristic Egyptian touches and elements of local colour.⁵¹ Herodotus apparently heard a large part of these narratives in Egypt or from people with ties to Egypt.⁵² However, he may have combined them with further scandalous tales about Cambyses, which he had picked up from Asiatic sources – whether in his native Caria, or in his familiar Ionian territories, or from his many informants about Persian matters and lore.⁵³ Darius had obviously taken care to spread the damning reports about his predecessor throughout the Achaemenid Empire.⁵⁴ The Greek historian

---

49 See Dandamaev 1976, 150, 153–157; Wallinga 1984, 407–411; Balcer 1987, 105, 109 f.; Dandamaev 1989, 101 f.; Högemann 1992, 336; Balcer 1995, 105, 109–111, 114 f.; Briant 2002, 103–105; Asheri/Lloyd/Corcella 2007, 459.
50 On Persian officials in occupied Egypt see Bresciani 1958, 132–157; Bresciani 1985, 508–519; Tuplin 1987, 119 f., 123–127, 136; Briant 1988, 137–143, 160–170; Ray 1988, 265–273; Högemann 1992, 212 f.; Briant 2002, 472–484; Ruzicka 2012, 20–22.
51 Cf. Reinhardt 1966, 157; Hofmann/Vorbichler 1980, 91 f., 105; Boyce 1982, 74 f., 81; Balcer 1987, 72, 89–93, 95; Balcer 1995, 107–109, 112; Asheri/Lloyd/Corcella 2007, 397, 432–434; Minunno 2008, 138.
52 Cf. Jacoby 1913, 427 f.; Hofmann/Vorbichler 1980, 91; Erbse 1992, 47 f., 50, 54; Asheri/Lloyd/Corcella 2007, 415.
53 Cf. Jacoby 1913, 428; Legrand 1949, 21–23, 25–27.
54 The text of the Inscription of Behistun was translated in various languages (Akkadian, Elamite, Aramaic, possibly also Greek) and spread throughout the Achaemenid territories. This is overtly stated towards the end of the inscription (DB IV § 70, 4.89–92): "This is the inscription which I have composed, in Aryan indeed. It was recorded both on clay tablets and on parchment. (...) Afterwards I sent this inscription everywhere in the provinces. The people cooperated in this" (Schmitt 2009, 87: ima dipiciçam, taya adam akunavam patišam ariyā; utā pavastāyā utā carmā gr̥ftam āha; [...] pasāva ima dipiciçam frāstāyam vispadā antar dahyāva; kāra hamātaxšatā). See further Kent 1953, 130, 132; Lecoq 1997, 212 f.; Asheri/Lloyd/Corcella 2007, 537;

would doubtless discover these reports during his long enquiries for the composition of his magnum opus.

4

The same composite amalgamation of layers from different origins can now be detected in the twofold episodic sequence comprising the murder of the Apis and Cambyses' death. The Memphite bull is an emblematic figure of Egyptian cult. On the other hand, the slaughter of consecrated oxen appears in ancient Iranian myth and cult as an important form of ritual sacrifice, prescribed by the gods and performed by great heroes. Much evidence in this respect is offered by the holy works of the *Avesta*, the sacred canon of the Zoroastrian faith, which provides a collection of hymns, prayers, and liturgies of the ancient Iranian religion. In the texts of this corpus, Ahura Mazda himself, the supreme god, is sometimes quoted demanding cattle sacrifice. According to Ahura Mazda's bidding, the head of an ox must be cooked as an offering to various spirits and heavenly powers (e. g. Vərəthraghna, the spirit of victory, and the bright stellar divinity Tištrya).[55] Another important figure with regard to bull sacrifice is Mithra, the god of righteousness and overseer of pacts, who was also formulaically hailed as the lord of wide pastures and presented as protector of cows and oxherds.[56] In the *Yašt*, a series of Avestan hymns addressed to various divinities

---

Kuhrt 2007, 149. Fragmentary copies of the translations have been found in Babylon (in Akkadian, on a stone inscription) and Egypt (in Aramaic, on a papyrus of Elephantine). See Kent 1953, 108; Dandamaev 1976, 48f., 76–78; Greenfield 1985, 701, 706, 708; Balcer 1987, 26–32, 67f.; Dandamaev 1989, 132; Porten/Yardeni 1993, 59–71; Lenfant 1996, 364, 376; Lecoq 1997, 54–57; Asheri 1999, 101f.; Kuhrt 2007, 136, 151; Schmitt 2009, 9. A Greek rendering or variant of the text of Behistun may ultimately lie behind Herodotus' narrative about Darius' ascension to kingship; see Köhnken 1980, 39–41; Brown 1982, 400, 402; Lewis 1985, 102f.; Cuyler Young 1988, 53; Erbse 1992, 52f.; Briant 2002, 100; Asheri/Lloyd/Corcella 2007, 392f.; Kuhrt 2007, 136; Brosius 2013, 662.

55 See *Yašt* 8.58, 14.50; Darmesteter 1883, 108, 244; Malandra 1983, 86f., 149; Rachet 1996, 182, 247; Alberti 2013, 328, 365; cf. Hinnells 1975b, 310; Russell 1994, 185.

56 See e.g. *Yasna* 1.3, 2.3, 6.2, 7.5; *Vidēvdād* 19.15; *Yašt* 2.4, 2.9, 6.5, 8.7, 10.1–15, 10.28, 10.39–52, 10.65, 10.86f., 10.112f., 19.35 etc.; Darmesteter 1880, lxi, lxiv, 208; Darmesteter 1883, 36–38, 86f., 95, 119–123, 126, 129–132, 135, 141, 148, 294; Mills 1887, 196, 204, 219, 223; Malandra 1983, 58–66, 69, 72, 91; Boyce 1984, 27–30; Hintze 1994, 196; Rachet 1996, 21, 25, 37, 41, 152, 172, 175, 186–195, 198, 202, 272; Skjærvø 2007, 3, 7, 83, 85, 95–97, 113, 147; Skjærvø 2011, 24f., 54f.; Alberti 2013, 90, 94, 106, 109, 289f., 318, 321f., 334–344, 347f., 351f., 393, 546. See also Boyce 1970, 80; Boyce 1975, 30, 60; Jafarey 1975, 55–61; Schwartz 1985, 658, 670; Sick 2004, 437–444, 451–461.

and holy powers, Mithra accepts sacrifices of cattle. Cows and bulls, along with other domestic animals, were ritually slain in his yearly autumn festival.⁵⁷ In the later Mithraic cult of the Roman period, it was standard to represent the god slaying a bull. It has repeatedly been argued, on the basis of diverse indications, that this portrayal may have old roots in the concepts or practices of early Iranian religion (although this remains a controversial hypothesis).⁵⁸ In general, cattle sacrifice seems to have had a profound cosmic significance in the most pristine form of ancient Iranian cosmological belief. It was considered a proper activity for the divine nature. At the beginning of creation, the god or gods themselves slew the primeval uniquely-created bull, as part of a beneficent sacrifice, from which earthly life (plants, animals, and men) came into existence. That initial divine sacrifice was then regularly re-enacted by men in religious worship.⁵⁹

---

57 See *Yašt* 10.119; Darmesteter 1883, 151; Boyce 1970, 70; Malandra 1983, 73; Rachet 1996, 203; Skjærvø 2007, 98f.; Skjærvø 2011, 56; Alberti 2013, 352f. On sacrifices in Mithra's festival see Boyce 1975, 139, 151, 172f.; Hinnells 1975b, 306–309; Beck 1984, 2069; Foltz 2013, 28f.

58 To summarize a few prominent examples: Many scholars seek the roots of the Mithraic tauroctony to the primordial bull sacrifice of ancient Iranian cosmogonic myth; see Lommel 1949, 212–218; Merkelbach 1984, 5–22, 193–206; Lincoln 1991, 76f., 89f.; Bivar 1994, 68; Kreyenbroek 1994, 173–181; Russell 1994, 185; Waldmann 1994, 265–274; Weiss 1998, 6f., 24f.; Näsström 2004, 109; Foltz 2013, 21, 24–26, 29f.; and the overviews of Hinnells 1975b, 290–293, 309f. and Beck 1984, 2068f., 2080. Merkelbach (1984) and Sick (2004, 444–462) further connect cattle sacrifice with Mithra's original nature as "god of pacts" (which are solidified through sacrificial ritual); both draw attention to Vedic and/or ancient Greek parallels. According to Boyce 1970, Mithra's bull-sacrifice is a development of the role played in ancient Zoroastrian religion by Haoma, the divinity who presided over religious offerings and performed the ritual slaughter of the victims; this latter function was at some point transferred to Mithra due to his strong connections with cattle and sacrificial practices. Hinnells (1975b, 304–312) finds strong parallels between the Mithraic tauroctony and ancient Iranian rituals and ideas of sacrifice. Some experts trace the Mithraic iconography of bull-killing (or individual motifs of it) back to Near-Eastern art of the second and first millennia B.C.: see Barnett 1975, 467f.; Bivar 1975, 96–105; Beck 1984, 2069; Bivar 1994, 64f.; Bivar 2005, 346–351; Foltz 2013, 20. See further Boyce 1975, 173; Hofmann/Vorbichler 1979, 176; Hofmann/Vorbichler 1980, 95; Asheri/Lloyd/Corcella 2007, 428f.

59 See Lommel 1949, 212–218; Boyce 1975, 138–141, 150, 156f., 210, 231, 244; Boyce 1984, 10; Merkelbach 1984, 10, 12–19, 199–206; Schwartz 1985, 645f., 657; Bivar 1994, 68; Kreyenbroek 1994, 173–181; Russell 1994, 185; Foltz 2013, 21, 29f., 224–226; cf. Boyce 1970, 69f., 79f.; Hinnells 1975b, 309f.; Malandra 1983, 175; Beck 1984, 2068f., 2080; Skjærvø 2005, 58. Overall, Balcer (1987, 91) and Minunno (2008, 141) are not convinced by the correlation with Mithraic or Iranian bull-sacrifices. But they overlook the fact that Iranian mythical and religious motifs run through the Herodotean narrative about Cambyses' madness.

On the level of human heroes, Yima, the archetypical first king and founder of civilization in Iranian myth, was regarded as the human originator of the sacrifice of cattle.[60] In the *Yašt* hymns, he is described as sacrificing thousands of oxen to specific deities.[61] Many other glorious hero-kings of ancient Iranian mythology are similarly said to perform the same sacrificial act in honour of divinities or celestial beings: Hoshang, Fereydun, Kai Kavus, Kai Khosrow, and others – all of them valiant rulers, regarded as mythical ancestors and models of the Iranian monarchs.[62] In historical times, the Persian kings maintained the magnificent offer of cattle victims as an expression of their royal piety. Xerxes sacrificed a thousand oxen when his army reached Troy (Hdt. 7.43); similar grand hecatombs are repeatedly ascribed to Cyrus (e.g. Hdt. 1.126.2; X. *Cyr.* 8.3.11–24, 8.3.33 f.).[63] The religious slaying of bulls, clearly the most highly regarded form of sacrifice, may have been mostly restricted to the circles of Iranian royalty and high nobility precisely because of its costliness; commoners would have preferred smaller victims (sheep or goats).[64]

Another type of confrontation between king and bull is pictured on many Achaemenid artworks (sculptures from the buildings at Persepolis, seals, and seal impressions on tablets from the same site). On these monuments, a heroized figure with kingly insignia and characteristics (commonly labelled "the royal hero" by scholars) is shown engaging in combat with rampant beasts or monsters. The bull (sometimes with wings or with a human head) figures prominently among those beasts and appears in many cases as the hero-king's adversary and victim. In the seal impressions, the image is occasionally accompanied by a cuneiform inscription which bears the Achaemenid monarch's name ("I Darius" or "Xerxes the Great King"). This iconographic conception has been interpreted as an exaltation of the Persian hero-ruler in his role as protector of the empire and the cosmic order, overcoming the forces of evil and chaos. It is thus significant that in many of these representations, the kingly character is portrayed again as a slayer of bulls. The "royal hero" is variously shown grasping the taurine animal

---

[60] This is implied by *Yasna* 32.8 (Mills 1887, 55, 61; Rachet 1996, 84; Alberti 2013, 160). See Boyce 1975, 93, 97; Hinnells 1975b, 308; Merkelbach 1984, 10; cf. Malandra 1983, 178.
[61] See *Yašt* 5.25, 9.8; Darmesteter 1883, 59, 112; Malandra 1983, 122; Rachet 1996, 161, 183 f.; Skjærvø 2007, 73; Skjærvø 2011, 98; Alberti 2013, 304, 331. See further Hofmann/Vorbichler 1980, 95.
[62] See e.g. *Yašt* 5.21, 5.33, 5.45, 5.49, 9.3, 9.13, 9.21; Darmesteter 1883, 58, 61, 65 f., 111, 113, 115; Malandra 1983, 122 f.; Rachet 1996, 160–163, 183–185; Skjærvø 2007, 72–75, 92 f.; Skjærvø 2011, 98 f.; Alberti 2013, 303 f., 306, 330–332. Cf. Schwartz 1985, 695; De Jong 1997, 358 f.
[63] Cf. Merkelbach 1984, 33 f.; Henkelman 2005, 159.
[64] See Boyce 1975, 150; Boyce 1982, 214 f.

by its head, neck, muzzle, leg, or horns. In a number of seals, he also threatens it with his sword or another kind of weapon. On the reliefs at Persepolis (from the doorjambs in Darius' palace and in the Throne Hall), the hero is actually stabbing the bull low in its belly with a dagger.[65] These scenes may bring to mind the Herodotean description of Cambyses attacking the Apis with his poniard; the mad Persian monarch was similarly intending to strike the holy beast in its belly (Hdt. 3.29.1: θέλων τύψαι τὴν γαστέρα τοῦ Ἄπιος), but missed and thrust his weapon into its thigh.

As transpires from all these materials, the killing of bulls (whether in ritual contexts or in mythical and panegyric representations) was for the ancient Iranians both a religious act of faith and a prime constituent of the idea of kingship. The Persian ruler was the earthly representative of Mithra, the divine judge and guarantor of order; he was also the heir of the primeval Yima and the other mythical monarchs. This made him by definition a holy slayer of cattle. Bull sacrifice was his traditional duty and an essential component of his royal identity. Further, the royal hero's iconographic combat and victory over taurine creatures could be read as a manifestation of his kingly power and a demonstration of his authority as protector of the realm.

In this light, the Apis episode once again displays the familiar mechanism of defamation that also determines many other features in the Herodotean portrait of Cambyses. The king's crime has been fashioned out of mythical or cultic elements of the ancient Persian tradition, which in their original context constituted a demonstration of divine worship or a heroic display of royal force. These were purposefully distorted by the enemies of Cambyses into a heinous act of sacrilege and madness. The devout Iranian sacrifice of holy cattle was misrepresented as an impious murder of an inviolable deified bull. What was in Iran a venerable offering to the godhead became in Egypt a bloody transgression of the most sacrosanct divine taboo. The royal hero's fight against the archetypical bull-monster was caricatured as the incontrollable frenzy of a crazy killer with a knife.[66]

---

[65] See Schmidt 1953, 136f., 226f. (and plates 117, 144); Schmidt 1957, 7f., 20–23 (and plates 3–5); Boyce 1982, 105f.; Garrison/Root 2001, 63–92, 169–181, 195f., 200f., 282–286, 309–319, 378f., 403f., 409f., 416–418; Kuhrt 2007, 473, 546f., 596 (and figures 11.37, 12.4); Garrison 2013, 582. For the interpretation of the images cf. Bivar 1975, 95f.; Calmeyer 1980, 59; Garrison/Root 2001, 54–60; Bivar 2005, 349–351. On the iconographic association of bulls and bull-like creatures with Achaemenid kingly power generally, see Boyce 1982, 103, 106; Root 2002, 197f.; Garrison 2013, 585–588.

[66] Cf. Merkelbach 1959, 155f. and Merkelbach 1984, 34f., who first pointed out the parallel between Cambyses' murder of the Apis and Mithraic bull-slaying.

A glimpse into the kind of tendentious tradition that lies behind Herodotus' narrative is afforded by another Near-Eastern historical text: the so-called *Chronicle of the Esagila* (i.e. Marduk's great sanctuary at Babylon) or *Weidner Chronicle*. This is an Akkadian literary composition in the form of a fictitious royal letter addressed by a ruler of Isin to a monarch of Babylon (or of Larsa). The fictional setting of their epistolary exchange apparently belongs to the late 19th or the early 18th century B.C., but the dating of the work itself is a different matter. A number of copies of the *Weidner Chronicle* are preserved on Neo-Assyrian and Neo-Babylonian tablets (from the first half of the first millennium B.C.). Its text contains late linguistic traits and orthographic conventions, which are otherwise paralleled only in writings and inscriptions of the Neo-Babylonian period. Such factors indicate that the entire composition was most probably created after about 1100 B.C. Elements of the content, such as the information provided about the cult and status of Marduk and the general ideological perspective of the work, also support a date in the late second millennium B.C.[67]

Within the aforementioned epistolary frame, the main portion of the Babylonian work conforms to the structure and style of a Near-Eastern chronicle; it lists a sequence of Mesopotamian kings from earliest antiquity, ranging from the remote Early Dynastic age (the time of Sumerian mythical heroes such as Enmerkar and Akka) to the Third Dynasty of Ur (at the end of the third millennium B.C.). For each one of these royal figures a brief narrative of events is provided, concerning specifically the king's behaviour towards the great temple of Marduk at Babylon and his actions with regard to the temple's cult, rituals, and offerings. At the end of each narrative, the text records the consequences of this particular kind of behaviour for the monarch's life and reign. In this way, the entire composition displays a clear theological stance and moral message: the kings who respected Marduk's worship and its holy offerings at the Esagila temple were rewarded by the god and prospered as a result. On the contrary, those rulers who disparaged Marduk's cult and committed impious acts were divinely punished and destroyed.[68] Such a religiously biased, theocentric view of history is percep-

---

[67] See Grayson 1975, 43f., 278f.; Grayson 1980, 180; Finkel 1980, 72, 74f.; Evans 1983, 108f.; Al-Rawi 1990, 1f.; Arnold 1994, 131; Millard 2003, 468; Glassner 2005, 263. For text and translation of the *Weidner Chronicle* see Grayson 1975, 145–151; Al-Rawi 1990; Arnold 1994, 133–138; Millard 2003, 468–470; Glassner 2005, 264–271.

[68] For this theological message see Grayson 1975, 43–45; Grayson 1980, 180; Evans 1983, 106–109; Van Seters 1983, 56, 85, 88f., 295f.; Assmann 1990, 19f.; Arnold 1994, 131f., 138–147; Pomponio 1998, 56f.; Millard 2003, 468; Glassner 2005, 263.

tible also in other Mesopotamian chronographies; it will later find its monumental expression in the historical books of the Hebrew Scripture.[69]

Alongside this spiritual orientation, the *Weidner Chronicle* has a notable propensity towards picturesque anecdotal narratives exploiting fairytale motifs and storylines. This is evident, for example, in the little story about Ku-Baba the tavern-keeper. The fishermen of the Esagila caught fish for the sacral meal of the great god Marduk, but the officers of the evil king Puzur-Nirah always seized their catch. One day, however, the fishermen stopped at Ku-Baba's tavern with their catch. The tavern-keeper offered them food and drink, and hurried to deliver the fish to the god's sanctuary. For this pious action, Marduk looked benevolently on Ku-Baba and entrusted her with the kingship over all the lands.[70] Similar is the tale of the fisherman Utu-hegal, who caught a nice fish at the seashore and intended to offer it to Marduk. Suddenly the savage Gutians (members of a barbarian mountain tribe which had overrun Babylonia) intervened and took the cooked fish out of Utu-hegal's hands before he could make his offering. Because of this, Marduk removed the Gutians from power and handed over the rule of the country to Utu-hegal.[71] These episodes are based on a widespread fairytale pattern: the rise of a humble hero thanks to his virtue. As in didactic *Märchen* or parables, the protagonist begins as a poor fellow in low circumstances (a common tavern or fish-boat), but he performs a pious deed and is divinely rewarded with the royal throne.

A different mythical structure is perceptible in another entry of the Babylonian work, concerning Amar-Sin, one of the Sumerian rulers of the Third Dynasty of Ur, who enjoyed a brief reign in the second half of the 21st century B.C. Like the Herodotean legend of Cambyses' demise, this story recounts the end of a sacrilegious king, which conforms to the scheme of *lo contrapasso*, an exact retaliation for his crimes. According to the chronicle, Amar-Sin did not respect the cult of the Esagila: he changed or falsified the traditional sacrifices of large oxen and sheep, which were offered in Marduk's temple at the New Year's festival (a very important religious feast in the Babylonian calendar). This statement is obviously meant to reprimand the king. Therefore, it must imply that Amar-Sin altered the animal sacrifices in a way detrimental to Marduk's cult or hieratic staff. Possibly the Sumerian ruler was held to have reduced, for example, the number of

---

[69] See Evans 1983; Van Seters 1983, 56–59, 85–91, 214–219, 238–246, 295f.; Assmann 1990, 18–26; Arnold 1994, 138–148.
[70] *Weidner Chronicle* 48–55 (reverse 6–13): see Grayson 1975, 148; Starr 1977, 159; Al-Rawi 1990, 5, 9; Arnold 1994, 135; Millard 2003, 469; Glassner 2005, 266f.
[71] *Weidner Chronicle* 65–68 (reverse 23–26): see Grayson 1975, 150; Al-Rawi 1990, 7, 10; Arnold 1994, 137; Millard 2003, 469; Glassner 2005, 266–269.

the victims or the duration of the ceremonies or to have imposed other limitations,[72] which were considered offensive to the faithful or detrimental to the priests' profits. Immediately after this misdeed, the Babylonian text notes the perpetrator's punishment. It was foretold that Amar-Sin would perish from being gored by an ox; but he died from a "bite of his shoe".[73]

The *Weidner Chronicle* records a very elliptical and summary form of the narrative, setting down only its barest outlines. Such is the general practice of this Mesopotamian composition throughout its chronographic section. The tales of the various kings are reduced to brief arid statements of the most essential events, without circumstantial details or any kind of storytelling embellishment. The text does not even mark the links between the individual incidents, but leaves them for the readers to deduce. For instance, in Amar-Sin's case it is not expressly acknowledged that the king's manner of death was a penalty for his religious wrongdoing. Neither is there any comment on the ironic parallelism between the falsified sacrifices of oxen and the fatal goring by an ox. The learned audience of the Babylonian work could be assumed to know the legends of those ancient kings from other historical writings or from collective popular tradition. They would thus be able to fill in the missing details from their own memory. Especially in the oral tradition, the stories might have circulated in much more detailed forms, expanded to proper folk novellas of adventure, horror, or wonder. The modern student is obliged to extrapolate the untold connections, ironies, and particulars, as far as possible, from the extant outlines.

In the case of Amar-Sin's death story, it is possible to detect the well-known motif of the prophecy coming true in an unexpected manner – a motif common in many ancient myths and especially favoured in the Herodotean legendarium. Amar-Sin was presumably given a prophecy (through some kind of divination or oracle)[74] that he would be mortally gored by an ox. This prediction came true in an unanticipated figurative sense. The reader is obviously expected to deduce that the king's footwear, which became the cause of his death, was made of ox-leather.[75] This leather shoe "bit" the king, that is, it was presumably too tight or constricting and injured his foot. Then the wound festered and Amar-

---

[72] Cf. Pomponio 1998, 53.
[73] *Weidner Chronicle* 72f. (reverse 30f.): see Finkel 1980, 73f.; Al-Rawi 1990, 7, 10; Arnold 1994, 137; Pomponio 1998, 52–55; Millard 2003, 469; Glassner 2005, 268f.
[74] This is implied by the vocabulary used in the Akkadian text; see Pomponio 1998, 53.
[75] This has been understood by Pomponio 1998, 55. For the use of leather shoes and sandals in ancient Mesopotamia see de Genouillac 1910, 157–159; de Genouillac 1939; Falkner 1971, 123f.; Sigrist 1981, 174f., 180, 187f.; Stol 1983, 534, 538–540, 542.

Sin died from the infection.⁷⁶ Thus, the goring by the ox in the omen turned out to be intended symbolically; the monarch was not pierced by the real animal's horns but gravely punctured on his foot by a product of ox-hide.

In this respect, Amar-Sin's death follows the principle of retribution, just like Cambyses' fatal accident. In both cases, the king commits an impious deed and perishes in a manner distinctively reflecting his crime. The Persian monarch stabs a holy bull on the thigh, and dies of a wound on his own thigh, inflicted by the same weapon. The Sumerian ruler falsifies the sacrifices of oxen, and the hide of an ox fittingly becomes the instrument of his doom.⁷⁷ The two narratives also present a series of notable similarities in circumstantial details. In both of them, the protagonist's sacrilege is connected with holy oxen: the Apis bull in Herodotus, the consecrated cattle offered to Marduk in the Babylonian chronicle. Further, both kings are hurt by an item they are wearing on their person: a shoe in one case, a dagger hanging from the belt in the other. In both cases, the fatal injury is inflicted on the lower limbs – the thigh of Cambyses, the foot of Amar-Sin. The medical cause of death seems to be similar in either instance: festering or infection of the wounded limb. Finally, both stories involve an oracle or prophecy predicting the king's end, which finally comes true in an unexpected sense. Amar-Sin's symbolic omen has been explained above. As for Cambyses, according to Herodotus, he had been warned by an oracle that he would die in a place called Agbatana. The Persian monarch believed all the while that this meant Ecbatana the capital of Media, the summer residence of the Achaemenid kings, where he might naturally retreat to spend his last years in old age. However, his fatal accident took place in a locality of Syria named precisely Agbatana, where the Persian army had camped (Hdt. 3.64.3–5).⁷⁸ This pattern of

---

76 On this point see Goetze 1947, 261, 265; Millard 2003, 470.
77 For the retribution and the unexpected verification of the omen in Amar-Sin's case, cf. Pomponio 1998, 55; Millard 2003, 470.
78 There has been debate over the historical identification of the Syrian "Agbatana" mentioned by Herodotus. Testimonia of subsequent Graeco-Roman sources about the Agbatana/Ecbatana of Syria seem to depend on Herodotus' account. Some scholars argue that no such township existed in ancient Syria. The place must have been made up in order to serve the legendary motif of the unexpected prophecy verification; see Aly 1969, 98; Dandamaev 1976, 147; Köhnken 1980, 46; Balcer 1987, 93–95, 106; Kuhrt 2007, 162; cf. Högemann 1986, who locates the site of Cambyses' death in the vicinity of Gaza. Other researchers propose various attested Syrian or Canaanite locations: the *Acbatana* on Mount Carmel mentioned by Pliny (*Nat.* 5.75); or the fortress Ecbatana in Bashan, east of the Sea of Galilee (J. *Vit.* 54–57); or the important Syrian city Hama (Biblical Hamath) on the bank of the river Orontes. This latter proposition is the most convincing one: Hama/Hamath could have sounded close to "Hagmatana" (the Old Persian name of

para prosdokian verification of a prophecy seems typically Herodotean.[79] Yet it is already prefigured in a Mesopotamian tale recorded several centuries before Herodotus' birth.

The *Weidner Chronicle* is not the only source for the story of Amar-Sin's end. Reports that this king died from goring by an ox or from the bite of his shoe are embedded in several Mesopotamian omen collections, on tablets dating from the Old Babylonian to the Neo-Assyrian period (from the early second to the first millennium B.C.).[80] It has even been proposed that all these omen texts should be interpreted in the same way as the brief narrative of the Akkadian epistolary chronicle: it had been presaged or decreed that Amar-Sin would be wounded and killed by an ox, but he died from the shoe-bite.[81] In any case, it seems that tales about the Sumerian monarch's strange manner of death were widespread in the Mesopotamian tradition for a long time. Possibly a religious legend of this type, about an impious king dying in a manner ironically corresponding to his sacrilegious acts and foretold by an unexpectedly verified prophecy, became known to the Persians after Cyrus' conquest of Babylon in 539 B.C. Indeed, through the close contacts of the Persian conquerors with the venerable Babylonian culture, much Mesopotamian narrative lore seems to have passed into the Iranian tradition.[82] Afterwards, the Persian circles hostile to Cambyses were in-

---

the Median Ecbatana) or "Ahmetha" (the Aramaic form of the same name). See Dandamaev 1989, 99f.; Yamauchi 1996, 389; Asheri/Lloyd/Corcella 2007, 462.

[79] On the typically Herodotean ring of this motif cf. Chiasson 1979, 133–135; Köhnken 1980, 44, 46; Lloyd 1988, 60; Erbse 1992, 54; Asheri 1999, 110; Bichler 2001, 276; Gould 2003, 300f.; Asheri/Lloyd/Corcella 2007, 462; Kuhrt 2007, 162. Some scholars (Köhnken, Bichler, Gould) draw special attention to the parallel with the similarly ambiguous oracle concerning the death of Cleomenes (Hdt. 6.75f. and 6.80); but cf. Dillery 2005, 404f. As rightly remarked by Aly (1969, 98) and Griffiths (1989, 58, 70f., 74), the motif is in essence a widespread folk narrative scheme, traceable in many legends and fairytales in the international popular tradition; cf. Pomponio 1998, 52, Griffin 2006, 52, and Asheri/Lloyd/Corcella 2007, 462f. for many examples from ancient myth or historiography.

[80] See Goetze 1947, 261, 265; Starr 1977, 160–162; Finkel 1980, 74; Grayson 1980, 190; Hallo 1991, 159f.; Pomponio 1998, 53–55.

[81] So Pomponio 1998, 54f., based on the parallel with the *Weidner Chronicle* and on the variant translation of a doubtful reading in the Old Babylonian omen texts. Other experts interpret differently the two kinds of wound recorded in the omens: they are distinguished as alternative traditions ("he died from being gored by an ox, or he died from the bite of a shoe") or harmonized as successive accidents ("he was injured by an ox and he died from the bite of a shoe"); see the references in the previous footnote.

[82] Indeed, Herodotus' tales about Cambyses' madness and crimes contain further material from Mesopotamian traditions. Hofmann/Vorbichler (1979, 134–140, 172 and 1980, 104) point out the parallels with the Babylonian defamatory narratives against the impious king Nabonidus.

spired by that old theological legend to fashion their own defamatory story about the end of the hated monarch. Of course, they adapted their damnatory narrative to the particular adventures and life circumstances of their target and furnished it with characteristic Iranian touches. The sacrilege was set in Egypt during Cambyses' domination there; the deadly accident took place en route, as the king was returning home from the Egyptian campaign; and the instrument of destruction was identified with the typical Persian *akinakes*. It was this principally Persian pseudo-historical creation that eventually reached Herodotus and formed the basis for his account of Cambyses' demise.

Exactly how the narrative was formed and developed over time, what its initial Persian shape was and which particular elements were subsequently added or altered by the Egyptian priests or by Herodotus himself[83] – all this is a matter of conjecture. Purely as an exercise in historical speculation, I may here forward one of the conceivable hypothetical scenarios. As noted above, Iranian myth and cult practice prominently involved the ritual slaying of cattle. The Persian circles, therefore, might have originally described how Cambyses falsified or distorted such traditional sacrifices of oxen, just like Amar-Sin in the Mesopotamian legend. In the sequel of the narrative, the impious Persian monarch would receive his punishment on the basis of the retaliation principle: he would die, for example, from the blow of an ox or from an injury inflicted by an object made of ox-related material (for instance, a scabbard fabricated of ox-hide or a blade forged out of ox-horn). Subsequently, this Persian story was transferred to Egypt and picked up by local enemies of Cambyses. The Egyptians naturally adapted the particulars to their own religious life. In their eyes, the consecrated ox *par excellence* was the holy Apis of Memphis; and they knew that an Apis had indeed expired around the beginning of Cambyses' rule in Egypt. Thus they altered the protagonist's initial sacrilege and presented him killing the sacred Memphite bull. The form of Cambyses' fatal injury was then adapted accordingly: he was shown dying from a wound inflicted on the same bodily part and by the very weapon which had stabbed the Apis.[84]

West (2003, 421–428) and Konstantakos (2008, 167–224) demonstrate how Cambyses' quarrel with Croesus (Hdt. 3.36) has been modelled on the *Story of Ahiqar*, an Aramaic novelistic composition of ultimate Assyrian provenance.

83 For example, Herodotus or another Greek intermediary may have added certain touches which recall Ionian rationalistic philosophy, such as the censorious attitude towards bodily and animalistic representations of the divinity (Hdt. 3.28.1, 3.29.1f., 3.37.2f.). See Hofmann/Vorbichler 1979, 66f.; Hofmann/Vorbichler 1980, 92, 95, 99f., 104f.

84 Cf. Reinhardt 1966, 157; Hofmann/Vorbichler 1980, 104f.; Yamauchi 1996, 387.

Such a hypothesis could explain how Persian and Egyptian elements were mingled within the story of Cambyses' death. Of course, alternative reconstructions are also imaginable. Only one thing can be ascertained with some confidence: the parallels between the Herodotean episode and the Asiatic legend of Amar-Sin indicate that the story of Cambyses' end ultimately originated in tendentious defamatory narratives of Persian provenance.[85] The rest is left to our imagination – but then who said that philologists and historians should be unimaginative people?[86]

---

[85] Cruz-Uribe 2003, 44 adduces a different legend as Herodotus' possible model: the story about Pharaoh Bocchoris and the Mnevis, the sacred bull of Heliopolis, reported in Aelian, *NA* 11.11. However, this latter tale does not present as many strong similarities to the Herodotean account. Bocchoris does not personally injure the sacred animal with a weapon; he only unleashes a wild bull against the Mnevis. Further, the holy ox suffers no harm in Aelian's narrative. On the contrary, the wild attacking bull trips and falls on a persea-tree; it is thus stricken down and killed by the Mnevis. Cruz-Uribe supposes that Aelian is reflecting an older Egyptian tradition known to Herodotus, who adapted and transferred it to Cambyses. However, since Aelian is a much later source, the opposite relationship is also likely: it may have been rather the Herodotean episode of the slaughter of the Memphite bull that influenced Aelian's tale. Cf. another later tradition, which presents the Persian king Artaxerxes III Ochos in the same role, killing a holy Apis (Ael. *NA* 10.28, *VH* 4.8; Plu *Mor.* 355c, 363c; Suda α 3201). This has clearly been modelled on the Herodotean narrative about Cambyses: see Schwartz 1949, 68–70, 74f.; Griffiths 1989, 76f.; Devauchelle 1995, 68–70; Chimko 2003, 54; Minunno 2008, 140f.; Lloyd 2014, 186. The killing of sacred animals is a recurrent motif in Egyptian narratives of bleak prophecy and national disaster (see Dillery 2005, 395f.); but the Apis is not involved in the known examples of this tradition.

[86] I am grateful to the editors, Professor Scott Farrington and Dr. Vasileios Liotsakis, for their invitation and their many salutary suggestions, which greatly improved my text. I am also deeply obliged to the two anonymous referees of the Trends in Classics Supplementary Volumes series, who offered incisive remarks and helped me supplement and refine my discussion.

Bibliography

Agut-Labordère, D. (2005), "Le sens du *Décret de Cambyse*", in: *Transeuphratène* 29, 9–16.
Alberti, A. (2013), *Avestā*, Novara.
Allam, S. (1975), "Ehe", in: W. Helck / E. Otto 1975, 1162–1181.
Al-Rawi, F.N.H. (1990), "Tablets from the Sippar Library. I. The 'Weidner Chronicle': A Supposititious Royal Letter Concerning a Vision", in: *Iraq* 52, 1–13.
Aly, W. (1969), *Volksmärchen, Sage und Novelle bei Herodot und seinen Zeitgenossen*, Göttingen.
Arnold, B.T. (1994), "The Weidner Chronicle and the Idea of History in Israel and Mesopotamia", in: A.R. Millard / J.K. Hoffmeier / D.W. Baker 1994, 129–148.
Asheri, D. (1999), "Erodoto e Bisitun", in: E. Gabba 1999, 101–116.
Asheri, D. / Lloyd, A. / Corcella, A. (2007), *A Commentary on Herodotus Books I–IV*, Oxford.
Assmann, J. (1990), "Guilt and Remembrance: On the Theologization of History in the Ancient Near East", in: *History and Memory* 2, 5–33.
Atkinson, K.M.T. (1956), "The Legitimacy of Cambyses and Darius as Kings of Egypt", in: *Journal of the American Oriental Society* 76, 167–177.
Baker, H.D. / Jursa, M. (eds.) (2005), *Approaching the Babylonian Economy*, Münster.
Bakker, E.J. / de Jong, I.J.F. / van Wees, H. (eds.) (2002), *Brill's Companion to Herodotus*, Leiden / Boston / Köln.
Balcer, J.M. (1987), *Herodotus & Bisitun. Problems in Ancient Persian Historiography*, Stuttgart.
Balcer, J.M. (1995), *The Persian Conquest of the Greeks 545–450 B.C.*, Konstanz.
Barnett, R.D. (1975), "A Mithraic Figure from Beirut", in: J.R. Hinnells 1975a, 466–469.
Bascom, W. (1965), "The Forms of Folklore: Prose Narratives", in: *The Journal of American Folklore* 78, 3–20.
Beck, R. (1984), "Mithraism since Franz Cumont", in: H. Temporini / W. Haase 1984, 2002–2115.
Belloni, L. (1994), *Eschilo. I Persiani*, Milan.
Bianchi, R.S. (1982), "Perser in Ägypten", in: W. Helck / W. Westendorf 1982, 943–951.
Bichler, R. (2001), *Herodots Welt. Der Aufbau der Historie am Bild der fremden Länder und Völker, ihrer Zivilisation und ihrer Geschichte*, Berlin.
Bivar, A.D.H. (1975), "Religious Subjects on Achaemenid Seals", in: J.R. Hinnells 1975a, 90–105.
Bivar, A.D.H. (1994), "Towards an Integrated Picture of Ancient Mithraism", in: J.R. Hinnells 1994, 61–73.
Bivar, A.D.H. (2005), "Mithraism: A Religion for the Ancient Medes", in: *Iranica Antiqua* 40, 341–358.
Boardman, J. / Hammond, N.G.L. / Lewis, D.M. / Ostwald, M. (eds.) (1988), *The Cambridge Ancient History, Second Edition*, vol. IV. *Persia, Greece and the Western Mediterranean c. 525 to 479 B.C.*, Cambridge.
Borgeaud, P. / Volokhine, Y. (2000), "La formation de la légende de Sarapis: une approche transculturelle", in: *Archiv für Religionsgeschichte* 2, 37–76.
Boyce, M. (1970), "Haoma, Priest of the Sacrifice", in: M. Boyce / I. Gershevitch 1970, 62–80.
Boyce, M. (1975), *A History of Zoroastrianism*, vol. I. *The Early Period*, Leiden / Köln.

Boyce, M. (1982), *A History of Zoroastrianism*, vol. II. *Under the Achaemenians*, Leiden / Köln.
Boyce, M. (1984), *Textual Sources for the Study of Zoroastrianism*, Chicago.
Boyce, M. / Gershevitch, I. (eds.) (1970), *W.B. Henning Memorial Volume*, London.
Brednich, R.W. (ed.) (2004), *Enzyklopädie des Märchens*, vol. XI, Berlin / New York.
Bresciani, E. (1958), "La satrapia d'Egitto", in: *Studi Classici e Orientali* 7, 132–188.
Bresciani, E. (1981), "La morte di Cambise ovvero dell'empietà punita: a proposito della 'Cronaca Demotica', verso, col. c, 7–8", in: *Egitto e Vicino Oriente* 4, 217–222.
Bresciani, E. (1985), "The Persian Occupation of Egypt", in: I. Gershevitch 1985, 502–528.
Briant, P. (1988), "Ethno-classe dominante et populations soumises dans l'empire achéménide: Le cas de l'Égypte", in: A. Kuhrt / H. Sancisi-Weerdenburg 1988, 137–173.
Briant, P. (2002), *From Cyrus to Alexander. A History of the Persian Empire*, Winona Lake.
Brosius, M. (2013), "Greek Sources on Achaemenid Iran", in: D.T. Potts 2013, 658–668.
Brown, T.S. (1982), "Herodotus' Portrait of Cambyses", in: *Historia* 31, 387–403.
Calmeyer, P. (1980), "Textual Sources for the Interpretation of Achaemenian Palace Decorations", in: *Iran* 18, 55–63.
Calmeyer, P. (1987), "Greek Historiography and Achaemenid Reliefs", in: H. Sancisi-Weerdenburg / A. Kuhrt 1987, 11–26.
Carradice, I. (ed.) (1987), *Coinage and Administration in the Athenian and Persian Empires*, Oxford.
Chiasson, C.C. (1979), *The Question of Tragic Influence on Herodotus*, Ph.D. Dissertation, Yale University.
Chiasson, C.C. (1982), "Tragic Diction in Herodotus: Some Possibilities", in: *Phoenix* 36, 156–161.
Chiasson, C.C. (2003), "Herodotus' Use of Attic Tragedy in the Lydian *Logos*", in: *Cl.Ant.* 22, 5–35.
Chimko, C.J. (2003), "Foreign Pharaohs: Self-Legitimization and Indigenous Reaction in Art and Literature", in: *Journal of the Society for the Study of Egyptian Antiquities* 30, 15–57.
Cogan, M. / Eph'al, I. (eds.) (1991), *Ah, Assyria ... Studies in Assyrian History and Ancient Near Eastern Historiography Presented to Hayim Tadmor*, Jerusalem.
Coleson, J. / Matthews, V. (eds.) (1996), *Go to the Land and I Will Show You. Studies in Honor of Dwight W. Young*, Winona Lake.
Collins, B.J. (ed.) (2002), *A History of the Animal World in the Ancient Near East*, Leiden / Boston / Köln.
Cook, J.M. (1985), "The Rise of the Achaemenids and Establishment of their Empire", in: I. Gershevitch 1985, 200–291.
Cruz-Uribe, E. (2003), "The Invasion of Egypt by Cambyses", in: *Transeuphratène* 25, 9–60.
Cuyler Young Jr., T. (1988), "The Early History of the Medes and the Persians and the Achaemenid Empire to the Death of Cambyses. The Consolidation of the Empire and its Limits of Growth under Darius and Xerxes", in: J. Boardman / N.G.L. Hammond / D.M. Lewis / M. Ostwald 1988, 1–111.
Dandamaev, M.A. (1976), *Persien unter den ersten Achämeniden (6. Jahrhundert v. Chr.)*, Wiesbaden.
Dandamaev, M.A. (1989), *A Political History of the Achaemenid Empire*, Leiden / New York / København / Köln.

Darmesteter, J. (1880), *The Zend-Avesta*, vol. I. *The Vendîdâd*, Oxford.
Darmesteter, J. (1883), *The Zend-Avesta*, vol. II. *The Sîrôzahs, Yasts, and Nyâyis*, Oxford.
de Genouillac, H. (1910), "Notes lexicographiques", in: *Revue d'Assyriologie et d'archéologie orientale* 7, 157–161.
de Genouillac, H. (1939), "La chaussure sumérienne", in: *Revue d'Assyriologie et d'archéologie orientale* 36, 43–45.
Dégh, L. (1996), "What Is a Belief Legend?", in: *Folklore* 107, 33–46.
De Jong, A. (1997), *Traditions of the Magi. Zoroastrianism in Greek and Latin Literature*, Leiden / New York / Köln.
Depuydt, L. (1995a), "Murder in Memphis: The Story of Cambyses's Mortal Wounding of the Apis Bull (ca. 523 B.C.E.)", in: *Journal of Near Eastern Studies* 54, 119–126.
Depuydt, L. (1995b), "Regnal Years and Civil Calendar in Achaemenid Egypt", in: *Journal of Egyptian Archaeology* 81, 151–173.
Depuydt, L. (1995c), "Evidence for Accession Dating under the Achaemenids", in: *Journal of the American Oriental Society* 115, 193–204.
Depuydt, L. (1996), "Egyptian Regnal Dating under Cambyses and the Date of the Persian Conquest", in: P. Der Manuelian 1996, 179–190.
Der Manuelian, P. (ed.) (1996), *Studies in Honor of William Kelly Simpson*, vol. I, Boston.
Derow, P. / Parker, R. (eds.) (2003), *Herodotus and his World. Essays from a Conference in Memory of George Forrest*, Oxford.
Devauchelle, D. (1995), "Le sentiment anti-perse chez les anciens Égyptiens", in: *Transeuphratène* 9, 67–80.
Devauchelle, D. (1998), "Un problème de chronologie sous Cambyse", in: *Transeuphratène* 15, 9–17.
Dewald, C. / Marincola, J. (eds.) (2006), *The Cambridge Companion to Herodotus*, Cambridge.
Dillery, J. (2005), "Cambyses and the Egyptian *Chaosbeschreibung* Tradition", in: *CQ* 55, 387–406.
Dodson, A.M. / Johnston, J.J. / Monkhouse, W. (eds.) (2014), *A Good Scribe and an Exceedingly Wise Man. Studies in Honour of W.J. Tait*, London.
Edzard, D.O. (ed.) (1983), *Reallexikon der Assyriologie und Vorderasiatischen Archäologie*, vol. VI, Berlin / New York.
Eichner, H. / Mumm, P.-A. / Panagl, O. / Winkler, E. (eds.) (2001), *Fremd und Eigen: Untersuchungen zu Grammatik und Wortschatz des Uralischen und Indogermanischen in memoriam Hartmut Katz*, Wien.
Erbse, H. (1992), *Studien zum Verständnis Herodots*, Berlin / New York.
Evans, C.D. (1983), "Naram-Sin and Jeroboam: The Archetypal *Unheilsherrscher* in Mesopotamian and Biblical Historiography", in: W.W. Hallo / J.C. Moyer / L.G. Perdue 1983, 97–125.
Falkner, M. (1971), "Fußbekleidung", in: E. Weidner / W. von Soden 1971, 123f.
Finkel, I.L. (1980), "Bilingual Chronicle Fragments", in: *Journal of Cuneiform Studies* 32, 65–80.
Foltz, R. (2013), *Religions of Iran from Prehistory to the Present*, London.
Friedrich, W.H. (1973), "Der Tod des Tyrannen: Die poetische Gerechtigkeit der alten Geschichtsschreiber – und Herodot", in: *Antike und Abendland* 18, 97–129.
Frizell, B.S. (ed.) (2004), *Pecus. Man and Animal in Antiquity*, Rome.

Gabba, E. (ed.) (1999), *Presentazione e scrittura della storia: Storiografia, epigrafi, monumenti*, Como.

Gammie, J.G. (1986), "Herodotus on Kings and Tyrants: Objective Historiography or Conventional Portraiture?", in: *Journal of Near Eastern Studies* 45, 171–195.

Garrison, M.B. (2013), "Royal Achaemenid Iconography", in: D.T. Potts 2013, 566–595.

Garrison, M.B. / Root, M.C. (2001), *Seals on the Persepolis Fortification Tablets*, vol. I. *Images of Heroic Encounter*, Chicago.

Garvie, A.F. (2009), *Aeschylus. Persae, with Introduction and Commentary*, Oxford.

Gershevitch, I. (ed.) (1985), *The Cambridge History of Iran*, vol. II. *The Median and Achaemenian Periods*, Cambridge.

Gippert, J. (2001), "Zum ‚eigenen' Tod des Kambyses", in: H. Eichner / P.-A. Mumm / O. Panagl / E. Winkler 2001, 15–26.

Glassner, J.-J. (2005), *Mesopotamian Chronicles*, Leiden / Boston.

Goetze, A. (1947), "Historical Allusions in Old Babylonian Omen Texts", in: *Journal of Cuneiform Studies* 3, 253–265.

Gould, J. (1989), *Herodotus*, London.

Gould, J. (2003), "Herodotus and the 'Resurrection'", in: P. Derow / R. Parker 2003, 297–302.

Grayson, A.K. (1975), *Assyrian and Babylonian Chronicles*, Locust Valley.

Grayson, A.K. (1980), "Assyria and Babylonia", in: *Orientalia* 49, 140–193.

Greenfield, J.C. (1985), "Aramaic in the Achaemenian Empire", in: I. Gershevitch 1985, 698–713.

Griffin, J. (2006), "Herodotus and Tragedy", in: C. Dewald / J. Marincola 2006, 46–59.

Griffiths, A. (1989), "Was Kleomenes Mad?", in: A. Powell 1989, 51–78.

Hallo, W.W. (1991), "The Death of Kings: Traditional Historiography in Contextual Perspective", in: M. Cogan / I. Eph'al 1991, 148–165.

Hallo, W.W. (ed.) (2003), *The Context of Scripture*, vol. I. *Canonical Compositions from the Biblical World*, Leiden / Boston.

Hallo, W.W. / Moyer, J.C. / Perdue, L.G. (eds.) (1983), *Scripture in Context II: More Essays on the Comparative Method*, Winona Lake.

Hansen, W. (2002), *Ariadne's Thread. A Guide to International Tales Found in Classical Literature*, Ithaca / London.

Harrison, T. (2000), *The Emptiness of Asia. Aeschylus' Persians and the History of the Fifth Century*, London.

Heinen, H. (ed.) (1983), *Althistorische Studien Hermann Bengtson zum 70. Geburtstag dargebracht*, Wiesbaden.

Helck, W. / Otto, E. (eds.) (1975), *Lexikon der Ägyptologie*, vol. I, Wiesbaden.

Helck, W. / Westendorf, W. (eds.) (1980), *Lexikon der Ägyptologie*, vol. III, Wiesbaden.

Helck, W. / Westendorf, W. (eds.) (1982), *Lexikon der Ägyptologie*, vol. IV, Wiesbaden.

Henkelman, W.F.M. (2005), "Animal Sacrifice and 'External' Exchange in the Persepolis Fortification Tablets", in: H.D. Baker / M. Jursa 2005, 137–165.

Herrenschmidt, C. (1987), "Notes sur la parenté chez les Perses au début de l'empire achéménide", in: H. Sancisi-Weerdenburg / A. Kuhrt 1987, 53–67.

Hinnells, J.R. (ed.) (1975a), *Mithraic Studies*, Manchester.

Hinnells, J.R. (1975b), "Reflections on the Bull-Slaying Scene", in: J.R. Hinnells 1975a, 290–312.

Hinnells, J.R. (ed.) (1994), *Studies in Mithraism*, Rome.
Hintze, A. (1994), *Der Zamyād-Yašt. Edition, Übersetzung, Kommentar*, Wiesbaden.
Hofmann, I. / Vorbichler, A. (1979), *Der Äthiopenlogos bei Herodot*, Wien.
Hofmann, I. / Vorbichler, A. (1980), "Das Kambysesbild bei Herodot", in: *Archiv für Orientforschung* 27, 86–105.
Högemann, P. (1986), "Über eine Notiz bei Strabo (XVI 4, 2) zur Klärung des Rückweges des Kambyses-Heeres aus Ägypten 522 v. Chr.", in: G. Maddoli 1986, 159–169.
Högemann, P. (1992), *Das alte Vorderasien und die Achämeniden. Ein Beitrag zur Herodot-Analyse*, Wiesbaden.
Hude, C. (1927), *Herodoti Historiae*, vol. I, Oxford.
Jacoby, F. (1913), "Herodotos (7)", in: *RE* Suppl. II, 205–520.
Jafarey, A.A. (1975), "Mithra, Lord of Lands", in: J.R. Hinnells 1975a, 54–61.
Johnson, J.H. (1994), "The Persians and the Continuity of Egyptian Culture", in: H. Sancisi-Weerdenburg / A. Kuhrt / M.C. Root 1994, 149–159.
Jones, M. (1990), "The Temple of Apis in Memphis", in: *Journal of Egyptian Archaeology* 76, 141–147.
Kahn, D. (2007), "Note on the Time-Factor in Cambyses' Deeds in Egypt as Told by Herodotus", in: *Transeuphratène* 34, 103–112.
Kent, R.G. (1953), *Old Persian. Grammar, Texts, Lexicon*, New Haven.
Klasens, A. (1945–1948), "Cambyses en Egypte", in: *Jaarbericht van het Vooraziatisch-Egyptisch Genootschap Ex Oriente Lux* 10, 339–349.
Köhnken, A. (1980), "Herodots falscher Smerdis", in: J. Latacz / G. Neumann / K. Nickau / E.-R. Schwinge / E. Siegmann 1980, 39–50.
Konstantakos, I.M. (2008), Ἀκίχαρος. Ἡ Διήγηση τοῦ Ἀχικὰρ στὴν ἀρχαία Ἑλλάδα, vol. II. Ἀπὸ τὸν Δημόκριτο στοὺς Περιπατητικούς, Athens.
Konstantakos, I.M. (2011), Θρύλοι καὶ παραμύθια γιὰ τὴ χώρα τοῦ χρυσοῦ. Ἀρχαιολογία ἑνὸς παραμυθιακοῦ μοτίβου, Athens.
Krauss, R. (1980), "Kambyses", in: W. Helck / W. Westendorf 1980, 303f.
Kreyenbroek, P.G. (1994), "Mithra and Ahreman in Iranian Cosmogonies", in: J.R. Hinnells 1994, 173–182.
Kuhrt, A. (2007), *The Persian Empire. A Corpus of Sources from the Achaemenid Period*, London / New York.
Kuhrt, A. / Sancisi-Weerdenburg, H. (eds.) (1988), *Achaemenid History*, vol. III. *Method and Theory*, Leiden.
Latacz, J. / Neumann, G. / Nickau, K. / Schwinge, E.-R. / Siegmann, E. (eds.) (1980), *Festschrift für Hartmut Erbse zum 65. Geburtstag*, Würzburg.
Lazenby, J.F. (1988), "Aischylos and Salamis", in: *Hermes* 116, 168–185.
Lecoq, P. (1997), *Les inscriptions de la Perse achéménide*, Paris.
Legrand, P.-E. (1949), *Hérodote. Histoires. Livre III. Thalie*, Paris.
Lenfant, D. (1996), "Ctésias et Hérodote ou les réécritures de l'histoire dans la Perse achéménide", in: *Revue des Études Grecques* 109, 348–380.
Lewis, D.M. (1985), "Persians in Herodotus", in: *The Greek Historians. Literature and History. Papers presented to A.E. Raubitschek*, Saratoga, 101–117.
Lincoln, B. (1991), *Death, War, and Sacrifice. Studies in Ideology and Practice*, Chicago / London.

Lloyd, A.B. (1975–1988), *Herodotus. Book II*, vols. I–III, Leiden / New York / København / Köln.
Lloyd, A.B. (1982), "The Inscription of Udjaḥorresnet: A Collaborator's Testament", in: *Journal of Egyptian Archaeology* 68, 166–180.
Lloyd, A.B. (1988), "Herodotus on Cambyses: Some Thoughts on Recent Work", in A. Kuhrt / H. Sancisi-Weerdenburg 1988, 55–66.
Lloyd, A.B. (2014), "The Egyptian Attitude to the Persians", in: A.M. Dodson / J.J. Johnston / W. Monkhouse 2014, 185–198.
Lommel, H. (1949), "Mithra und das Stieropfer", in: *Paideuma* 3, 207–218.
Maddoli, G. (ed.) (1986), *Strabone. Contributi allo studio della personalità e dell'opera*, vol. II, Perugia.
Malandra, W.W. (1983), *An Introduction to Ancient Iranian Religion. Readings from the Avesta and Achaemenid Inscriptions*, Minneapolis.
Merkelbach, R. (1959), "Zwei Vermutungen zur Mithrasreligion", in: *Numen* 6, 154–156.
Merkelbach, R. (1984), *Mithras*, Königstein.
Millard, A. (2003), "The Weidner Chronicle", in: W.W. Hallo 2003, 468–470.
Millard, A.R. / Hoffmeier, J.K. / Baker, D.W. (eds.) (1994), *Faith, Tradition, and History: Old Testament Historiography in its Near Eastern Context*, Winona Lake.
Mills, L.H. (1887), *The Zend-Avesta*, vol. III. *The Yasna, Visparad, Âfrînagân, Gâhs, and Miscellaneous Fragments*, Oxford.
Minunno, G. (2008), "Aspetti religiosi nella conquista assira e persiana dell'Egitto", in: *Egitto e Vicino Oriente* 31, 127–143.
Munson, R.V. (1991), "The Madness of Cambyses (Herodotus 3.16–38)", in: *Arethusa* 24, 43–65.
Myres, J.L. (1953), *Herodotus. Father of History*, Oxford.
Näsström, B.-M. (2004), "The Sacrifices of Mithras", in: B.S. Frizell 2004, 108–111.
Nielsen, F.A.J. (1997), *The Tragedy in History. Herodotus and the Deuteronomistic History*, Sheffield.
Nilsson, M.P. (1967), *Geschichte der griechischen Religion*, vol. I. *Die Religion Griechenlands bis auf die griechische Weltherrschaft*, Munich.
Nilsson, M.P. (1972), *Greek Folk Religion*, Philadelphia.
Parker, R.A. (1941), "Persian and Egyptian Chronology", in: *The American Journal of Semitic Languages and Literatures* 58, 285–301.
Pelling, C. (ed.) (1997a), *Greek Tragedy and the Historian*, Oxford.
Pelling, C. (1997b), "Aeschylus' *Persae* and History", in: C. Pelling 1997a, 1–19.
Pomponio, F. (1998), "Presagi ingannevoli", in: *Die Welt des Orients* 29, 52–57.
Porten, B. / Yardeni, A. (1993), *Textbook of Aramaic Documents from Ancient Egypt*, vol. III. *Literature, Accounts, Lists*, Jerusalem.
Porter, B. / Moss, R.L.B. (1974), *Topographical Bibliography of Ancient Egyptian Hieroglyphic Texts, Reliefs, and Paintings*, vol. III. *Memphis. Part 1*, Oxford.
Posener, G. (1936), *La première domination perse en Égypte. Recueil d'inscriptions hiéroglyphiques*, Cairo.
Potts, D.T. (ed.) (2013), *The Oxford Handbook of Ancient Iran*, Oxford.
Powell, A. (ed.) (1989), *Classical Sparta. Techniques Behind her Success*, London.
Quack, J.F. (2011), "Zum Datum der persischen Eroberung Ägyptens unter Kambyses", in: *Journal of Egyptian History* 4, 228–246.

Rachet, G. (1996), *Avesta. Le livre sacré des Anciens Perses*, vol. I. Zoroastre, Paris.
Ray, J.D. (1988), "Egypt 525–404 B.C.", in: J. Boardman / N.G.L. Hammond / D.M. Lewis / M. Ostwald 1988, 254–286.
Reinhardt, K. (1966), *Vermächtnis der Antike. Gesammelte Essays zur Philosophie und Geschichtsschreibung*, Göttingen.
Röhrich, L. / Uther, H.-J. / Brednich, R.W. (2004), "Sage", in: R.W. Brednich 2004, 1017–1049.
Rollinger, R. / Truschnegg, B. / Bichler, R. (eds.) (2011), *Herodot und das Persische Weltreich*, Wiesbaden.
Root, M.C. (2002), "Animals in the Art of Ancient Iran", in: B.J. Collins 2002, 169–209.
Russell, J.R. (1994), "On the Armeno-Iranian Roots of Mithraism", in: J.R. Hinnells 1994, 183–193.
Ruzicka, S. (2012), *Trouble in the West. Egypt and the Persian Empire, 525–332 BCE*, Oxford.
Saïd, S. (2002), "Herodotus and Tragedy", in: E.J. Bakker / I.J.F. de Jong / H. van Wees 2002, 117–147.
Sancisi-Weerdenburg, H. / Kuhrt, A. (eds.) (1987), *Achaemenid History*, vol. II. *The Greek Sources*, Leiden.
Sancisi-Weerdenburg, H. / Kuhrt, A. / Root, M.C. (eds.) (1994), *Achaemenid History*, vol. VIII. *Continuity and Change*, Leiden.
Schmidt, E.F. (1953), *Persepolis*, vol. I. *Structures, Reliefs, Inscriptions*, Chicago.
Schmidt, E.F. (1957), *Persepolis*, vol. II. *Contents of the Treasury and Other Discoveries*, Chicago.
Schmitt, R. (2009), *Die altpersischen Inschriften der Achaimeniden. Editio minor mit deutscher Übersetzung*, Wiesbaden.
Schwartz, J. (1949), "Les conquérants perses et la littérature égyptienne", in: *Bulletin de l'Institut Français d'Archéologie Orientale* 48, 65–80.
Schwartz, M. (1985), "The Old Eastern Iranian World View According to the Avesta. The Religion of Achaemenian Iran", in: I. Gershevitch 1985, 640–697.
Sick, D.H. (2004), "Mit(h)ra(s) and the Myths of the Sun", in: *Numen* 51, 432–467.
Sigrist, M. (1981), "Le travail des cuirs et peaux à Umma sous la dynastie d'Ur III", in: *Journal of Cuneiform Studies* 33, 141–190.
Skjærvø, P.O. (2005), *Introduction to Zoroastrianism*, Cambridge.
Skjærvø, P.O. (2007), *Zoroastrian Texts*, Cambridge.
Skjærvø, P.O. (2011), *The Spirit of Zoroastrianism*, New Haven / London.
Skjærvø, P.O. (2013), "*Avesta* and Zoroastrianism under the Achaemenids and Early Sasanians", in: D.T. Potts 2013, 547–565.
Spiegelberg, W. (1914), *Die sogenannte Demotische Chronik des Pap. 215 der Bibliothèque Nationale zu Paris nebst den auf der Rückseite des Papyrus stehenden Texten*, Leipzig.
Starr, I. (1977), "Notes on Some Published and Unpublished Historical Omens", in: *Journal of Cuneiform Studies* 29, 157–166.
Stol, M. (1983), "Leder(industrie)", in: D.O. Edzard 1983, 527–543.
Stucky, R.A. (1976), "Achämenidische Ortbänder", in: *Archäologischer Anzeiger* 1976, 13–23.
Temporini, H. / Haase, W. (eds.) (1984), *Aufstieg und Niedergang der römischen Welt*, vol. II.17.4, Berlin / New York.
Thompson, D.J. (1988), *Memphis under the Ptolemies*, Princeton.

Tuplin, C. (1987), "The Administration of the Achaemenid Empire", in: I. Carradice 1987, 109–166.
Van De Mieroop, M. (2011), *A History of Ancient Egypt*, Chichester.
Van Seters, J. (1983), *In Search of History. Historiography in the Ancient World and the Origins of Biblical History*, New Haven / London.
Vercoutter, J. (1975), "Apis", in: W. Helck / E. Otto 1975, 338–350.
Vittmann, G. (2011), "Ägypten zur Zeit der Perserherrschaft", in: R. Rollinger / B. Truschnegg / R. Bichler 2011, 373–429.
Waldmann, H. (1994), "Mithras Tauroctonus", in: J.R. Hinnells 1994, 265–277.
Wallinga, H.T. (1984), "The Ionian Revolt", in: *Mnemosyne* 37, 401–437.
Walser, G. (1983), "Der Tod des Kambyses", in: H. Heinen 1983, 8–18.
Weidner, E. / von Soden, W. (eds.) (1971), *Reallexikon der Assyriologie und Vorderasiatischen Archäologie*, vol. III, Berlin / New York.
Weiss, M. (1998), "Mithras, der Nachthimmel: Eine Dekodierung der römischen Mithras-Kultbilder mit Hilfe des Awesta", in: *Traditio* 53, 1–36.
Wesselmann, K. (2011), *Mythische Erzählstrukturen in Herodots Historien*, Berlin / Boston.
West, S. (2003), "Croesus' Second Reprieve and Other Tales of the Persian Court", in: *CQ* 53, 416–437.
Yamauchi, E. (1996), "Cambyses in Egypt", in: J. Coleson / V. Matthews 1996, 371–392.

Vasileios Liotsakis
Narrative Defects in Thucydides and the Development of Ancient Greek Historiography

Abstract: Following up Donelli's and Konstantakos' papers concerning Herodotus' narratives on Near-Eastern rulers, this study elaborates first the way in which Thucydides adopts and adapts his predecessor's narrative method. The two test cases are the digression on Sitalces' expedition against Macedonia in book 2 and the account of the Athenians' lust in books 4 and 5. Second, this paper examines Thucydides' innovation of shaping stereotypical episodes on international relationships, and through this observation explains some of the well-known peculiarities of book 8. The conclusion of this examination is that although these three narrative samples appear to be unusual and inconsistent with their context, they may also be very enlightening with regard to Thucydides' effort to develop a new method of historical writing that would supercede traditional narrative models of his age.

A significant difficulty for every historian lies in explaining events "by emplotment", or the effort to give a comprehensive narrative form to the information (s)he has collected that invariably reflects the author's interpretative perspective.[1] As a result, the historical narrative is both informative as well as interpretative. Were the ancient historians concerned with this twofold process? And if they were, what problems of information and interpretation did they face? Last but not least, did they try to improve the interpretative models of their predecessors or even to create totally new models? I will confine my focus to Thucydides and the way he uses both traditional and innovative narrative models in his effort to offer an informative as well as interpretative account.

One of Thucydides' most prominent interpretative perspectives is his belief that the past can be very useful for understanding the present and predicting the future.[2] In Grethlein's terms, Thucydides uses past events as examples which can prove the continuity and the regularity of the historical development.[3]

---

[1] In White's (1973, 7 ff.) terms, this type of historical writing is defined as "explanation by emplotment".
[2] See most recently Kallet 2006, 335; Raaflaub 2013, 7.
[3] Grethlein 2010, 511.

In this paper, I suggest that this way of seeing the past sometimes created inconsistencies in the Thucydidean narrative, which nevertheless went hand in hand with the development of historical writing.[4] I will present three test cases. Two of them have been considered by many scholars as signs of the imperfection or incompleteness of the Thucydidean work. I will suggest instead that such unusual narratives are indications of the development and improvement of fifth-century historiography concerning a) the use of ethnographic data, b) the criticism of imperialism and c) the ideology of international relations. These narratives reflect Thucydides' struggle to negotiate, in a way different than Herodotus,[5] the intersection of information and interpretation.

The three test-cases can also be categorized as follows:

Narrative model a': although this serves Thucydides' goal of rendering his work a possession for all time on the macro-structure level, the kind and the amount of its information disrupts the coherence of its immediate context on the micro-structure level. Moreover, this model follows a traditional near-eastern way of storytelling, also found in Herodotus.

Narrative model b': This model serves Thucydides' goal to render his work a possession for all time, but in contrast to the previous model, it is less informative for the sake of internal coherence, which is why Thucydides is later forced to supply some additional information omitted in this narrative model. As in the previous model, this one likewise stems from a popular tradition, followed also by Herodotus.

Narrative model c': This model serves Thucydides' goal to render his work a possession for all time, but its distinctive features have been considered by modern scholars narrative imperfections which Thucydides would have emended if his death had not prevented him. This way of writing does not originate from any tradition and is Thucydides' innovation.

---

[4] On the relationship between Classical historiography and narrative techniques see Sommer 2006, 58, 79–88; Marincola 2007 I, 2–4; Schwinge 2008, 9 n. 2–3 with bibl.; Christodoulou 2013, 226.

[5] For a comprehensive as well as inclusive collection of the discussion on the relationship between the two historians see Foster/Lateiner 2012.

1 Sitalces' digression: the use of ethnographic data

The first test case comes at the end of book 2 (95–101). In the winter of 429 BC, Sitalces, the Odrysian king of the Thracians and ally of the Athenians, campaigned against the Macedonian king Perdiccas, both to punish him for not fulfilling an old promise and to help the Athenians against the Chalcidians and the Bottiaeans. He gathered a sizable army by calling under his command all the nations he ruled. Nevertheless, he was forced to abandon the campaign because the Athenians never helped him and his army was starving and confronting a strong winter. Thucydides structures his narrative as follows: the reasons for the expedition (2.95); the gathering of the nations and the preparation of the army (2.96); the extent and the great wealth of the Odrysian empire (2.97); the route to Macedonia up to the city Doberus (2.98); the Macedonian kingdom (2.99); the retreat of the Macedonians inside their walls and forts, while the Odrysians conquer some cities and plunder others (2.100); Sitalces, after negotiating with Perdiccas and laying siege to the Chalcidians and the Bottiaeans, decides to return home due to the lack of supplies and the strong winter (2.101).

This digression has raised both complaints and confusion. On the one side, there are those who consider it incongruent with its context. According to Gomme, there is no need for so many ethnographic and geographic details, especially since the event narrated is unimportant; therefore, he argues that Thucydides is merely satisfying his desire to share with his audience his knowledge about Thrace.[6] Hornblower follows him, although he questions that the event is unimportant.[7] Most recently, Hawthorn suggested that the digression is partly a way for Thucydides to "share the Greeks' disdain for what they regarded as less civilized peoples".[8]

On the other side, there are those who contend that the digression fits in very well with the general narrative and is thematically linked to the Athenians' foreign policy.[9] However, there has been no consensus even between these scholars. Some insist that Thucydides uses Sitalces' situation to criticize the Athenians' diplomatic and strategic mistakes.[10] Others argue that, on the contrary, Thucy-

---

[6] *HCT* II, 241.
[7] *COT* I, 371.
[8] Hawthorn 2014, 82.
[9] Münch 1935, 41; Stahl 1966, 13, 92–97; Connor 1984, 77–78; Rusten 1989, 242–245; Badian 1993, 179–184; Konishi 2008, 658–668.
[10] Stahl 1966, 92; Connor 1984, 78.

dides records the event in order to explain, excuse, or even justify some of his compatriots' political decisions.[11]

Most of the views presented above appear reasonable. Indeed, Thucydides could have omitted some information about the peoples and the geomorphology of Macedonia and Thrace without causing any serious deficiency to the overall history. However, Hornblower justifiably questions Gomme's view that the event itself is trivial. Territorial changes in the North would affect Athenian economic and dipolomatic aspirations, and Thucydides, by including this episode, may have wished to show how fragile the diplomatic *status quo* can be. Besides, we should not forget that Sitalces' campaign was one more proof of Thucydides' programmatic statement that the Peloponnesian War was the greatest ever, affecting even the barbarians (2.23.2). For this reason, although Sitalces' campaign did not ultimately change the borders between Macedonia and the Odrysian kingdom, Thucydides would hardly leave it out of the *History*.

However, a debate about whether this digression is connected to its context, because it focuses solely on the (ir)relevance of the episode to Athenian policy, prevents us from reaching a multi-perspective evaluation of its ethnographic elements. There are, of course, more questions to be answered concerning, first, the narrative function of the ethnographic information in the inner plot of the story, second, the degree to which it is necessary for adequately understanding the story, and third, the semantic load of this information. In addition to being informative, the episode may even carry moral messages.

Moreover, if we examine all these questions in comparison to Herodotus, then, apart from a multi-dimensional penetration of the logic of the episode, we may shed some new light on the development of Classical historiography with regard to ethnography.[12] As many critics have already observed, in this case Thucydides chose to present ethnographic and geographic information in a Herodotean way or – to put it more carefully – in a way which may have been usual in works of ethnography of that period, although due to the lack of surviving fragments of such works, Herodotus sometimes appears to be Thucydides' sole benchmark. The similarities between the digression about Sitalces' campaign and Herodotus are the following: a) the calculation of distances both

---

[11] Badian 1993, 182. See also Konishi (2008, 658–668), who suggests that Thucydides both vindicates Pericles' opinion that the Athenian empire influences even the most distant allies and at the same time distracts the reader from the political turmoil in Athens due to Pericles' death. For Sitalces' digression as an effort of distraction from the political life of Athens cf. Connor 1984, 78.
[12] For the relationship between ethnography and history in the ancient world see, for example, Dench 2008.

for a light-armed person and a ship;[13] b) the measurement of time in days and nights;[14] c) some similarities in terms of vocabulary,[15] and d) Thucydides' comment on the Scythians' lack of prudence as an answer to Herodotus' claims about their wisdom.[16]

Of course, the question is which passages of Herodotus might be parallel to the Sitalces digression. The answer lies in its plot. Sitalces' story is a narrative about a powerful ruler, the leader of an enormous army, who launches an ambitious military campaign that falls short of its aims due to the leader's failure to protect his soldiers from the hostile land. This, as is well known, is one of Herodotus' favorite plots, the most characteristic examples being the wars of Cyrus against the Massagetae, Cambyses against the Ethiopians, and Darius against the Scythians.

In the first book of Herodotus, when Cyrus wishes to subjugate the Massagetae, he first tries to do so by asking their queen Tomyris to marry him. When she rejects his proposal, he campaigns against the Massagetae. Tomyris suggests to him that he should leave her land and let the two armies fight in Persia. However, Cyrus, following Croesus' advice, refuses. First, he defeats the third part of Tomyris' army, including her son. In the final battle, however, the Persians are defeated and Cyrus dies. Tomyris cuts off his head and puts it in a bag full of blood, taking her revenge for all the sufferings he put her through (1.201–216).

In book 3, Herodotus narrates another failed expedition, that of Cambyses against the Ethiopians. Just like Cyrus, Cambyses tries to achieve his goal initially by means of diplomacy. He sends to the Ethiopian king envoys carrying gifts (a purple garment, a necklace and bracelets made of gold, an alabaster container of myrrh, and Phoenician wine). The delegates' real purpose was to see the so-called 'Table of the Sun' (a meadow full of roasted meat) and to collect information about the Ethiopian kingdom. The Ethiopian ruler, informed of Cambyses' deceit, spurns the envoys' offerings and, after leading them to the 'Table of the Sun', the fountain of longevity, and the state prisons, sends them back to Cambyses. He, full of hatred and blinded by arrogance, seizes an army without any serious preparation and leads it to Ethiopia. His soldiers, as they run out of

---

13 Bloomfield 1830, 274; Krüger 1847; *HCT* II, 242; Rusten 1989, 242.
14 *HCT* II, 242.
15 Bloomfield 1830, 276; Krüger 1847, 268–270; Classen/Steup 1966, 264.
16 Krüger 1847, 269; Classen/Steup 1966, 263. For the passages that prove that Thucydides had read Herodotus' work, see Canfora 1982.

supplies, start eating each other, forcing Cambyses to abandon the campaign (3.17–25).[17]

In book 4, we read of Darius' failure at Scythia. The Persian conqueror did not take into account the fact that the Scythians, being nomads, did not have their own land, which they would be compelled to fight for. As a result, he never manages to face their army, as they were always retreating. Darius, after losing some part of his army, gives up his efforts and leaves them unharmed (4.1–142).

Thucydides' narrative about Sitalces shares specific motifs with all these stories:
a) Attempts by a king to rule the elements of nature: Cyrus bridges the river Araxes (Hdt. 1.205.2). Darius builds his own bridges at the Bosporus and Istrus (4.85–88; 97.1). Similarly, Thucydides mentions that Sitalces passed through the mountain Cercine by using a road he had constructed in a previous campaign against the Paionians (2.98.1).
b) The antithesis between the king's wealth or military power and his eventual failure: Cyrus, blinded by his good luck, disregards Croesus' and Tomyris' warnings that his luck will not help him forever (Hdt. 1.204.2; 206.1; 207.1–2). In Cambyses' case, the wealth and the huge army of the Persians are outweighed by the Ethiopians' wisdom and strength as well as by their rough land. Darius attacks Scythia in the hope that no nation can resist his prosperity (4.1.1). Accordingly, Sitalces' εὐδαιμονία and his enormous army do not suffice to help him achieve his goal.
c) The king's inability to protect his army: Cyrus and Darius sacrifice the weakest of their soldiers in order to defeat their enemies (1.211; 3.25.6–7). Cambyses loses some of his men due to starvation (3.134–136). Similarly, Sitalces' army faces the lack of supplies and the hostile climatic conditions (2.101.5).
d) The *wise advisor* motif:[18] Croesus advises Cyrus to fight the Massagetae in their land and not in Persian territory (1.207). In Darius' narrative we find three advisors, Artabanus, Coes and Gobryes (4.83.1–2; 97–98; 134–135). In Sitalces' story we have Seuthes (2.101.5–6).

This narrative model of the *impious and frivolous ruler* originated and was widely prevalent in the traditions of the Near East, which undoubtedly influenced

---

17 On Cambyses' hubris in Herodotus, see Konstantakos in this volume.
18 On this motif in Herodotus and Thucydides, see Marinatos 1980; Pelling 1991; Rogkotis 2006, 58 f.

Herodotus.[19] More specifically, the Herodotean tale of Cambyses' abortive expedition against the Aethiopians has been connected to the description of the campaigns of Nabonidus, the last king of Babylon, as told in the Neo-Babylonian *Verse Account of Nabonidus*,[20] to the traditions about the Iranian king Kai Kāūs (going back to the 1st millennium), as well as to tales about biblical rulers like Sennacherib.[21] Similarly, the Herodotean narrative of Cyrus' campaign against the Massagetae has also been compared to the old Iranian legends of Kai Kāūs and Kai Khosrow.[22] Furthermore, Herodotus' account to Darius' invasion of Scythian recalls similar oriental traditions.[23]

All of these examples indicate that Thucydides composed his own story on the basis of a traditional Near-Eastern narrative model, which he borrowed from Herodotus. However, Thucydides very carefully focuses on the coherence of his narrative not only by confining the ethnographic information but also by emphasizing those details that serve his compositional and interpretative goals. On the contrary, in many cases, Herodotus offers so many details irrelevant to the economy of his stories that the plot can become loquacious and loose. In Cyrus' story, he dedicates many digressions to the nations neighboring the Scythians and their customs (1.202–203; 215–216). In the chapters about Cambyses and the Ethiopians, although he is much more careful and most of the folklore elements are absolutely necessary for the characterization of Cambyses, he still mentions superfluous data like their burial customs (3.24). As for the Scythian *logos*, there is no need to enumerate the rich information – unconnected to the plot – about the Scythians' gods, their sacrifices, their military customs, or their neighbors (4.1–13; 16–31; 36–45; 59–80; 94–96).

Thucydides abandons Herodotus' enthusiasm for 'ethnography for ethnography's sake' and confines such overload to the nations conquered by the Macedonians (2.99). For, as I will try to explain in the following paragraphs, the rest of the ethnographic details in Sitalces' tale concern the historian's narrative and interpretive goals. Of course, even in this case, Thucydides' choice should be connected to Herodotus, as the latter, despite his informational exaggerations,[24] had

---

[19] Konstantakos 2011, 317. On rulers in Herodotus, see also Donelli and Konstantakos in this volume.
[20] Hofmann-Vorbichler 1979, 134–140.
[21] Konstantakos 2008, 196–199; Konstantakos 2011, 121–129.
[22] Duleba 1995, 24–29.
[23] Konstantakos 2008, 159–160.
[24] On this matter, see, collectively, Jacoby 1913, 361; Fornara 1971, 1–3; De Jong 2002, 245–266.

already paved the way for a more creative exploitation of ethnography on a narrative level.[25] The information in the very beginning of the story that the Massagetae are a populous nation of strong men (μέγα ... καὶ ἄλκιμον) (1.201) creates three cross-references, as the story unfolds: first, it explains why Cyrus tried to defeat their army by using a stratagem and not open battle (1.211). This is also the reason why Tomyris complains that the two armies should have faced each other, so that her soldiers would have had the chance to take advantage of their strength (κατὰ τὸ καρτερόν, 1.212.2). Third, it foreshadows the magnitude of the last battle and the Persians' defeat (1.214). We find a similar narrative setting in Darius's story. There is, for instance, the detail that the Scythians are nomads (4.46.2–3). The reader recalls this important element when Darius chases them in vain. The Scythians explain to him that they have absolutely no reason to face him, as they have no land to protect, and he gives up running behind them (4.127.1–2). The information about the Scythians' nomadic way of life confirms the admonition of the wise adviser, Artabanus, namely, that they are hard to subdue (4.83.1–2). Additionally, it foreshadows the failure of the Persian expedition and serves the characterization of Darius as an arrogant and frivolous commander.

In Cambyses' case, we find the perfected version of this use of ethnography. Herodotus takes full advantage of almost all the characteristics of the Ethiopians, with the exception of their burial customs, in order to stress Cambyses' immorality and the Ethiopians' superiority over the Persians.[26] Within the story, there is a diffusive antithesis between the Ethiopian features and the Persian gifts. First, the Persian golden jewelry means nothing to the Ethiopians, as they have so much gold in their land that they use it even to make handcuffs for their prisons. Second, the Persian foods fail to offer them longevity, unlike the Ethiopian water. The Ethiopian monarch gets excited only about Cambyses' wine, which is not Persian but Phoenician. Finally, the Ethiopians are so strong that Cambyses' decision to subdue such a powerful nation seems to be completely misguided.

Thucydides abandons the Herodotean model in which only a small part of the ethnographic data is smoothly incorporated into the inner logic of the story. He chooses instead a more coherent model like Cambyses' story, in which the presence of almost all the information is justified by its energetic effect on the way the reader perceives the plot development and penetrates the

---

[25] On the various functions of the ethnographic data in Herodotus' narrative, see Mash 2010 (humor); Thomas 2000 (as a means of persuasion); Thomas 2011, 237–254 (political propaganda); for the mythical character of ethnography in Herodotus see Baragwanath-Bakker 2012.
[26] Cf. Konstantakos 2011, 113–142.

meaning of the events. In Sitalces' digression, when recording the plethora of the nations that followed Sitalces in his campaign (2.96), Thucydides offers additional details only about the Getae and the Thracian inhabitants of the mountain Rhodope. The first were mounted archers (ἱπποτοξόται) and the latter were knife-carriers (μαχαιροφόρων). Neither clarification is offered *per se*; both prepare the readers for later, when they read that the Getae constituted a large part of the kings' cavalry and that the Thracian knife-carriers were the best of his infantry (2.98.4). Moreover, Thucydides includes the Agrianians, the Laeaeans, the Treres and the Tilataeans, only because they inhabit the borders of the Odrysian kingdom (2.96.3–4). In this way, the reader is oriented concerning the extent of the empire.[27]

Even more important is the role of the information concerning the Odrysians' countless incomes (2.87). Thucydides pays close attention to the gift exchange between the Odrysian king and his tributaries, in order to emphasize the conqueror's financial power. He closes this chapter with a comment that the Odrysian kingdom was the richest among those lying in the area between the Ionian Sea and the Hellespont. As in the Herodotean stories, Thucydides contrasts the invader's prosperity to his final setback. The historian's means are the techniques of a) narration by negation[28] and b) irony through the ring composition.[29] As for the first, in ch. 2.101.2–4 we read that due to the presence of such an imposing armada the Greeks south of Macedonia and the barbarians of the north feared that Sitalces would attack them as well. Though the reader is prepared for such a possible development, nothing happens: Sitalces leaves Macedonia.[30] The Odrysian king is inferior to the reputation that derives from his wealth and power.[31] Thucydides reinforces the irony of Sitalces' ineffectiveness through a ring composition. In the beginning of the digression, we read that Sitalces invaded Macedonia partly because of an unfulfilled promise made to him by Perdiccas (2.95.1–2). Thucydides ends his story by saying that Perdiccas fulfilled his promise, but not to Sitalces. Perdiccas had promised to Seuthes, Sitalces' councilor, to give him his daughter in marriage if Seuthes convinced Sitalces to remove his army from Macedonia (2.101.5–6). The antithesis between the two promises creates a tragic irony at the expense of Sitalces.

---

27 On geographic and ethnographic information as an interpretative means in historiography, see Baumann's study on Diodorus' *Bibliotheke* in this volume.
28 Hornblower 1994b, 152–158.
29 On the ring composition in Thucydides, see Katicic 1957; Connor 1985, 29–30, 251.
30 Cf. 5.50.4. For this chapter see Hornblower 2004, 284; *COT* III, 134.
31 Cf. Stahl 1966, 93.

Is Thucydides imitating Herodotus here, or is he merely sharing parallel folktale material with him?[32] The answer to this question depends on whether Thucydides had access to sources other than Herodotus (either oral or written) that included such stories. Still, such a line of inquiry should stop exactly at the point where our knowledge about Thucydides' life ends. It is more important to have in mind that Thucydides' account of Sitalces resembles Herodotus' accounts in terms not only of content but also of style. For this reason, I believe that we deal with deliberate allusions. By narrating Sitalces' failure in such a way that the resulting account echoes the failures of Cyrus, Cambyses, and Darius, Thucydides accomplishes a great deal. First, he includes Sitalces in a tradition of imperialistic failures during ambitious conquests, thereby pointing out the continuity of historical development. Finally, he uses Sitalces' narrative as a prelude – on the macro-structure level – to the difficulties of the Athenian army, on the one hand, during their distant expedition to Sicily in books 6 and 7 and of the Spartan army, on the other, during their distant expedition in the Aegean in book 8. Nevertheless, it is impossible to deny that on a micro-structure level, Thucydides interrupts the smooth presentation of the events by giving an – indeed unusually – detailed digression. Still, he is much briefer in doing so than Herodotus, so in this respect, I suggest, he tries to improve a traditional, Herodotean narrative model, in order to be both informative and interpretative.

2 From Sphacteria to the peace of Nicias and the analepsis of 5.15–16: criticism on imperialism

The second narrative defect concerns book 4 and the analepsis of it in chapters 15–16 of book 5. In book 4, Thucydides narrates the three-year period between the Athenians' success at Pylos and their defeat at Amphipolis (4.3–5.11).[33] In 424 BC, the Athenians succeed in taking Pylos and capturing 200 Spartan hoplites on the island of Sphacteria. Very confident after their success, the Athenians press the Spartans with successive invasions in the Peloponnese. Moreover, they manage to occupy Cythera, an island of great strategic importance for the Spartans. Nevertheless, these successes are followed by failures. The Athenians are defeated by the Boeotians at Delion and at the same time see their northern alliance with Thrace falling apart due to the Spartan general Brasidas' campaign. In 422, the two sides make an annual truce and a year later, they fight each other

---

[32] On Herodotus and story-telling traditions, cf. Donelli and Konstantakos in this volume.
[33] For the narrative organization of book 4, see Babut 1981 and 1986.

at Amphipolis. The Spartans win the battle and the opportunity to make peace on very favorable terms. It is the Peace of Nicias.

In the flashback to this long narrative (5.15–16), Thucydides' focus shifts. He stresses how both sides were gradually losing their appetite for war. However, the discrepancy between the two passages is that in the latter, Thucydides gives some new information about the efforts of the Spartan king Pleistoanax and the Athenian Nicias to reach a peace agreement during that period. The question is, then, why Thucydides did not give this information in the main narrative. According to the historian, Pleistoanax was attacked by his political rivals every time Sparta had a loss. So, one could justifiably wonder why Thucydides did not record these political charges against Pleistoanax after the Spartan losses of Pylos (4.15) and Cythera (4.53–56).[34] Elsewhere, we learn that, while Brasidas was sending messages to Sparta asking for reinforcements, the most powerful politicians of Sparta disagreed with him and were intending to make peace with the Athenians (4.108.7). Pleistoanax was probably among these powerful Spartans, but he is not even mentioned by the historian. The same question arises regarding Nicias. In the main narrative there had been at least two opportunities for Thucydides to inform us about Nicias' peace efforts. The first was when we learn that the Athenians regretted not accepting the Spartan offer while besieging the Spartan hoplites in Sphacteria (4.27.2). Second, in the flash-back, we read that after their defeat at Delion, the Athenians started to want a peace (5.15.2).

Thucydides could have mentioned Pleistoanax and Nicias' peace efforts plenty of times in his main narrative. Therefore, his flashback might be an attempt to correct either an accidental mistake or a conscious omission, and one can decide which by focusing on the central interpretative axes of the main narrative. One of these is the Athenians' good luck in Pylos. Throughout the whole narrative, Thucydides explains their victory there as a result of good fortune (4.3.1; 12.3; 14.3; 17; 65.4).[35] Whoever the focalizer is, the Spartans, the Greeks, even the Athenians themselves, the facts are a great surprise in comparison with the general expectations. But the most central idea of the narrative is Athenian greed.[36] The text is full of statements that the Athenians overestimated their good luck and therefore got greedy and falsely hoped that they could get whatever they wished (4.21.2; 65.4). Athenian greed is presented through an antithesis with a third axis, Spartan diffidence, a central antithesis of the whole

---

[34] For the scholarship on this issue and further discussion, see *COT* II, 262f.
[35] For scholarship on the luck concerning the events at Pylos, see Liotsakis 2015, 303 n. 94.
[36] For the scholarship on the Athenian greed in these chapters see Balot 2001, 163–165.

work (4.55–57).³⁷ Finally, the Athenian failures at Delion, Thrace, and Amphipolis serve the last interpretative axis, a universal principle which punishes the Athenians for overestimating their good luck.³⁸

This interpretative model echoes Croesus' story in Herodotus.³⁹ Here is a summary of this narrative: In a period when Croesus has reached the apex of power, Solon visits him. When Croesus tries to make a show of his wealth and prosperity, Solon reminds him of the fact that Croesus' present welfare stems merely from good luck and therefore is temporary and fragile. According to Solon, if Croesus wants to see whether he is indeed the happiest man in the world, he should not consider his present state but instead wait to see the whole course, and especially the end, of his life. Croesus concludes that Solon is an unwise man and lets him go. Afterwards, the gods punish Croesus for his hubristic belief that he is the happiest of all men: his son dies and the Persian king Cyrus deprives him of his kingdom. When Cyrus captures Croesus, he binds him in a fire, but Croesus regrets not listening to Solon's advices, begs the god Apollo for mercy and is saved from the fire by a sudden rain sent by the god.⁴⁰

To begin with an essential difference between the two cases, Croesus' story is dominated by the supernatural to such a degree that, while reading it, we feel that we are reading a fairytale.⁴¹ On the contrary, Thucydides' narrative of the Athenians' greed is a rationalistic analysis. However, in both cases, we read a similar narrative: overestimation of the present prosperity → calamities → regret. In the Thucydidean narrative, after the Athenian success at Pylos and Sphacteria, the Spartan envoys ask the Athenians to accept their peace offer. The Spartans advise them not to believe that their present good luck will last forever. However, the Athenians, carried away by their present success, feel omnipotent and, greedy as they are, reject the peace offer. Still, here follow their losses in the battles at Delion and Amphipolis, which make them regret not accepting the Spartans' truce. The similarities between the two narratives are the following:

---

37 Schwartz 1929, 103–104; Finley 1942, 112–113; Gundert 1968; Edmunds 1975, 89–93; Crane 1992, 240–244; Cartledge-Debnar 2006, 562; Ober 2006, 138, 145–147.
38 On the religious connotations of the punishment of the Athenians, see Liotsakis 2015, 303–309.
39 Hdt. 1.29–94. For the scholarship on the narrative structure and logic of Croesus' novella, see Liotsakis 2015, 304 n. 95.
40 Hdt. 1.28–87.
41 Some of the story's supernatural elements are a) the god-punisher of hubristic behavior, b) Adrastus' curse, c) the dream revealing the death of Croesus' son, d) Croesus' mute son who miraculously speaks and thereby saves his father from death at the very last moment, and e) Apollo as the *deus ex machina* in Croesus' escape from the pyre.

a) One's false impression that one can manage everything: Croesus, having conquered almost all the neighboring nations (πάντων; πάντας), has everything (πάντα) and thinks that he is the happiest of all men (πάντων). Similarly, the Athenians are convinced that there is nothing (μηδέν) that can oppose to them.
b) The overestimation of the present: Herodotus purposely opens his narration by stressing that Solon visits Croesus exactly when the latter has reached the peak of his prosperity. The introductory delineation of Croesus' acme depicts a present which is overly valued and therefore falsely considered to last forever, which is why Croesus considers Solon a fool given that the latter takes the end of one's life as a more reliable criterion for the measurement of happiness than the present itself (τὰ παρέοντα ἀγαθά). Similarly, the Athenians refuse to accept the Spartans' peace offer, because they are misled by the positive developments of the present (παροῦσαν νῦν ῥώμην; παρούσῃ εὐτυχίᾳ; τῇ παρούσῃ τύχῃ).
c) The advice: In both cases, the admonitions follow the same logic: good luck is not eternal and human life unfolds in an unpredictable way, with an abundance of developments and reversals (Solon: πολλὰ ἰδεῖν ... πολλὰ παθεῖν ... οὐδὲν ὅμοιον // Spartans: πλεῖσται μεταβολαί). For this reason, everything is ephemeral. Humans should always have in mind that they are captives of their calamities (Solon: πᾶν ἐστι ἄνθρωπος συμφορῇ // Spartans: ἐς τὰς ἡμετέρας νῦν ξυμφορὰς) and this is the most useful knowledge (Solon: ἐπιστάμενον // Spartans: δι' ἐμπειρίαν; γνῶτε).
d) Here follow the failures that lead the arrogant to the realization of their mistakes. Croesus loses both his son and his kingdom, while the Athenians lose the battles of Delion and Amphipolis.
e) In both cases, the narrative ends with the protagonist's regret.

These similarities could explain why Thucydides excluded Pleistoanax and Nicias' diplomatic efforts from his story. Although due to the stylistic affinities already presented it is my personal belief that Thucydides follows Herodotus consciously here,[42] it would be more economical to confine my analysis to mentioning the undeniable fact that, in this case, Thucydides obviously shares with Herodotus the Greek traditional way of storytelling, i.e. that of ὕβρις → ἄτη → νέμεσις → τίσις.[43] In this way, he included the Athenians in a diachronic

---

[42] The themes introduced in the dialogue of Croesus and Solon resonate not only in Herodotus' work (cf. Donelli in this vol.) but also in Thucydides'.
[43] On this element in Herodotus see Konstantakos this volume.

tradition of cases where arrogance is punished by super-human forces, in order to share with his readers the general conclusion that in human history those who overestimate their happiness or their good luck fail in the end. This conclusion is based, as we have seen, on general ideas such as good fortune, the false hopes it creates, and Athenian lust. In Thucydides' mind, these general factors have affected the past and will continue to affect the present and the future. These general factors – and not Nicias' and Pleistoanax' diplomatic efforts – led to the peace of Nicias. For this reason, I suggest, Thucydides omitted the political activity of the two men in the main narrative.

However, by adding Nicias and Pleistoanax's diplomatic efforts to the analepsis, the historian essentially admits that the traditional Herodotean model he has exploited is imperfect. That model might have helped him make his work a possession for all time, but it undermines the second historiographical principle, that is, it does not aid the completeness of information. The inclusion of additional details about Nicias and Pleistoanax can be regarded as a moment of meta-history, i.e. Thucydides' implicit criticism of the inadequacy of traditional interpretative models. As said above, this sudden interest in individuals in chapters 15–16 has been considered a sign of imperfection or even incompleteness of book 5. I suggest instead that these chapters are the result of Thucydides' effort to overcome the inefficacy of the popular topos of ὕβρις → ἄτη → νέμεσις → τίσις he had followed not in book 5 but in book 4.

3 Chios' revolt in book 8: narrative innovations concerning international relations

The third narrative inconsistency is one of the most famous in Thucydidean scholarship and concerns book 8. While in the first part of the book, Alcibiades is left mainly in the background, in the second part his actions are the main cohesive element of the narrative. This difference between the two parts of book 8 has been the basis of much discussion and negative criticism, with the most prevalent theory being that book 8 is a draft and Thucydides, if death had not stopped him, would have reworked its narrative structure.[44] In light of this debate, I will examine a single episode, the revolt of Chios (8.1–24). The plot of the episode is as follows: after the Athenian disaster in Sicily, all Greeks believe

---

44 Jerzykowski 1842; Mewes 1868; Fellner 1880; Holzapfel 1893; Prenzel 1903; Wilamowitz 1908; Rawlings 1981; *HCT* V. For the opposite side see Hellwig 1876; Cüppers 1884; Kunle 1909; Patwell 1978; Erbse 1989; Rood 1998; Williams 1998; *COT* III; Greenwood 2011.

that Athens will collapse very soon. Chios, one of Athens' most powerful allies, joins the Spartans and leads other Athenian allies to revolt. However, after the successive revolts of Clazomenae, Erythrae, and Miletus, the Athenians regain control of the situation; they suppress the Lesbians' revolt, land on Chios and start besieging the city.

Alcibiades definitely has an important role in these events. He convinced the Spartans to focus on Chios and not Lesbos (8.6.3). Moreover, he encouraged the disheartened Spartans not to abandon their expedition to the island (8.12). Thus, in both cases, Thucydides had ample opportunity to analyze Alcibiades' influence on the Spartan decisions. The question is the same as with Nicias and Pleistoanax, that is, why Thucydides omits such details. Again, the answer lies in the narrative structure of the episode. If we compare it with the other revolt episodes of the *History*, we will see that it is comprised of the four basic motifs of such narratives. There are four more revolt episodes in the whole work: the revolt of Potidaea in book 1, at Acarnania in book 2, of Lesbos in book 3, and the disruption of the Peloponnesian League in book 5. In all these episodes, just like in the narrative of Chios, Thucydides follows a typical technique of presentation, always pointing out the same issues, that is, a) the strategic value of a central city, b) fear, c) the urgent need for rapid precautions, and d) secret negotiations.[45]

a. Key cities

The first motif is the strategic importance of one or more cities for the surrounding area. Thucydides always brings the matter to the foreground through the same syllogism: if the powerful city revolts, then her neighbors will follow. In ch. 56–65 of book 1, the Corinthians and the Macedonian king Perdiccas jointly organize the defection of the Thracians from the Athenian alliance. Potidaea has the central role. According to Thucydides, the Athenians, immediately after winning a sea-battle at Sybota against the Corinthians, focus on Potidaea, because they fear that her citizens will revolt and also rouse the coterminous cities. Similarly, Perdiccas colludes with the Chalcidians and the Bottiaeans in the hope that, if these cities are on his side, he will be more effective against the Athenians. In book 2, during their failed effort to abandon the Athenian Empire (2.80–82), the Ambraciots and the Chaonians ask the Spartans for help, arguing that a potential defection of Acarnania from Athens would mean very probably that Za-

---

45 On affinities between similar episodes, see Low in this volume.

cynthus, Cephallonia and even Naupactus will follow (2.80.1). When the Peloponnesian army enters Acarnania, they initially decide to attack Stratus, the most powerful city in Acarnania, in the belief that if they bring it under their power, the rest of the cities will follow (2.81.8). In the Lesbos narrative (3.2–19 and 25–51), Thucydides points out the significance of the island for the conservation of Athenian hegemony through the feelings of the Athenians themselves. When they are informed of the Lesbians' planned revolt, they become very anxious because they believe that having such a strong enemy would be a heavy load for them (3.3.1). The Lesbian envoys, for their part, try to convince the Peloponnesians to send ships explaining that if the Spartans help Lesbos against Athens, they will have a very powerful naval city, which will inspire the rest of the Ionians to revolt (3.13.7). In book 4, Thucydides narrates Brasidas' efforts to turn the Thracian allies of Athens (4.78–88, 102–116). In this case, Amphipolis is the key city. Like the previous examples, Amphipolis' revolt was the main reason that the rest of the Thracians – apart from Brasidas' ingenious diplomacy – dared leave the Athenian alliance (4.108.1–3). In book 5, Mantinea (5.29.2) and Tegea (5.32.3–4) are the key cities during the gradual dissolution of the Spartan hegemony. Last comes the narrative about Chios' revolt in book 8. Thucydides' syllogism remains the same: The Athenians are afraid that the Ionians will follow Chios' example (8.15.1).

Apart from its similarity on a syllogistic level – i.e., the powerful city causes the revolts of its smaller neighbors – Chios' case resembles the other examples linguistically:[46] for Stratus, we read πόλιν μεγίστην (2.81.8), Concerning Lesbus the Athenians consider the danger μέγα ἔργον (3.3.1), while as for Amphipolis ἐς μέγα δέος κατέστησαν (4.108.1). Accordingly, the Corinthians think that Tegea is μέγα μέρος (5.32.3), and in Chios' narrative, the Athenians felt a μέγαν κίνδυνον given that they have to deal with a μεγίστης πόλεως (8.15.1). The concept of magnitude is present in all the examples.

Another observation, however, is more important for understanding the narrative organization of 8.1–24. In some of the cases above, the focus on the key city is particularly intense. In Potidaea's story, the strategic place of the Thracian cities, with the Athenians (δείσαντες) and Perdiccas (νομίζων) as the focalizers, constitutes the source of the majority of the tactical movements and unifies the whole episode.[47] One could say the same about the Acarnanian episode. From the very first comment on the key city Stratus up to the end of his narra-

---

[46] On verbal similarities between typical narratives in Thucydides see also Romilly 1956, 42–47.
[47] The city's role for Thrace is emphasized by the fact that the battle of Potidaea is the culmination of this episode (Rademaker/Buijs 2011, 115–138).

tion, Thucydides focuses exclusively on this μεγίστην city. From 2.83 onwards, he offers no further detail in regard to the situation in the rest of Acarnania and passes to the sea-battle of Patrae (2.83–84). Thucydides obviously omits anything that does not concern the key city. Therefore, one might justifiably conclude that the omission of information due to the focus on the key city is usual in Thucydides' revolt narrations, and this may explain the Chians' dominant presence in 8.1–24 more satisfactorily than Wilamowitz and Andrewes' conjecture that the information of the episode comes exclusively from Chian informants.

b. Fear

The place of a city in the anarchic world of diplomacy defines its fate. In addition, the chaotic situation of international relations spreads fear. It has been justifiably argued that the most prevalent diachronic factor in the *History* is fear, an emotion which unifies all political phenomena to such a degree that from this point of view, the whole work is a constant speculation about this emotion.[48] Fear, just like hope, is present in almost every decision. In Thucydides, it is the predominant regulator of human behavior.[49]

Fear is a motif of the revolt narratives as well. It is the most important source of moves in Thucydides' diplomatic chessboard. From the first chapter of the Chian episode, Thucydides describes the psychological situation in Athens when the news about the Sicilian disaster arrives (8.1.1–4). The atmosphere of fear that is created from the very beginning of the narrative casts the Athenians' consequent efforts in the in the shadow of agony and timorousness. The Athenians' enemies feel quite the same. The Chians anxiously wait for forty Peloponnesian ships, fearing that the Athenians will forestall their attempts (8.7). Still, the Spartans send the ships, though delayed due to their fear (8.11.3). The reader watches exactly the same situation in the rest of the revolt episodes as well, as the following table can show:

Book 1: Revolts of the Thracian cities	δείσαντες (1.56.2); δεδιώς (1.57.4); δεδιότες περὶ τῷ χωρίῳ (1.60.1); δεδιότες μὴ σφίσιν οἱ Ποτειδαιᾶται καὶ οἱ ξύμμαχοι γενομένοις δίχα ἐπιθῶνται (1.64.1)

---

[48] Romilly 1956, 119–127; Proctor 1980, 177–191; Crane 1996; Desmond 2006, 359–360; Luginbill 2011, 39–59, 73–75, 86–88, 102–103, 153–155, 186–187, 193–194.
[49] Luginbill 1999, 65–81; Forde 1995, 147–148; Ahrensdorf 1997, 241–243; Chittick/Freyberg-Inan 2001, 69–90; Welch 2003, 304 and 306f.; Waltz 2010, 270, 389 n. 10.

Book 3: Revolts of Mytilene	δείσαντες (3.3.1); φοβούμενοι μὴ οὐχ ἱκανοὶ ὦσι Λέσβῳ πάσῃ πολεμεῖν (3.4.3); οὐκ ἔτι ἀδεεῖς ἦμεν (3.10.4); τὸ δὲ ἀντίπαλον δέος μόνον πιστὸν ἐς ξυμμαχίαν (3.11.2); τό τε ναυτικὸν ἡμῶν παρεῖχέ τινα φόβον μή ποτε καθ' ἓν γενόμενον ἢ ὑμῖν ἢ ἄλλῳ τῳ προσθέμενον κίνδυνον σφίσι παράσχῃ (3.11.6); οἱ μὲν ἡμᾶς ἐν τῷ πολέμῳ δεδιότες ἐθεράπευον, ἡμεῖς δὲ ἐκείνους ἐν τῇ ἡσυχίᾳ τὸ αὐτὸ ἐποιοῦμεν· ὅ τε τοῖς ἄλλοις μάλιστα εὔνοια πίστιν βεβαιοῖ, ἡμῖν τοῦτο ὁ φόβος ἐχυρὸν παρεῖχε, δέει τε τὸ πλέον ἢ φιλίᾳ κατεχόμενοι ξύμμαχοι ἦμεν· (3.12.1); ἐκφοβῆσαι (3.13.1); καὶ τὸ ἡμέτερον δέος βούλεται (3.14.2); μέγα τὸ δέος ἐγένετο (3.33.2)
Book 4: Revolts of the Thracian cities	δείσαντες οἵ τε ἐπὶ Θρᾴκης ἀφεστῶτες Ἀθηναίων καὶ Περδίκκας ἐξήγαγον τὸν στρατόν… Περδίκκας φοβούμενος δὲ καὶ αὐτὸς τὰ παλαιὰ διάφορα τῶν Ἀθηναίων (4.79.2); διὰ του καρποῦ τὸ δέος ἔτι ἔξω ὄντος (4.84.2); περὶ τοῦ καρποῦ φόβῳ (4.88.1); δεδιὼς καὶ τὴν ἀπὸ τῆς Θάσου τῶν νεῶν βοήθειαν (4.105.1); πρὸς τὸν φόβον (4.106.1); ἐς μέγα δέος κατέστησαν/ἐφοβοῦντο (4.108.1)
Book 5: Peloponnesian revolts	δείσαντες τοὺς Λακεδαιμονίους (5.29.1); φοβούμενοι οἱ πολλοὶ ὥρμηντο πρὸς τοὺς Ἀργείους (5.29.3); ὠρρώδησαν (5.32.4); δεδιότες (5.38.3); ἔδεισαν μὴ μονωθῶσιν (5.40.1); φοβούμενοι (Ε 40.3); δείσαντες (5.44.3); οἱ δὲ Ὀρχομένιοι δείσαντες...ξυνέβησαν (5.61.5)
Book 8: Revolt of Chios	περιειστήκει ἐπὶ τῷ γεγενημένῳ φόβος (8.1.1); πρὸς τὸ παραχρῆμα περιδεές (8.1.4); δεδιότων μὴ οἱ Ἀθηναῖοι τὰ πρασσόμενα αἴσθωνται (8.7); ἀθυμήσαντες (8.11.3)

c. Secret negotiations

Fear brings distrust between states.[50] For this reason, one more permanent characteristic of the Thucydidean revolts are the secret negotiations of the aspiring defectors with Athens and Sparta. In order to succeed in leaving the one or the other side, the Greek cities secretly send ambassadors to Sparta, while at the same time they parley with the Athenians in Attica.

In Potidaea's episode, the city's deputies visit Athens, in order to dissuade the Athenians from imposing preventive measures. However, as the Potidaeans suspect that they will not achieve anything positive in Athens, they simultaneously send some other emissaries to Sparta in order to ensure help from Pelo-

---

50 Korab-Karpowicz 2006, 234.

ponnese (1.58.1).⁵¹ In book 3, the Mytilenaeans secretly prepare their revolt, however, the Tenedians, the Methymnaeans, and some of their own citizens reveal the facts to the Athenians (3.2.3). After the Athenian fleet arrived at the island in order to suppress the revolt, the Mytilenaeans visit Attica and try to convince the Athenians to withdraw from their land, while other Mytilenaeans are secretly sent to Sparta, as it was clear that their compatriots would not persuade the Athenians (3.4.5). In Brasidas' case in Thrace, the anti-Athenian sentiment is covered by secrecy not only in Thrace but also in Berdiccas' court due to the fear that everyone feels for the Athenians (4.79.2; 108.3). The same situation is described in the Chian narrative as well (8.7).

Regarding these secret negotiations, Thucydides implicitly expresses a bitter irony about the hopes of those who want to revolt. Their efforts to keep their plans secret are always belied by the plot development. The historian thereby reveals the vanity of the conviction of the allies of Athens that the Spartans are in a position to free them from Athens. Specifically, concerning the events in Thrace in book 2 and in the narrative on the Ionian war, there is an antithesis between the adverb κρύφα and the phrase ὧν αἰσθόμενοι οἱ Ἀθηναῖοι (4.108.6 in Thrace's case), or an escalation of information, which begins as the Chians' fear (8.7: δεδιότων μὴ οἱ Ἀθηναῖοι τὰ πρασσόμενα αἴσθωνται) turns into the partial knowledge of the Athenians (8.8.2: διατριβῆς ἐγγιγνομένης, οἱ Ἀθηναῖοι ᾐσθάνοντο; 8.10.1: καὶ κατάδηλα μᾶλλον αὐτοῖς τὰ τῶν Χίων ἐφάνη), and ends as secure information (8.15.1: ἐς δὲ τὰς Ἀθήνας ταχὺ ἀγγελία τῆς Χίου ἀφικνεῖται) that initiates the allies' failure.⁵²

d. Speed – urgency – precaution

Another motif is the emphasis on the urgent character of the situation and the precautionary measures the protagonists must take. Consistently, the purpose of either sides is to act first. This motif is, of course, closely connected to the more general antithesis of the *slow Spartans-fast Athenians*.⁵³ The "race" of the opponents is vigorously presented through a) verbs and b) adverbs or adverbial phrases, all indicating quickness. The decisions are to be fulfilled immediately,

---

51 Although the text does not support the view that the mission of the Potidaean envoys to Sparta was made secretly, see Kagan 2009, 108.
52 The phrase μηνυταὶ γίγνονται in Lesbos' case can be seen in the same way.
53 Cf. Schwartz 1929, 103–104; Finley 1942, 112–113; Gundert 1968; Edmunds 1975, 89–93; Crane 1992, 240–244; Cartledge/Debnar 2006, 562; Ober 2006, 138, 145–147.

everyone moves very fast, and there is a quick sequence of events and a minimization of time between them through the use of the adverb εὐθύς.

Thucydides uses the verbs προκαταλαμβάνειν, ἐπείγειν/ἐπείγεσθαι and φθάνειν, as well as compounds beginning with the prefix προ-.[54] Moreover, the three first verbs are used in the same frequency, a total of five times each in typical revolt narratives. The verb προκαταλαμβάνειν appears once in Potidaea's case for the Athenians' desire to prevent potential revolts (1.57.6); twice in Mytilene's narrative, the first in the pro-Athenian informers' advice to the Athenians (3.2.3) and the second for the intentions of the Athenians themselves (3.3.1); once in the case of Thrace for Thucydides' plan to defend Eione (4.104.5); and finally twice in book 5 for the Spartans (5.30.1; 57.1). The verb ἐπείγειν/ἐπείγεσθαι is used once in a compound form for the Athenians' hastiness concerning Potidaea (1.61.3); once in book 3 (3.2.3); once in the case of Thrace for Thucydides' hurry (4.105.1); twice in book 8 for the Chians (8.7) and the Spartans (8.9.1). Compound verbs are also used a total of four times (1.57.1; 3.12.3; 13.1; 4.105.1).

The use of the verb φθάνειν is of great interest with regard to the narrative of Chios. This verb is always used for naval routes: in Mytilene's case, the Spartan Meleas and Hermaeondas do not manage to arrive at Lesbos in time (3.5.2); the verb is used also in the case of Thrace for Thucydides' route from Thasos to Amphipolis (4.104.5) and appears thrice in book 8 in Chios' narrative (8.12.1; 17.2; 17.3), which indicates, if anything, that the style in the case of Chios is purposely polished. Thucydides chooses to give the description of the naval routes in the narrative of Chios by using the most usual verb in such cases and moreover in different forms (φθήσονται; φθάσαι; φθάσαντες).

The stylistic sophistication in the Chian narrative is indicated also by the use of adverbs, specifically forms of the adverb ταχέως and prepositional phrases with the noun τάχος. In four out of six revolt narratives, Thucydides uses such types more than once and always in different forms. In Mytilene's narrative we read κατὰ τάχος, διὰ ταχέων, διὰ τάχους, ἐν τάχει, ὅτι τάχιστα and ὑπὸ σπουδῆς. In the case of Thrace, we find κατὰ τάχος, ἐν τάχει and διὰ τάχους. In the chapters about the disruption of the Peloponnesian League, we have ὡς τάχιστα, κατὰ τάχος and ἐν τάχει. In book 8, Thucydides pays the same attention to the *variatio*: here we read ὡς τάχιστα, διὰ τάχους and ταχύ.

Many scholars have noticed the rattling rhythm in the revolt narratives in Thucydides. Connor observed that in Potidaea's case the story unfolds in a con-

---

54 Cf. also the type βιάσασθαι in Potidaea's narrative for the route of the Corinthian general Aristeus to Potidaea (1.63.1).

cise and quick narrative.⁵⁵ Macleod also points out Thucydides' emphasis on the element of precaution and the use of compound verbs beginning with the prefix προ- in the Mytileneans' words in book 3,⁵⁶ while Zumbrunnen focuses on the immediacy of the Athenians' reaction when they hear of the creation of an alliance between Sparta and Mytilene.⁵⁷ These observations, along with what I have presented concerning the special stylistic elaboration, may give a satisfactory answer to three complaints about book 8, with regard to a) the concise character of the narration, b) the lack of emotions and c) the absence of speeches.

To those who consider the compendious presentation in book 8 an indication of its unfinished condition, one may offer two objections. First, the quick narration is a typical element of all the revolt narratives and not only of Chios' case in the last book. Therefore, at least concerning the first twenty four chapters of the book, we are justified in saying that the fast rhythm is not the result of the fact that Thucydides is merely taking notes, but it proves instead that he is very carefully exploiting a typical narrative method. Second, the author's strong interest in style through the choice of φθάνειν and the variation of the adverbial phrases further strengthens the conclusion that the narrative acceleration is intentional.

As for the ostensibly cold and spiritless character of such a rapid narrative, the speed may be considered the author's effort to stress more vividly the protagonists' emotions. The chaotic situation in the international arena causes the fear of the cities: Athens' and Sparta's anxiety that they will lose control of Greece; the subjects' fear of potential retaliation; the individuals' anxiety that their careers will be destroyed by failure. In the Chian narrative, all of the above are revealed through constant haste. The Chians are in a hurry to accept the Spartans' help, before the Athenians learn their plans. The Spartans intend to support them immediately, although they do not succeed in doing so. On the opposite side, The Athenians are informed of the Chians' revolt and act rapidly. Alcibiades is keen to convince everyone that Chios' revolt is his own accomplishment. All these feelings, the insecurity of the weak, the strong's lust for power, the individuals' arrogant ambition, are emphasized by the element of acceleration. In other words, the speed of the narrative reflects Thucydides' effort to intensify all these emotions.

---

55 Connor 1984, 36 n. 38.
56 Macleod 1983, 90. Cf. The debate of the Corcyrians and the Corinthians (1.32–43), where Thucydides uses similar compounds (for their use there, see Debnar 2011, 126, n. 61). This is one more episode concerning alliances, where Thucydides uses the preposition προ-.
57 Zumbrunnen 2008, 62–66 and 86.

Regarding the absence of speeches,[58] Zumbrunnen's thoughts are very illuminating. He observes that in Mytilene's narrative, one of the means Thucydides uses in order to stress the immediacy of the Athenians' reaction is the omission of speeches.[59] This is the case also in the rest of the revolt narratives. Indeed, in Mytilene's story, the Mytileneans' speech and the debate of Cleon and Diodotus lie at the beginning and the end of the fast narrative, so that they frame it without interrupting it. One could say the same about Brasidas' speeches in book 4. His speech to the Acanthians lies at the beginning of the revolts, while in the quick narrative on Amphipolis' revolt there is no speech. Similarly, we find no speeches in the narratives of Acarnania, Potidaea and the Peloponnesian defections. Given all these, in the Chian episode there are no speeches perhaps due to Thucydides' intention not to interrupt the fast narrative rhythm, which is consistent with the rest of the revolt episodes.

This narrative model is Thucydides' own invention, an innovative one, since it does not occur in Herodotus. Thucydides is much more confident in the use of his own interpretative model than he was in the first two cases. While in Sitalces' case and the case of Nicias and Pleistoanax he corrects the Herodotean models, in this case he does not add anything about Alcibiades. I suggest this means that he considers his new narrative model both informative enough and interpretative, even if it contrasts with the rest of book 8. Indeed, this episode serves Thucydides' desire to offer an account of the past useful for the present and the future. By following his typical narrative method for revolt episodes in the Chian narrative, he offers one more example which proves that history repeats itself in a regular way. The price in terms of narrative organization is Alcibiades' absence and thus the antithesis with the rest of book 8. Nevertheless, such a narrative inconsistency is not a sign of incompleteness, as has been very often argued, but a necessary imperfection and an indication of Thucydides' effort to consolidate his way of interpreting revolts.

Undoubtedly, in the *History*, there are certain passages that do not fit in well with their context or perhaps omit important information. However, such passages can also be very enlightening, and they illustrate how Thucydides tried to reconcile two basic goals of his art, informing and interpreting. Besides that, these parts of the *History* reveal the method Thucydides used in order to develop the historiography of his age by combining the traditional norms he borrowed from his predecessors with his own principles. For example, in a work where ethnog-

---

[58] For a discussion on the very issue of the speeches in Thucydides, see Feddern and Harris in this volume.
[59] Zumbrunnen 2008, 51–56.

raphy is almost absent, Sitalces' narrative indicates that although Thucydides left ethnography out of the *History*, he did so only after examining in depth the function of ethnographic data in Herodotus' account – or perhaps even in other works – embracing some of his predecessor's methods and imitating him while improving the narrative techniques that integrate ethnographic information in the plot and meaning of the story. One can observe a similar process of working on traditional models in the connection between book 4 and its flashback in 5.15–16 concerning imperialism. Lastly, in book 8, narrative inconsistencies go hand in hand with narrative innovations with regard to international relations.

List of Abbreviations

COT = Hornblower, S. (1991–2008), *A Commentary on Thucydides*, vols. I–III, Oxford.
HCT = Gomme, A.W. / Andrewes, A. / Dover, K.J. (1945–1981), *A Historical Commentary on Thucydides*, vols. I–V, Oxford.

Bibliography

Ahrensdorf, P.J. (1997), "Thucydides' Realistic Critique of Realism", in: *Polity* 30, 231–265.
Babut, D. (1981), "Interprétation historique et structure littéraire chez Thucydide: Remarques sur la composition du livre IV", in: *BAGB* 40, 417–439.
Babut, D. (1986), "L' episode de Pylos-Sphactérie chez Thucydide: L' agencement du récit et les intentions de l' historien", in: *RPh* 60, 59–79.
Badian, E. (1993), *From Plataea to Potidaea. Studies in the History and Historiography of the Pentecontaetia*, Baltimore.
Bakker, E.J. / De Jong, I.J.F. / van Wees, H. (eds.) (2002), *Brill's Companion to Herodotus*, Leiden.
Baragwanath, E. / de Bakker, M. (eds.) (2012), *Myth, Truth, and Narrative in Herodotus*, Oxford.
Balot, R.K. (2001), *Greed and Injustice in Classical Athens*, Princeton / Oxford.
Bloomfield, S.T. (1830), *The History of the Peloponnesian War*, London.
Canfora, L. (1982), "Tucidide erodoteo", in: *QS* 16, 77–84.
Cartledge, P. / Debnar, P. (2006), "Sparta and the Spartans in Thucydides", in: A. Rengakos / A. Tsakmakis 2006, 559–587.
Chittick, W.O. / Freyberg-Inan, A. (2001), "'Chiefly for Fear, Next for Honour, and Lastly for Profit': An Analysis of Foreign Policy Motivation in the Peloponnesian War", in: *RIS* 27, 69–90.
Christodoulou, P. (2013), "Thucydides' Pericles. Between Historical Reality and Literary Representation", in: A. Tsakmakis / M. Tamiolaki 2013, 225–254.
Classen J. / Steup, J. (1966), *Thukydides, II*, Berlin.

Connor, W.R. (1984), *Thucydides*, Princeton.
Crane, G. (1992), "The Fear and Pursuit of Risk: Corinth on Athens, Sparta and the Peloponnesians (Thucydides 1.68 – 71, 120 – 121)", in: *TAPhA* 122, 227 – 256.
Crane, G. (1996), *The Blinded Eye. Thucydides and the New Written Word*, Lanham.
Cüppers, Fr. J. (1884), *De octavo Thucydidis libro non perpolito*, Münster.
Debnar, P. (2004⁴), *Speaking the Same Language. Speech and Audience in Thucydides' Spartan Debates*, Ann Arbor.
Debnar, P. (2011), "Rhetoric and Character in the Corcyra Debate", in: G. Rechenauer / V. Pothou 2011, 115 – 130.
De Jong, I.J.F. (2002), "Narrative Unity and Units", in: E.J. Bakker / I.J.F. De Jong / H. van Wees 2002, 245 – 266.
Dench, E. (2007), "Ethnography and History", in: J. Marincola 2007 I, 493 – 503.
Desmond, W. (2006), "Lessons of Fear: A Reading of Thucydides", in: *CPh* 101, 359 – 379.
Duleba, W. (1995), *The Cyrus Legend in the Šāhnāme*, Kraków.
Edmunds, L. (1975), *Chance and Intelligence in Thucydides*, Cambridge.
Erbse, H. (1989), *Thukydides-Interpretationen*, Berlin / New York.
Fellner, T. (1880), *Forschung und Darstellungsweise des Thukydides. Gezeigt an einer Kritik des Achten Buches*, Vienna.
Finley, J.H. (1942), *Thucydides*, Oxford.
Flower, M. / Toher, M. (eds.) (1991), *Georgica. Greek Studies in Honour of George Cawkell*, London.
Forde, S. (1995), "International Realism and the Science of Politics: Thucydides, Machiavelli, and Neorealism", in: *ISQ* 39, 141 – 160.
Fornara, C.W. (1971), *Herodotus. An Interpretative Essay*, Oxford.
Foster, E. / Lateiner, D. (eds.) (2012), *Thucydides and Herodotus*, Oxford.
Greenwood, E. (2006), *Thucydides and the Shaping of History*, Duckworth.
Grethlein, J. (2010), *The Greeks and their Past. Poetry, Oratory and History in the Fifth-Century BCE*, Cambridge.
Gundert, H. (1968), "Athen und Sparta in den Reden des Thukydides", in: H. Herter 1968, 114 – 134.
Hawthorn, G. (2014), *Thucydides on Politics. Back to the Present*, Cambridge.
Hellwig, P. (1876), *De Thucydidei operis libri octavi indole ac natura*, Halle.
Herter, H. (ed.) (1968), *Thukydides*, Darmstadt.
Hofmann, I. / Vorbichler, A. (eds.) (1979), *Der Äthiopenlogos bei Herodot*, Vienna.
Holzapfel, L. (1893), "Doppelte Relationen im VIII. Buche des Thukydides", in: *Hermes* 28, 435 – 464.
Hornblower, S. (ed.) (1994a), *Greek Historiography*, New York / Oxford.
Hornblower, S. (1994b), "Narratology and Narrative Techniques in Thucydides", in: S. Hornblower 1994a, 131 – 66.
Hornblower, S. (2004), *Thucydides and Pindar. Historical Narrative and the World of Epinikian Poetry*, Oxford.
Jacoby, F. (1913), "Herodotos (7)", in: *RE* Suppl. II, 205 – 520.
Jerzykowski, A. (1842), *Octavo historiae Thucydideae libro extremam manum non accessisse demonstratur*, Breslau.
Kagan, D. (2009), *Thucydides. The Reinvention of History*, New York.

Kallet., L. (2006), "Thucydides' Workshop of History and Utility Outside the Text", in: A. Rengakos / A. Tsakmakis 2006, 335–368.
Konishi, H. (2008–2009), *Power and Structure in Thucydides. An Analytical Commentary* vols. I–III, Amsterdam.
Konstantakos, I.M. (2008), *Ἀκίχαρος. Ἡ Διήγηση τοῦ Ἀχικὰρ στὴν ἀρχαία Ἑλλάδα*, vol. II. *Ἀπὸ τὸν Δημόκριτο στοὺς Περιπατητικούς*, Athens.
Konstantakos, I.M. (2011), *Θρύλοι καὶ παραμύθια γιὰ τὴ χώρα τοῦ χρυσοῦ. Ἀρχαιολογία ἑνὸς παραμυθιακοῦ μοτίβου*, Athens.
Korab-Karpowicz, W.J. (2006), "How International Relations Theorists Can Benefit by Reading Thucydides", in: *The Monist* 89, 232–244.
Krüger, K.W. (1847), *ΘΟΥΚΥΔΙΔΟΥ ΞΥΓΓΡΑΦΗ*, Berlin.
Kunle, L. (1909), *Untersuchungen über das achtes Buch des Thukydides*, Freiburg.
Lallot, J. / Rijksbaron, A. / Jacquinod, B. / Buijs, M. (eds.) (2011), *The Historical Present in Thucydides. Semantics and Narrative Function = Le présent historique chez Thucydide. Sémantique et function narrative*, Leiden.
Liotsakis, V. (2015), "Texts of Religious Content in Thucydides and the Ancient Implied Reader", in: *RFIC* 143, 278–317.
Luginbill, R.D. (1999), *Thucydides on War and National Character*, Boulder.
Luginbill, R.D. (2011), *Author of Illusions. Thucydides' Rewriting of the History of the Peloponnesian War*, Newcastle.
Macleod, C. (1983), *The Collected Essays of Colin Macleod*, Oxford.
Marinatos, N. (1980), "Nicias as a Wise Adviser and Tragic Warner in Thucydides", in: *Philologus* 124, 305–310.
Marincola, J. (ed.) (2007), *A Companion to Greek and Roman Historiography*, vols. I–II, Oxford.
Mash, M.C. (2010), *Humor and Ethnography in Herodotus' Histories*, (diss.), Chapel Hill.
Mewes, W. (1868), *Untersuchungen über das Achte Buch der Thukydideischen Geschichte*, Brandenburg.
Ober, J. (2006), "Thucydides and the Invention of Political Science", in: A. Rengakos / A. Tsakmakis 2006, 131–159.
Patwell, J.M. (1978), *Grammar, Discourse, and Style in Thucydides' Book Eight*, Philadelphia.
Pelling, C.B.R. (1991), "Thucydides' Archidamus and Herodotus' Artabanus", in: M. Flower / M. Toher 1991, 120–142.
Prenzel, K. (1903), *De Thucydidis libro octavo quaestiones*, Berlin.
Proctor, D. (1980), *The Experience of Thucydides*, Warminster.
Raaflaub, K.A. (2013), "*Ktēma es aiei*: Thucydides' Concept of "Learning Through History" and Its Realization in His Work", in: A. Tsakmakis / M. Tamiolaki 2013, 3–21.
Radermaker, A. / Buijs, M. (2011), "A Tale of Two Involuntary Encounters: Linguistics and the Persuasive Function of the Historical Present in Two Thucydidean Battle Scenes (1.45–51 and 1.56–66)", in: J. Lallot / A. Rijksbaron / B. Jacquinod / M. Buijs 2011, 115–138.
Rawlings, H.R. (1981), *The Structure of Thucydides' History*, Princeton.
Rechenauer, G. / Pothou, V. (eds.) (2011), *Thucydides – a Violent Teacher. History and its Representations*, Göttingen.
Rengakos, A. / Tsakmakis, A. (eds.) (2006), *Brill's Companion to Thucydides*, Leiden.
Rogkotis, Z. (2006), "Thucydides and Herodotus: Aspects of their Intellectual Relationship", in: A. Rengakos / A. Tsakmakis 2006, 57–86.

Rollinger, R. / Truschnegg, B. / Bichler, R. (eds.) (2011), *Herodot und das Persische Weltreich*, Wiesbaden.
Romilly, J. de (1956), *Histoire at raison chez Thucydide*, Paris.
Rood, T.C.B. (1998), *Thucydides. Narrative and Explanation*, Oxford.
Rusten, J.S. (ed.) (1989), *Thucydides, The Peloponnesian War, Book II*, Cambridge.
Schwartz, E. (1929), *Das Geschichtswerk des Thukydides*, Hildesheim.
Schwinge, E.R. (2008), *Komplexität und Transparenz. Thukydides. Eine Leseanleitung*, Heidelberg.
Sommer, K. (2006), *Techne und Geschichte. Eine Diskursgeschichtliche Studie zu Thukydides*, Bonn.
Stahl, H.P. (1966), *Thukydides. Die Stellung des Menschen im geschichtlichen Prozess*, Munich.
Thomas, R. (2000), *Herodotus in Context. Ethnography, Science and the Art of Persuasion*, Cambridge.
Thomas, R. (2011), "Herodotus' Persian Ethnography", in: R. Rollinger / B. Truschnegg / R. Bichler 2011, 237–254.
Tsakmakis, A. / Tamiolaki, M. (eds.) (2013), *Thucydides Between History and Literature*, Berlin / Boston.
Waltz, K. (2010), *Theory of International Politics*, Waveland.
Welch, D.A. (2003), "Why International Relations Theorists Should Stop Reading Thucydides", in: *RIS* 29, 301–319.
Wilamowitz, U. (1908), "Thukydides VIII", in: *Hermes* 43, 578–618.
Williams, M.F. (1998), *Ethics in Thucydides. The Ancient Simplicity*, London / New York / Oxford.
Zumbrunnen, J. (2008), *Silence and Democracy. Athenian Politics in Thucydides' History*, Pennsylvania.

Vera Mariantonia Grossi
Thucydides and Poetry. Ancient Remarks on the Vocabulary and Structure of Thucydides' *History*

Abstract: This paper investigates the ancient perception of the links between Thucydides' *History* and (Homeric) poetry. The relationship between historiography and poetry connects the present contribution to Donelli's analysis of Herodotus' relationship with epic and lyric tradition. Adopting the same approach as Feddern's paper – namely the idea that ancient sources may provide an interesting point of view to address issues of modern criticism – I move from the ancient debate about the poetic style in prose writing (a concern that also underlies Polybius' accusations of Phylarchus' exploitation of tragedy, the subject of Farrington's contribution), and proceed to discuss how the ancient rhetorical tradition dealt with the similarity between Thucydidean and Homeric narrative technique. The second part of my contribution aims to show how the concept of Homeric emulation operates in the *corpus* of Thucydides' *scholia* and to describe the interaction between ancient Thucydidean and Homeric studies.

Thucydides' relationship with poetry has been richly explored by modern scholars: stylistic features and narrative situations that seem to derive from tragedy and epic have been identified in his work; the Sicilian narrative in the sixth and seventh book has often been examined for its intertextual relationship to Homeric vocabulary, motifs and characters; and the influence of the epic model on the narrative construction of the *History* has also been matter of recent inquiries.[1]

---

[1] On the influence of the language of tragedy and epic on Thucydides' vocabulary, see Smith 1891; Smith 1892; Smith 1900; see also Wolcott 1898 for a helpful study on Thucydides' introduction of new words into literary usage. A tragic pattern in Th. 3.113 has been interestingly examined by Lapini 1991; cf. also Macleod 1983, 140–158 for an account of the tragic elements in Thucydides' narration and speeches. Specific points of contact between the Sicilian narrative and Homer's epic have been investigated by Frangoulidis 1993; Mackie 1996; Allison 1997; Zadorojnyi 1998; Rood 1998a, who provides a rich discussion of earlier studies and a broader analysis of literary allusion in Thucydides. Rengakos (2006a, 183–185) argues that the influence of Homer on ancient historiography was above all a matter of narrative technique and offers a detailed inquiry into the borrowing of epic narrative strategies in Herodotus' and Thucydides' works (on the same topic see also Rengakos 2006b). As for the role of the poetic

DOI 10.1515/9783110496055-005

Ancient scholars also used to reflect upon Thucydides' relationship to poetry; in this contribution, I will consider that point of view. I will first examine some texts concerning the topic and try to sketch their theoretical context while focusing on ancient sources that regard Thucydides as an emulator of Homer.[2] In the second part of this paper, I will introduce some examples from the *corpus* of Thucydides' *scholia* and from a papyrus commentary on the second book of the *History*, in order to show how the concept of Homeric emulation was concretely employed by ancient scholars commenting on Thucydides' text.

The first to point out a stylistic affinity between Thucydides' work and poetry was Dionysius of Halicarnassus. In his *Second Letter to Ammaeus*, Dionysius states that Thucydides aspired to create and to introduce a kind of style which was neither wholly prose nor entirely verse, but a combination of the two (*Amm.* 2.2):[3]

> τούτῳ γὰρ Θουκυδίδης τῷ ἀνδρὶ ἐπιβαλὼν καὶ τοῖς ἄλλοις ὧν πρότερον ἐμνήσθην, καὶ συνιδών, ἃς ἕκαστος αὐτῶν ἔσχεν ἀρετάς, ἴδιόν τι γένος χαρακτῆρος, οὔτε πεζὸν αὐτοτελῶς οὔτ' ἔμμετρον ἀπηρτισμένως, κοινὸν δέ τι καὶ μικτὸν ἐξ ἀμφοῖν ἐργασάμενος εἰς τὴν ἱστορικὴν πραγματείαν ἐσπούδασεν εἰσαγαγεῖν·

> Following after him [sc. Herodotus] and the others whom I mentioned before, and perceiving their several qualities, Thucydides aspired to form and to introduce into the writing of history an individual kind of style which was neither absolute prose nor wholly verse, but a mixture containing elements of both.

After this assertion, he lists in detail the most distinctive features of the historian's style. He first concentrates on Thucydides' vocabulary, the essential quality

---

tradition in the development of Greek historiography, Donelli's contribution at the beginning of the present volume provides an illuminating exploration of the multiple levels of Herodotus' engagement with both epic and lyric poetry.

[2] Most of the ancient sources I will consider (Dionysius of Halicarnassus, Theon, Marcellinus) are also taken into account by Feddern in his discussion of Thucydides' methodology: for an examination of the approach of those sources to Thucydides' *History*, see his contribution in this collection.

[3] For Dionysius' works I follow the text and, with minor changes, the translation of Usher 1974–1985. The *Second Letter to Ammaeus* was written as a sort of illustration of chapter 24 of the earlier essay *On Thucydides*, a description of the historian's style whose text is fully quoted at the beginning of the *Letter*. It is worthwhile noting that in *Th.* 24 Dionysius simply attributes to Thucydides the introduction into the ἱστορικὴν πραγματείαν of "an individual style which had been overlooked by his predecessors" (ἴδιόν τινα χαρακτῆρα καὶ παρεωραμένον ἅπασι), while in *Amm.* 2.2 he clarifies that such style's peculiarity consisted in its poetic character. The following sections of the text, to which I refer below, occur identically both in *Th.* 24 and *Amm.* 2.2. For a helpful commentary on *Th.* 24 (=*Amm.* 2.2) see Pavano 1958, 89–101.

of which is that it is quite distant from everyday language: ἐπὶ μὲν τῆς ἐκλογῆς τῶν ὀνομάτων τὴν τροπικὴν καὶ γλωττηματικὴν καὶ ἀπηρχαιωμένην καὶ ξένην λέξιν παραλαμβάνων πολλάκις ἀντὶ τῆς κοινῆς καὶ συνήθους τοῖς κατ' αὐτὸν ἀνθρώποις ("in his choice of words he preferred those which were metaphorical, rare, archaic and outlandish to those which were common and familiar to his contemporaries"). The use of such terms produces a vocabulary that Dionysius defines, in a word, as ποιητικόν: "poetic" in the sense of "artificial," "the result of an artistic intention," and therefore remote from ordinary language.[4]

It is worthwhile to consider the role Thucydides plays in Dionysius' classification of the literary styles. In the eventual system, which the scholar develops in the treatise *On Demosthenes* (37–41), Thucydides is mentioned, together with the poets Aeschylus and Pindar, as a representative of the most elevated kind of style, the so called αὐστηρὰ ἁρμονία, the style "which is noble, austere, grand in conception and has an old-fashioned flavour" (γεννικὴ καὶ αὐστηρὰ καὶ μεγαλόφρων καὶ τὸ ἀρχαιοπρεπὲς διώκουσα, *Dem.* 39):[5]

> καὶ παραδείγματα δὲ αὐτῆς ποιητῶν μὲν καὶ μελοποιῶν ἥ τ' Αἰσχύλου λέξις ὀλίγου δεῖν πᾶσα καὶ ἡ Πινδάρου, χωρὶς ὅτι μὴ τὰ Παρθένεια καὶ εἴ τινα τούτοις ὁμοίας ἀπαιτεῖ κατασκευάς· διαφαίνεται δέ τις ὁμοία κἂν τούτοις εὐγένεια καὶ σεμνότης ἁρμονίας τὸν ἀρχαῖον φυλάττουσα πίνον. συγγραφέων δὲ λαμπρότατός τε καὶ μάλιστα τῶν ἄλλων κατορθῶν περὶ ταύτην τὴν ἰδέαν Θουκυδίδης.

> There are examples of this style, in poetry spoken or sung, in nearly all the verse of Aeschylus and Pindar, except that Pindar's *Partheneia* and other poems of that kind require a different style, though even in these a certain similar nobility and solemnity of style is still

---

4 Cf. *Amm.* 2.2: ἵνα δὲ συνελὼν εἴπω, τέσσαρα μέν ἐστιν ὥσπερ ὄργανα τῆς Θουκυδίδου λέξεως, τὸ ποιητικὸν τῶν ὀνομάτων, τὸ πολυειδὲς τῶν σχημάτων, τὸ τραχὺ τῆς ἁρμονίας, τὸ τάχος τῆς σημασίας ("I may summarise the instruments, so to speak, of Thucydides' style as follows: there are four–artificiality of vocabulary, variety of figures, harshness of word-order, rapidity of signification"). On the meaning of τὸ ποιητικόν in this passage see Nicolai 1992, 245–246. Usher rightly translates τὸ ποιητικὸν τῶν ὀνομάτων as "artificiality of vocabulary," which is substantially equivalent to Aujac's *la fabrication de mots*. A slightly different, but also effective rendering is Pavano's *il sapore poetico dei vocaboli*.

5 In this section of *On Demosthenes*, the critic adopts essentially the same theory as in chapters 21–24 of the treatise *On Composition* (on the relative chronology of the two essays see the *status quaestionis* in de Jonge 2008, 20–25, with quotation of further literature). In *Comp.* 22, Dionysius included in the group of the exponents of the first style, along with Pindar, Aeschylus, and Thucydides, also Antimachus of Colophon, Empedocles, and Antiphon, but, as it came to selecting examples from these authors, he considered it to be "enough to cite Pindar among the poets, Thucydides among the prose writers; for these are the best writers in the austere style of composition" (ποιητῶν μὲν οὖν Πίνδαρος ἀρκέσει παραληφθείς, συγγραφέων δὲ Θουκυδίδης· κράτιστοι γὰρ οὗτοι ποιηταὶ τῆς αὐστηρᾶς ἁρμονίας). Note that the types of literary composition cross the dividing line between prose and poetry.

apparent, preserving the patina of antiquity. The most brilliant and successful exponent of this style among the historians is Thucydides.

We should notice that Dionysius' attitude towards Thucydides is complex and oscillates between admiration and criticism. When presenting his theoretical classification of the literary styles, Dionysius regards the historian as "the most successful exponent" of the loftiest style. Yet, in the first century BC debate on the imitation of Thucydides, Dionysius takes a stand against those who believed Thucydides could serve as a stylistic model for historical composition. According to Dionysius, in fact, history should not contain too much artistry (it should not be too ποιητικόν), because it should be accessible to the broadest possible public. Thucydides, on the contrary, rises above common language to such an extent that he becomes obscure, and restricts the benefit of reading history to the narrow public that can cope with his difficult style (*Th.* 50–51).

Dionysius' position against the imitation of Thucydides should be considered in the context of the wider debate which interested the rhetoricians from Aristotle onwards about the legitimacy of using the ποιητικόν, the poetic style, in prose writing: a topic the philosopher had dealt with in his *Rhetoric* (1404a–b). Dionysius' criticism of Thucydides' poetic, artificial language is clearly related to Aristotle's view that expressions departing from normal linguistic usage, although convenient for the solemnity of poetry, do not have the clarity which is required for prose writing.[6]

In order to understand Dionysius' attitude towards the ποιητικόν in (Thucydidean) prose, attention should be paid to a passage in the treatise *On Thucydides* which immediately precedes the above mentioned description of the historian's style (*Th.* 24 = *Amm.* 2.2). In this passage (*Th.* 23), Dionysius argues for the superiority of Herodotus over his predecessors on the grounds that he was the first to develop, along with the so-called ἀναγκαῖαι ἀρεταί, the "essential virtues" of style (purity of language, clarity and brevity), also the "additional" (ἐπίθετοι) virtues (sublimity, eloquence, dignity, magnificence). Herodotus, consequently, "made his prose style resemble the finest poetry by its persuasiveness, its charm and its utterly delightful effect" (παρεσκεύασε τῇ κρατίστῃ ποιήσει τὴν πεζὴν φράσιν ὁμοίαν γενέσθαι πειθοῦς τε καὶ χαρίτων καὶ τῆς εἰς ἄκρον ἡκούσης ἡδονῆς ἕνεκα). It is clear that this association with poetry has to be understood as a positive remark on Herodotus' style, while the poetic character of the Thu-

---

[6] For an account of the debate on the ποιητικόν in the rhetorical tradition see Nicolai 1992, 61–83. As for the ancient concern of the proper relationship of poetry to historiography, one may also compare Polybius' accusations on Phylarchus' exploit of tragedy, on which see Farrington's analysis in this collection.

cydidean prose is the object of Dionysius' criticism. Dionysius does value prose resembling the aesthetic impact of poetry: his point seems to be that Herodotus succeeded in developing both the essential and the additional qualities of style, while Thucydides, who raised the latter to their highest level, did not always preserve the former.[7]

The topic of poetic style in prose also occurs in later treatises, such as Theon's *Progymnasmata*, a handbook of rhetorical exercises probably composed in the first century AD.[8] Theon testifies that later rhetoricians inherited the Aristotelian concern for a necessary stylistic distinction between prose and poetry. In fact, in the chapter devoted to narrative (διήγησις), Theon points out that narration should aim at clarity, a requirement one may satisfy avoiding, among others, poetic, metaphorical, archaic, and outlandish words, that is to say, the very features of Thucydides' vocabulary criticized by Dionysius (*Prog.* 80.8–10, 81.8–10):[9]

> σαφὴς δὲ ἡ διήγησις γίνεται διχόθεν, ἐξ αὐτῶν τῶν ἀπαγγελλομένων πραγμάτων, καὶ ἐκ τῆς λέξεως τῆς ἀπαγγελίας, ἧς τὰ πράγματα. [...] κατὰ δὲ τὴν λέξιν φυλακτέον τῷ σαφηνίζοντι τὸ ποιητικὰ ὀνόματα λέγειν καὶ πεποιημένα καὶ τροπικὰ καὶ ἀρχαῖα καὶ ξένα καὶ ὁμώνυμα.

---

[7] A recent, comprehensive study on Dionysius' ideas on prose and poetry and their relationship to the Aristotelian tradition is found in de Jonge 2008, 329–366 (357–358 on *Th.* 23). According to the scholar, Dionysius, who retained Aristotle's differentiation between prose and poetry and didactically objected to the excessive use of poetic diction in prose, had nevertheless a more complicated attitude towards poetic prose. Especially in the treatise *On Composition*, Dionysius was concerned with the similarities between prose and poetry that share the common aim of producing an artistic effect on the public: in this perspective, which is critical rather than didactic, he did appreciate prose having the aesthetic impact of poetry. A similar tension between a critical and a didactic attitude becomes evident in Dionysius' analysis of the Melian dialogue, cf. Grossi 2015, 41–45.

[8] On Theon's chronology see Butts 1987, 1–6; Kennedy 2003, 1–3; Patillon 1997, vii–xvi who dates the rhetor at the beginning of the imperial age.

[9] Here and below I follow the text of Patillon 1997. Translations of Theon are borrowed and adapted from Kennedy 2003. According to Theon's theory (on which see Patillon 1997, 140–142), a narration should keep to the three "virtues" of clarity, concision, and credibility (Theon, *Prog.* 79, 20–21: ἀρεταὶ δὲ διηγήσεως τρεῖς, σαφήνεια, συντομία, πιθανότης), which should be observed both in respect to the subjects and the style. Theon's statements about the words to avoid for clarity's sake are indebted to the Aristotelian tradition, which, as seen above, also operates in Dionysius' discussion on the Thucydidean style, but they do not contain any reference or criticism of the historian. Theon explicitly refers to Thucydides in the discussion of clarity in the subject-matter (*Prog.* 80, 12–26), where he mentions the fact that the historian made his narration unclear by dividing the account of the events into summers and winters, thus breaking the narration of a single subject into several different sections, a remark which is evidently derived from Dionysius (cf. D. H. *Th.* 9 and see below, n. 16).

The narration becomes clear from two sources: from the very subject matter being reported and from the style of the report containing the subject matter. [...] As for style, in aiming at clarity one should avoid words which are poetic and coined and metaphorical and archaic and foreign and homonym.

A further example may be found in the treatise *On Style* which has come down under the name of Demetrius of Phalerum and was possibly composed in the first century BC.[10] In his discussion of the "elevated" (μεγαλοπρεπής) kind of style, the author of the treatise states that "a touch of poetic diction adds to the elevation of prose". Yet the writer should not simply imitate the poets, as Herodotus does, but use them in his own, original way (ἰδίως χρώμενος), as Thucydides does (*Eloc.* 112–113):

> τὸ δὲ ποιητικὸν ἐν λόγοις ὅτι μὲν μεγαλοπρεπές, καὶ τυφλῷ δῆλόν φασι, πλὴν οἱ μὲν γυμνῇ πάνυ χρῶνται τῇ μιμήσει τῶν ποιητῶν, μᾶλλον δὲ οὐ μιμήσει, ἀλλὰ μεταθέσει, καθάπερ Ἡρόδοτος. Θουκυδίδης μέντοι κἂν λάβῃ παρὰ ποιητοῦ τι, ἰδίως αὐτῷ χρώμενος ἴδιον τὸ ληφθὲν ποιεῖ, οἷον ὁ μὲν ποιητὴς ἐπὶ τῆς Κρήτης ἔφη· "Κρήτη τις γαῖ' ἐστι μέσῳ ἐνὶ οἴνοπι πόντῳ, καλὴ καὶ πίειρα, περίρρυτος" [*Od.* 19.172–173]. ὁ μὲν δὴ ἐπὶ τοῦ μεγέθους ἐχρήσατο τῷ "περίρρυτος", ὁ δὲ Θουκυδίδης [4.64.3] ὁμονοεῖν τοὺς Σικελιώτας καλὸν οἴεται εἶναι, γῆς ὄντας μιᾶς καὶ περιρρύτου, καὶ ταῦτα πάντα εἰπών, "γῆν" τε ἀντὶ νήσου καὶ "περίρρυτον" ὡσαύτως, ὅμως ἕτερα λέγειν δοκεῖ, διότι οὐχ ὡς πρὸς μέγεθος, ἀλλὰ πρὸς ὁμόνοιαν αὐτοῖς ἐχρήσατο.

> A touch of poetic diction adds to the elevation of prose. Even a blind man can see that, as the proverb has it. Still some writers imitate the poets quite crudely. Or rather, they do not imitate them, but transfer them to their pages, as Herodotus has done. Thucydides acts otherwise. Even if he does borrow something from a poet, he uses it in his own way and so makes it his own property. Homer, for instance, says of Crete: "a land there is, called Crete, in the midst of the wine-dark sea, fair, fertile, wave-encompassed" [*Od.* 19.172–173]. Now Homer has used the word "wave-encompassed" to indicate the great size of

---

10 Modern scholars unanimously reject the traditional attribution to Demetrius of Phalerum. The date of the treatise is uncertain, but the most recent contributions on the question are inclined to assign it to the first half of the first century BC: see Dihle 2007 and Dührsen 2005, who also discusses the authorship of the work, arguing for its ascription to Demetrius of Magnesia. The author of the treatise adopts a peculiar classification system which set the different styles of writing into four categories (*Eloc.* 36: ἰσχνός, μεγαλοπρεπής, γλαφυρός, δεινός): the relation of this system to Dionysius' theory of composition has drawn attention also because of its central importance for establishing the relative chronology of the two authors (see on this point Dihle 2007, 299–300; Dührsen 2005, 246–247). According to Dührsen' analysis the treatise *On Style* would be earlier than Dionysius's works; a different interpretation has been proposed by Calcante 2004, who dates its composition between the first and the second version of Dionysius' treatise *On Demosthenes*. Marini 2007, 8–16 follows Rhys Roberts 1902, 49–64 in dating the work to the second half of the first century AD. On the origin of Demetrius' theory of styles see also Chiron 1993, xli-cvii. Text and translation are quoted from Rhys Roberts.

the island. Thucydides [4.64.3], on his part, holds the view that Greek settlers in Sicily should be at one, as they belong to the same land and that a wave-encompassed one. Although he employs throughout the same terms as Homer – "land" in place of "island" and "wave-encompassed" – he seems nevertheless to be saying something different. The reason is that he uses the words with reference not to size but to concord.

As is evident, Demetrius is himself concerned with the ways poetic diction should be used in prose, but he approaches the topic with a different attitude than Dionysius, who disapproved of Thucydides for "writing like a poet". He, on the contrary, appreciates Thucydides as a good emulator of Homer. According to Demetrius, Thucydides' ability consists in using an epic word like περίρρυτος ("encircled by the sea") to express a different meaning from the one implied in the Homeric context from which the word is borrowed. Homer, he says, uses the adjective to indicate the great size of the island of Crete. Thucydides, on the other hand, puts it in the mouth of Hermocrates in his address to the Siceliots to be at one, since they share a single land and one that is "encircled by the sea".[11] The epic word in Thucydides effectively conveys the idea of Sicily's isolation, which serves the purpose of Hermocrates' argument.[12]

Let us now explore the topic of Thucydides' emulation of Homer through a text that is well known to those who deal with ancient Thucydidean scholarship: the *Life of Thucydides* attributed to Marcellinus, a biography that was probably

---

11 Cf. Th. 4.64.3: οὐδὲν γὰρ αἰσχρὸν οἰκείους οἰκείων ἡσσᾶσθαι, ἢ Δωριᾶ τινὰ Δωριῶς ἢ Χαλκιδέα τῶν ξυγγενῶν, τὸ δὲ ξύμπαν γείτονας ὄντας καὶ ξυνοίκους μιᾶς χώρας καὶ περιρρύτου καὶ ὄνομα ἓν κεκλημένους Σικελιώτας ("for there is no disgrace in kinsmen giving way to kinsmen, a Dorian to a Dorian or a Chalcidian to men of the same race, since we are, in a word, neighbours and together are dwellers in a single land and that encircled by the sea, and we are called by a single name, Siceliots"). Here and below, I refer to the text of Thucydides in the edition by Alberti 1972–2000, while translations are borrowed, with slight adjustments, from Forster Smith 1956–1958. Note that Thucydides' manuscripts unanimously read μιᾶς χώρας καὶ περιρρύτου, while according to Demetrius, Thucydides used the word γῆ (not χώρα), instead of νῆσος. Demetrius also refers to the sentence as it would be pronounced by Thucydides himself, not by Hermocrates (ὁ δὲ Θουκυδίδης ὁμονοεῖν τοὺς Σικελιώτας καλὸν οἴεται εἶναι). According to Chiron 1993, 106, Demetrius may not be aware of the exact context of the passage he mentions, possibly because he knows the quotation from another source, probably a collection of examples.

12 See the *scholion ad l.* (262, 2–4): "καὶ περιρρύτου": τοῦτο οὐ παρέργως τέθεικεν, ἀλλ' ἐμφῆναι βουλόμενος ὅτι οὐκ ἔστιν ἡμῖν εἰς τοὺς ἄλλους κοινωνία, διὰ τὸ νησιώτας εἶναι sc² ("and that encircled by the sea": he [sc. Thucydides] does not use this word cursorily, but aims to make clear that "we do not have relations with other people because we are islanders"). For references to the Thucydidean *scholia*, I give the page and line number of the edition by Hude 1927. Translations, when provided, are my own.

compiled as an introduction to Thucydides for students of rhetoric.¹³ In chapter 35 of the *Life*, it is stated that the historian "was an emulator of Homer in the subjects' arrangement (the so called οἰκονομία) and of Pindar in the noble and lofty style" (ζηλωτὴς δὲ γέγονεν ὁ Θουκυδίδης εἰς μὲν τὴν οἰκονομίαν Ὁμήρου, Πινδάρου δὲ εἰς τὸ μεγαλοφυὲς καὶ ὑψηλὸν τοῦ χαρακτῆρος). This concept of Thucydides as an exponent of the most elevated kind of style, as well as the comparison between him and Pindar, may have been borrowed from Dionysius of Halicarnassus.¹⁴

In the next pages I will focus on Marcellinus' statement that Thucydides imitated Homer's οἰκονομία. This assertion, too, should be considered in the light of Dionysius' work. In fact, a large part of Dionysius' treatise *On Thucydides* is devoted to demonstrating that the historian is deficient in that aspect of literary composition which is technically called οἰκονομικόν, that is to say the subjects' arrangement.¹⁵ According to Dionysius (*Th.* 9), this consists in the subjects' division (διαίρεσις), order (τάξις) and development (ἐξεργασία):

> ἃ δ' ἐλλιπέστερον κατεσκεύασε καὶ ἐφ' οἷς ἐγκαλοῦσιν αὐτῷ τινες, περὶ τὸ τεχνικώτερον μέρος ἐστὶ τοῦ πραγματικοῦ, τὸ λεγόμενον μὲν οἰκονομικόν, ἐν ἁπάσαις δὲ γραφαῖς ἐπιζητούμενον, ἐάν τε φιλοσόφους προέληταί τις ὑποθέσεις ἐάν τε ῥητορικάς. ταῦτα δὲ ἐστὶ τὰ περὶ τὴν διαίρεσιν καὶ τὰ περὶ τὴν τάξιν καὶ τὰ περὶ τὰς ἐξεργασίας.

> One aspect of his [*sc.* Thucydides'] composition is less satisfactory, and has given rise to some criticism. It concerns the more artistic side of the presentation of subject-matter, that which is called arrangement, which is required in every kind of writing, whether one selects philosophical or rhetorical themes. It consists of division, order and method of development.

---

13 The material for this biographical compilation has mainly been gathered from a commentary on Thucydides or a collection of *scholia*, as it is evident from the heterogeneous character of the *Life*, and from its full title in the E manuscript (*Palatinus Heidelbergensis Gr.* 252, dating back to the tenth century AD), namely Μαρκελλίνου ἐκ τῶν εἰς Θουκυδίδην σχολίων περὶ τοῦ βίου αὐτοῦ Θουκυδίδου καὶ τῆς τοῦ λόγου ἰδέας (other manuscripts have the title in the abridged form Μαρκελλίνου περὶ τοῦ Θουκυδίδου βίου καὶ τῆς ἰδέας αὐτοῦ: see Alberti 1972–2000, I, 1). I am inclined to believe that Marcellinus, as the title in E suggests, was not the author or compiler of the Thucydidean *Life* that is traditionally designated with his name, but the author of a lost, late ancient commentary on the historian upon which the biography, as well as our *scholia*, probably rely. For a *status quaestionis* on the origin and attribution of Marcellinus' *Life* see Piccirilli 1985, xv-xxx. An interesting study on the biography's structure is found in Luzzatto 1993b. I follow the text of the *Life* in the edition by Alberti 1972–2000, the translation is my own.

14 D. H. *Dem.* 39, *Comp.* 22 (on these passages see above). Explicit reference to Dionysius, who is one of the sources of Marcellinus' *Life*, is made in *Vit. Thuc.* 53.

15 Thucydides' treatment of the subject-matter, discussion of whom extends over chapters 9–20, appears to be the central issue of the treatise: on this point see Pavano 1958, xxviii–xxxix.

Having defined the three main aspects of the subjects' arrangement, Dionysius proceeds to discuss the (inadequate) treatment they receive in Thucydides' work (*Th.* 9–20)[16]. In respect to the τάξις ("order"), Dionysius (*Th.* 10–12) criticizes Thucydides because his narration did not follow the "natural order" of the events. Although the historian pointed out in the introduction that the real cause of the war was to be found in the growth of Athenian power, he did not start his narration from this argument, but from the events in Epidamnus, Corcyra, and Potidaea, events that he believed to be mere pretexts for the war. Only later, in the *Pentecontaetia*, did he deal with the 50 years after the Persian War, when Athens advanced to the height of its power. According to Dionysius, on the contrary, it would have been appropriate to adopt the "natural order", which requires previous events to have precedence over later ones, and true causes to be stated before the false ones (*Th.* 11):

ἐχρῆν δὲ αὐτὸν ἀρξάμενον τὰς αἰτίας τοῦ πολέμου ζητεῖν πρῶτον ἀποδοῦναι τὴν ἀληθῆ καὶ ἑαυτῷ δοκοῦσαν. ἥ τε γὰρ φύσις ἀπῄτει τὰ πρότερα τῶν ὑστέρων ἄρχειν καὶ τἀληθῆ πρὸ τῶν ψευδῶν λέγεσθαι, ἥ τε τῆς διηγήσεως εἰσβολὴ κρείττων ἂν ἐγίνετο μακρῷ, τοιαύτης οἰκονομίας τυχοῦσα.

But he ought to have stated at the beginning of his enquiry into the true causes of the war the cause which he considered to be the true one: for not only was it a natural requirement that prior events should have precedence over later ones, and true causes be stated before false ones, but the start of his narrative would have been far more powerful if he had adopted this arrangement.

---

[16] In respect to διαίρεσις, Thucydides is criticized for having introduced, instead of the traditional division by places and time, the new organization by the summer/winter, which according to Dionysius destroyed the continuity of the narration breaking it up into small sections recording actions which occurred in many different places, thus leading to great obscurity (*Th.* 9). Concerning the elaboration (ἐξεργασία), Dionysius considers Thucydides to be at fault for giving too much space to unimportant matters or, on the other hand, for giving too little development to episodes requiring more thorough treatment (*Th.* 13–20). Dionysius had also dealt with Thucydides' treatment of the subject matter in the lost treatise *On Imitation*, where he drew a comparison between him and Herodotus in respect to the contents' arrangement. As we know from the full quotation of this passage in *Pomp.* 3, Dionysius argued for Herodotus' superiority in the choice of the subject, in the choice of a suitable starting point and conclusion for his account, in the selections of which events to include and which to omit from the narration, in the distribution and collocation of the material in its proper place and even in his own attitude to the described events. On the evolution of this framework into the theory of the three aspects of the οἰκονομικόν which is expressed in the treatise *On Thucydides* see, again, Pavano 1958, xxviii–xxxix.

So, according to Dionysius, the main fault of Thucydides' work, in respect to the τάξις, is that "it does not begin at the natural starting-point" (τὸ μὴ τὴν κατὰ φύσιν ἔχειν ἀρχήν, *Th.* 12).[17]

As seen above, the word οἰκονομία refers to the way an author should present the subject matter in order to achieve his artistic purpose (cf. Dionysius' statement ἥ τε τῆς διηγήσεως εἰσβολὴ κρείττων ἂν ἐγίνετο μακρῷ, τοιαύτης οἰκονομίας τυχοῦσα in the above quoted passage). In Dionysius' system τάξις is an aspect of the οἰκονομία, and "not the least important one" (οὐκ ἐλάχιστον), as he states in *Th.* 9. In his review of Thucydides' work, Dionysius identifies the good τάξις with the *natural* τάξις, but the ancient rhetorical tradition did in some cases regard the deviation from the natural order as a desirable artistic device.[18]

In this respect, a very interesting analysis of Thucydides' narrative may be found in a passage of Theon's *Progymnasmata*, again in the chapter devoted to διήγησις. Theon deals with the rhetorical techniques that produce the ἀναστροφὴ τῆς τάξεως, that is variation of the natural order of narration. As a first example, he introduces the narrative structure of Homer's *Odyssey*, and compares it with that of Thucydides' *History*. Homer, he says, begins his work with Odysseus being with Calypso, goes back to the hero's previous adventures and then continues the narration bringing it to the end with Odysseus arriving in Ithaca. Thucydides, as well, starts with the events regarding Epidamnus, goes back to the *Pentecontaetia* and then takes up the narration of the Peloponnesian war (86.7–20):

> τὴν δὲ ἀναστροφὴν τῆς τάξεως πενταχῶς ποιησόμεθα· καὶ γὰρ ἀπὸ τῶν μέσων ἐστὶν ἀρξάμενον ἐπὶ τὴν ἀρχὴν ἀναδραμεῖν, εἶτα ἐπὶ τὰ τελευταῖα καταντῆσαι, ὅπερ ἐν Ὀδυσσείᾳ Ὅμηρος πεποίηκεν· ἤρξατο μὲν γὰρ ἀπὸ τῶν χρόνων, καθ' οὓς Ὀδυσσεὺς ἦν παρὰ Καλυψοῖ, εἶτα ἀνέδραμεν ἐπὶ τὴν ἀρχὴν μετά τινος οἰκονομίας γλαφυρᾶς· ἐποίει γὰρ τὸν Ὀδυσσέα τοῖς Φαίαξι τὰ καθ' ἑαυτὸν διηγούμενον· εἶτα συνάψας τὴν λοιπὴν διήγησιν ἔληξεν εἰς τὰ τελευταῖα, μέχρι τοὺς μνηστῆρας ἀπέκτεινεν Ὀδυσσεὺς καὶ πρὸς τοὺς γονέας αὐτῶν φιλίαν ἐποιήσατο. καὶ Θουκυδίδης δὲ ἀπὸ τῶν περὶ Ἐπίδαμνον ἀρξάμενος ἀνέδραμεν ἐπὶ τὴν Πεντηκονταετίαν, ἔπειτα κατῆλθεν ἐπὶ τὸν Πελοποννησιακὸν πόλεμον.

---

17 It also does not have a proper conclusion (*Th.* 12: πρόσεστι δὲ τούτῳ καὶ τὸ μὴ εἰς ἃ ἔδει κεφάλαια τετελευτηκέναι τὴν ἱστορίαν), since the historian has not brought the narration down to the end of the war.

18 In later sources the term τάξις seems even to acquire the narrow sense of "natural order", in contrast with οἰκονομία, which comes to mean the "artistic order": for an illuminating illustration of this terminological shift and more generally on the concept of οἰκονομία and τάξις in the ancient rhetorical tradition see Meijering 1987, 134–148. Cf. also Grisolia 2001, 11–13 and Nünlist 2009, 23–24, who focuses on the meaning "plot" that the word οἰκονομία acquires in Greek *scholia*.

We shall do the inversion of the natural order in five ways.¹⁹ It is possible to begin in the middle and run back to the beginning, then to jump to the end, which Homer did in *Odyssey*. He began with the period when Odysseus was with Calypso, then went back to the beginning in an elegant arrangement; for he had Odysseus narrate each of his own adventures to the Pheacians; then, after taking up the rest of the narration, he continued to the end at the point where Odysseus killed the suitors and made friends with their relatives. Also, Thucydides, after starting with the events about Epidamnus, went back to the fifty years before the war and then took up the Peloponnesian war.

As seen here, what Dionysius considered to be a fault in the order of Thucydides' *History* is described by Theon as an exemplary rhetorical technique (note the expression μετά τινος οἰκονομίας γλαφυρᾶς), which is also found in the *Odyssey*.²⁰ Marcellinus' assertion that Thucydides imitated Homer's οἰκονομία may refer to the very feature described by Theon, namely to the fact that the historian did not narrate the events in their chronological order, but used a complex flashback technique which made his first book resemble the structure of Homer's *Odyssey*.²¹ Marcellinus' comparison between Thucydides and Homer implies a positive judgment and possibly a defense of Thucydides' οἰκονομία against Dionysius' criticism.²²

---

19 Patillon prints πενταχῶς following the Armenian translation, while the Greek manuscripts read πολλαχῶς ("in many ways"). Theon, in fact, lists *five* types of ἀναστροφή, which correspond to the five possible alterations of the chronological order (beginning-middle-end): the first and the second type of ἀναστροφή (namely the combinations middle-beginning-end and end-middle-beginning) are concretely illustrated through examples from Thucydides and Herodotus (Hdt. 3.1), while the other three (middle-end-beginning; end-beginning-middle; beginning-end-middle) are merely abstract combinations.
20 Whereas in *Prog.* 80, 12–26 Theon seems to agree with Dionysius' criticism of the division of Thucydides' *History* (see above, n. 9), note that the debate about the inclusion of the ποιητικόν in prose writing appears to be a matter of style, especially of vocabulary, which does not touch the subjects' organization.
21 Modern scholarship is also concerned with the affinity between the epic narrative technique and the temporal structuring of Thucydides' *History:* see Rengakos 2006a, 183–190; Rengakos 2006b. For a general study of Thucydides' presentation of time in its connection with the historian's interpretation of the past see Rood 1998b, 109–130. The question of chronology and inverse order in Homer's narrative is discussed in the Homeric *scholia:* see Nünlist 2009, 88–89.
22 Note that in *Vit. Thuc.* 53, Marcellinus explicitly defends the style of Thucydides against Dionysius' objections. Moreover, Dionysius' views on Thucydides' οἰκονομία seem to have had a significant echo in later Thucydidean studies, as testified by the commentary on the second book of the *History* preserved by P. Oxy 6.853, dating back to the second century AD (on which see below). The opening section of the commentary (coll. I, 7–III, 35) contains a polemic against Dionysius and a defence of Thucydides on the three points of the division of the work into summers and winters, the unity of the narration, and the exposition of the causes of the

In chapter 37 of Marcellinus' *Life*, it is also asserted that Homer was the most important stylistic model for Thucydides, and the historian emulated him "in choice of words and in precise combination of them, and in strength of explanation, and in beauty and swiftness" (μάλιστα δὲ πάντων, ὅπερ εἴπομεν, ἐζήλωσεν Ὅμηρον καὶ τῆς περὶ τὰ ὀνόματα ἐκλογῆς καὶ τῆς περὶ τὴν σύνθεσιν ἀκριβείας, τῆς τε ἰσχύος τῆς κατὰ τὴν ἑρμηνείαν καὶ τοῦ κάλλους καὶ τοῦ τάχους).[23] As mentioned above, the so-called Marcellinus' biography was probably compiled from a late ancient commentary on Thucydides as an introduction to the reading of the *History*. The assertion about Thucydides' emulation of Homer corresponds to the practice of reading and commenting on the historian with an eye towards epic poetry, the evidence of which may be found in the *corpus* of Thucydides' *scholia*.[24]

The high number of quotations from the *Iliad* and the *Odyssey* in the *scholia* to Thucydides is partially due to the fact that ancient grammarians generally gave examples of figures of speech and explained stylistic patterns by introducing parallels from Homer.[25] Yet there are more Homeric quotations in Thucydides' *scholia* than in the *corpus* of any other Greek prose writer. No Homeric parallel appears in the small body of the *scholia* to Herodotus; there are 7 quotations from Homer in the *scholia* to Aeschines, 20 in the *scholia* to Demosthenes, 43 in the *scholia* to Plato, while Homeric quotations in the *scholia* to Thucydides number 92. These statistics suggest that ancient scholars perceived a kind of affinity between epic poetry and Thucydides' *History*, and when commenting on it, they

---

war. See Grenfell/Hunt 1908, 137–138. On Marcellinus' comments on Thucydides' οἰκονομία and their relation to Dionysius see also Esposito Vulgo Gigante 1981–1982; Piccirilli 1985, 130–131. Marcellinus may allude to (and reject) Dionysius' criticism also in *Vit. Thuc.* 57, the passage about Thucydides' speeches that is discussed by Feddern in this volume.

[23] The expression ὅπερ εἴπομεν refers to the assertion about the imitation of Homer's οἰκονομία in *Vit. Thuc.* 35.

[24] As it is known, the *scholia* to Thucydides are edited by Hude 1927, but a new edition by Klaus Alpers (on the basis of Alexander Kleinlogel's legacy) has been announced and is now awaited. Traces of valuable, ancient exegetic material in the Thucydidean *scholia* are mixed with several late and less interesting remarks, which form the main part of the *corpus*. There is no ultimate scholarly agreement about the date of origin of the Thucydides' *scholia*, but the extant collection was probably compiled in the ninth century AD. I extensively deal with this crucial question in my doctoral dissertation, "Tucidide nell'esegesi antica. Traduzione e commento degli scoli al libro primo delle *Storie*", discussed in May 2015 at the University of Verona; cf. Alpers 2013, 87–99; Kleinlogel 1998; Kleinlogel 2011; Luzzatto 1993a. A fundamental study on the nature of the Thucydides' *scholia* is found in Luschnat 1954; see also de Jonge 2011; Grossi 2013.

[25] See e.g. the *scholia* on Th. 1.25.4 (28, 7–11); 33.2 (35, 4–6); 89.3 (71, 13–15); 2.47.3 (140, 2–7); 3.3.3 (164, 12–15); 3.4.1 (164, 25–27); 40.8 (190, 17–20); 42.4 (191, 24–26).

made reference to Homeric verses they believed to be emblematic of such an affinity.

Next, I will provide some examples of this phenomenon.²⁶ We have just seen that, according to Marcellinus's *Life*, Thucydides emulated Homer "in choice of words" (*Vit. Thuc.* 37). There are, as well, several *scholia* stating that Thucydides made use of Homeric words or expressions. An example may be found in the speech held by the Plataeans in Th. 3.53–59, where the expression ἐπικαλούμεθα τοὺς κεκμηκότας ("we call upon the departed") occurs (3.59.2). The *scholion* to the passage (201, 12–14) comments that the participle κεκμηκότας resembles the Homeric form καμόντας and draws a parallel between Thucydides' usage of the word and a verse of the *Iliad* ("τοὺς κεκμηκότας": τοὺς νεκρούς. [καὶ] Ὅμηρος [*Il.* 3.278] "καὶ οἳ ὑπένερθε καμόντας" ABFGMc²). This passage of Thucydides displays, in fact, the first prose occurrence of the participle of κάμνω to indicate the dead.²⁷

Another case is found in 6.8.4, where Thucydides introduces Nicias' speech with the following words:

καὶ ὁ Νικίας ἀκούσιος μὲν ᾑρημένος ἄρχειν, νομίζων δὲ τὴν πόλιν οὐκ ὀρθῶς βεβουλεῦσθαι, ἀλλὰ προφάσει βραχείᾳ καὶ εὐπρεπεῖ τῆς Σικελίας ἁπάσης, μεγάλου ἔργου, ἐφίεσθαι, παρελθὼν ἀποτρέψαι ἐβούλετο, καὶ παρῄνει τοῖς Ἀθηναίοις τοιάδε.

And Nicias, who had been elected to the command against his will, and thought the city had not come to a right decision, but that, with a slight and specious pretext, it was the conquest of all Sicily, a great undertaking, at which they aimed, came forward with the purpose of averting this, and advised the Athenians as follows.

The *scholion* (331, 10–12) remarks on the use of the adjective μέγας in the sense of "over-great", which it rightly records as Homeric, and points to a similar expression in *Il.* 10.401 ("μεγάλου ἔργου ἐφίεσθαι": Ὅμηρος [*Il.* 10.401]· "ἦ ῥά νύ τοι μεγάλων δώρων ἐπεμαίετο θυμός" BFMc2: "a great undertaking, at which they aimed": Homer [*Il.* 10.401]: "surely on great rewards was your heart set" BFMc2).²⁸

---

26 In the following sections, references to Homer's text are to the edition by West 1998–2000, while translations are borrowed from Murray/Wyatt 1999. In quotations from Homeric *scholia* I give the volume, page and line number of Erbse 1969–1988. Translations of the *scholia*, if provided, are my own.
27 According to Smith 1891, 19, the form κεκμηκότες in the sense of "the dead" is "evidently borrowed directly from tragedy, though as old as Homer".
28 For the use of μέγας in the sense of "over-great", which is actually a Homeric and poetic use, see *LfrgE* III 69, 51–54; 74, 34–61, which records *Od.* 11.474 (σχέτλιε, τίπτ' ἔτι μεῖζον ἐνὶ φρεσὶ μήσεαι ἔργον;: "what hardier deed than this will you essay, rash man?", with allusion

A similar instance may be found in the commentary on the second book of the *History*, which has survived in P. Oxy. 6. 853 (= MP³ 1536 = LDAB 4069), dating back to the second half of the second century AD.²⁹ The papyrus fragments also display some Homeric quotations, suggesting that the scholarly practice of drawing parallels between Thucydidean passages and Homeric verses was quite ancient. An example may be taken from the speech of Archidamus in the second book, where the expression ἐς ἔργον καθίστανται ("rush into action") occurs (2.11.7). The author of the commentary notes that the word ἔργον in this context means "war". He qualifies such a usage as "Homeric" (ὁμηρικῶς) and quotes as proof *Il.* 4.539 (col. VII, ll. 9 – 11: ἔργ]ον δὲ τὸν πόλεμον [ὁ]μ[ηρικῶς], ἔνθά κεν οὐκέτι ἔργον ἀνὴρ ὀνόσαιτο μετελθών).³⁰

Other *scholia* remark upon the epic style of a whole section or description, as is the case of Th. 6.24.3. As seen above, in this passage Nicias makes an unsuccessful attempt to dissuade the Athenians from sailing against Sicily. Having re-

---

to Odysseus' evocation of the dead). According to LSJ⁹, 1880 the expression μέγα ἔργον occurs with this (negative) meaning also in *Od.* 3.261 (μάλα γὰρ μέγα μήσατο ἔργον: "for monstrous was the deed he [sc. Aegisthus] devised") and Pi. *N.* 10.64; A. *A.* 1546.

29 For a recent description of the papyrus see Ippolito/Pellé 2002, 571–572. See also Körte 1913, 256–257. A general study on the commentary is provided by Voltz 1911, 35–58, while Luschnat 1954, 25–29 and Maehler 1977 discuss the papyrus' relationship to the *corpus* of the Thucydides' *scholia*.

30 In the Thucydidean passage, Archidamus warns the Peloponnesians that they should expect the Athenians to risk a battle, as soon as they will see the enemies wasting their land: "for with all men, when they suffer an unwonted calamity, it is the sight set then and there before their eyes which makes them angry, and when they are angry they do not pause to think but rush into action" (πᾶσι γὰρ ἐν τοῖς ὄμμασι καὶ ἐν τῷ παραυτίκα ὁρᾶν πάσχοντάς τι ἄηθες ὀργὴ προσπίπτει· καὶ οἱ λογισμῷ ἐλάχιστα χρώμενοι θυμῷ πλεῖστα ἐς ἔργον καθίστανται). The commentary refers to *Il.* 4.539–544 (ἔνθά κεν οὐκέτι ἔργον ἀνὴρ ὀνόσαιτο μετελθών ... πολλοὶ γὰρ Τρώων καὶ Ἀχαιῶν ἤματι κείνῳ \ πρηνέες ἐν κονίῃσι παρ' ἀλλήλοισι τέταντο: "then a man could not any more enter into the battle and make light of it ... for multitudes of Trojans and Achaeans were that day stretched beside one another with faces in the dust"). Note that reference to the same episode, namely the battle scene that closes the *Iliad*'s fourth book, is also found in the *scholion* to Th. 2.11.4 (again Archidamus' speech, where the Peloponnesian king states that "the events of war cannot be foreseen, and attacks are generally sudden and furious": ἄδηλα γὰρ τὰ τῶν πολέμων, καὶ ἐξ ὀλίγου τὰ πολλὰ καὶ δι' ὀργῆς αἱ ἐπιχειρήσεις γίγνονται). The *scholion* (117, 15–16) focuses on Archidamus' allusion to the sudden (ἐξ ὀλίγου) explosion of military action and points to the description of Ἔρις in *Il.* 4.442, which, ὀλίγη μὲν πρῶτα, grows into the battle (Ὅμηρος [*Il.* 4.442]· "ἥ τ' ὀλίγη μὲν πρῶτα κορύσσεται" ABFGc²). Cf. *Il.* 4.440–443: καὶ Ἔρις ἄμοτον μεμαυῖα \ Ἄρεος ἀνδροφόνοιο κασιγνήτη ἑτάρη τε \ ἥ τ' ὀλίγη μὲν πρῶτα κορύσσεται, αὐτὰρ ἔπειτα \ οὐρανῷ ἐστήριξε κάρη καὶ ἐπὶ χθονὶ βαίνει ("and Strife who rages incessantly, sister and comrade of man-slaying Ares; she first rears her crest only a little, but then her head is fixed in the heavens while her feet tread on earth").

ported his ineffective speech, Thucydides states that "upon all (*sc.* Athenians) alike fell an eager desire to sail" (καὶ ἔρως ἐνέπεσε τοῖς πᾶσιν ὁμοίως ἐκπλεῦσαι). The *scholion* (340, 25–26) briefly quotes from the second book of the *Iliad*, drawing an analogy between the situation described by Thucydides and the Homeric one, where the goddess Athena instills into the Greeks the desire to fight, so that "war became sweeter than returning to their native land" ("ἔρως ἐνέπεσε τοῖς πᾶσιν": Ὅμηρος [*Il.* 2.453]· "τοῖσι δ' ἄφαρ πόλεμος γλυκίων γένετο").[31]

A last and very interesting case is found in the description of the battle of Syracuse in Thucydides' seventh book. In 7.71.4, the historian assumes the point of view of the army on land as it observes the sea battle from the shore, the outcome of which is still uncertain:

> ἦν τε ἐν τῷ αὐτῷ στρατεύματι τῶν Ἀθηναίων, ἕως ἀγχώμαλα ἐναυμάχουν, πάντα ὁμοῦ ἀκοῦσαι, ὀλοφυρμὸς βοή, νικῶντες κρατούμενοι, ἄλλα ὅσ' ἂν ἐν μεγάλῳ κινδύνῳ μέγα στρατόπεδον πολυειδῆ ἀναγκάζοιτο φθέγγεσθαι.

> In the same Athenian army one might hear, so long as the combatants were fighting on equal terms, every kind of cry at the same time, laments, shouting, "we are winning", "we are beaten", and all the divers kinds of cries that a great army in great danger would be constrained to utter.

As the Syracusans succeed in routing the Athenians and pursuing them to land (7.71.5), Thucydides describes the reaction of the army on the shore in the following way (7.71.6):

> ὁ δὲ πεζὸς οὐκέτι διαφόρως, ἀλλ' ἀπὸ μιᾶς ὁρμῆς οἰμωγῇ τε καὶ στόνῳ πάντες δυσανασχετοῦντες τὰ γιγνόμενα, οἱ μὲν ἐπὶ τὰς ναῦς παρεβοήθουν, οἱ δὲ πρὸς τὸ λοιπὸν τοῦ τείχους ἐς φυλακήν, ἄλλοι δὲ καὶ οἱ πλεῖστοι ἤδη περὶ σφᾶς αὐτοὺς καὶ ὅπη σωθήσονται διεσκόπουν.

> As for the army on land, their emotions were no longer at variance, but with one impulse they all broke forth into wailing and groaning, being scarcely able to bear what was happening, and ran along the shore, some to the ships, in order to help their comrades, some to what remained of their wall, in order to guard it; while still others, and these the great number, were now concerned only about themselves and how they might be saved.

---

31 Cf. *Il.*2.453–454: τοῖσι δ' ἄφαρ πόλεμος γλυκίων γένετ' ἠὲ νέεσθαι \ ἐν νηυσὶ γλαφυρῇσι φίλην ἐς πατρίδα γαῖαν ("and to them at once war became sweeter than to return in their hollow ships to their dear native land"). Smith 1900, 73 includes the word ἔρως in the group of terms which Thucydides borrows "from Homer or the Epic, apparently directly".

The *scholion* to the first passage (7.71.4) comments on the expression ὀλοφυρμὸς βοή, νικῶντες κρατούμενοι and refers to the above mentioned battle's description at the end of the *Iliad*'s fourth book, namely to a couple of verses which describe the confusion of wailing and shouts of triumph (401, 26–29: "ὀλοφυρμὸς κτλ.": Ὅμηρος [*Π.* 4, 450–451]· "ἔνθα δ' ἅμ' οἰμωγή τε καὶ εὐχωλὴ πέλεν ἀνδρῶν ὀλλύντων τε καὶ ὀλλυμένων" ABFvc²).[32]

The *scholion* to the second scene (7.71.6) focuses on the expression ἀπὸ μιᾶς ὁρμῆς οἰμωγῇ τε καὶ στόνῳ πάντες, and especially on the word οἰμωγή, and also points to a Homeric parallel, namely to *Il.* 22. 408–410, where the poet describes the lament rising throughout Troy after Hectors' death (402, 2–4: "οἰμωγῇ τε καὶ στόνῳ": Ὅμηρος [*Π.* 22.409]· "κωκυτῷ τ' εἴχοντο καὶ οἰμωγῇ κατὰ ἄστυ" ABCFM).[33]

Strikingly, not only Thucydides' but also Homer's commentators appear to be aware that Thucydides' narrative, especially his description of the Sicilian defeat in the seventh book, had a kind of Homeric patina. In fact, if we turn to the *scholia* to the Homeric verses in question, we unexpectedly find quotations from Thucydides. We have seen that the *scholion* to Th. 7.71.4 quotes from *Il.* 4.450–451. The exegetical *scholion* to *Il.* 4.450 (1, 523, 62–65) also refers to Th. 7.71.4, suggesting that Homer's passage provided inspiration for the historian, as well as for Gorgias, the rhetor who is traditionally considered, from Aristotle onwards, to have introduced poetic style into prose writing:[34]

> "οἰμωγή τε καὶ εὐχωλή": Θουκυδίδης (7.71.4) "πάντα ὁμοῦ ἀκοῦσαι" φησὶν "ὀλοφυρμὸς βοή, κρατοῦντες κρατούμενοι". καὶ Γοργίας (82 B 27 D.-K.)· "ἀνεμίσγοντο δὲ λιταῖς ἀπειλαὶ καὶ εὐχαῖς οἰμωγαί". T

> "the wailing and the shout of triumph": Thucydides (7.71.4) says "[*sc.* one might] hear every kind of cry at the same time, laments, shouting, "we are winning", "we are beaten"". And Gorgias (82 B 27 D.-K.): "threats were mixed with supplications, and wailing with prayers". T

---

[32] Cf. *Il.* 4.450–451: ἔνθα δ' ἅμ'οἰμωγή τε καὶ εὐχωλὴ πέλεν ἀνδρῶν \ ὀλλύντων τε καὶ ὀλλυμένων, ῥέε δ' αἵματι γαῖα ("then were heard alike the wailing and the shout of triumph of the slayers and the slaves, and the earth flowed with blood").

[33] Cf. *Il.* 22.408–411: ᾤμωξεν δ' ἐλεεινὰ πατὴρ φίλος, ἀμφὶ δὲ λαοὶ \ κωκυτῷ τ' εἴχοντο καὶ οἰμωγῇ κατὰ ἄστυ. \ τῷ δὲ μάλιστ' ἄρ' ἔην ἐναλίγκιον ὡς εἰ ἅπασα \ Ἴλιος ὀφρυόεσσα πυρὶ σμύχοιτο κατ' ἄκρης ("and a piteous groan did his father utter, and around them the people were given over to wailing and groaning throughout the city. To this was it most like, as though all beetling Ilios were utterly burning with fire").

[34] On this point, see Nicolai 1992, 242–244. On Gorgias' influence on Thucydides' style see Finley 1939.

Concerning Th. 7.71.6, the *scholion* to the passage refers to the description of the lamentations for Hector's death in *Il.* 22.408–410. The exegetical *scholion* to *Il.* 22.410 (5, 343, 47–48) refers, as well, to Thucydides ("ὡσεὶ ἅπασα": καὶ Θουκυδίδης [7.75.5]· "οὐδὲν γὰρ ἄλλο ἢ πόλει ἁλισκομένη ἐῴκεσαν" T). Granted, the quotation is not precisely taken from 7.71.6, but from a close passage in 7.75.5, where Thucydides describes the retreat of the Athenian army from Sicily: the author of the Homeric *scholion* seems to point to the fact that in both Homer's and Thucydides' passages, the feeling of dejection described is so great that it can be compared with the destruction of a entire city.³⁵

It is evident that the Thucydidean quotations occurring in the *scholia* to Homer do not, strictly speaking, contribute to the interpretation of the poet. The *scholia* to *Il.* 4.450–451 and 22.410 seem rather to adopt a Thucydidean perspective: they are interested in introducing parallels from the historian, even if they are not essential for the explanation of the poet's words. On the other hand, the quotations from the *Iliad* are central to the purpose of the *scholia* to Thucydides, aiming to show that the historian, especially in his Sicilian narrative, took Homer's poetry as a model. One may consequently suggest that the references to Thucydides in the T *scholia* to the *Iliad* rely on an ancient commentary on the historian, which pointed to Homer as a model for the Sicilian account. This commentary may have been consulted by a Homeric scholar with a special interest in Thucydides or even composed by a commentator of the poet, which would explain why its fragments have survived in the *corpus* of the *Iliad*'s *scholia*.³⁶

In conclusion, my analysis of the ancient observations of the links between Thucydides and poetry has started from the traditional debate concerning the inclusion of the poetic style into prose writing. In this respect, Dionysius of Halicarnassus criticizes Thucydides for the obscurity caused by his excessive use of the poetic style, while Demetrius focuses on the elevation resulting from Thucy-

---

35 The Homeric passage has been quoted above. Cf. Th. 7.75.5: κατήφειά τέ τις ἅμα καὶ κατάμεμψις σφῶν αὐτῶν πολλὴ ἦν. οὐδὲν γὰρ ἄλλο ἢ πόλει ἐκπεπολιορκημένῃ ἐῴκεσαν ὑποφευγούσῃ, καὶ ταύτῃ οὐ σμικρᾷ ("There was also a general feeling of dejection and much self-condemnation. For indeed they looked like nothing else than a city in secret flight after a siege, and that no small city"). Note that Thucydides' manuscripts unanimously read ἐκπεπολιορκημένῃ, while the *scholion* to the *Iliad* has ἁλισκομένῃ. Homeric allusions in Thucydides' account of the withdrawal of the Athenians in 7.75 have been examined by Allison 1997.
36 This is not the place to give a full account of the Thucydidean quotations occurring in the exegetical *scholia* to the *Iliad*, but it may be useful to briefly mention that other T *scholia* seem to support this theory, since they also display a kind of "Thucydidean perspective": see *schol. Il.* 16.280 (4, 229, 74–77) and 21.9b (5, 124, 62–63). Cf. also the A *scholion* to *Il.* 23.144 (5, 392, 36–393,42), with the interesting parallel in *schol.* Th. 1.109 (82, 4).

dides' peculiar and successful use of epic words. In respect to the subject matter, while Dionysius condemns Thucydides for his "unnatural" disposition of the material, other rhetorical sources (Theon, Marcellinus' *Life*), which display a different understanding of οἰκονομία, point to the similarity between Thucydidean and Homeric narrative technique, proposing both of them as models for imitation (Theon). Finally, Homeric allusion in Thucydides' narrative appears to be a central issue in ancient Thucydidean studies. The reading of both scholiastic *corpora* reveals that there was a kind of interaction between ancient Thucydidean and Homeric scholarship: scholars commenting on Thucydides used to make reference to Homeric poetry, which they believed to have provided inspiration for the historian, and the result of their exegetical activity has in some cases even penetrated into the *corpus* of the *scholia* to Homer.

List of Abbreviations

LfgrE = *Lexikon des frühgriechischen Epos*, vols.I–IV, Göttingen, 1955–2010.

Bibliography

Alberti, I.B. (ed.) (1972–2000), *Thucydidis Historiae*, vols. I–III, Rome.
Alpers, K. (2013), *Untersuchungen zu Johannes Sardianos und seinem Kommentar zu den Progymnasmata des Aphthonios. Zweite, durchgesehene und verbesserte Auflage*, Braunschweig.
Allison, J.W. (1997), "Homeric Allusions at the Close of Thucydides' Sicilian Narrative", in: *AJPh* 118, 499–516.
Angiolillo, R. / Elia, E. / Nuti, E. (eds.) (2015), *Crisi. Immagini, interpretazioni e reazioni nel mondo greco, latino e bizantino*. Atti del Convegno Internazionale Dottorandi e Giovani Ricercatori Torino, 21–23 ottobre 2013, Alexandria.
Aujac, G. (ed.) (1991), *Denys d'Halicarnasse, Opuscules Rhétoriques. Tome IV. Thucydide, Seconde Lettre à Ammée*, Paris.
Butts, J.R. (ed.) (1987), *The Progymnasmata of Theon. A New Text With Translation and Commentary*, Ann Arbor.
Calcante, C.M. (2004), "Il *De Elocutione* di Demetrio e il *De Demosthene* di Dionigi di Alicarnasso", in: *RIL* 138, 99–124.
Chiron, P. (ed.) (1993), *Démétrios, Du style*, Paris.
de Jonge, C.C. (2008), *Between Grammar and Rhetoric. Dionysius of Halicarnassus on Language, Linguistics and Literature*, Leiden.
de Jonge, C.C. (2011), "Dionysius of Halicarnassus and the *Scholia* on Thucydides' Syntax", in: S. Matthaios / F. Montanari / A. Rengakos 2011, 451–478.
Dihle, A. (2007), "Zur Datierung der Schrift des Demetrios *Über den Stil*", in: *RhM* 148, 298–313.

Dührsen, N.C. (2005), "Wer war der Verfasser des rhetorischen Lehrbuchs *Über den Stil* (Περὶ ἑρμηνείας)?", in: *RhM* 150, 242–271.
Eldamaty, M. / Trad, M. (eds.) (2002), *Egyptian Museum Collections Around the World. Studies for the Centennial of the Egyptian Museum*, Cairo, I.
Erbse, H. (ed.) (1969–1988), *Scholia graeca in Homeri Iliadem*, vols. I–VII, Berlin.
Esposito Vulgo Gigante, G. (1981–1982), "Il *Bios* tucidideo di Marcellino e lo *zelos* omerico", in: *AFLN* 24, 5–16.
Finley, J.H. (1939), "The Origins of Thucydides' style", in: *HSPh* 50, 35–84.
Forster Smith, C. (ed.) (1956–1958), *Thucydides, History of the Peloponnesian War*, vols. I–IV, London.
Frangoulidis, S.A. (1993), "A Pattern from Homer's 'Odyssey' in the Sicilian Narrative of Thucydides", in: *QUCC* 44, 95–102.
Frösén, J. / Purola, T. / Salmenkivi, E. (eds.) (2007), *Proceedings of the 24th International Congress of Papyrology*. Helsinki, 1–7 August 2004, Helsinki, II.
Grenfell, B.P. / Hunt, A.S. (eds.) (1908), *The Oxyrhynchus Papyri. Part VI*, London.
Grisolia, R. (2001), Οἰκονομία. *Struttura e tecnica drammatica negli scoli antichi ai testi drammatici*, Napoli.
Grossi, V. (2013), "Tradizioni locali attiche negli scoli a Tucidide. Note su alcuni scoli all'*Archeologia*", in: *Lexis* 31, 254–271.
Grossi, V. (2015), ""Anche se il nostro impero sarà spento, noi non ne paventiamo la fine": la crisi dei sistemi di potere in Tucidide, *Storie* 5.91", in: R. Angiolillo / E. Elia / E. Nuti 2015, 41–56.
Hude, C. (ed.) (1927), *Scholia in Thucydidem ad optimos codices collata*, Leipzig.
Ippolito, F. / Pellé, N. (2002), "Greek Historians in Cairo", in: M. Eldamaty / M. Trad 2002, 569–579.
Kennedy, G.A. (ed.) (2003), *Progymnasmata. Greek Textbooks of Prose Composition*, Leiden.
Kleinlogel, A. (1998), "Beobachtungen zu den Thukydidesscholien II", in: *Philologus* 142, 11–40.
Kleinlogel, A. (2011), "Beobachtungen zu den Thukydidesscholien III. Aus dem Nachlass hrsgg. von Klaus Alpers", in: *Philologus* 155, 257–271.
Körte, A. (1913), "Literarische Texte mit Ausschluß der christlichen", in: *APF* 6, 221–268.
Lapini, W. (1991), "Tucidide tragico: noterella su 3.113.1–6", in: *Sileno* 17, 121–137.
Luzzatto, M.J. (1993), "Itinerari di codici antichi: un'edizione di Tucidide tra il II ed il X secolo", in: *MD* 30, 167–203.
Luzzatto, M.J. (1993), "Scholia tardoantichi: il commentario di Marcellino a Tucidide", in: *QS* 38, 111–115.
Luschnat, O. (1954), "Die Thukydidesscholien", in: *Philologus* 98, 14–58.
Macleod, C. (1983), *Collected Essays*, Oxford.
Marini, N. (ed.) (2007), *Demetrio, Lo Stile*, Rome.
Matthaios, S. / Montanari, F. / Rengakos, A. (eds.) (2011), *Ancient Scholarship and Grammar. Archetypes, Concepts and Contexts*, Berlin.
Meijering, R. (1987), *Literary and Rhetorical Theories in Greek Scholia*, Groningen.
Mackie, C.J. (1996), "Homer and Thucydides: Corcyra and Sicily", in: *CQ* 46, 103–113.
Maehler, H. (2007), "Das Thukydides-Hypomnema P.Oxy. 853 und die Scholien", in: J. Frösén / T. Purola / E. Salmenkivi 2007, 587–593.

Montanari, F. / Rengakos, A. (eds.) (2006), *La poésie épique grecque: métamorphoses d'un genre littéraire*. Entretiens sur l'antiquité classique 52, Vandoeuvres-Genève 22–26 Aout 2005, Geneva.
Murray, A.T. / Wyatt, W.F. (eds.) (1999), *Homer, Iliad*, Cambridge / London.
Nicolai, R. (1992), *La storiografia nell'educazione antica*, Pisa.
Nünlist, R. (2009), *The Ancient Critic at Work. Terms and Concepts of Literary Criticism in Greek Scholia*, Cambridge.
Patillon, M. (ed.) (1997), *Aelius Théon, Progymnasmata*, Paris.
Pavano, G. (ed.) (1958), *Dionisio di Alicarnasso, Saggio su Tucidide*, Palermo.
Piccirilli, L. (ed.) (1985), *Storie dello storico Tucidide*, Genova.
Rengakos, A. (2006a), "Homer and the Historians: the Influence of Epic Narrative Technique on Herodotus and Thucydides", in: F. Montanari / A. Rengakos 2006, 183–214
Rengakos, A. (2006b), "Thucydides' Narrative: the Epic and Herodotean Heritage", in: A. Rengakos / A. Tsamakis 2006, 279–300.
Rengakos, A. / Tsakmakis, A. (eds.) (2006), *Brill's Companion to Thucydides*, Leiden.
Rhys Roberts, W. (ed.) (1902), *Demetrius, On Style*, Cambridge.
Rood, T. (1998a), "Thucydides and his Predecessors", in: *Histos* 2, 230–267.
Rood, T. (1998b), *Thucydides. Narrative and Explanation*, Oxford.
Smith, F. (1891), "Traces of Tragic Usage in Thucydides", in: *TAPhA* 22, 16–21.
Smith, F. (1892), "Poetic Words in Thucydides", in: *TAPhA* 23, 48–51.
Smith, F. (1900), "Traces of Epic Usage in Thucydides", in: *TAPhA* 31, 69–81.
Usher, S. (ed.) (1974–1985), *Dionysius of Halicarnassus, The Critical Essays*, vols. I–II, London.
Voltz, E. (1911), *Die Thukydidespapyri*, Strasbourg.
West, M.L. (ed.) (1998–2000), *Homeri Ilias*, vols. I–II, Munich / Stuttgart / Leipzig.
Wolcott, J.D. (1898), "New Words in Thucydides", in: *TAPhA* 29, 104–157.
Zadorojnyi, A.V. (1998), "Thucydides' Nicias and Homer's Agamemnon", in: *CQ* 48, 298–303.

Stefan Feddern
Thucydides' *Methodenkapitel* in the Light of the Ancient Evidence

Abstract: In this article, I will attempt to throw light on the *Methodenkapitel* from an ancient point of view (for the interpretation of ancient remarks on Thucydides, cf. Grossi's paper in this volume). In particular, I analyze the evidence of Dionysius of Halicarnassus, Marcellinus, and Palaephatus not only because of an interest in the history of scholarship, but also in the hope of resolving, or at least bringing nearer to a solution, four problems of modern scholarship concerning Thucydides' *Methodenkapitel*: the expression ἐκ τοῦ παρατυχόντος, the supplement τά after καί in the relative clause of the ἔργα-sentence, the meaning of λογογράφοι just before the *Methodenkapitel* (Th. 1.21.1), and especially the meaning of τὰ δέοντα in the second speech sentence. The conclusion that τὰ δέοντα has to be understood as τὸ πρέπον in terms of appropriateness (cf. Harris' paper in this volume) might lead to a better understanding of Thucydides' speeches as speeches-in-character. For an interpretation of Thucydides' literary techniques, cf. also Liotsakis' paper in this volume.

Thucydides' statements in the so-called *Methodenkapitel* concerning his account of the events (ἔργα) and the speeches (λόγοι) of the *Peloponnesian War* have been the subject of numerous investigations. Especially with regard to the speeches, modern scholars have presented many points and continue to offer much discussion, often extremely controversially.[1]

---

[1] Cf. Woodman 1988, 11: "The account which Thucydides gives of his speeches is one of the most discussed and controversial passages of Greek literature." For the most relevant literature on the *Methodenkapitel*, cf. (in chronological order) Schütrumpf 2011; Pelling 2009; Scardino 2007, 399–416; Shanske 2007, 157 f.; Köhnken 2006 (1993); Rood 2006; Vössing 2005; Grethlein 2004; Bonelli 2003; Moles 2001, 198–219; Plant 1999; Porciani 1999; Winton 1999; Garrity 1998; Shrimpton 1998; Tsakmakis 1998; Moles 1993, 104–107; Swain 1993; Badian 1992; Bicknell 1990; Develin 1990; Flory 1990; Porter 1990; Erbse 1989; Iglesias Zoido 1989; Marincola 1989; Plant 1988; Hornblower 1987, 45–72; Walbank 1985; Macleod 1984 (1974); Egermann 1983; Trédé 1983; Loriaux 1982; Rokeah 1982; Wilson 1982; Cogan 1981; Schepens 1980; Kagan 1975; Macleod 1975; Luschnat 1974; Egermann 1972; Tompkins 1972; Luschnat 1970; Erbse 1968 (1953); Wille 1968 (1965); Wimmer 1966; Glucker 1964; Rokeah 1962; Egermann 1961; Rohrer 1959; Schmid 1954/1955; Gomme 1937; Patzer 1937; Grosskinsky 1936.

DOI 10.1515/9783110496055-006

Thucydides' programmatic statements comprise two sentences about the speeches and one about the events of the *Peloponnesian War*:[2]

(1) Καὶ ὅσα μὲν λόγῳ εἶπον ἕκαστοι ἢ μέλλοντες πολεμήσειν ἢ ἐν αὐτῷ ἤδη ὄντες, χαλεπὸν τὴν ἀκρίβειαν αὐτὴν τῶν λεχθέντων διαμνημονεῦσαι ἦν ἐμοί τε ὧν αὐτὸς ἤκουσα καὶ τοῖς ἄλλοθέν ποθεν ἐμοὶ ἀπαγγέλλουσιν· ὡς δ' ἂν ἐδόκουν ἐμοὶ ἕκαστοι περὶ τῶν αἰεὶ παρόντων τὰ δέοντα μάλιστ' εἰπεῖν, ἐχομένῳ ὅτι ἐγγύτατα τῆς ξυμπάσης γνώμης τῶν ἀληθῶς λεχθέντων, οὕτως εἴρηται. (2) τὰ δ' ἔργα τῶν πραχθέντων ἐν τῷ πολέμῳ οὐκ ἐκ τοῦ παρατυχόντος πυνθανόμενος ἠξίωσα γράφειν, οὐδ' ὡς ἐμοὶ ἐδόκει, ἀλλ' οἷς τε αὐτὸς παρῆν καὶ παρὰ τῶν ἄλλων ὅσον δυνατὸν ἀκριβείᾳ περὶ ἑκάστου ἐπεξελθών.

(1) As to the speeches that were made by different men, either when they were about to begin the war or when they were already engaged therein, it has been difficult to recall with strict accuracy the words actually spoken, both for me as regards that which I myself heard, and for those who have brought me reports from various other sources. Therefore the speeches are given in the language in which, as it seemed to me, the several speakers would express, on the subjects under consideration, the sentiments most befitting the occasion, though at the same time I have adhered as closely as possible to the general sense of what was actually said. (2) But as to the facts of the occurrences of the war, I have thought it my duty to give them, not as ascertained from any chance informant nor as seemed to me probable, but only after investigating with the greatest possible accuracy each detail, in the case both of the events in which I myself participated and of those regarding which I got my information from others.[3]

Two modern scholars who were concerned with Thucydides' *Methodenkapitel* have already taken into account the critical essay *De Thucydide* of Dionysius of Halicarnassus. First, Franz Egermann used it in order to resolve two problems inside the ἔργα-sentence: one connected with the expression ἐκ τοῦ παρατυχόντος, and one concerning a problem of textual criticism. Second, Adolf Köhnken analyzed the critical essay *De Thucydide* in order to answer the question how the term τὰ δέοντα has to be understood.

Egermann entered the debate surrounding the expression ἐκ τοῦ παρατυχόντος in two articles from 1961 and 1972.[4] He contradicted the *communis opinio*, represented by Otto Luschnat[5] among others, who held the view that the participle, being masculine, referred to a person and therefore meant "from the first person [sc. I met]". In contrast, Egermann proposed that ἐκ τοῦ παρατυχόντος had the function of an adverb and meant "at chance". One of his arguments

---

[2] Th. 1.22.1–2.
[3] Smith's 1999 (1928), 39 translation. Unless otherwise indicated, the translations of the Greek are my own.
[4] Cf. Egermann 1961, 436f. and 1972, 586–590.
[5] Cf. Luschnat 1970, 1181.

against Luschnat's view was that πυνθάνεσθαι ἐκ with the genitive of a person is not attested in Thucydides.⁶

In response to Egermann, Luschnat conceded that πυνθάνεσθαι ἐκ with the genitive of a person is not attested in Thucydides.⁷ However, he referred to evidence in Sophocles, who connects πυνθάνεσθαι ἐκ with the genitive of a person once.⁸

Egermann, in turn, did not accept Luschnat's evidence from Sophocles.⁹ He objected that the construction in question did not correspond to Thucydides' use of language. Further, he found a telling argument that τοῦ παρατυχόντος is neuter in the fact that Dionysius of Halicarnassus, when he cites Thucydides' programmatic statements, omits the participle πυνθανόμενος, from which evidence it becomes clear that for him ἐκ τοῦ παρατυχόντος had the function of an adverb: οὐκ ἐκ τοῦ παρατυχόντος ἠξίωσα γράφειν.¹⁰

In subsequent scholarship, Egermann's argument, relying on the evidence of Dionysius of Halicarnassus, has met with challenges. Köhnken objected that structural considerations make it more probable that the expression ἐκ τοῦ παρατυχόντος is a masculine participle and refers to a witness. If the expression has this meaning, the sources of information mentioned in the ἔργα-sentence would form a chiasm:

Informants: οὐκ ἐκ τοῦ παρατυχόντος πυνθανόμενος
Thucydides himself ("I"): οὐδ' ὡς ἐμοὶ ἐδόκει
Thucydides himself ("I"): οἷς τε αὐτὸς παρῆν
Informants: καὶ ⟨τὰ⟩ παρὰ τῶν ἄλλων [...] ἐπεξελθών

Further, the participles πυνθανόμενος and ἐπεξελθών would be parallel if both of them refer to informants, i.e. to persons. Additionally, Köhnken objects that in Egermann's interpretation, the participle πυνθανόμενος would be superfluous because it would be enough to say οὐκ ἐκ τοῦ παρατυχόντος ἠξίωσα γράφειν.¹¹

Egermann also tried to resolve a problem of textual criticism with the help of *De Thucydide*. Specifically, he considered whether it is necessary to add τά after καί in order to connect the two relative clauses in the ἔργα-sentence (οἷς τε αὐτὸς παρῆν καὶ ⟨τὰ⟩ παρὰ τῶν ἄλλων ὅσον δυνατὸν ἀκριβείᾳ περὶ ἑκάστου ἐπεξελθών). Previously, Egermann – like many researchers – had viewed Ullrich's sup-

---

6 Cf. Egermann 1972, 588f.
7 Cf. Luschnat 1974, 766f.
8 S. *OC* 1266: τἀμὰ μὴ ἐξ ἄλλων πύθῃ.
9 Cf. Egermann 1983, 47.
10 D.H. *Th*. 20 (I 356.8 Usener/Radermacher).
11 Cf. Köhnken 2006 (1993), 486.

plement τά as indispensable because οἷς τε αὐτὸς παρῆν and ⟨τὰ⟩ παρὰ τῶν ἄλλων formed the two objects of ἐπεξελθών that are connected by τε [...] καί.[12] At this point, he changed his view because Dionysius of Halicarnassus transmits the sentence in the same form as the manuscripts of Thucydides.[13] According to Egermann, the correct understanding of the sentence depends upon the insight that without any alteration of the text, one must mentally supply the relative pronoun ἅ behind καί, and that this second relative pronoun is suggested and justified by the first, οἷς.[14] For this phenomenon, he adduces some parallels:

οὗ ἐνδεής ἐστι καὶ [sc. ὃ] μὴ ἔχει;[15]

ἅς γέ τις ἀπαλλάξειεν ἄν, εἰ μελετῷ ἐκ νέου, καὶ [sc. αἵ] πρὸς οὐδὲν ἀγαθὸν ἐνοῦσαι δρῶσιν;[16]

τὸ πνεῦμα, ὅπερ ἀναμένων τε περιέπλει καὶ [sc. ὃ] εἰώθει γίγνεσθαι ἐπὶ τὴν ἕω;[17]

οὓς εὖ παθών τις καὶ αὐτὸς δεόμενος προσηγάγετο ξυμμάχους καὶ [sc. ὧν] πολιτείας μετέλαβεν.[18]

Egermann's new position, based on the evidence of Dionysius of Halicarnassus, seems completely justified. The textual structure that raises doubts has to be described in the following way: the relative pronoun of the second of two connected relative clauses is not repeated although the predicate of the second relative clause requires a different case than the first one.[19]

In light of the results that Egermann obtained from Dionysius of Halicarnassus, it seems considerable advances are possible using this method, as his results concerning the problem of textual criticism show. On the other hand, the evidence of Dionysius of Halicarnassus does not always supply a striking and simple solution, as the problem connected with the expression ἐκ τοῦ παρατυχόντος shows. Köhnken rightly cast doubt on the certainty with which Egermann claimed that ἐκ τοῦ παρατυχόντος had the function of an adverb and meant "at

---

12 Cf. Egermann 1972, 593 n. 3. For the supplement, cf. Ullrich 1846, 63f. n. 150.
13 Cf. D.H. *Th.* 20 (I 356.9–10 Usener/Radermacher).
14 Cf. Egermann 1983, 49f. and 53, who speaks of a "ἅ subaudiendum".
15 Pl. *Smp.* 201b1.
16 Pl. *R.* 8.559a3–4.
17 Th. 2.84.2.
18 Th. 3.55.3.
19 Cf. the Greek grammar of Kühner/Gerth 1955, 432.

chance", though Köhnken's arguments themselves do not seem to represent the final answer in this debate.[20]

Nevertheless, Köhnken himself turned to Dionysius of Halicarnassus' *De Thucydide* in order to resolve a problem connected with Thucydides' *Methodenkapitel*, namely, the problem of τὰ δέοντα. In scholarship, the question of how to regard Thucydides' speeches in light of his own statements has traditionally been answered in the categories of "objectivity" and "subjectivity",[21] and the most common answer is that they have to be regarded as subjective.[22]

Another tendency in scholarship before Köhnken's publication was to adduce parallels for the expression τὰ δέοντα in order to highlight its rhetorical character.[23] Several scholars found a parallel in the programmatic statement at the beginning of Gorgias' *Helen*:[24]

---

20 This is not the place to fully address the question of ἐκ τοῦ παρατυχόντος. In a future commentary on the *Methodenkapitel*, I will try to give detailed answers to the many problems it contains. Schepens 1980, 126–138 brings the syntactical problems of the ἔργα-sentence nearer to a solution. At the end of this article, these problems, to which the question about the supplement τά belongs, are analyzed in the light of Palaephatus' evidence.

21 There was also the older opinion according to which the speeches expressed the "ideal reality"; cf. Meyer 1899, 384–387; Patzer 1937, 37; Erbse 1968 (1953), 338f.; Erbse 1989, 133 and the critical remarks in Wille 1968 (1965), 707 and Hornblower 1987, 45f. According to Rokeah 1982, 389–395 (cf. also Rokeah 1962), the term τὰ δέοντα forms an expression with περὶ τῶν αἰεὶ παρόντων. He translates the whole expression as "the things most relevant to the ever-current issues" and challenges the conventional view that the expression means "what they had to say on the several occasions", found, for example, in Gomme 1945, 140 ad Th. 1.22.1–3. Glucker 1964, 1f. already criticized Rokeah because he adduced no parallel for τὰ δέοντα in the sense of "the relevant". Moreover, it does not seem likely that the expression has such a general meaning because in debates with contradicting views and as a principle for all the speeches it is difficult to imagine (and would contradict Arist. *Po*. 9.1451a36–b5 and the practice of ancient historiography) that a historian ignores the particular situation and words and turns to "the things most relevant to the ever-current issues". For the universal in Thucydides' speeches, cf. also Hammond 1973.

22 Shrimpton 1998, 72 already criticized the tendency of modern scholarship to use these categories in order to interpret the *Methodenkapitel*. He objects on the grounds that the term "objectivity" is a term of 19th century psychology and consequently runs the risk of anachronism. Shrimpton's objection has to be taken seriously; nevertheless, it requires modification. The problem of anachronism does not arise because no methodological objection can be made against the approach of explaining ancient theoretical statements in modern terms as long as the ancient and modern categories correspond to one another. Rather, the problem seems to be that the modern terms "objectivity" and "subjectivity" are not clearly defined and therefore do not seem to supply a contrast that would be helpful in the interpretation of the *Methodenkapitel*.

23 Cf. Macleod 1984 (1974), 52; Macleod 1975, 39f.; Hornblower 1987, 45–52; Iglesias Zoido 1989, 129f.; Tsakmakis 1998, 248f.; Scardino 2007, 405f.

> τοῦ δ' αὐτοῦ ἀνδρὸς λέξαι τε τὸ δέον ὀρθῶς καὶ ἐλέγξαι τοὺς μεμφομένους Ἑλένην [...].
>
> The same man whose duty it is to say rightly what has to be said, must also refute those who criticize Helena [...].

Swain denies that this parallel is evidence that Thucydides expresses the subjective aspect of τὰ δέοντα. For, while Gorgias is talking about himself, Thucydides gives an account of what the respective speakers regarded as necessary to say.[25] Indeed, the parallel in Gorgias does not seem to contribute much to a better understanding of the expression in Thucydides, but for another reason: When Gorgias uses τὸ δέον, he probably means that one must praise praiseworthy things and criticize that which deserves criticism, as the context shows.[26] Due to this quantitative meaning of τὸ δέον ("the truth, the whole truth, and nothing but the truth"), the same man whose duty it is to say rightly what has to be said, must also refute those who criticize Helen, because, according to Gorgias, she deserves no criticism.

Another parallel these scholars cited in order to demonstrate the rhetorical character of τὰ δέοντα is an oration of Isocrates where he describes the sophists in the following manner:[27]

> περὶ μὲν τῶν μελλόντων εἰδέναι προσποιούμενοι, περὶ δὲ τῶν παρόντων μηδὲν τῶν δεόντων μήτ' εἰπεῖν μήτε συμβουλεῦσαι δυνάμενοι.
>
> [sc. men] who pretend to have knowledge about the future, but are not able to say anything of what has to be said nor to give counsel about the present.

Despite the fact that τὰ δέοντα is connected with εἰπεῖν, there is nothing else that suggests a relationship with Thucydides' statement. Isocrates is obviously saying that the sophists have no knowledge about the present. Therefore, τὰ δέοντα has almost the meaning of the truth. In contrast, Thucydides says that his speeches are not identical with the actual speeches the speakers gave, but that they contain τὰ δέοντα. While Isocrates' use of τὰ δέοντα refers to the truth in the sense of knowledge of the world, in Thucydides the expression designates the relationship between the speeches as given and the speeches as Thucydides represents them.

---

[24] Gorg. *Hel.* 2 (Gorg. fr. 11.2 Buchheim 1989, 4). Among others, Macleod 1975, 39 f. and Hornblower 1987, 46 f. adduced this parallel.
[25] Cf. Swain 1993, 42, who sees the objectivity in what the respective speakers regarded as necessary to say.
[26] Cf. Gorg. *Hel.* 1 (Gorg. fr. 11.1 Buchheim 1989, 2).
[27] Isoc. 13.7–8.

Colin Macleod, in turn, argues that τὰ δέοντα functions as a persuasive strategy, and compares two passages in Aristotle:[28]

> τοῦτο δέ ἐστιν τὸ λέγειν δύνασθαι τὰ ἐνόντα καὶ τὰ ἁρμόττοντα.[29]
>
> That is to be able to say the relevant und fitting things.
>
> φανερόν [...] ὅτι οὐ τὸ πεῖσαι ἔργον αὐτῆς [sc. τῆς ῥητορικῆς], ἀλλὰ τὸ ἰδεῖν τὰ ὑπάρχοντα πιθανὰ περὶ ἕκαστον.[30]
>
> It is obvious that it is not her duty [sc. of rhetoric or oratory, respectively] to persuade, but to see that what is persuasive in every case.

However, these parallels do not seem to support Macleod's view. In the first passage, Aristotle defines the qualitative part of tragedy that he calls διάνοια. It is not apparent how this citation confirms the opinion that τὰ δέοντα means "the necessary" in the sense of "the persuasive". Likewise, the expression τὰ ὑπάρχοντα πιθανά, which Aristotle uses in order to designate the task of rhetoric, that is to recognize the persuasive elements, does not seem to be a convincing parallel for Thucydides' use of τὰ δέοντα.[31]

Given this state of the scholarship, Köhnken took a very promising approach to give an answer to the question of the precise meaning of τὰ δέοντα, namely, to take into account *De Thucydide*. Dionysius' statements make it clear that he understood τὰ δέοντα in the sense of τὸ πρέπον ("the fitting"). His understanding becomes clear through the criterion for the evaluation of the Melian Dialogue (Th. 5.85–111), which he roots in the principle that Thucydides formulated at the beginning of his work:[32]

> λείπεται δὴ σκοπεῖν, εἰ τοῖς τε πράγμασι προσήκοντα καὶ τοῖς συνεληλυθόσιν εἰς τὸν σύλλογον προσώποις ἁρμόττοντα πέπλακε διάλογον 'ἐχόμενος ὡς ἔγγιστα τῆς συμπάσης γνώμης τῶν ἀληθῶς λεχθέντων', ὡς αὐτὸς ἐν τῷ προοιμίῳ τῆς ἱστορίας προείρηκεν.
>
> So it remains to examine whether he has made the dialogue appropriate to the circumstances and befitting the persons who came together at the conference, "keeping him as close

---

[28] Cf. Macleod 1975, 40. Cf. also Macleod 1984 (1974), 52. Shanske (2007, 157 f.) and Plant (1999, 69) follow Macleod.
[29] Arist. *Po.* 6.1450b4–5.
[30] Arist. *Rh.* 1.1355b9–11.
[31] There is a parallel for τὰ δέοντα in the sense here needed: Gorg. fr. 6.2 Buchheim 1989, 72; I will return to it later after considering which must be the sense in Thucydides.
[32] D.H. *Th.* 41 (I 395.17–22 Usener/Radermacher).

as possible to the general sense of what was really said", as he himself announced in the proem of his history.³³

Obviously, the indirect question beginning with εἰ is a paraphrase of the comparative clause in Thucydides (ὡς δ' ἂν ἐδόκουν ἐμοὶ ἕκαστοι περὶ τῶν αἰεὶ παρόντων τὰ δέοντα μάλιστ' εἰπεῖν).³⁴

In another chapter, Dionysius uses the same criterion of appropriateness for the evaluation of Thucydides' speeches, when he analyzes the dialogue between Archidamus and the Plataeans in the second book (Th. 2.71f.):³⁵

> [...] καὶ λόγους ἀποδίδωσιν, οἵους εἰκὸς ἦν ὑπὸ ἀμφοτέρων εἰρῆσθαι, τοῖς ⟨τε⟩ προσώποις πρέποντας καὶ τοῖς πράγμασιν οἰκείους [...].
>
> [...] and he reports such speeches as were likely to have been given by each side, speeches that were suited to the speakers and appropriate to the subject [...].³⁶

According to Köhnken, Dionysius of Halicarnassus reasons that Thucydides used creative freedom in the composition of the speeches, as the verb πέπλακε shows, but he made the speeches congruent with the respective situations and persons, and the ξύμπασα γνώμη τῶν ἀληθῶς λεχθέντων.³⁷ This highly debated expression raises problems of its own, especially for the phrase τὰ ἀληθῶς λεχθέντα. To address it, Köhnken once again turns to Dionysius, particularly to his criticism of the third Periclean speech (Th. 2.60–64).³⁸ Dionysius believes that Thucydides should have made Pericles say appeasing words, and justifies his criticism in the following way:³⁹

> τοῦτο γὰρ ἦν πρέπον τῷ μιμεῖσθαι βουλομένῳ συγγραφεῖ τὴν ἀλήθειαν.
>
> For this would have been appropriate for a historian who wants to represent the truth.

When Dionysius uses the expression μιμεῖσθαι [...] τὴν ἀλήθειαν, his meaning, Köhnken contends, is not to reproduce the words Pericles uttered, but, as the verb μιμεῖσθαι shows, "to write in a realistic and credible manner".⁴⁰ For this rea-

---

33 Pritchett's 1975, 33 translation with minor changes.
34 The fact that Dionysius speaks of a dialogue instead of a speech is due to the context of the passage he analyzes.
35 D.H. *Th.* 36 (I 383–384 Usener/Radermacher).
36 Pritchett's translation (Pritchett 1975, 28).
37 Cf. Köhnken 2006 (1993), 473.
38 Cf. D.H. *Th.* 43–45.
39 D.H. *Th.* 45 (I 402.2–4 Usener/Radermacher).
40 Cf. Köhnken 2006 (1993), 474: "realistisch und glaubwürdig schreiben".

son, Köhnken believes that it is not sufficient to argue, as Pritchett does, that "Dionysius' preoccupation concerning τὸ πρέπον is the direct result of his rhetorical training and leads to criticisms which are not convincing [...]."[41] Rather, as Dionysius explicitly refers to Thucydides' programmatic statements, Köhnken contends one must examine whether Dionysius understood Thucydides' intentions correctly. That is, one must examine whether τὰ δέοντα has the sense of τὸ πρέπον so that Thucydides wrote speeches that befit the given situations and the persons speaking, and whether he sought not authenticity, but credibility in his speeches.[42]

Köhnken himself, after an examination of the *Methodenkapitel* in the light of modern scholarship, concludes that Dionysius' understanding of τὰ δέοντα is mistaken. He admits that authenticity is not Thucydides' professed aim, but he argues that Thucydides does not promise rhetorical probability in Dionysius' sense either.[43] According to Köhnken, Dionysius' criticism of Thucydides' speeches, above all, has a heuristic value *ex negativo*: it shows their lack of distinctive features concerning place and time.[44]

Because he takes into account Dionysius' criticisms, Köhnken's approach to determining the precise meaning of τὰ δέοντα is very promising; nevertheless, his results are not convincing. He draws a conclusion that could be the result of analyzing Thucydides' speeches, but his conclusion does not follow organically out of his argument. The reader would like to know, particularly, why the understanding of τὰ δέοντα in the sense of τὸ πρέπον is mistaken, and is left desiring a deeper understanding of the expression. In the following discussion, I will reconsider the question of whether τὰ δέοντα means τὸ πρέπον in terms of appropriateness.[45]

---

[41] Pritchett 1975, 128 n. 3 ad D.H. *Th.* 44.
[42] Cf. Köhnken 2006 (1993), 474 f.
[43] Cf. Köhnken 2006 (1993), 488: "Der Redensatz des Methodenkapitels verspricht aber auch nicht rhetorische 'Wahrscheinlichkeit' im Sinne des Dionysios, sondern unter Berücksichtigung von Ziel und Auswirkung tatsächlicher politischer Stellungnahmen die nach Auffassung des Thukydides für die gegebene historische Situation wesentlichen Argumente (τὰ δέοντα περὶ τῶν αἰεὶ παρόντων) [...] im Munde einer oder mehrerer der jeweils beteiligten Personen."
[44] Cf. Köhnken 2006 (1993), 489.
[45] The view that τὰ δέοντα means τὸ πρέπον in terms of appropriateness is not totally new in modern scholarship; cf. Walbank 1985, 245: "There is a contradiction between the two ideas of recording what was actually said and recording what the historian thought the speakers would have said [...] on the various occasions. The criterion of the one is quite simply the truth, the criterion of the other is suitability, τὸ πρέπον [...], a concept which was frequently to arise in connection with the rhetorical theory about speeches in history." Hornblower 1987, 45–52 understands τὰ δέοντα as "appropriate" and acknowledges (p. 46) that the "rhetorical approach to

There are two reasons to revisit Köhnken's assertion that Dionysius' understanding of τὰ δέοντα does not give justice to Thucydides' programmatic statements. First, it seems possible, maybe even probable that τὰ δέοντα does essentially mean τὸ πρέπον and that Thucydides' speeches, according to his own statements, follow the rules of speeches-in-character.[46] Second, we find a similar interpretation of τὰ δέοντα in Marcellinus' ancient biography of Thucydides:[47]

> οἶμαι δὲ οὐκ ἀγνοίᾳ σχηματισμοῦ τοῦ κατὰ διάνοιαν παρεῖναι τὸν Θουκυδίδην τὸ τοιοῦτον, ἀλλὰ τοῖς ὑποκειμένοις προσώποις πρέποντας καὶ ἁρμόζοντας συντιθέντα τοὺς λόγους· οὐ γὰρ ἔπρεπε Περικλεῖ καὶ Ἀρχιδάμῳ καὶ Νικίᾳ καὶ Βρασίδᾳ, ἀνθρώποις μεγαλόφροσι καὶ γενναίοις καὶ ἡρωικὴν ἔχουσι δόξαν, λόγους εἰρωνείας καὶ πανουργίας περιτιθέναι, ὡς μὴ παρρησίαν ἔχουσι φανερῶς ἐλέγχειν καὶ ἄντικρυς μέμφεσθαι καὶ ὅτι οὖν βούλονται λέγειν. διὰ τοῦτο τὸ ἄπλαστον καὶ ἀνηθοποίητον ἐπετήδευσε, σῴζων κἂν τούτοις τὸ προσῆκον καὶ τῇ τέχνῃ δοκοῦν· τεχνίτου γὰρ ἀνδρὸς φυλάξαι τοῖς προσώποις τὴν ἐπιβάλλουσαν δόξαν καὶ τοῖς πράγμασι τὸν ἀκόλουθον κόσμον.

> I think, however, that not from ignorance of any figure of thought did Thucydides leave such things out, but that he puts together the speeches that suit and harmonize with the given person. For it was not suitable to Pericles, and Archidamus, and Nicias, and Brasidas—high-minded men, and well born, and having heroic reputations—to ascribe to them speeches of irony and knavery, as if they do not possess the frankness to accuse openly and to censure without disguise and to say whatever they wish to say. For this reason, he pursued the sincere and un-characterized [sc. form of speeches], preserving also herein the fitting and the skillful. For it belongs to the skilled man to keep watch over the reputation bestowed on the persons, and to apply to the deeds the corresponding embellishment.[48]

As Marcellinus says, Thucydides composed the speeches with the goal that they were suitable to the speaking persons (οἶμαι [...] τὸν Θουκυδίδην [...] τοῖς ὑποκειμένοις προσώποις πρέποντας καὶ ἁρμόζοντας συντιθέντα τοὺς λόγους). This assertion is very similar to the view of Dionysius (λείπεται δὴ σκοπεῖν, εἰ τοῖς τε πράγμασι προσήκοντα καὶ τοῖς συνεληλυθόσιν εἰς τὸν σύλλογον προσώποις ἁρμόττοντα πέπλακε διάλογον). The main difference is that Marcellinus does not speak about the respective situations, but focuses on the appropriateness of the speeches to the respective persons.

Thucydides has enormously deepened or understanding of the speeches". However, he sees a risk of over-valuing it (p. 49), especially the *Rhetoric to Alexander*, because the rhetorical theory might have followed his practice. In this paper, I will argue that the understanding of τὰ δέοντα in terms of appropriateness does not only offer a deeper understanding of Thucydides' programmatic statements, but also that there is no contradiction in them.
46 The degree to which Thucydides' speeches are speeches-in-character will be discussed below.
47 Marcellin. *Vit. Thuc.* 57. For Marcellinus' *Life of Thucydides*, cf. Grossi's paper in this volume.
48 Burns' (2010, 24) translation with minor changes.

On the other hand, Marcellinus says that Thucydides' speech technique is ἀνηθοποίητος. This rare term, first attested in a Cicero letter,[49] normally means, "not giving an exact delineation of character".[50] Given this meaning, there seems to be a contradiction in Marcellinus' statements, because on the one hand, he affirms twice that Thucydides' speeches are suitable to the speaking persons,[51] but on the other hand, he designates them with the term ἀνηθοποίητος.[52]

The problem of the apparent contradiction in his statements can possibly be resolved if it is assumed that the adjective does not have the exclusive meaning of not showing the personal element at all. Therefore, it is a question of degree, and it must be stressed that ἀνηθοποίητος has the meaning "not giving *exact* delineation of character".

In Marcellinus' judgment, Thucydides' speeches, to a certain extent, are speeches-in-character. The extent to which they are so is expressed in negative terms, and in comparison with Demosthenes' speeches.[53] They are speeches-in-character, but they do not give an exact delineation of character because figures of thought like irony, knavery, and self-correction, which are not suitable to noble persons like Pericles and Archidamus, do not occur in Thucydides'

---

[49] Cf. Cic. *Att.* 10.10.6: *iuvenem nostrum non possum non amare sed ab eo nos non amari plane intellego. nihil ego vidi tam ἀνηθοποίητον, tam aversum a suis, tam nescio quid cogitans.*

[50] Cf. LSJ s.v. ἀνηθοποίητος.

[51] Marcellinus affirms not only at the beginning of the chapter that Thucydides' speeches are suitable to the speaking persons, but also in the same sentence where he says that they are ἀνηθοποίητος: διὰ τοῦτο τὸ ἄπλαστον καὶ ἀνηθοποίητον ἐπετήδευσε, σῴζων κἀν τούτοις τὸ προσῆκον καὶ τῇ τέχνῃ δοκοῦν.

[52] Friedrich Zucker (1953), in a semasiological investigation of ἀνηθοποίητος, argues that the common feature in the figures that Marcellinus contends Thucydides did not use is the indirect element. Therefore, the meaning of τὸ ἄπλαστον καὶ ἀνηθοποίητον, according to Zucker, is direct diction. In order to harmonize this meaning of ἀνηθοποίητος with that in the Cicero letter, Zucker concludes that the best translation of the adjective would be "repellent" (cf. Zucker 1953, 9: "abweisend"). However, the translation of ἀνηθοποίητος with "repellent" ("abweisend") does not seem to make sense in Marcellinus' statements about Thucydides' style. It could make sense in the Cicero letter, where Cicero is talking about a person, his nephew Quintus. However, even here the meaning "unprincipled" (cf. LSJ s.v. ἀνηθοποίητος) is more probable: Quintus has not yet found the right principles that guide his life. With regard to Thucydides' style, it can hardly be assumed that Marcellinus says that his speeches are repellent.

[53] The pronoun τὸ τοιοῦτον at the beginning of chapter 57 obviously refers to the figures of thought mentioned at the end of the previous chapter; cf. Marcellin. *Vit. Thuc.* 56: [...] ποικιλώτατος μὲν ἐν τοῖς τῆς λέξεως σχήμασι, κατὰ δὲ τὴν διάνοιαν τοὐναντίον ἀσχημάτιστος· οὔτε γὰρ εἰρωνείαις οὔτε ἐπιτιμήσεσιν οὔτε ταῖς ἐκ πλαγίου ῥήσεσιν οὔτε ἄλλαις τισὶ πανουργίαις πρὸς τὸν ἀκροατὴν κέχρηται, τοῦ Δημοσθένους μάλιστα ἐν τούτοις ἐπιδεικνυμένου τὴν δεινότητα.

speeches. This is why Marcellinus formulates the almost paradoxical sentence that Thucydides' speeches are not speeches-in-character in the strict sense because Thucydides took into account what suited the speaking persons' character and skill (διὰ τοῦτο τὸ ἄπλαστον καὶ ἀνηθοποίητον ἐπετήδευσε, σῴζων κἂν τούτοις τὸ προσῆκον καὶ τῇ τέχνῃ δοκοῦν).

Marcellinus seems to classify Thucydides' speeches as ἀνηθοποίητος for two reasons. First, he apparently conceives of a scale of possible degrees in which a speech can reflect the individual character (ἦθος) of a person. In Demosthenes' speeches, he sees the maximum delineation of character fulfilled. Thucydides' speeches, in turn, fall short in comparison with those of Demosthenes; they are ἀνηθοποίητος. Nevertheless, this does not mean that Thucydides' speeches do not reflect the character of the speaking person at all. Rather, there are at least three degrees of speeches-in-character that have to be distinguished:

> speeches-in-character in a maximum sense: Demosthenes' speeches
> speeches-in-character in an intermediate sense: Thucydides' speeches
> speeches-in-character with a minimum or no delineation of character.

For this reason, the best translation of ἀνηθοποίητος in Marcellinus' biography of Thucydides might be "not giving a maximum delineation of character".

The second reason why Thucydides' speeches are classified as ἀνηθοποίητος seems to be the fact that they are speeches that are characteristic for a group of noble persons. When Marcellinus explains why figures of thought like irony and self-correction do not occur in Thucydides' speeches by arguing that it is not suitable to noble persons like Pericles and Archidamus to make use of those figures, he does not refer to the single character of each single person, but regards them as a group of noble men with high reputations.

Dionysius' and Marcellinus' interpretation that τὰ δέοντα carries the sense of τὸ πρέπον seems to be the key for an adequate understanding of the expression, even though this observation might demand some qualification. Nevertheless, some arguments suggest that it is probable that Dionysius' and Marcellinus' interpretations lead to a better understanding of the problematical expression. First, there are the verbal correspondences between Thucydides' programmatic statements and Dionysius' and Marcellinus' interpretation of them, especially in the case of Dionysius. Specifically, Dionysius mentions that the speech must fit both the persons (τὰ πρόσωπα) and the circumstances (τὰ πράγματα); Thucydides mentions the persons in the form of ἕκαστοι, and circumstances in the form of τὰ αἰεὶ παρόντα.[54] Second, interpreting τὰ δέοντα as τὸ πρέπον

---

[54] As it has already been shown that Dionysius' interpretation of Thucydides' programmatic

allows one to see Thucydides' speeches as what they obviously are – at least in the formal sense: speeches-in-character (Gr. προσωποποιΐα). A look at the instructions about the προσωποποιΐα in the ancient progymnasmata confirms this view. They demand emphatically that speeches-in-character consider various parameters, most importantly the speaking person, the addressed person and the circumstance, as Theon shows:[55]

> πρῶτον μὲν τοίνυν ἁπάντων ἐνθυμηθῆναι δεῖ τό τε τοῦ λέγοντος πρόσωπον ὁποῖόν ἐστι, καὶ τὸ πρὸς ὃν ὁ λόγος, τήν τε παροῦσαν ἡλικίαν, καὶ τὸν καιρόν, [...] καὶ τὴν ὑποκειμένην ὕλην, περὶ ἧς οἱ μέλλοντες λόγοι ῥηθήσονται· ἔπειτα δὲ ἤδη πειρᾶσθαι λόγους ἁρμόττοντας εἰπεῖν. πρέπουσι γὰρ δι' ἡλικίαν ἄλλοι ἄλλοις.
>
> First of all, then, one should have in mind what the personality of the speaker is like, and to whom the speech is addressed: the speaker's age, the occasion [...]; also the general subject which the anticipated speeches are going to discuss. Then one is ready to try to say appropriate words. Different ways of speaking befit different ages of life.[56]

Indeed, Theon does not use the term τὰ δέοντα (or a similar term) with regard to what the impersonated figure has to say.[57] However, that is no lexical problem in the strict sense that we are dealing with. It is not problematic to translate τὰ δέοντα in Thucydides' programmatic statements as "the necessary" or "what is / was needed". More to the point is the question of whether it is reasonable to assume that Thucydides lays open his rules of προσωποποιΐα when he says that he made his speakers say τὰ δέοντα in the respective situations.[58]

As both Thucydides and Theon address the person speaking and the situation, one must assume that they are speaking about the same thing, i.e. about the appropriateness of the speech to the person speaking and the respective circumstances. The real question is what, in that relationship of speech to speaker and circumstance, Thucydides refers to when he speaks about 'the necessary', and a quite easy or even probable answer is that he means that the person speak-

---

statements is quite similar to Marcellinus', it is not necessary to make evident the correspondences between Thucydides' programmatic statements and Marcellinus' interpretation of it.
55 Theon, *Prog.* 10 ed. L. Spengel *Rhet.* ii p. 115 (Patillon/Bolognesi 1997, 70).
56 Kennedy's 2003, 47 f. translation with minor changes.
57 Theon uses the word δεῖ for the instructions he gives, that is to teach the possible composer of a προσωποποιΐα what he has to do.
58 In an abstract sense, the awareness for the speaking person develops from the Aristotelian communication model that distinguishes the three *genera causarum* by the three parameters speaking person, addressee and topic; cf. Arist. *Rh.* 1358a36–b8.

ing and the demands of each respective circumstance necessarily determine what will make a speech appear appropriate.⁵⁹

While the parallels for τὰ δέοντα discussed at the beginning of this paper were not convincing, there is indeed a parallel for τὰ δέοντα in the sense of τὸ πρέπον ("the fitting") in Gorgias:⁶⁰

> [...] τοῦτον νομίζοντες θειότατον καὶ κοινότατον νόμον, τὸ δέον ἐν τῷ δέοντι καὶ λέγειν καὶ σιγᾶν καὶ ποιεῖν ⟨καὶ ἐᾶν⟩, [...] ὑβρισταὶ εἰς τοὺς ὑβριστάς, κόσμιοι εἰς τοὺς κοσμίους, ἄφοβοι εἰς τοὺς ἀφόβους, δεινοὶ ἐν τοῖς δεινοῖς.

> [...] this they regarded as the most divine and common law, to say the necessary in the necessary [sc. circumstances] and to be silent about it, to do it ⟨and to let it be⟩, [...] violent towards the violent, honest towards the honest, unafraid against the unafraid, terrible in the terrible.

Gorgias speaks about the brave ancestors of the Greeks who fought in the Persian wars and whose greatest virtue was appropriateness. This appropriateness is associated with the same term as in Thucydides (τὸ δέον). It is incorporated into a wider concept because in Gorgias it not only comprises the speeches, but also the actions of the Greek ancestors. However, as in Thucydides, τὸ δέον / τὰ δέοντα is one of three parameters in the respective concept: the persons (the Greek ancestors / the participants of the Peloponnesian War) say what is necessary (τὸ δέον / τὰ δέοντα) in the respective circumstances (ἐν τῷ δέοντι / περὶ τῶν αἰεὶ παρόντων).

The assumption that τὰ δέοντα describes the appropriateness of the speech is supported by Aristotle, who in the 15th chapter of his *Poetics* speaks about the characters (τὰ ἤθη), after finishing his instructions about the plot (ὁ μῦθος = ἡ τῶν πραγμάτων σύστασις):⁶¹

> χρὴ δὲ καὶ ἐν τοῖς ἤθεσιν ὁμοίως ὥσπερ καὶ ἐν τῇ τῶν πραγμάτων συστάσει ἀεὶ ζητεῖν ἢ τὸ ἀναγκαῖον ἢ τὸ εἰκός, ὥστε τὸν τοιοῦτον τὰ τοιαῦτα λέγειν ἢ πράττειν ἢ ἀναγκαῖον ἢ εἰκὸς καὶ τοῦτο μετὰ τοῦτο γίνεσθαι ἢ ἀναγκαῖον ἢ εἰκός.

---

59 For the term that designates necessity, one may compare Quintilian (*Inst.* 3.8.49): *Ideoque longe mihi difficillimae videntur prosopopoeiae, in quibus ad relicum suasoriae laborem accedit etiam personae difficultas: namque idem illud aliter Caesar, aliter Cicero, aliter Cato suadere debebit*. "That is why by far the most difficult ones [sc. exercises] seem to me to be speeches-in-character, in which in addition to the remaining effort of the *suasoria* is added the difficulty of the person: Caesar must advise the same thing in a different way than Cicero, and in a different way than Cato."
60 Gorg. fr. 6.2 Buchheim 1989, 72. Tsakmakis (1998, 248 n. 29 and 32) adduces this parallel.
61 Arist. *Po.* 15.1454a33–36.

With regard to the characters as well as with regard to the plot-construction, you must search always what is necessary or plausible. Consequently, a specific man says or does specific things out of necessity or plausibility, and this happens after that out of necessity or plausibility.

Aristotle here combines two requirements that follow the principle of plausibility or even necessity. First, everything that a person says or does must be appropriate, either plausibly or necessarily, for his character. Second, the sequence of events and speeches must unfold according to the principle of plausibility or necessity.[62] These two requirements form the fundamental law, and a consequence of that law is that the character of a person must be appropriate.[63]

When we compare these statements with Thucydides' programmatic statements in the second speech-sentence, we have to be aware of the differences as well as the similarities. Of course, the Aristotelian phrase τὸ ἀναγκαῖον ἢ τὸ εἰκός is not identical with the expression τὰ δέοντα in Thucydides. The fact that the terms are not identical should not be a serious problem. More important is the fact that Aristotle speaks about the deeds and the speeches of the characters, while Thucydides refers only to speeches. More significantly, in Aristotle, the phrase τὸ ἀναγκαῖον ἢ τὸ εἰκός has a more general meaning than τὰ δέοντα – if we accept that τὰ δέοντα carries the sense of τὸ πρέπον – because for Aristotle, the befitting is just one way the principle of plausibility or even necessity of the character manifests itself.

The question of whether τὰ δέοντα in Thucydides has to be understood in the sense of the more general τὸ ἀναγκαῖον ἢ τὸ εἰκός in Aristotle is almost impossible to answer. What can be said is that τὰ δέοντα at least comprises the befitting and that it is possible that it also comprises other aspects like consistency, but the standards that Aristotle sets for tragedy are probably higher than those that Thucydides declares for his speeches.

The Aristotelian parallel invites an analysis of a further aspect of Thucydides' speeches. As Gerrit Kloss has shown, in the ninth chapter of the *Poetics*, the categories of plausibility and of necessity describe the motivated sequence of events.[64] Therefore, the expression τὰ δέοντα in Thucydides might imply that his

---

[62] Cf. Schmitt 2011, 534 ad loc.
[63] Cf. Arist. *Po.* 15.1454a16–28, especially 22: δεύτερον δὲ τὸ ἁρμόττοντα ("Second, the characters must be appropriate"). The other requirements are that the character should be (1) good, (3) similar to the recipients, and (4) consistent. Cf. also the examples for violation of these requirements ib. 28–33.
[64] Cf. Kloss 2003. For the relevant passage in the ninth chapter of the *Poetics*, cf. *Po.* 9.1451a36–38: Φανερὸν δὲ ἐκ τῶν εἰρημένων καὶ ὅτι οὐ τὸ τὰ γενόμενα λέγειν, τοῦτο ποιητοῦ ἔργον ἐστίν, ἀλλ' οἷα ἂν γένοιτο καὶ τὰ δυνατὰ κατὰ τὸ εἰκὸς ἢ τὸ ἀναγκαῖον.

speeches stand together with the deeds of the war in a relationship of motivation. The degree in which they do so—according to Thucydides' programmatic statements—is uncertain. Maybe the speeches do not reflect a high degree of motivation in the sense that, in the first place, certain events cause a speaker to react by giving his opinion or taking a particular position in a speech, and in the second, the speeches themselves are in turn the cause for the following events. However, it seems that the expression τὰ δέοντα in connection with περὶ τῶν αἰεὶ παρόντων implies that the speeches are motivated by the events of the war.

Reconsidering Thucydides' second speech-sentence this way, we may detect two functions the speeches fulfill. First, they are speeches-in-character (the specific manner in which they are so will be analyzed subsequently), in which the speaking persons say what is appropriate for them to say in a given situation. Second, the speeches-in-character are motivated by the events of the war.

Speeches-in-character can take into account the character of the speaking person in different degrees. For instance, it is possible to create a speech-in-character that regards all the individual details that belong to a person: the age, the thoughts, the stylistic choices of constructions, words and collocations, even the figures of speech that are typical for him. On the other hand, a speech in character can take into account the character of the speaking person in a more general way, attributing to the person thoughts and diction that belong to a group of persons like generals, soldiers, or politicians.

In order to determine precisely the extent to which Thucydides' speeches are speeches-in-character according to his own statements, a systematic investigation of Thucydides' actual speeches could be useful.[65] In the present investigation, it is only possible to formulate a hypothetical answer to this question based mainly on Thucydides' programmatic statements.

These statements seem to indicate that Thucydides' speeches are speeches-in-character in the sense that they reflect the character of the speaking person in a broader sense. The formulation Thucydides uses to designate the speaking persons, in particular, the word ἕκαστοι, points in this direction (ὡς δ' ἂν ἐδόκουν ἐμοὶ ἕκαστοι περὶ τῶν αἰεὶ παρόντων τὰ δέοντα μάλιστ' εἰπεῖν). As a distributive pronoun, ἕκαστος refers to an individual person, but in the plural much of the distributive meaning is lost. Furthermore, and this is the decisive point, Thucydides does not use the term for character in the strict sense (ἦθος). Likewise, Di-

---

[65] For a study of the speeches, cf. Wimmer 1966. On the other hand, analyzing the actual speeches in order to better understand Thucydides' programmatic statements perhaps raises new problems because it is possible that theory and practice do not correspond to one another.

onysius of Halicarnassus and Marcellinus do not speak of character in the strict sense (ἦθος) when they explain Thucydides' programmatic statements, but use the more general term "person" (τὰ πρόσωπα).

The likeliest conclusion, therefore, is that Thucydides makes his speakers speak as the respective (group of) persons and the respective situations require. In Marcellinus' terms, the literary technique Thucydides employs in his speeches is ἀνηθοποίητος in the sense that the speeches do not present a maximum delineation of the individual character, but reflect the group to which the speaking person belongs and the demands of a given situation. In this sense, Thucydides' speeches are fictional speeches-in-character, although they try to be realistic.[66]

This conclusion can be compared with and is partly supported by Tompkins' results, gained out of a case study in which he analyzed Thucydides' stylistic characterization of Nicias and Alcibiades. While former scholarship had judged that Thucydides' speeches only mark the stronger lines of character,[67] Tompkins has shown that there are differences in the manner in which Nicias and Alcibiades speak.[68] The main difference Tompkins detects between Nicias and Alcibiades is that Nicias tends to a high level of complexity, as the high degree of subordination shows, while Alcibiades tends to a paratactic style with initial καί. Most interestingly, his investigation does not conceal that there are stylistic differences within a single speaker.[69]

Therefore, Thucydides' actual speeches make the conclusion highly probable that they are speeches-in-character that pay attention to the speakers and the circumstances. However, the question of to which extent Thucydides' speeches are speeches-in-character according to his own statements, is difficult to answer. Tompkins' results seem to lead to the general conclusion that *some* of Thucydides' speeches reveal stylistic characterization of the individual characters. But as a general rule, both Thucydides' programmatic statements and the im-

---

[66] The term "realistic" designates a lower degree of fictionalization; cf. Zipfel 2001, 107. Thucydides' speeches are fictional speeches-in-character. However, Thucydides has made his speakers speak as those kinds of men speak in those kinds of situations.

[67] Cf. Jebb 1907, 404: "[...] the words ascribed to them rarely do more than mark the stronger lines of the character; they seldom reveal new traits of a subtler kind." Cf. also Blass 1868, 229 f. and 238.

[68] Cf. Tompkins' 1972, 183 programmatic statement: "If it can be shown that Thucydidean speakers do vary significantly in their manners of speaking, and moreover that there is a particular aptness of styles to speakers, the canonical denial of differentiated styles must be challenged [...]."

[69] Tompkins 1972, 200 states that despite Nicias' predilection for concessive clauses, there are speeches in which there are none or just a few (6.20–23; 6.68; 7.11–15), and explains this discrepancy by looking at the circumstances surrounding each speech.

pression of his actual speeches point in the direction that Thucydides did not take into account the individual character of every single speaking person.

Another problem that can be brought nearer to a solution with the help of ancient evidence, in this case with evidence from Palaephatus, is the problem of the meaning of λογογράφοι in Thucydides. Palaephatus was a peripatetic mythographer of the late fourth century BCE who composed a work entitled "On unbelievable things" (Περὶ ἀπίστων).[70] In the introduction of his compilation,[71] Palaephatus makes some remarks on his method. Above all, he expresses his view that all stories (of miraculous events) are true in principle because the names and stories would not exist if the respective events had never taken place.[72] On the other hand, he believes that, since what happened in the past happens in the present and will happen again in the future, whatever does not exist in the present, never existed.[73]

After stating these philosophical remarks on his method,[74] Palaephatus asserts that the poets distorted many reports of real events:[75]

> γενομένων δέ τινα οἱ ποιηταὶ καὶ λογογράφοι παρέτρεψαν εἰς τὸ ἀπιστότερον καὶ θαυμασιώτερον, τοῦ θαυμάζειν ἕνεκα τοὺς ἀνθρώπους.
>
> To some of the things that happened, the poets and authors have given a quite unbelievable and miraculous character in order to astonish people.

As the scholarship concerned with Palaephatus has shown,[76] this statement shares some remarkable parallels with those of Thucydides, who expresses a very similar view just before the *Methodenkapitel*:[77]

---

[70] For the date, cf. Hawes 2014, 38 and 227–238. Theon mentions Palaephatus and his work in his instructions for the refutation of a narration; cf. Theon, *Prog.* 6 ed. L. Spengel *Rhet.* ii p. 96.4–6 (Patillon/Bolognesi 1997, 61): καὶ Παλαιφάτῳ τῷ Περιπατητικῷ ἐστιν ὅλον βιβλίον περὶ τῶν ἀπίστων ἐπιγραφόμενον.

[71] For the introduction, cf. Santoni 1998/1999; Hawes 2014, 39–48.

[72] Cf. Palaeph. 1.5–9 Festa: ἐμοὶ δὲ δοκεῖ γενέσθαι πάντα τὰ λεγόμενα (οὐ γὰρ ὀνόματα μόνον ἐγένοντο, λόγος δὲ περὶ αὐτῶν οὐδεὶς ὑπῆρξεν· ἀλλὰ πρότερον ἐγένετο τὸ ἔργον, εἶθ' οὕτως ὁ λόγος ὁ περὶ αὐτῶν).

[73] Cf. Palaeph. 1.9–2.3 Festa: ὅσα δὲ εἴδη καὶ μορφαί εἰσι λεγόμεναι καὶ γενόμεναι τότε, αἳ νῦν οὐκ εἰσί, τὰ τοιαῦτα οὐκ ἐγένοντο. εἰ γάρ ⟨τί⟩ ποτε καὶ ἄλλοτε ἐγένετο, καὶ νῦν τε γίνεται καὶ αὖθις ἔσται. ἀεὶ δὲ ἔγωγε ἐπαινῶ τοὺς συγγραφέας Μέλισσον καὶ Λαμίσκον τὸν Σάμιον "ἐν ἀρχῇ" λέγοντας "ἔστιν ἃ ἐγένετο, καὶ νῦν ἔσται". Both the text and the sense, especially of the last sentence, are debated; cf. Hawes 2014, 41f.

[74] Cf. Hawes 2014, 42.

[75] Palaeph. 2.4–6 Festa.

[76] Cf. Santoni 1998/1999, 11.

[77] Th. 1.21.1.

ἐκ δὲ τῶν εἰρημένων τεκμηρίων ὅμως τοιαῦτα ἄν τις νομίζων μάλιστα ἃ διῆλθον οὐχ ἁμαρτάνοι, καὶ οὔτε ὡς ποιηταὶ ὑμνήκασι περὶ αὐτῶν ἐπὶ τὸ μεῖζον κοσμοῦντες μᾶλλον πιστεύων, οὔτε ὡς λογογράφοι ξυνέθεσαν ἐπὶ τὸ προσαγωγότερον τῇ ἀκροάσει ἢ ἀληθέστερον, ὄντα ἀνεξέλεγκτα καὶ τὰ πολλὰ ὑπὸ χρόνου αὐτῶν ἀπίστως ἐπὶ τὸ μυθῶδες ἐκνενικηκότα, ηὑρῆσθαι δὲ ἡγησάμενος ἐκ τῶν ἐπιφανεστάτων σημείων ὡς παλαιὰ εἶναι ἀποχρώντως.

Still, from the evidence that has been given, any one would not err who should hold the view that the state of affairs in antiquity was pretty nearly such as I have described it, not giving greater credence to the accounts, on the one hand, which the poets have put into song, adorning and amplifying their theme, and, on the other, which the chroniclers have composed with a view rather of pleasing the ear than of telling the truth, since their stories cannot be tested and most of them have from lapse of time won their way into the region of the fabulous so as to be incredible. He should regard the facts as having been made out with sufficient accuracy, on the basis of the clearest indications, considering that they have to do with early times.[78]

Both Thucydides and Palaephatus consider how historical truth can be distorted. In the case of Thucydides, the distorted objects fall more obviously into the category of historical events. Palaephatus notices a distortion from truth with regard to fictive stories, from the modern point of view, that belong to the realm of myth; but in Palaephatus' eyes, they are historical in their core. The people who are responsible for the distortion from truth are identical, because both Thucydides and Palaephatus blame the poets and the λογογράφοι. Finally, even the intentions of those who – in the judgment of Thucydides and Palaephatus – distort reality are similar: according to Palaephatus, the poets and the λογογράφοι want to astonish the people. Thucydides claims that their intention is to glorify and to entertain the audience.

This parallel between Thucydides and Palaephatus is not only remarkable in itself. It also helps to resolve the problem of the meaning of λογογράφοι in Thucydides that arose when Jonas Grethlein cast doubt on the common understanding that the term designates "authors" or "prose authors". One of his arguments is that this meaning is not attested in classical literature. In his opinion, λογογράφοι in Thucydides means "orators".[79] But the parallel in Palaephatus makes clear that the meaning "orators" does not make sense, and that the meaning "authors" or "prose authors" should be assumed for both Thucydides and Palaephatus.[80]

---

[78] Smith's [1999 (1928)], 37 translation.
[79] Cf. Grethlein 2004.
[80] Grethlein 2004, 213 does not accept the parallel to Palaephatus because he regards his work as a compendium that is full of interpolations. Nevertheless, not even the most decisive defender

However, there are further significant parallels between Thucydides and Palaephatus. Palaephatus, for instance, after his remarks on the relationship between unbelievable tales and reality, makes the following statements about his method in the collection and investigation of the unbelievable tales:[81]

> ἐπελθὼν δὲ καὶ πλείστας χώρας ἐπυνθανόμην τῶν πρεσβυτέρων ὡς ἀκούοιεν περὶ ἑκάστου αὐτῶν, συγγράφω δὲ ἃ ἐπυθόμην παρ' αὐτῶν. καὶ τὰ χωρία αὐτὸς εἶδον ὡς ἔστιν ἕκαστον ἔχον, καὶ γέγραφα ταῦτα οὐχ οἷα ἦν λεγόμενα, ἀλλ' αὐτὸς ἐπελθὼν καὶ ἱστορήσας.
>
> I have visited many places and have asked the elder inhabitants what they heard about every single one of these [sc. tales]; what I learned from them, I document. And I myself have seen the localities, what each one is like, and I wrote down not just the sorts of things that were said, but what I myself examined and investigated.[82]

These remarks on method echo the ἔργα-sentence inside Thucydides' *Methodenkapitel*. Like Thucydides, Palaephatus praises the value of autopsy and face-to-face interview. The echo is especially clear in Palaephatus' last sentence, because in both examples, the object of the presentation is determined through a negative and a positive element: Thucydides, in his presentation of the events of the war, does not want to follow chance information, but makes sure that both what he himself witnessed and the reports of his informants come under close scrutiny. Analogously, Palaephatus does not simply believe the witnesses he interviewed, but undertakes a critical examination of the reports.

Again, this parallel between Thucydides and Palaephatus is not only remarkable in itself, but also helps to resolve a problem of the *Methodenkapitel*. Schmid held the view that οἷς τε αὐτὸς παρῆν καὶ ⟨τὰ⟩ παρὰ τῶν ἄλλων were the objects of ἀλλ' [sc. ἠξίωσα γράφειν].[83] Schepens argued, with Egermann, against Schmid that there would be no meaningful opposition between the events of the war (τὰ ἔργα τῶν πραχθέντων ἐν τῷ πολέμῳ) on the one side and what Thucydides himself witnessed and what he got to know from his informants on the other side.

---

of the compendium hypothesis holds the view that the introduction to Περὶ ἀπίστων is the product of a later compilation and, therefore, full of interpolations; cf. Hawes 2014, 39f.
81 Palaeph. 2.5–9 Festa.
82 The verb ἐπέρχομαι (or the participle ἐπελθών, respectively) in the last sentence is ambiguous, because it can designate both the local visits that Palaephatus made—in this sense the verb is used at the beginning of the cited passage (ἐπελθὼν δὲ καὶ πλείστας χώρας)—and the discussion and critical examination of his observations. Here, it has probably the latter meaning, because the object ταῦτα refers to the written stories; cf. ἐπεξελθών in Thucydides. Therefore, ἐπελθών καὶ ἱστορήσας are synonyms. Stern (1996, 29), Santoni (2000, 53), and Hawes (2014, 45) understand the participle ἐπελθών here in the former sense.
83 Cf. Schmid 1954/1955, 224.

For, first he says that he is not going to report the events of the war, and then he adds that he is going to report them.[84] However, this argument cannot be accepted because the opposition that Thucydides formulates is not between the object of the presentation (the events of the war), but between the manner of investigation: he does not write down the events uncritically, but he scrutinizes events critically, both those he himself witnessed and those he got to know from his informants. It is this sentiment that Palaephatus echoes: he does not write down the tales just like they were told, but after he has scrutinized them.

Additionally, the parallel in Palaephatus helps to explain a further point regarding the structure of the difficult ἔργα-sentence. The expression καὶ παρὰ τῶν ἄλλων remains to be explained syntactically, and it seems that Palaephatus' formulation συγγράφω δὲ ἃ ἐπυθόμην παρ' αὐτῶν parallels the Thucydidean expression.

Egermann argued that the correct understanding of the ἔργα-sentence demands that, without any alteration of the text, the reader must mentally supply the relative pronoun ἃ behind καί. The parallels he adduced convincingly showed that the supplement ⟨τὰ⟩ is not necessary: οἷς τε αὐτὸς παρῆν καὶ [sc. ἃ] παρὰ τῶν ἄλλων.[85] Nonetheless, a question remained concerning the predicate of the second relative clause. Egermann did not give his opinion on this question.[86]

The parallel in Palaephatus affirms the assumption that the predicate of the second relative clause in Thucydides' ἔργα-sentence is [sc. ἐπυνθανόμην] and that the predicate is omitted by brachylogy. It is possible to reconstruct the omitted predicate out of the predicate of the first relative clause (παρῆν) and out of the former πυνθανόμενος. Therefore, Thucydides' ἔργα-sentence syntactically has to be explained this way: τὰ δ' ἔργα τῶν πραχθέντων ἐν τῷ πολέμῳ οὐκ ἐκ τοῦ παρατυχόντος πυνθανόμενος ἠξίωσα γράφειν, οὐδ' ὡς ἐμοὶ ἐδόκει, ἀλλά [sc. ἠξίωσα γράφειν τὰ ἔργα τῶν πραχθέντων ἐν τῷ πολέμῳ] οἷς τε αὐτὸς παρῆν καὶ [sc. ἃ] παρὰ τῶν ἄλλων [sc. ἐπυνθανόμην] ὅσον δυνατὸν ἀκριβείᾳ περὶ ἑκάστου ἐπεξελθών.

I would like now to discuss the conclusions of this investigation: hopefully, some problems of modern scholarship concerning Thucydides' *Methodenkapitel* have been brought nearer to a solution with the help of the evidence of Dionysius of Halicarnassus, Marcellinus, and Palaephatus. The results presented here

---

84 Cf. Schepens 1980, 127f. and Egermann 1961, 438 and 445f.
85 Egermann 1983, 49f. and 53.
86 It seems that Egermann (1983, 50 n. 3) postulated an ellipsis of a form of εἶναι, as his translation makes clear: "sowohl das, bei welchem ich selbst zugegen war, wie das, welches von den anderen ist".

might motivate scholars to pay more attention to the ancient evidence. In addition, the results might suggest that the ἔργα-sentence can be explained syntactically as cited above and that the expression τὰ δέοντα in the second speech-sentence must be understood in a sense that reflects that Thucydides' speeches are motivated by the events of the war and that they are speeches-in-character that follow the rule of appropriateness without taking into account the individual character of every single speaking person.

Bibliography

Adcock, F.E. (1963), *Thucydides and his History*, Cambridge.
Andrewes, A. (1962), "The Mytilene Debate: Thucydides 3.36–49", in: *Phoenix* 16, 64–85.
Badian, E. (1992), "Thucydides on Rendering Speeches", in: *Athenaeum* 80, 187–190.
Benedetti, F. (ed.) (2003), *Studi di filologia e tradizione greca in memoria di Aristide Colonna*, Naples.
Bettenworth, A. (ed.) (2006), *Adolf Köhnken. Darstellungsziele und Erzählstrategien in antiken Texten*, Berlin.
Bicknell, P. (1990), "Thucydides, 1.22: A Provocation", in: *AC* 59, 172–178.
Blass, F. (1868), *Die attische Beredsamkeit. Vol. 1. Von Gorgias bis zu Lysias*, Leipzig.
Bonelli, G. (2003), "Tucidide 1, 22, 1", in: F. Benedetti 2003, 155–164.
Buchheim, T. (1989), *Gorgias von Leontinoi. Reden, Fragmente und Testimonien*, Hamburg.
Burns, T. (2010), "Marcellinus' *Life of Thucydides*, Translated, With an Introductory Essay", in: *Interpretation* 38, 3–25.
Classen, J. / Steup, J. (1919⁵), *Thukydides. Bd. 1: Einleitung. Erstes Buch*, Berlin.
Cogan, M. (1981), *The Human Thing. The Speeches and Principles of Thucydides' History*, Chicago.
De Ste. Croix, G.E.M. (1972), *The Origins of the Peloponnesian War*, London.
Develin, R. (1990), "Thucydides on Speeches", in: *AHB* 4, 58–60.
Diller, H. / Diller, I. (eds.) (1968), *Ernst Kapp. Ausgewählte Schriften*, Berlin.
Egermann, F. (1961), "Zum historiographischen Ziel des Thukydides", in: *Historia* 10, 435–447.
Egermann, F. (1972), "Thukydides über die Art seiner Reden und über seine Darstellung der Kriegsgeschehnisse", in: *Historia* 21, 575–602.
Egermann, F. (1983), "Zu den Grundbegriffen der thukydideischen Geschichtsschreibung", in: H. Heinen 1983, 44–55.
Erbse, H. (1953), "Über eine Eigenheit der thukydideischen Geschichtsbetrachtung", in: *RhM* 96, 38–62.
Erbse, H. (1968), "Über eine Eigenheit der thukydideischen Geschichtsbetrachtung", in: H. Herter 1968, 317–343.
Erbse, H. (1989), *Thukydides-Interpretationen*, Berlin.
Festa, N. (1902), *Palaephati Περὶ ἀπίστων*, Leipzig.
Flashar, H. / Gaiser, K. (eds.) (1965), *Synusia. Festgabe für Wolfgang Schadewaldt zum 15. März 1965*, Pfullingen.

Flory, S. (1990), "The Meaning of τὸ μὴ μυθῶδες (1.22.4) and the Usefulness of Thucydides' History", in: *CJ* 85, 193–208.
Garrity, T.F. (1998), "Thucydides 1.22.1: Content and Form in the Speeches", in: *AJPh* 119, 361–384.
Gill, C. / Wiseman, T.P. (eds.) (1993), *Lies and Fiction in the Ancient World*, Exeter.
Glucker, J. (1964), "A Misinterpretation of a Passage in Thucydides", in: *Eranos* 62, 1–6.
Gomme, A.W. (1937), "The Speeches in Thucydides", in: idem, *Essays in Greek History and Literature*, Oxford, 156–189.
Gomme, A.W. (1945), *A Historical Commentary on Thucydides*. vol. I, Oxford.
Grethlein, J. (2004), "Logográphos und Thuc. 1.21.1", in: *Prometheus* 30, 209–216.
Grosskinsky, A. (1936), *Das Programm des Thukydides*, Berlin.
Hakkert, A.M. (ed.) (1993), *Offenheit und Interesse. Studien zum 65. Geburtstag von Gerhard Wirth*, Amsterdam.
Hammond, N.G.L. (1973), "The Universal and the Particular in the Speeches of Thucydides, with Special Reference to that of Hermokrates at Gela", in: P.A. Stadter 1973, 49–59.
Harrison, S.J. (ed.) (2001), *Texts, Ideas, and the Classics. Scholarship, Theory, and Classical Literature*, Oxford.
Hawes, G. (2014), *Rationalizing Myth in Antiquity*, Oxford.
Heinen, H. (ed.) (1983), *Althistorische Studien. Hermann Bengtson zum 70. Geburtstag dargebracht von Kollegen und Schülern*, Wiesbaden.
Herter, H. (ed.) (1968), *Thukydides*, Darmstadt.
Hornblower, S. (1987), *Thucydides*, London.
Hornblower, S. (1991), *A Commentary on Thucydides*. vol. I, Oxford.
Huart, P. (1973), *γνώμη chez Thucydide et ses contemporains (Sophocle – Euripide – Antiphon – Andocide – Aristophane). Contribution à l'histoire des idées à Athènes dans la seconde moitié du Ve siècle av. J.-C.*, Paris.
Iglesias Zoido, J.C. (1989), "Acercamiento a la polémica sobre Tucídides I, 22, 1", in: *Anuario de estudios filológicos* 12, 125–132.
Jebb, R.C. (1907), "The speeches of Thucydides", in: idem, *Essays and Addresses*, Cambridge, 359–445.
Jones, H.S. / Powell, J.E. (1900/1902), *Thucydidis Historiae*, Oxford.
Kagan, D. (1975), "The Speeches in Thucydides and the Mytilene Debate", in: *YCIS* 24, 71–94.
Kapp, E. (1930), "Besprechung: Wolfgang Schadewaldt, die Geschichtsschreibung des Thukydides", in: *Gnomon* 6, 76–100.
Kapp, E. (1968), "Besprechung: Wolfgang Schadewaldt, die Geschichtsschreibung des Thukydides", in: H. Diller / I. Diller 1968, 7–29.
Kennedy, G.A. (2003), *Progymnasmata. Greek Textbooks of Prose Composition and Rhetoric*, Leiden.
Kloss, G. (2003), "Möglichkeit und Wahrscheinlichkeit im 9. Kapitel der Aristotelischen Poetik", in: *RhM* 146, 160–183.
Köhnken, A. (1993), "Antike und moderne Thukydideskritik. Der Redensatz Thuk. 1,22,1 in seinem Kontext", in: A.M. Hakkert 1993, 5–30.
Köhnken, A. (2006), "Antike und moderne Thukydideskritik. Der Redensatz Thuk. 1,22,1 in seinem Kontext", in: A. Bettenworth 2006, 471–489.

Kühner, R. / Gerth, B. (1955⁴), *Ausführliche Grammatik der griechischen Sprache. Satzlehre, Zweiter Teil*, Hannover.
Kurz, D. (1970), *AKPIBEIA. Das Ideal der Exaktheit bei den Griechen bis Aristoteles*, Göppingen.
Loriaux, R. (1982), "Les discours de Thucydide (I, 22)", in: *LEC* 50, 289–292.
Lüdtke, W. (1930), *Untersuchungen zum Satzbau des Thukydides (Das sog. Anakoluth)*, Borna / Leipzig.
Luschnat, O. (1970), "Thukydides", in: *RE Suppl.* 12, 1085–1354.
Luschnat, O. (1974), "Thukydides. Nachträge", in: *RE Suppl.* 14, 760–786.
Macleod, C. (1974), "Form and Meaning in the Melian Dialogue", in: *Historia* 23, 385–400.
Macleod, C. (1975), "Rhetoric and History (Thucydides, VI, 16–18)", in: *QS* 1, 39–65.
Macleod, C. (1984), "Form and Meaning in the Melian Dialogue", in: idem, *Collected Essays*, Oxford, 52–67.
Maddalena, A. (1951), *Thucydidis Historiarum liber 1,1. Introduzione, testo critico e commento con traduzione e indici*, Florence.
Marincola, J.M. (1989), "Thucydides 1.22.2", in: *CPh* 84, 216–223.
Meyer, E. (1899), *Forschungen zur alten Geschichte. Band 2: Zur Geschichte des Fünften Jahrhunderts v. Chr.*, Halle.
Moles, J.L. (1993), "Truth and Untruth in Herodotus and Thucydides", in: C. Gill / T.P. Wiseman 1993, 88–122.
Moles, J.L. (2001), "A False Dilemma: Thucydides' *History* and Historicism", in: S. J. Harrison 2001, 195–219.
Patillon, M. / Bolognesi, G. (1997), *Aelius Théon. Progymnasmata*, Paris.
Patzer, H. (1937), *Das Problem der Geschichtsschreibung des Thukydides und die thukydideische Frage*, Berlin.
Pelling, C. (2009), "Thucydides' Speeches", in: J.S. Rusten 2009, 176–187.
Plant, I. (1988), "A Note on Thucydides I 22,1: ἡ ξύμπασα γνώμη = General Sense?", in: *Athenaeum* 66, 201f.
Plant, I. (1999), "The Influence of Forensic Oratory on Thucydides' Principles of Method", in: *CQ* 49, 62–73.
Pohlenz, M. (1919), "Thukydidesstudien I", in: *Nachrichten von der Königlichen Gesellschaft der Wissenschaften zu Göttingen. Philologisch–historische Klasse*, 95–138.
Pohlenz, M. (1936), "Die thukydideische Frage im Lichte der neueren Forschung", in: *Göttingische Gelehrte Anzeigen* 198, 281–300.
Poppo, E.F. / Stahl, J.M. / Böhme, G. (1886³), *Thucydidis De bello Peloponnesiaco libri octo. Vol. 1, Sect. 1*, Leipzig.
Porciani, L. (1999), "Come si scrivono i discorsi. Su Tucidide I 22, 1 ἂν ... μάλιστ' εἰπεῖν", in: *QS* 49, 103–135.
Porter, St.E. (1990), "Thucydides 1.22.1 and Speeches in Acts: Is there a Thucydidean View?", in: *NT* 32, 121–142.
Pritchett, W.K. (1975), *Dionysius of Halicarnassus. On Thucydides*, Berkeley.
Rengakos, A. / Tsakmakis, A. (eds.) (2006), *Brill's Companion to Thucydides*, Leiden.
Rohrer, K. (1959), "Über die Authentizität der Reden bei Thukydides", in: *WS* 72, 36–53.
Rokeah, D. (1962), "A Note on Thucydides I,22,1", in: *Eranos* 60, 104–107.
Rokeah, D. (1982), "τὰ δέοντα περὶ τῶν αἰεὶ παρόντων. Speeches in Thucydides: Factual Reporting or Creative Writing?", in: *Athenaeum* 60, 386–401.

Rood, T. (2006), "Objectivity and Authority: Thucydides' Historical Method", in: A. Rengakos / A. Tsakmakis 2006, 225–249.
Ros, J.G.A. (1938), *Die μεταβολή (Variatio) als Stilprinzip des Thukydides*, Nijmegen.
Rusten, J.S. (1989), *Thucydides. The Peloponnesian War. Book 2*, Cambridge.
Rusten, J.S. (ed.) (2009), *Oxford Readings in Classical Studies. Thucydides*, Oxford.
Santoni, A. (1998/1999), "Sulla prefazione del Περὶ ἀπίστων di Palefato", in: *Kléos* 2/3, 9–18.
Santoni, A. (2000), *Palefato. Storie incredibili*, Pisa.
Scardino, C. (2007), *Gestaltung und Funktion der Reden bei Herodot und Thukydides*, Berlin.
Schadewaldt, W. (1929), *Die Geschichtschreibung des Thukydides. Ein Versuch*, Berlin.
Schepens, G. (1980), *L' ,autopsie' dans la méthode des historiens grecs du Ve siècle avant J.-C.*, Brussels.
Schmid, W. (1954/1955), "Zu Thukydides I 22, 1 und 2", in: *Philologus* 99, 220–233.
Schmitt, A. (2011²), *Aristoteles. Poetik*, Berlin.
Schütrumpf, E. (2011), "'As I Thought that the Speakers Most Likely Might Have Spoken...'. Thucydides *Hist* 1.22.1 on Composing Speeches", in: *Philologus* 155, 229–256.
Schwartz, E. (1919), *Das Geschichtswerk des Thukydides*, Bonn.
Schwartz, E. (1926), "Review of F. Taeger 1925", in: *Gnomon* 2, 65–82.
Shanske, D. (2007), *Thucydides and the Philosophical Origins of History*, Cambridge.
Shrimpton, G.S. (1998), "Accuracy in Thucydides", in: *AHB* 12, 71–82.
Smith, C.F. (1999), *Thucydides. In Four Volumes*. vol. I, London.
Stadter, P.A. (ed.) (1973), *The Speeches in Thucydides. A Collection of Original Studies With a Bibliography*, Chapel Hill.
Stern, J. (1996), *Palaephatus. Περὶ ἀπίστων, On Unbelievable Tales. Translation, Introduction and Commentary*, Wauconda.
Swain, S. (1993), "Thucydides 1.22.1 and 3.82.4", in: *Mnemosyne* 46, 33–45.
Taeger, F. (1925), *Thukydides*, Stuttgart.
Tompkins, D.P. (1972), "Stylistic Characterization in Thucydides: Nicias and Alcibiades", in: *YCIS* 22, 181–214.
Trédé, M. (1983), "ἀκρίβεια chez Thucydide", in: *Mélanges Edouard Delebecque*, Aix-en-Provence, 405–415.
Tsakmakis, A. (1998), "Von der Rhetorik zur Geschichtsschreibung: Das 'Methodenkapitel' des Thukydides (1,22,1–3)", in: *RhM* 141, 239–255.
Ullrich, F.W. (1846), *Beiträge zur Erklärung des Thukydides. Band 2: Die Entstehung des thukydideischen Geschichtswerkes*, Hamburg.
Usener, H. / Radermacher, L. (1899/1929), *Dionysii Halicarnasei opuscula*, vols. I-II, Leipzig.
Vössing, K. (2005), "Objektivität oder Subjektivität, Sinn oder Überlegung? Zu Thukydides' γνώμη im ‚Methodenkapitel' (1,22,1)", in: *Historia* 54, 210–215.
Walbank, F.W. (1985), "Speeches in Greek Historians", in: idem, *Selected Papers. Studies in Greek and Roman History and Historiography*, Cambridge, 242–261.
West, W.C. (1973), "A Bibliography of Scholarship on the Speeches in Thucydides, 1873–1970", in: P.A. Stadter 1973, 124–165.
Wille, G. (1965), "Zu Stil und Methode des Thukydides", in: H. Flashar / K. Gaiser 1965, 53–77.
Wille, G. (1968), "Zu Stil und Methode des Thukydides", in: H. Herter 1968, 683–716.
Wilson, J. (1982), "What Does Thucydides Claim For His Speeches?", in: *Phoenix* 36, 95–103.

Wimmer, H. (1966), *Die thukydideischen Reden in der Beleuchtung durch den λόγοι-Satz*, Diss. Munich.
Winton, R.I. (1999), "Thucydides, I.22.1", in: *Athenaeum* 87, 527–533.
Woodman, A.J. (1988), *Rhetoric in Classical Historiography. Four Studies*, London.
Zipfel, F. (2001), *Fiktion, Fiktivität, Fiktionalität. Analysen zur Fiktion in der Literatur und zum Fiktionsbegriff in der Literaturwissenschaft*, Berlin.
Zucker, F. (1953), "Ἀνηθοποίητος. Eine semasiologische Untersuchung aus der antiken Rhetorik und Ethik", in: *Sitzungsberichte der deutschen Akademie der Wissenschaften zu Berlin. Klasse für Sprachen, Literatur und Kunst*, Jahrgang 1952 Nr. 4, Berlin.

Edward M. Harris
Alcibiades, the Ancestors, Liturgies, and the Etiquette of Addressing the Athenian Assembly

Abstract: This study shows how Thucydides might portray speakers departing from the implicit rules of conduct in the Assembly as a way of revealing an important aspect of their character (cf. Feddern's study in this volume). In Thucydides' account of the Sicilian Expedition, Alcibiades gives a speech to the Assembly in response to Nicias' proposal that the Athenians abandon their plan to invade Sicily. In this speech, Alcibiades replies to Nicias' attacks on his character by mentioning his recent victories in the chariot race at Olympia and his generous funding for liturgies. These activities enhance not only his personal reputation but also the fame of his own ancestors (Th. 6.16). Though scholars have noted the unusual features of Alcibiades' speech (see, for example, Tompkins [1972]), none has observed that speakers in Thucydides and Xenophon and Demosthenes, when addressing the Assembly, never mention their own ancestors or their own liturgies. When those speaking to the Assembly mention ancestors, they are always the ancestors of the entire community. This is also true for those speaking before the Assembly in other Greek cities, for example, Sparta and Syracuse. The only exception to this rule is foreign ambassadors who recall how their ancestors have helped the community as a way of enhancing their credibility. In this regard, the etiquette observed in the Assembly was very different from that followed in the law courts where litigants often cited their own liturgies or the achievements of their ancestors.

During the debate about the Sicilian expedition, Nicias attacks the motives of his rival Alcibiades. In Thucydides' version of his speech, Nicias charges his opponent (without naming him) for promoting the expedition for selfish reasons and claims that he is too young to assume command (Th. 6.12.2). Nicias alleges that Alcibiades needs money to pay for his horses and hopes to profit from the expedition. He warns the Athenians that those who spend lavishly in private life should not be trusted with public administration. Alcibiades replies to these charges by defending his spending on chariots and liturgies (Th. 6.16.1–3). Alcibiades could have replied briefly to Nicias' charges by denying his rival's allegations about his motives; instead, he boasts about entering seven chariots at the

Olympic games and winning first, second, and fourth places.[1] He adds that he has also provided many choruses. Alcibiades argues that his spending brings fame not only to himself and his ancestors,[2] but also to Athens by giving outsiders an impression of strength and power.[3]

When addressing the Assembly at Athens (and, as we will see, in other Greek city-states), speakers often mention the common ancestors of the entire community, but they never mention their own ancestors.[4] And speakers in the Assembly never discuss their own liturgies or victories in Panhellenic games. Alcibiades is unusual for discussing both of these topics and for drawing attention to his own family and his own liturgies, thereby violating two of the unwritten rules of deliberative oratory. This in turn reveals an aspect of his character, which Thucydides (Th. 6.15.4) calls his ἀνομία, his defiance of convention.[5] This essay will study the references to the ancestors in deliberative speeches in Thucydides, Xenophon and Demosthenes. It will also show that those speaking in the Assembly avoid their own liturgies or political achievements. Finally, this essay will contrast the discursive protocols observed by speakers in the Assembly with those of litigants addressing the law courts, where it was permissible to mention one's ancestors and liturgies.

One would not expect someone like Cleon or Diodotus in the debate about Mytilene to mention his ancestors because neither man appears to have come from a distinguished family. Thucydides (3.41) only gives the name and patronymic of Diodotus and says nothing about his social background, and no other source supplies any other details. Although we know the name of Cleon's father, there is no information about his more distant relatives. On the other

---

[1] Isocrates (16.34) and Plutarch (*Alc.* 11.2) quoting Euripides, state that Alcibiades won first, second and third places. For a discussion of the relationship between these passages and Thucydides see Dover in Gomme/Andrewes/Dover 1970, 246–47.
[2] Dover in Gomme/Andrewes/Dover 1970, 246 thinks that this phrase can be interpreted in three ways: "he may mean that men felicitate (or ought to felicitate) his dead ancestors for what he himself does (cf. ii.11.9 and Isoc. vii.56), or that credit for what he does belongs to his ancestors in so far as then enabled him, by accumulating wealth and establishing a tradition of political and military ambition, to do it, or (sc. ἔφερεν) that horse-racing brought renown to his ancestors and brings it to him."
[3] For a similar justification of Alcibiades' spending see X. *HG.* 1.2.12.
[4] See Mann 2007, 209: "Offensiv setzt er außerdem seine Abstammung ein: Seine Vorfahren sowie spätere echte Verwandte und solche, welche die Verwandtschaft nur postulierten, partizipierten an seinem Ruhm: dies läßt umgekehrt den Schluß zu, daß auch er vom Ruhm seiner Vorfarhen profitiere – ein Gedanke, der in den thukydideischen Reden anderer Demagogen nicht anzutreffen ist." On the topic of ancestors in general see Jost 1936.
[5] On Alcibiades as "Normenübertreter" see Mann 2007, 199–229.

hand, Cleon's father Cleaenetus appears to have won as *choregos* for Pandionis in the men's dithyramb at the Dionysia of 460/59 (*IG* ii² 2318, line 34), which would indicate that Cleon should have been able to perform liturgies, but he does not mention them in his speech.⁶ By contrast, Pericles had many distinguished ancestors. His father Xanthippus married into the powerful family of the Alcmeonidae (Hdt. 6.131.2) and captured Sestos in 478 BCE (Th. 1.89.1). Yet in neither of his speeches that Thucydides has him deliver before the Athenian Assembly does Pericles talk about his family background (Th. 1.140–44; 2.60–64). When Pericles mentions the ancestors in his speech to the Assembly just before the war's outbreak, they are the ancestors of all the Athenians who abandoned Attica during the Persian invasion, drove back the invaders and have thereby set an example for every Athenian to imitate (Th. 1.144). In his speech to the Assembly during the plague, Pericles does not claim that his advice deserves to be followed because of his ancestors. Instead he reminds the Athenians how their collective ancestors won an empire, which they handed down to their descendants, and urges them to live up to their example (Th. 2.62). Pericles was the successful *choregos* in 473/2 for the trilogy of Aeschylus that included *Persians* (*IG* ii² 2318, lines 9–11) and certainly had the wealth to perform other liturgies,⁷ but these are never even alluded to in either of his speeches to the Assembly. Nicias does not appear to have had distinguished ancestors, but we know from other sources that Nicias was a very wealthy man and performed many liturgies.⁸ Despite his impressive record, Nicias does not mention his liturgies in speeches to the Assembly during the debate in 415 (Th. 6.9–14, 20–23).

Speakers addressing the Athenian Assembly in Xenophon's *History of Greece* observe the same rules. When speaking at the debate about the generals in 406 BCE, Euryptolemus does not attempt to persuade the Athenians by mentioning his ancestors or his public service (X. *HG*. 1.7.16–33). Euryptolemus was a cousin of Alcibiades (X. *HG*. 1.4.19) and therefore counted many distinguished men among his ancestors, going all the way back to Megacles in the sixth century BCE.⁹ In a similar way, Cephisodotus does not bring up either of these topics in his speech to the Assembly in 369 BCE (X. *HG*. 7.1.12–14).

We find the same respect for these informal rules in Demosthenes' speeches to the Assembly. Demosthenes' ancestors were not famous for winning major vic-

---

6 On Cleon's family and wealth see Davies 1971, 318–9.
7 On Pericles' wealth see Davies 1971, 459–60.
8 For Nicias' wealth and liturgies see Th. 7.86.4 and Plu. *Nic.* 3.1; 11.2; and 15.2 with Davies 1971, 403–4, though there is good reason to question the figure of 1,000 slaves given by X. *Vect.* 4.14. For rumors about his fortune being exaggerated see Lys. 19.47.
9 On Euryptolemus and his family connections see Davies 1971, 377–78.

tories, but his father was a wealthy man (D. 27.9–11), whose property qualified him for inclusion in a *symmoria* (D. 27.7).¹⁰ Demosthenes performed many liturgies, starting with a trierarchy in 363 (D. 30.15–17) and serving again in 360/59 (Aeschin. 3.51–52), around 357 (D. 18.99; 21.161) and sometime before 353/2, probably during the Social War (*IG* ii² 1613, lines 186–96). He also sponsored a feast for his tribe and was a *choregos* for the Panathenaea before 349/8 (D. 21.156) and volunteered to be *choregos* at the men's dithyramb for the Dionysia in 349/8 (Dem. 21 *passim*).¹¹ Despite this impressive record, Demosthenes never mentions his liturgies in any of his speeches to the Athenian Assembly (D. 1–6, 8–10, 13–16). In fact, he criticizes his opponent Meidias for boasting about his liturgies at every meeting of the Assembly and calls his behavior annoying (ἀποκναίει), tedious (ἀηδίᾳ) and boorish (ἀναισθησίᾳ), a clear sign of his arrogance (D. 21.153). When Demosthenes mentions his own actions, it is always his advice in the Assembly (D. 5.9–10).

Like other speakers in the Assembly, Demosthenes mentions only the ancestors of all the Athenians.¹² In the *Third Olynthiac*, Demosthenes (3.21) reminds the Athenians that their ancestors were more interested in promoting the public good than in courting popularity. In the same speech, Demosthenes (3.23–24) reminds them how their ancestors ruled the Greeks for forty-five years, brought more than ten thousand talents to the Acropolis, had the Macedonian king as their subject and erected many trophies. He challenges them not to abandon the post assigned them by their ancestors (D. 3.36). In the *Second Philippic*, Demosthenes (6.11. Cf. 8.49; 10.15) recalls that when offered the chance to rule over the Greeks in return for obedience to the Great king, their ancestors rejected the proposal. In several speeches, Demosthenes holds up the ancestors as an example for the Athenians to imitate.¹³ But the practice of praising the ancestors could be overdone; in one passage, Demosthenes (14.1) ruefully notes that many speakers find favor with the Assembly by praising the ancestors but do not accomplish anything.¹⁴

---

10 On Demosthenes' ancestors see Davies 1971, 113–23.
11 For Demosthenes' liturgies see Davies 1971, 135–37.
12 The only speech composed for delivery to the Assembly that contains the names of the speaker's ancestors is [Andocides] *On the Peace* (3.6, 29) where Andocides, the speaker's grandfather, who negotiated peace with Sparta, and his uncle Epilycus, who concluded a treaty with the Persian king, are named. However, this speech is a forgery probably dating from the Hellenistic period. See Harris 2000. This deviation from standard practice in the Assembly can be used as another argument against the speech's authenticity. Note that, even though Alcibiades alludes to his ancestors, he does not refer to any of them by name.
13 E.g., D. 9.41, 74; 10.46, 73; 11.21–2; 12.22; 14.29, 30, 40, 41; 15.33, 35.
14 In one place Demosthenes (13.12) imagines this criticism being leveled at himself.

What is interesting to note is that the unwritten rule against mentioning one's own ancestors is observed in speeches given before Assemblies in Sparta and in Sicily reported by Thucydides. One would not expect the ephor Sthenelaidas to mention his own ancestors, because five new ephors were elected every year, and, most probably, came from undistinguished families.[15] But King Archidamus was a member of the royal family and could trace his lineage back to Heracles. Despite his royal background, Archidamus does not mention his ancestors in his speech to the Spartan Assembly about Athenian violations of the peace treaty (Th. 1.80–85). When addressing the Peloponnesian army at the isthmus, he recalls how their common ancestors have fought together inside and outside the Peloponnese and urges them not to fall below the standard set by their ancestors, but never speaks about his own royal ancestors (Th. 2.11).

In the debate at Syracuse before the arrival of the Athenian expedition, neither Hermocrates nor Athenagoras make any reference to their ancestors or discuss their public service (Th. 6.33–40). Thucydides (6.72.1) says that Hermocrates had displayed his qualities in war, which implies that he had led the Syracusans to victory, and was famous for his personal courage, but in his speeches Hermocrates never even alludes to his public service.[16] Thucydides describes Athenagoras as leader of the democratic party and one who has great influence with the people, which implies a record of public service. But Athenagoras does not discuss these topics in his speech to the Assembly at Syracuse.[17]

The only exception to the convention that one should not mention one's own ancestors when speaking before the Assembly is the case of ambassadors addressing a foreign Assembly. For instance, when Callias, the torch-bearer of the Eleusinian Mysteries (X. *HG.* 6.3.3) and a member of the *genos* of the Kerykes, addressed the Spartan Assembly in 371 about a peace treaty, he reminded the Spartans how his grandfather had been the *proxenos* of the Spartans at Athens and handed this position to his descendants. He also points out that during wars the Athenians elected his ancestors as generals and, when they wished to end a war, they sent his ancestors as ambassadors to make peace (X. *HG.* 6.3.4). Xenophon implies that Callias was more boastful than others, but his allusions to his ancestors serve an important diplomatic purpose. As a foreigner, his words might appear suspect. To build trust, therefore, he recalls his traditional position

---

15 On ephors at Sparta see Richer 1998.
16 On Hermocrates see Westlake 1969, 174–202.
17 Hermocrates does not mention his ancestors also when he addresses the congress at Gela (Th. 4.59–64) and when he speaks before the Assembly at Camarina (Th. 676–80), but in these cases he speaks as an ambassador of his city, not as a leader in the Assembly of his own city.

as *proxenos* for the Spartans and his ancestors' role in making peace.[18] Even though he mentions his family's achievements, he does so to enhance his credibility as an ambassador, which in turn helps him to perform his public duty as a representative of the Athenian state. In similar fashion, Polydamas of Pharsalus in 375 BCE reminds the Spartan Assembly that his ancestors have traditionally served as Spartan *proxenoi* in Thessaly and that he holds the title of Spartan benefactor (*euergetes*) (X. HG. 6.1.4). Unlike Callias, Polydamas does not appear to have been sent on an official mission, but like Callias he recalls his ancestors to show the Spartans that they have trusted his family in the past, which is aimed at enhancing his credibility. He is also similar to Callias insofar as he uses his position for what he believes is in the best interests of his native country (X. HG. 6.1.4–17).

When speaking before the Spartan Assembly, Alcibiades mentions his ancestors for reasons that are partly similar, partly different. On the one hand, Alcibiades admits that he has to overcome the suspicions against him because he is an Athenian, whose country is at war with Sparta and because he himself stirred up opposition to Sparta in the Peloponnese (Th. 6.89.1 with Th. 5.45–48). To reassure the Spartans that he has their best interests at heart, he reminds them that his ancestors were their *proxenoi* (cf. Th. 5.43). After they renounced the position, Alcibiades took up the position again. He also mentions that his family has always been hostile to tyranny – he does this to create a bond between his own political views and those of the Spartans, who traditionally opposed tyranny.[19] He then distances himself from Athenian democracy. Like Callias, he uses his ancestors to enhance his credibility with his audience and thereby encourage them to take his arguments seriously. Unlike Callias, however, he mentions his ancestors as a way of advancing his personal goals to the detriment of Athenian interests. His departure from traditional practice when speaking in Sparta bears a striking similarity to his violation of the informal rules when speaking before the Assembly at Athens.

The mention of ancestors by *proxenoi* when addressing a foreign Assembly finds an interesting parallel in contemporary Athenian inscriptions (see Appendix). When inscriptions mention someone's ancestors (πρόγονοι), this occurs only in proxeny decrees or other decrees for foreigners, not in decrees for

---

[18] As one of the referees observes, one might compare how Glaucus mentions his ancestors in his speech to Diomedes when they meet as strangers on the battlefield in *Il.* 6.145–211. In this case however the two characters meet as enemies only to discover that they have a relationship of *xenia*.

[19] See Debnar 2001, 205–6.

Athenians.[20] The earliest example of such a decree was enacted in 412/11, which states that Eurytion, his father Potamodorus and their ancestors have been *proxenoi* and benefactors of the Athenians (*IG* i³ 97, lines 5–11). There are several examples from the fourth century BCE: the services of ancestors to the Athenian *demos* in the past are used as one of the reasons for granting the honors and privileges of a *proxenos* (see the Appendix). By contrast, decrees of honors for Athenians in the fourth century do not mention ancestors.[21]

The contrast between the etiquette observed by speakers in the Assembly and the practices of the litigants speaking before the Athenian courts is quite striking. It was not unusual for those speaking in court to mention their ancestors.[22] In *On the Mysteries*, delivered at his trial for impiety in 400/399, Andocides (1.141, 147–149) reminds the court how his ancestors held many offices and were generous to destitute citizens. Menexenus, a litigant in a speech of Isaeus (5.40–42), tells the court that his ancestors performed many liturgies, made financial contributions to the war, and served as trierarchs and set up dedications such as tripods for their choregic victories in the temples of Dionysus and Pythian Apollo. They also dedicated bronze and marble statues on the Acropolis and died fighting for Athens. In a speech about his mother's dowry, the litigant Mantitheus tells the judges that his mother was married to Cleomedon, whose father was the general Cleon (D. 40.25). In a speech delivered at his scrutiny, Evander states that his father died fighting in Sicily and his ancestors fought against tyrants (Lys. 26.21–22). Even Aeschines (2.147), who did not belong to a famous family, says that his father was a member of the same phratry as the Eteobutadae, who held the priesthood of Athena Polias, and had been banished by the Thirty and fought in Asia as a mercenary.[23] And it was also common for those speaking in court to mention their public service.[24]

The findings of this essay shed some light on Thucydides' method in composing the speeches in his history. In the preface to his history, Thucydides (1.22.1) states that for the speeches in his history he tries to have each speaker say "what was called for" or "what was appropriate" (τὰ δέοντα) in each situation while at the same time keeping as close as possible to the overall argument

---

20 On Athenian proxeny decrees see Walbank 1978 and Culasso-Gastaldi 2004.
21 See for example the honorary decree for Demosthenes preserved at Plu. *Mor.* 850f–851b.
22 It was also not unusual for litigants to attack the ancestors of their opponents (e.g. Aeschin. 3.171–172; D. 18.258–260), but that is a separate issue.
23 For discussion see Harris 1995, 21–29, 183–84. One might add the speech of Alcibiades' son, in which he speaks at great length about his father's career, but this speech may not be genuine (Isoc. 16.4–38).
24 For a list of all mentions of public service in forensic oratory see Harris 2013a, 387–99.

(τῆς ξυμπάσης γνώμης) of what was really said (τῶν ἀληθῶς λεχθέντων).²⁵ As Feddern has argued in his essay in this volume, this statement has two aspects: what is said in the speeches is appropriate for the situation and is also appropriate for the character of the person who is making the speech.²⁶ I would suggest that the arguments are not only rhetorically suitable but also appropriate in a given venue. In other words, when a speaker in Thucydides makes a speech about going to war, he not only presents arguments designed to convince his audience that this is the correct policy to adopt, but also conforms to the normal standards of etiquette in the Assembly, that is, what was "appropriate." As we have observed, speakers in the Assembly did not normally mention their ancestors or remind their audience about their liturgies. This appears to have been traditional practice in the speeches one reads in Thucydides and Xenophon and in the deliberative speeches of Demosthenes. When speakers mention ancestors, they are almost always the ancestors of everyone in the community. It has recently been observed that in his deliberative speeches, Demosthenes does not accuse his opponents of deceiving their audience. This kind of charge was only permitted in the courts.²⁷ The practice is the same for those addressing the Assembly in Thucydides: with one notable exception these speakers do not accuse their opponents of deceiving their audience.²⁸

On the other hand, Thucydides in some cases has a speaker depart from, or even violate, the rules of etiquette in the Assembly in order to reveal something about his character. The most notorious example is Cleon, who delivers a speech in the debate about Mytilene that adopts the language and arguments of law court speeches, which were out of place in the Assembly.²⁹ Cleon is therefore not only violent in his emotions (Th. 3.36.6: βιαιότατος), but also does violence to the rhetorical conventions of the Assembly. Diodotus rightly points out that Cleon's manner of speaking is not appropriate for the Assembly because he uses arguments normally employed only in the courts (Th. 3.44.4). In this sense, one might even argue that what Thucydides has Cleon do is not "to say what is appropriate" to the situation (τὰ δέοντα εἰπεῖν), but quite the contrary. One should not fault Thucydides for departing from the principles he sets out for the speeches in his preface because what Cleon says is appropriate to his character (τὰ δέοντα in the second sense). Thucydides has Cleon say what is "in-

---

25 Badian (1992) translates the phrase "the entire intention" of what was actually said.
26 For discussion of this phrase see, for instance, Hornblower (1987 45–52), who does not however discuss the kind of "appropriateness" discussed here.
27 Kremmydas 2013.
28 See Harris 2013b, 102–3.
29 Th. 3.37–40 with Harris 2013b.

appropriate" as a way of revealing his unscrupulous tactics and his dishonest character. What Thucydides has Cleon say may not be appropriate for the Assembly but it is appropriate for Cleon. In much the same way, Thucydides has Alcibiades violate two of the unwritten rules of speaking in the Assembly, avoiding talk of one's own liturgies and refraining from mentioning one's ancestors, in order to reinforce a point he has made in the narrative about Alcibiades' defiance of convention (Th. 6.15.4).[30] And when Alcibiades mentions his ancestors in his speech to the Spartan Assembly after his flight from Athens, Thucydides has him do so in a way that perverts the normal convention used by speakers when addressing a foreign Assembly. Dover has claimed that "With one obvious exception (Sthenelaidas, i.86), there is (i.e. in Thucydides' speeches) very little individual characterization of speakers."[31] This does not do justice to Thucydides' artistry: the historian sometimes has his speakers depart from the conventions of speaking in the Assembly to set them apart from other speakers and to bring out the distinctive features of their characters.[32]

Appendix
Athenian Proxeny Decrees Mentioning the Services of the Honorand's Ancestors

- *IG* i³ 97 (412/1), lines 5–11 – Eurytion, his father Potamodorus and their ancestors have been *proxenoi* and benefactors of the Athenians.
- *IG* ii² 17 (394/3), lines 5–7 (cf. 24–5) – The ancestors of Sthorys of Thasos have been *proxenoi* and benefactors of the Athenians.
- *IG* ii² 31 (386/5), lines 5–9 – Hebryzelmis, the king of the Odrysians, is praised for being a good man and is voted all the privileges his ancestors received.
- *IG* ii² 79 (before 378/7) – In a fragmentary decree, the honorand and his ancestors are praised (lines 1–4), and he is granted the titles of *proxenos* and benefactor (lines 7–8).

---

30 Cf. Mann 2007, 209: "Diese Argumentation is formal kein Gesetzesverstoß, aber er begibt sich damit außerhalb der eingespielten politischen Kommunikation zwischen Demos und Demagogos – nicht zufällig verwendet Thukydides den Begriff *paranomia*."
31 Dover 1973, 23. Compare Hornblower (1987) 57: "there is more characterization in Thucydides than is sometimes allowed." Hornblower cites Macleod 1983, 68–87.
32 For other examples of Thucydides' characterization of individual speakers see Tompkins 1972, Tompkins 1993, and Tompkins 2012.

- *IG* ii² 110 (before 378/7), line 21 – The ancestors of Menelaus of Pelagonia are praised as benefactors in an honorary decree for Menelaus.
- *IG* ii² 172 (before 353/2) – Democharis, the son of Nymphaeus, is praised along with his ancestors (lines 21–26) and the *proxenia*, which his ancestors held, is renewed (lines 4–8).
- *IG* ii² 181 (before 353/2) – The word πρόγονοι is restored in line 3, in what appears to be an award of *proxenia*.
- *IG* ii² 187 (before 353/2), lines 3–5 – A phrase indicating that the honorand's ancestors were *proxenoi* and benefactors is plausibly restored.
- *IG* ii³ 294 (349/8), lines 8–14 (= *IG* ii² 206) – Theogenes of Naucratis is awarded the titles of *proxenos* and *euergetes* because he and his ancestors have helped the Athenian people and those coming to Naucratis on private and public business now and earlier.
- *IG* ii³ 316 (= *IG* ii² 237) (338/7), lines 8–13 – The Acarnanians Phormion and Carphinas are praised for maintaining the good will toward the Athenian people that their ancestors handed down to them, and bringing a force to fight alongside the Athenians.
- *IG* ii² 304 (before 336/5), line 3 – Ancestors mentioned in fragmentary decree, probably for a foreigner.
- *IG* ii³ 358 (328/7?) (= *IG* ii³ 399), lines 5–9 – The ancestors of Eurylochus of Cydonia and his father Acesandrus are praised for their good deeds to the Athenian people.
- *IG* ii³ 361 (327/6), lines 24–34 (= *IG* ii² 356) – The name of the honorand who receives a gold crown is lost (Thymondas?), but the services of his ancestors Pharnabazos and Artabazus are mentioned as well as the fact that his father Mentor saved Greek soldiers serving in Egypt when the Persian conquered the country (D. S. 16.42–51).
- *IG* ii³ 375 (323/2), lines 41–48 (= *IG* ii² 365) – Lapyris of Cleonae who is an Athenian *proxenos* is praised and invited for dinner at the *prytaneion*. The secretary of the Council is ordered to inscribe the decree on the same stele containing the grant of *proxenia* to his ancestor Echembrotus of Cleonae.
- In *IG* ii³ 413 (340/39?) (= *IG* ii² 234), lines 11–12 and in *IG* ii³ 430 (337?) (= *IG* ii² 283), lines 11–2 a phrase about the good will of the ancestors is plausibly restored.

Bibliography

Badian, E. (1992), "Thucydides on Rendering Speeches," in: *Athenaeum* 80, 187–90.
Culasso-Gastaldi, E. (2004), *Le prossenie ateniesi del IV secolo a.C.: gli onorati asiatici*, Alexandria.
Davies, J.K. (1971), *Athenian Propertied Families. 600–300 B.C.*, Oxford.
Debnar, P. (2001), *Speaking the Same Language. Speech and Audience in Thucydides' Spartan Debates*, Ann Arbor.
Dover, K.J. (1973), *Thucydides* (= Greece and Rome: New Surveys in the Classics 7), Oxford.
Flensted-Jensen, P. / Nielsen, T.H. / Rubinstein, L. (eds.) (2000), *Polis and Politics. Studies in Ancient Greek History*, Copenhagen.
Gomme, A.W. / Andrewes, A. / Dover, K.J. (1945–1986), *A Historical Commentary on Thucydides*, Oxford.
Gribble, D. (1999), *Alcibiades and Athens. A Study in Literary Presentation*, Oxford.
Harris, E.M. (1995), *Aeschines and Athenian Politics*, Oxford / New York.
Harris, E.M. (2000), "The Authenticity of Andocides' De Pace: A Subversive Essay" in: P. Flensted-Jensen / T.H. Nielsen / L. Rubinstein 2000, 479–505.
Harris, E.M. (2013a), *The Rule of Law in Action in Democratic Athens*, Oxford.
Harris, E.M. (2013b), "How to Address the Athenian Assembly: Rhetoric and Political Tactics in the Debate about Mytilene", in: *CQ* 63, 94–109.
Hornblower, S. (1987), *Thucydides*, London.
Hornblower, S. (1991–2008), *A Commentary on Thucydides*, vols. I-III, Oxford.
Jost, K. (1936), *Das Beispiel und Vorbild der Vorfahren bei den attischen Rednern und Geschichtschreibern bis Demosthenes*, Paderborn.
Kremmydas, C. (2013), "The Discourse of Deception and Characterization in Attic Oratory", in: *GRBS* 53, 51–89.
Macleod, C. (1983), *Collected Essays*, Oxford.
Mann, C. (2007), *Die Demagogen und das Volk. Zur politischen Kommunikation im Athen des 5. Jahrhunderts v. Chr*, Berlin.
Parry, A. (ed.) (1972), *Studies in Fifth-Century Thought* (= Yale Classical Studies 22), Cambridge.
Richer, N. (1998), *Les Éphores. Études sur l'histoire et sur l'image de Sparte (VIIIe-IIIe siècle avant J.-C*, Paris.
Rosen, R.M. / Farrell, J. (eds.) (1993), *Nomodeiktes. Greek Studies in Honor of Martin Ostwald*, Ann Arbor.
Tompkins, D. (1972), "Stylistic Characterization in Thucydides: Nicias and Alcibiades" in: A. Parry 1972, 181–214.
Tompkins, D. (1993), "Archidamus and the Question of Characterization in Thucydides" in: R.M. Rosen / J. Farrell 1993, 94–111.
Tompkins, D. (2013), "The Language of Pericles" in: A. Tsakmakis / M. Tamiolaki 2013, 447–64.
Tsakmakis, A. / Tamiolaki, M. (eds.) (2013), *Thucydides between History and Literature*, Berlin.
Walbank, M. (1978), *Athenian Proxenies of the Fifth Century B.C.*, Toronto.
Westlake, H.D. (1969), *Essays on the Greek Historians and Greek History*, Manchester.

II Greek Narrators of the Past Under Rome

Scott Farrington
The Tragic Phylarchus

Abstract: I argue that when Polybius attacks Phylarchus for confusing the ends of history and tragedy, he does so with a traditional conception of tragedy, its narrative elements, and its effects in mind. Most importantly, Phylarchus aims to arouse ἔκπληξις in his readers, and he employs many elements of tragic style to do so. The extant fragments of Phylarchus help interpret precisely what Polybius conceives as the fundamental differences between tragedy and historiography. Like Baumann's contribution to this volume, my arguments concern how emotion might be aroused appropriately in historiography. For a discussion of tragedy and other elements of "historical fiction" in Herodotus, see the contribution by Konstantakos. For a discussion of emotion, particularly fear, in Thucydides, see Liotsakis in this volume.

One of the most divisive issues in Polybian scholarship is the nature of his attack on Phylarchus, in which Polybius alleges that his predecessor confused the ends of tragedy and history. Though some scholars accept Polybius's criticism,[1] the more common reaction is to discount his comments and defend Phylarchus on various grounds.[2] But whether scholars defend Phylarchus or Polybius's attack

---

1 Most recently, Eckstein (2013, 316) has argued that: "the Phylarchus digression...needs to be taken in good part on its own terms as historiographical critique." For a thorough discussion of the history of the debate, see Eckstein 2013, 314–316. Another recent summary appears at Marincola 2013, 73 n. 1. To these and the works cited therein add Rutherford 2011; Vanhaegendoren 2010; Foulon 2008; McCaslin 1985.
2 E.g. Walbank/Habicht 2010, 412 n. 123: "P. is just as biased as he accuses Phylarchus to be." Walbank 1957–1979 *ad* 2.56.6: "Phylarchus voices contemporary opinion better than P...". Phylarchus's most strident supporters are, first, Schepens (2005, 164): "Phylarchus, though an unconditional admirer of Cleomenes, does not deserve to be slighted as a sensational novelist on account of the vividness and amount of emotional detail in his description of the destruction of Mantinea – a real 'tragic' event which he may just have narrated in an appropriate manner", and second, Haegemans/Kosmetatou 2005. Both were anticipated by McCaslin (1985). A distinct subset of support for Phylarchus comes in various misstatements like the following (Brown 1958, 94): "Phylarchus, who lived through the events he describes, wrote an account of the period which differs materially from that of Aratus...". In fact, Polybius never asserts any material differences between the two sources. He does not, for instance, suggest that Aratus reported that he and Antigonus did not sack Mantineia or that they did not slaughter (perhaps a large portion) of the male citizens. Polybius asserts (twice, in fact, Plb. 2.58.9 and 12) that the city was pillaged and the free population was sold into slavery, which was clearly also the core

on him, they tend to agree on two central facts. First, Phylarchus wrote tragic history,[3] or at least exhibited the qualities attributed to tragic history.[4] Second, Polybius wrote tragic history, too, or at least did most everything he accused Phylarchus of doing, whether through simple patriotism, or outright hypocrisy, or a profound lack of self-awareness, or perhaps just an apparatchik's knack for splitting hairs.[5] Both points, I contend, demand reconsideration, especially because, when defining the precise nature of "tragic history," very little agreement exists. This style of historiography began as peripatetic,[6] but quickly became Aristotelian.[7] Its connection to Aristotle and the Peripatos has been questioned and revived, but through all the swings of the pendulum one constant has remained: however it arose, tragic history manipulates the emotions through the vivid presentation of dramatic reversals of fortune and lamentable scenes,[8] and Polybius rejects, or at least pretends to reject, the arousal of the emotions.[9]

---

narrative for Phylarchus (Plb. 2.56.7–8). He differs only on two matters of fact in the entire attack: first, Polybius asserts that Aristomachus was not tortured before he was killed, and second that the booty from Mantineia did not amount to 6000 talents as Phylarchus reports. His other objections are qualitative, not quantitative: i.e., that whatever happened to the Mantineians or to Aristomachus was just, not an outrage as Phylarchus has suggested, or that Phylarchus does not provide enough context to judge the events from a reasoned point of view.

3 E.g. Rebenich 1997, 267. Foulon 2008, 687: "Cette thèse a largement prévalu à partir du milieu du XXe siècle, au point qu'elle est devenue comme un credo universel et que l'existence d'une telle historiographie ne fait plus de doute."

4 E.g. Tuplin 2011, 169.

5 E.g. Walbank, 1972, 39–40; McCaslin 1985, 95; Sacks 1981, 166; Haegemans/Kosmetatou 2005, 136; Schepens 2005, 162–3 and n. 60, but the idea is already in Schwartz 1897, 562. We find this opinion even among Polybius's defenders: Boncquet 1982, 280–81: "While accepting that other motives could influence Polybius's polemics in practice, I would like to sketch here a theoretical frame, the result of Polybius's deeper convictions about the method of the true historian, although he perhaps did not always manage to adhere to his own theory." On emotion in Polybius generally, cf. Marincola 2003. Marincola (2013) argues that Polybius only restricts certain kinds of emotional narration, vivid description, and tales of peripeteiai from historiography; therefore, these elements, though present in Polybius, do not constitute moments of 'tragic history', cf. esp. 80–85.

6 Schwartz 1897, 560.

7 First in Scheller 1911, 67. Developed most fully in von Fritz 1956 and Zegers 1959, esp. 6. See also Walbank 1957–1979 *ad* 2.56.9. The notion has persisted, e.g. Leigh 1997, 36–7.

8 The position is well summarized at Marincola 2013, 72–73. The notion persists even, or perhaps especially, in tangential considerations of Phylarchus, e.g. Morgan 2011, 558. See, further, Walbank 1957–79 *ad* 2.56–63 and Sacks 1981, 144.

9 E.g. Brown 1958, 95: "This account [Phylarchus on the sack of Mantineia] he [i.e. Polybius] attacks on several grounds. The first is really a criticism of style. The historian, unlike the tragedy writer, should not try to stir the emotions."

This traditional point of view focuses primarily on the subject matter of the history and the emotions it arouses – a focus that no matter how it is clothed is primarily Aristotelian in nature.¹⁰ Consequently, this position represents an oversimplification of Polybius's criticism of Phylarchus, of his concept of the nature of tragedy, and of the critical appreciation of tragedy in the Greek literary tradition. I shall offer an alternative view. To avoid overvaluing Peripatetic definitions of tragedy, I will proceed by first considering Polybius's conception of tragedy before looking for precedents in earlier literary criticism. I shall argue that tragic ἔκπληξις, the profound mental disturbance that tragedy inflicts upon its spectators, is central to Polybius's concept of tragedy. Furthermore, when Polybius uses this term, he is borrowing from a traditional critical vocabulary in which this term had a consistent if not technical meaning.¹¹ In this tradition, the depiction of emotional events is only a single element in a complex system designed to produce ἔκπληξις. Equally important is the literary style in which those events are related. Tragedy, as Polybius and others conceive it, must narrate its emotional scenes in a tragic style in order to achieve its full emotional impact.

1 Polybius on tragic ἔκπληξις

In the attack on Phylarchus, Polybius draws a distinction between the aims of tragedy and historiography. The stated reason for his polemical tangent is to convince the readers to reject Phylarchus's account and accept the account of Poly-

---

10 Cf., e.g., Vanhaegendoren 2010, 421, who refers also to Fromentin 2001, 77. Even when scholars attempt to take the study beyond the limits of Aristotle, his influence somehow persists, e.g. Leigh 1997, 36: "the narrative of the tragic historian – in so far as it presents the events as they happened and allows them to speak for themselves – is consonant with the criteria of dramatic presentation and therefore thoroughly Aristotelian in character." Similarly, Foulon 2008, 700: "Il se situe dans une perspective aristotélicienne qui est celle de la separation des genres, mais en meme temps, il opera un renversement de l'ordre hiérarche aristotélicien...".
11 *pace* Schepens 2005, 162: "...Polybius uses the reference to tragedy in a loose, non-technical manner, indicating sensational, semi-fictional, or excessively elaborated descriptions which he deems inappropriate or disproportionate in relation to the intrinsic importance of the event described. Polybius, to be sure, was not opposed to vivid and detailed description of the events of history, which bring about a 'reality effect'..." and Walbank 1985 (1938), 213: "Polybius is deliberately using [the word 'tragedy'] in a loose and vulgar sense...". The tendency to discount the technical nature of Polybius's vocabulary has inspired studies that do the same, e.g. Vanhaegendoren 2010, 412: "j'utilise les termes "dramatisation" et "dramatiser" dans un sens large et non théorique...".

bius, which is based primarily on Aratus. He begins his attack just after he narrates Cleomenes' sack of Megalopolis (223 BCE), and he focuses first on Phylarchus's account of the capture of Mantinea by Antigonus. He charges that Phylarchus, eager to arouse the pity and anger of his Greek audience and determined to evoke pity and tears with a lurid account of the cruelty of Antigonus and Aratus, introduces[12] scenes of wailing women and families being led off together into slavery. At this point, Polybius invokes the comparison to tragedy (Plb. 2.56.10):[13]

> δεῖ τοιγαροῦν οὐκ [ἐκπλήττειν][14] τὸν συγγραφέα τερατευόμενον διὰ τῆς ἱστορίας τοὺς ἐντυγχάνοντας οὐδὲ τοὺς ἐνδεχομένους λόγους ζητεῖν καὶ τὰ παρεπόμενα τοῖς ὑποκειμένοις ἐξαριθμεῖσθαι, καθάπερ οἱ τραγῳδιογράφοι, τῶν δὲ πραχθέντων καὶ ῥηθέντων κατ' ἀλήθειαν αὐτῶν μνημονεύειν πάμπαν, ⟨κ⟩ἂν πάνυ μέτρια τυγχάνωσιν ὄντα.
>
> It is therefore necessary that the historian not drive the readers from their wits with sensationalism in histories nor seek the possible utterances and the consequences of the events, as writers of tragedies do, but rather recall, with absolute truth, the very things that were said and done, even if these happen to be entirely ordinary.

Polybius levels this criticism at the narrative elements Phylarchus employs and the end for which he employs them. Like a tragedian, Phylarchus relates astounding tales comprised of every possible utterance and all conceivable consequences in order to astound the readers. His narrative paralyzes the senses with a vivid presentation of all the things Antigonus and the Mantineans might possibly have uttered and all the imaginable consequences of the sack.

The actual subjects of tragic history – sieges and the besieged, victors and the vanquished, masters and the enslaved – are indeed favorites of tragedy.[15] On the other hand, Polybius himself describes the sack of Mantinea in 223

---

[12] The theatrical nature of the verb P. employs – εἰσάγειν – has received some attention, e.g., Walbank 1957–1979 ad loc., Schepens 2005, 152. Cf. Pl. R. 2.381d5–7: μηδὲ Πρωτέως καὶ Θέτιδος καταψευδέσθω μηδείς, μηδ' ἐν τραγῳδίαις μηδ' ἐν τοῖς ἄλλοις ποιήμασιν εἰσαγέτω Ἥραν ἠλλοιωμένην, ὡς ἱέρειαν ἀγείρουσαν... (Neither let anyone tell lies about Proteus or Thetis, nor introduce Hera in their tragedies, or in any of their other poems, disguised as a priestess collecting alms....) Text of Plato's *Republic* is from Burnet 1968, IV. All translations of Greek are my own unless otherwise noted.
[13] For the text of Polybius, I use Büttner-Wobst 1962–1967.
[14] On the emendation, cf. Walbank 1957–1979 ad loc.
[15] One thinks immediately of the *Trojan Women*, for instance. Ostwald (2002, 25) argues for a more fundamental connection between tragedy and historiography: "Men bear the ultimate responsibility for what they do and suffer, but, as in Aeschylus and in Thucydides, their experiences can bring them an insight that can be trained by a close study of the past to recognize social symptoms and prepare themselves for what is likely to be in store for them."

BCE, the very same event that Phylarchus describes, and again the type of event often depicted in tragedies.¹⁶ The distinction between historiography and tragedy upon which Polybius insists, therefore, must not hinge upon the subject matter alone or in the emotions inherent in any narration of great misfortune; rather, the distinction lies in the aim of each genre and the full complement of narrative techniques that each genre uses to achieve its individual aim.¹⁷

History aims at the truth, which is, in Polybius's opinion, sometimes bland. At other times, the truth might well astound the reader and arouse powerful emotions. Unlike historiography, tragedy will never choose truth over an astounding effect on the audience. The verb Polybius uses to name that astounding effect, ἐκπλήττειν, and related forms, recurs again and again. He employs it, for instance, in the very next sentence (Plb. 2.56.11):

> τὸ γὰρ τέλος ἱστορίας καὶ τραγῳδίας οὐ ταὐτόν, ἀλλὰ τοὐναντίον. ἐκεῖ μὲν γὰρ δεῖ διὰ τῶν πιθανωτάτων λόγων ἐκπλῆξαι καὶ ψυχαγωγῆσαι κατὰ τὸ παρὸν τοὺς ἀκούοντας, ἐνθάδε δὲ διὰ τῶν ἀληθινῶν ἔργων καὶ λόγων εἰς τὸν πάντα χρόνον διδάξαι καὶ πεῖσαι τοὺς φιλομαθοῦντας...

> For the purposes of history and tragedy are not the same, but opposites. In tragedy, one must use the most convincing accounts to drive the audience from its wits and to beguile them for the moment. In history, on the other hand, one must use the truest deeds and words to teach and persuade for all time those who are eager to learn.

The purpose of tragedy, stated twice, is to strike readers senseless.

In order to fully understand his attack on Phylarchus, which is a necessary first step to understanding either the nature and quality of Phylarchus's history or the sincerity and trustworthiness of Polybius's criticism, we must first examine Polybius's concept of tragic ἔκπληξις. In fact, his conception of tragedy is complex; for him, tragedy is not made of vivid descriptions of emotional reversals of fortune alone. Certainly, tragedy or tragic history can present peripeteiai and arouse pity, anger, and fear to achieve the goal of stupefaction (Plb. 2.56.13):

> ...τὰς πλείστας ἡμῖν ἐξηγεῖται τῶν περιπετειῶν, οὐχ ὑποτιθεὶς αἰτίαν καὶ τρόπον τοῖς γινομένοις, ὧν χωρὶς οὔτ' ἐλεεῖν εὐλόγως οὔτ' ὀργίζεσθαι καθηκόντως δυνατόν ...

---

16 Walbank (1972, 39–40) gives a long list of emotional events in the *Histories*. They are: the mutiny at Alexandria (Plb. 15.25–33), the capture of Abydus (Plb. 16.30–4), Hasdrubal's surrender (Plb. 38.20), the fall of the house of Philip (Plb. 23.10–11), the ruin of 146 BCE (Plb. 38.1–4, 16.7).

17 Polybius similarly distinguishes epic poetry from other genres according to its aim (τέλος), cf. Plb. 34.4.1–5.

> ...he narrates most of these peripeteiai for us without suggesting the why and the how for the things that happened, in the absence of which it is impossible to pity with good reason or to be angered appropriately...

But Polybius's criticism here does not suggest that these elements belong exclusively to tragedy or tragic history. On the contrary, Polybius suggests that peripeteiai, properly treated, are well at home in historical narrative, as are the emotional reactions they arouse, as long as the reactions are reasonable and appropriate.

In fact, Polybius stresses that "shocking peripeteiai" are both a natural and a necessary subject of history (Plb. 3.4.4–6):

> ἐπεὶ δ' οὐκ αὐτοτελεῖς εἰσιν οὔτε περὶ τῶν κρατησάντων <οὔτε περὶ τῶν> ἐλαττωθέντων αἱ ψιλῶς ἐξ αὐτῶν τῶν ἀγωνισμάτων διαλήψεις, διὰ τὸ πολλοῖς μὲν τὰ μέγιστα δοκοῦντ' εἶναι τῶν κατορθωμάτων, ὅταν μὴ δεόντως αὐτοῖς χρήσωνται, τὰς μεγίστας ἐπενηνοχέναι συμφοράς, οὐκ ὀλίγοις δὲ τὰς ἐκπληκτικωτάτας περιπετείας, ὅταν εὐγενῶς αὐτὰς ἀναδέξωνται, πολλάκις εἰς τὴν τοῦ συμφέροντος περιπεπτωκέναι μερίδα, προσθετέον ἂν εἴη ταῖς προειρημέναις πράξεσι ...

> Unsupported judgments drawn from the contests themselves are never sufficient, whether regarding the conquerors or the conquered, since for many people those victories that seem to be the greatest, whenever people do not make use of them as they ought, bring the greatest disasters, and for not a few people, the most shocking peripeteiai, whenever people suffer these nobly, oftentimes change suddenly into the category of an advantage; therefore, I must append to the aforementioned events... [information about how the Romans ruled].

The inclusion of the most shocking reversals is perfectly appropriate – sometimes absolutely necessary – in historiography. The arousal of emotions alone does not constitute tragic history.[18]

In fact, Polybius records many scenes that *he* considers both shocking and tragic. Take, for instance, an episode during Molon's rebellion in which Molon routs the opposing forces, led by an Achaean mercenary named Xenoetas. Convinced that Molon had fled, Xenoetas' men encamped across the river from their allies and celebrated by becoming thoroughly drunk. Before long, Molon reappeared with his men, and slaughtered his enemies (Plb. 5.48.5–10):

> καθόλου δὲ ποικίλη τις ἦν ἀκρισία περὶ τὰ στρατόπεδα καὶ κυδοιμός· πάντες γὰρ ἐκπλαγεῖς καὶ περιδεεῖς ἦσαν, ἅμα δὲ καὶ τῆς ἀντίπερα παρεμβολῆς ὑπὸ τὴν ὄψιν οὔσης ἐν πάνυ βραχεῖ διαστήματι, τῆς μὲν τοῦ ποταμοῦ βίας καὶ δυσχρηστίας ἐξελανθάνοντο διὰ τὴν ἐπιθυμίαν τὴν πρὸς τὸ σῴζεσθαι, κατὰ δὲ τὴν παράστασιν καὶ τὴν ὁρμὴν τὴν πρὸς τὴν σωτηρίαν

---

[18] For a similar distinction between history that arouses the emotions and tragic history in Diodorus Siculus, cf. Baumann in this volume.

ἐρρίπτουν ἑαυτοὺς εἰς τὸν ποταμόν, ἐνίεσαν δὲ καὶ τὰ ὑποζύγια σὺν ταῖς ἀποσκευαῖς, ὡς τοῦ ποταμοῦ κατά τινα πρόνοιαν αὐτοῖς συνεργήσοντος καὶ διακομιοῦντος ἀσφαλῶς πρὸς τὴν ἀντίπερα κειμένην στρατοπεδείαν. ἐξ ὧν συνέβαινε τραγικὴν καὶ παρηλλαγμένην φαίνεσθαι τοῦ ῥεύματος τὴν φαντασίαν, ὡς ἂν ὁμοῦ τοῖς νηχομένοις φερομένων ἵππων, ὑποζυγίων, ὅπλων, νεκρῶν, ἀποσκευῆς παντοδαπῆς.

And generally, there was a turbulent confusion and uproar throughout the camp. For the men were shocked out of their minds and terrified, and because the encampment on the other side of the river was within sight and a very short distance away, they completely forgot the force of the river's current and its disadvantageous position because of their desire to save themselves, and because of their desperation and their impulse for salvation, they hurled themselves into the river, and they also threw in the pack animals still with their baggage, as if the river, due to some goodwill toward them would lend a hand and ferry them safely across to the camp on the opposite bank. From which facts, it happened that the image of the stream appeared tragic and frenzied, as together, borne along with the swimmers, were horses, pack animals, arms, corpses, baggage of every description.

He recounts the men's ἔκπληξις and calls the scene tragic. The inclusion of scenes characterised by great emotion is generally considered a violation of Polybius's own rejection of tragic history, but such a conclusion is only true if tragic history is nothing more than a narrative that arouses the emotions. Polybius's very willingness to include emotional scenes suggests that such a definition of 'tragic history' is unsound.

Polybius stresses the emotional nature of the scenes he includes that are characterised by ἔκπληξις so emphatically that it is hard to believe that he could expect their presence to go unnoticed or unremarked. As a matter of fact, he explicitly states that he recorded the intrigues between Perseus and Eumaeus because he saw them first hand and was so stunned that he had no choice but to record them (Plb. 29.5.3):

οὐ μὴν ἀλλὰ κατηνέχθην ἐπὶ τὸ γράφειν κεφαλαιωδῶς τὸ δοκοῦν, καὶ δι' ὧν εἰκότων καὶ σημείων ἐπὶ ταύτης ἐγενόμην τῆς γνώμης, ὑπάρχων κατὰ τοὺς αὐτοὺς καιροὺς καὶ μᾶλλον ἑτέρων ἐκπληττόμενος ἕκαστα τῶν γενομένων.

But I was not dissuaded from writing in summary fashion what I thought, nor the probabilities and indications through which I formed my opinion, because I was there at that time, and I was more astounded at each thing that happened than anyone else was.

Polybius simply does not object to the inclusion of emotionally stunning events in historical narrative. It is furthermore clear that Polybius expects his reader to experience emotion as they read his narrative; however, for Polybius, the reader of historiography does not necessarily experience the exact emotions depicted.

As he explains,[19] a natural reaction when witnessing a free man being beaten is outrage, an emotion perhaps present in the depiction of the beaten man. On the other hand, if the witness understands that the free man struck first and was beaten in response, the response is one of satisfaction. And if the free man is beaten for correction or discipline, those who witness the beating experience feelings of approbation, regardless of any emotions depicted in the narrative. Polybius seems to suggest, therefore, that tragedy merely depicts events out of context and therefore can only arouse the most immediate emotional response. His own conception of how tragedy affects the emotions, therefore, is similar to Plato's opinions, namely, that the audience gives in and experiences emotions similar to those depicted.[20] In historiography, the same is not necessarily true.

As we have seen, Polybius complains that Phylarchus depicts his peripeteiai in ways that do not allow the reader to experience the appropriate emotional response (Plb. 2.56.13). Instead of narrating the events and allowing the reader to experience the emotions that arise from a thorough understanding of the chain of cause and effect that produced any particular outcome, Phylarchus intends rather to make his readers feel pity and make them sympathetic to his account (Plb. 2.56.7): σπουδάζων δ' εἰς ἔλεον ἐκκαλεῖσθαι τοὺς ἀναγινώσκοντας καὶ συμπαθεῖς ποιεῖν τοῖς λεγομένοις. (He is eager to arouse the readers to pity and to make them sympathetic to the things he says.) We could understand that Polybius is accusing Phylarchus of trying to instill in the reader a political bias similar to his own.[21] That is, he is trying to make them sympathetic to his opinions. There is another interpretation, however, that is more appropriate to the nature of tragedy. Like a tragedian, what Phylarchus does – or is alleged to do – is to cause the reader to experience the same emotions that are depicted in the history.

This type of sympathy is what we find described in Plato's *Ion*. Ion, like the spectators, experiences the emotions he describes, and that experience is described as ἔκπληξις (Pl. *Ion* 535b1–c8):[22]

ΣΩ.: Ἔχε δή μοι τόδε εἰπέ, ὦ Ἴων, καὶ μὴ ἀποκρύψῃ ὅτι ἄν σε ἔρωμαι· ὅταν εὖ εἴπῃς ἔπη καὶ ἐκπλήξῃς μάλιστα τοὺς θεωμένους, ...τότε πότερον ἔμφρων εἶ ἢ ἔξω σαυτοῦ γίγνῃ καὶ παρὰ

---

19 2.56.14.
20 See, e.g., *R*. 10.605c–d.
21 On his bias, c.f. McCaslin 1985, *passim*; Haegemans/Kosmetatou 2005, 127, 138 and Schepens 2005, 144–5, 155–7, who asserts that Polybius is silent regarding Phylarchus's politics. For a discussion of how Diodorus Siculus arouses sympathy, see Baumann in this vol.
22 The text of the *Ion* is from Burnet 1968, III. Of course, the *Ion* is concerned with epic, though for Plato, Homer is the preeminent tragedian. Cf., Pl. *R*. 10.595c1–3, 10.598d7–8, 10.607a2–3.

τοῖς πράγμασιν οἴεταί σου εἶναι ἡ ψυχή οἷς λέγεις ἐνθουσιάζουσα, ἢ ἐν Ἰθάκῃ οὖσιν ἢ ἐν Τροίᾳ ἢ ὅπως ἂν καὶ τὰ ἔπη ἔχῃ;
ΙΩΝ: Ὡς ἐναργές μοι τοῦτο, ὦ Σώκρατες, τὸ τεκμήριον εἶπες· οὐ γάρ σε ἀποκρυψάμενος ἐρῶ. ἐγὼ γὰρ ὅταν ἐλεινόν τι λέγω, δακρύων ἐμπίμπλανταί μου οἱ ὀφθαλμοί· ὅταν τε φοβερὸν ἢ δεινόν, ὀρθαὶ αἱ τρίχες ἵστανται ὑπὸ φόβου καὶ ἡ καρδία πηδᾷ.

Soc.: Come on then, tell me this, Ion, and don't hold back what I'm going to ask you. When you recite your poem well and drive your spectators out of their senses to the utmost degree...are you in your senses then? Or are you beside yourself and does your soul – in ecstasy from the things you are saying – think it is at the event, whether that's in Ithaca, or Troy or wherever the poems lead it?
Ion: How vivid this proof you speak of is for me, Socrates. I shall answer, and not hide anything from you. It's true: whenever I say anything pitiable, my eyes fill full of tears. And whenever something fearful or dreadful, the hair stands straight up on my terrified head and my heart pounds.

We see this sympathy again in the *Phaedrus*, where Socrates emphasizes its contagious aspect (Pl. *Phdr.* 234d1–6):[23]

Δαιμονίως μὲν οὖν, ὦ ἑταῖρε, ὥστε με ἐκπλαγῆναι. καὶ τοῦτο ἐγὼ ἔπαθον διὰ σέ, ὦ Φαῖδρε, πρός σε ἀποβλέπων, ὅτι ἐμοὶ ἐδόκεις γάνυσθαι ὑπὸ τοῦ λόγου μεταξὺ ἀναγιγνώσκων· ἡγούμενος γὰρ σὲ μᾶλλον ἢ ἐμὲ ἐπαΐειν περὶ τῶν τοιούτων σοὶ εἱπόμην, καὶ ἑπόμενος συνεβάκχευσα μετὰ σοῦ τῆς θείας κεφαλῆς.

[Your speech was] Divine, my friend, and so I was driven from my wits. And I felt this because of you, Phaedrus, as I watched you, I thought you lit up from the speech as you read it. And because I thought that you understood these things more than I, I followed you, and following, I joined in Bacchic revelry with your divine perfection.

We find a similar understanding of sympathy in Aristotle's *Politics* (Arist. *Pol.* 8.1340a12–13):[24] ἔτι δὲ ἀκροώμενοι τῶν μιμήσεων γίγνονται πάντες συμπαθεῖς, καὶ χωρὶς τῶν ῥυθμῶν καὶ τῶν μελῶν αὐτῶν. (And furthermore, everyone who listens to imitations becomes *sympathetic*, even apart from the rhythm and melodies alone.) In the context of this passage, Aristotle is speaking specifically of music, but his focus widens when he asserts that all imitation evokes sympathy.[25] Polybius is not simply accusing Phylarchus of attempting to instill

---

23 The text of the *Phaedrus* is from Burnet 1968, II.
24 Text of the *Politics* is from Ross 1964.
25 And furthermore, music and tragedy are both fundamentally mimetic and somewhat intertwined: Arist. *Po.* 1.1447a13–16 (Text from Kassel 1968): ἐποποιία δὴ καὶ ἡ τῆς τραγῳδίας ποίησις ἔτι δὲ κωμῳδία καὶ ἡ διθυραμβοποιητικὴ καὶ τῆς αὐλητικῆς ἡ πλείστη καὶ κιθαριστικῆς πᾶσαι τυγχάνουσιν οὖσαι μιμήσεις τὸ σύνολον. (Indeed, epic and the poetry of tragedy and also comedy and dithyramb and most flute and kithara playing, speaking generally, are all, as it turns out, mimetic.); Arist. *Po.* 26.1462a14–17: ἔπειτα διότι πάντ' ἔχει ὅσαπερ ἡ ἐποποιία

certain political beliefs in his readers. He complains also about the method by which Phylarchus achieves his aims; namely, he presents a vivid description of the mental paralysis of the townsfolk, brought on by anger and pity, in order to produce a similar paralysis induced by similar emotions in his readers. Phylarchus does not allow the reader to experience the emotion that would be appropriate, given all the facts. It might well be that it is only in Polybius's biased view that the emotions Phylarchus elicits are inappropriate. But whether or not Phylarchus sincerely believes that Mantineia was a violent travesty is beside the point for Polybius. It is Phylarchus's duty to narrate the events in such a way that the reader can draw his own conclusions, emotional or otherwise, based on a complete retelling of the events. To simply elicit ἔκπληξις by its depiction is the province of tragedy.

Polybius is not the first author to associate the goal of tragedy with ἔκπληξις. We find a similar view, for instance, in the *Poetics*. In chapter 6, the catharsis of tragic emotions is the genre's primary end. Later, however, Aristotle restates the end of tragedy with different vocabulary (Arist. *Po*. 25.1460b23–26): ἀδύνατα πεποίηται, ἡμάρτηται· ἀλλ' ὀρθῶς ἔχει, εἰ τυγχάνει τοῦ τέλους τοῦ αὑτῆς (τὸ γὰρ τέλος εἴρηται), εἰ οὕτως ἐκπληκτικώτερον ἢ αὐτὸ ἢ ἄλλο ποιεῖ μέρος. [It is a mistake to include impossibilities, but it is possible to do so correctly, if they achieve the goal of tragedy (which I have stated), that is, if they make this or another part more emotionally shattering.] Elizabeth Belfiore has argued that Aristotle speaks of ἔκπληξις as a type of tragic fear in this passage.[26] If she is right, it is possible that Aristotle is restating his innovative description of cathartic tragedy in a more traditional vocabulary of ekplectic tragedy.

The author of *On the Sublime* is more direct and unambiguously asserts that the goal of tragedy is to arouse ἔκπληξις ([Longin.] 15.2):[27] …τέλος ἐστὶν ἔκπληξις… (…the goal [of tragedy] is mental paralysis…) When Polybius makes ἔκπληξις a defining feature of tragedy, therefore, he assumes a position that is consistent with a long traditon of dramatic criticism.

(καὶ γὰρ τῷ μέτρῳ ἔξεστι χρῆσθαι), καὶ ἔτι οὐ μικρὸν μέρος τὴν μουσικήν [καὶ τὰς ὄψεις], δι' ἧς αἱ ἡδοναὶ συνίστανται ἐναργέστατα. (Next, [tragedy] has whatever epic has (for it can also use hexameters), and no lesser a share of music [and spectacle], through which the pleasure is contrived in the most vivid way.).

26 Belfiore 1992, 221–222.
27 Text is from Russell 1964.

2 The elements of tragedy

Polybius's attack reveals that he considers the arousal of ἔκπληξις to require a combination of narrative elements. As I have already shown, the narration of emotional scenes alone does not constitute a tragedy. Polybius is not the only ancient critic to consider tragedy to be comprised of several parts. Aristotle, for instance, defines six parts of tragedy.[28] Plutarch presents a similarly complex picture. For him, the visual aspect of tragedy is the most important. Second is the wondrous sound. Third, story or plot, and fourth, the emotions. Finally is the pleasure of the words.[29]

Therefore, Polybius's complex view of tragedy reflects a long tradition that considered that the tragic effect was produced not by any single element of tragedy alone, but through a combination of subject matter, diction, spectacle, and other elements. In fact, a combination of such elements, as R. B. Rutherford's recent comprehensive treatment suggests, is perhaps best termed "tragic style".[30]

In the attack on Phylarchus, Polybius identifies several elements of tragic history, but for the rest of this study, I will focus on sensationalism (τερατεῖαι)

---

28 Arist. *Po.* 6.1450a7–10: ἀνάγκη οὖν πάσης τῆς τραγῳδίας μέρη εἶναι ἕξ, καθ' ὃ ποιά τις ἐστὶν ἡ τραγῳδία· ταῦτα δ' ἐστὶ μῦθος καὶ ἤθη καὶ λέξις καὶ διάνοια καὶ ὄψις καὶ μελοποιία. (Necessarily, therefore, the parts of every tragedy are six, according to which tragedy of whatever sort is [composed]. These are plot, character, diction, thought, spectacle, and song.).

29 Plu. *Mor.* <5> 348b11–c8: ἤνθησε δ' ἡ τραγῳδία καὶ διεβοήθη, θαυμαστὸν ἀκρόαμα καὶ θέαμα τῶν τότ' ἀνθρώπων γενομένη καὶ παρασχοῦσα τοῖς μύθοις καὶ τοῖς πάθεσιν ἀπάτην, ὡς Γοργίας φησίν [DK 82 B 23], ἣν ὅ τ' ἀπατήσας δικαιότερος τοῦ μὴ ἀπατήσαντος, καὶ ὁ ἀπατηθεὶς σοφώτερος τοῦ μὴ ἀπατηθέντος. ὁ μὲν γὰρ ἀπατήσας δικαιότερος, ὅτι τοῦθ' ὑποσχόμενος πεποίηκεν· ὁ δ' ἀπατηθεὶς σοφώτερος· εὐάλωτον γὰρ ὑφ' ἡδονῆς λόγων τὸ μὴ ἀναίσθητον. (But tragedy flourished and was celebrated, because it was the spectacle – the sound and sight the people of that time enjoyed – and it furnished deception through stories and emotions. As Gorgias says, "He who deceives is more just than he who has not, and he who is deceived is wiser than the one who is not." The one who has deceived is more just because he promised to do it, and he did it. And the one who was deceived is wiser because not being easily swept up by the pleasure of the words is senselessness.) Text of Plutarch is from Nachstädt 1971, II.

30 Cf., e.g., Rutherford 2012, 18: [In the *Frogs*,] "The actual criticisms of the tragedians relate to both form (vocabulary, music) and content or moral impact (Aeschylus inspired men to heroism and war, Euripides corrupts them with decadent ideas). Lines are cited and criticised for swollen or extravagant compounds (924–6, 928–30, 937), redundancy of language (1154, 1173), monotony of construction (1177–1248, on the younger poet's prologues). Form and content come together in the attack on the 'the Muse of Euripides', for loose and effeminate metre and music are associated with 'low' or ignoble subject matter in the brilliant parody of monody (1329–63 and context cf. 849). The blend of technical and moral fault-finding is typical of much ancient criticism."

and the narration of possible utterances (τοὺς ἐνδεχομένους λόγους). The best place to probe for these elements is in the *Histories* of Phylarchus, and therefore our best opportunity to consider whether Polybius's criticism is in any way fair, is in the extant fragments of Phylarchus. In addition to the challenges inherent in the study of any fragmentary author, two particular problems distort the interpretation of these fragments. The first is the influence of Polybius's criticism. Details that might otherwise escape notice entirely become amplified – perhaps unduly – in the search for tragic history. The second distortion is the fact that a significant majority, roughly half of those collected by Jacoby, are recorded by Athenaeus. This author, even if questions of how faithfully he reproduced his sources are set aside, seems to have employed criteria for selecting fragments that coincidentally reinforce Polybius's criticism.[31] Therefore, conclusions drawn from a study of the fragments will never provide absolute answers to questions about the nature of Phylarchus's *Histories*. Nevertheless, given that the overwhelming majority of the surviving fragments tend to corroborate Polybius's description of Phylarchus's content, it can be safely concluded that Phylarchus did – at least occasionally – indulge in the kinds of narration that Polybius describes. Given that my purpose is not to argue that Phylarchus is untrustworthy or chronically prone to tragic style, but rather to elucidate Polybius's conceptions of tragedy, tragic history, and historiography, the standard of proof that the fragments allow – especially since it is the only evidence available at all – must suffice.

As Polybius suggests, Phylarchus's fragments do reveal an interest in sensational tales.[32] Many of the fragments contain sensational detail in the broadest sense. For instance, Phylarchus records that Ariamnes provided lavish feasts for all Celts, and any passers-by, for a year (F2); Milon of Croton ate a whole bull (F3); the Byzantians rent out their beds, wives included (F7); Demetrius wittily insulted Lysimachus (F12); the Iberians are so stingy, they drink only water and eat only one meal a day (F13); the water of the Arabian Gulf causes priapism

---

[31] Brunt (1980) argues that Athenaeus generally reproduces his sources reliably. See, e. g., 480: "he quotes Herodotus in twelve passages more or less verbatim, and provides substantially accurate paraphrases in four others." Vanhaegendoren (2010, 425) concurs: "le fragment [he is speaking particularly of FGrHist 81F24] dans son ensemble est probablement très proche de, sinon identique à la mise en forme qu' avait ce passage dans l'ouevre de Phylarque. Tout d'abord, Athéné a tendance à "citer" assez fidèlement." Olson (2015), on the other hand, stresses that Athenaeus's idiosyncratic criteria for selection does not allow any safe conclusions regarding the nature or character of any complete work of any author quoted. It is a conclusion already central to Brunt's argument, cf. 494.

[32] cf. Jacoby 1963 *ad* FGrHist81F2: "sind θαυμάσια und ἴδια in menge vorhanden."

(F17); the Aetolian Kouretes are fastidious with their hair (F23); Sandrokottos of India sent Seleucus some aphrodisiacs (F35b); those who drink from a spring in Kleitor can no longer tolerate the smell of wine (F63); Egyptian beans had never been sown outside of Egypt, or if they had, they never bore fruit, so when Alexander II of Epirus learned some had grown in a marsh near the river Thyamis, he placed a guard over them, whereupon the marsh dried up (F65); to purge the city Elaeusa of a plague, the king Demophon, following an oracle, selected by lot and sacrificed a noble daughter every year, but because he refused to include his own daughters in the lottery, the nobleman Mastusius, whose own daughter had been sacrificed, killed the king's daughters, mixed their blood with wine in a bowl, and served it to the king who learned the truth and had Mastusius and the bowl tossed into the sea thereafter called 'Mastusian' in which there is a harbor called 'the Bowl' (F69); Dimoetes married his niece, but after he learned of her incestuous affair with her brother, she cursed him as she hanged herself, and when he found the corpse of a woman washed up on the beach, he loved it until it decomposed to a point where he was forced to bury it at which time he killed himself at the corpse's tomb (F71); whomever a Thibian looks upon, or breathes on, or speaks to, grows sick (F79a), and Thibians have two pupils in one eye and one in the shape of a horse in the other, and they cannot sink in water (F79b); every night, before going to sleep, every Skythian puts a white pebble in his quiver if he passed the day without pain, and a black one if he did not, and when a Skythian dies, his family counts his pebbles to see if he had a happy life (F83).

Much of his sensationalism concerns animals. He records that it often rains fish, tadpoles, and frogs (F4a); the nymph Cyrene killed a lion (F16); a Milesian, Koiranus, saved a dolphin from a fisherman's net, was later rescued from a shipwreck by a dolphin, and, when he died, a pod of dolphins followed his funeral procession (F26); Egyptians rear and train asps, and at the snap of a finger, the asps come to the table and eat barley groats (F27); one asp, whose whelp killed her master's son, killed the offending whelp and never returned to the house (F28); the dying queen of India entrusted her child to an elephant named Nicaea, who would whisk away flies from the baby's cradle and rock it if the baby cried (F36); a young boy's pet eagle nursed him when he fell sick and threw itself on his pyre when he died (F61a, b).

Some of his sensationalism is mythical. He tells us Daphne loved Leucippos and Apollo loved Daphne (F32a), and after she became a tree, she gained the gift of prophesy, and she was the Pasiphaë who had a temple at Thalamae (F32b); the magistrates of the Sybarites, after they killed a Crotonian embassy, thought they saw Hera vomiting bile in the agora, and a spring of blood appeared in her temple (F45); Phayllus, who loved the wife of the Oetaean chief Ariston, promised her anything, so she asked for a necklace that hung in the temple of Athena Pronoia that was once Eriphyle's, and, when he gave it to her, she wore it until, like Eriphyle, she burned in a fire started by her youngest son (F70).

He also shows an interest in sensational superlatives. He asserts that Antiochus was a spectacular drunk (F6); Isanthes surpassed everyone in wantonnes (F20); Timosa the concubine of Oxyartos was the most beautiful of women (F34).

Even if, as Schepens argues, it would be "foolhardy to deduce the true nature and value of Phylarchus' historiography from the fragments which survive in Athenaeus," these episodes, regardless of their historicity, certainly sound like the kind of tangential, sensational, and titillating material that Polybius tends to reject and can obviously cast light on Polybius's opinions about the elements of what he calls "tragic history."[33] In fact, certain fragments of Phylarchus closely resemble material that Polybius explicitly rejects. Fragment 33, for instance, preserved by Lydus (Joannes Laurentius), records that neither women nor dogs nor flies enter the temple of Kronos.[34] It is possible, of course, that women could be restricted from a sacred space. The exclusion of dogs would prove somewhat more difficult, particularly when roasting sacrificial meat, though perhaps desirable, particularly when roasting sacrificial meat.[35] Excluding flies, no matter how desirable, would require nothing short of a miracle.[36] Though Polybius does not speak directly of the temple of Kronos and its miraculous characteristics, he does comment on similar assertions by historiographers when he ridicules reports that statues of Artemis Cindyas or Artemis Astias are

---

33 Schepens 2005, 161. Of the 29 fragments I mention above, 13 (16, 17, 27, 28, 32a, 32b, 64a, 64b, 69, 70, 71, 79a, 79b) are preserved in authors other than Athenaeus. Lendle's conclusion (1992, 199), to which Schepens (2005, 161) subscribes, "die von Polybios in bezug auf die Frage der Glaubwürdigkeit des Phylarchos aufgestellte und von Plutarch nachgesprochene Behauptung...wird weder durch erhaltene Fragmente noch durch die plutarchische Erzählung noch durch die von Polybios beigebrachten Beweismittel erhärtet" is narrowly focused on the issue of Phylarchus's credibility.
34 FGrHist 81F33: ἐν δὲ τῶι κατ' αὐτὸν (sc. Κρόνον) ἱερῶι, ὥς φησι Φύλ‹αρχος ἐν τῆι ἑ›πτακαιδεκάτηι καὶ Μένανδρός γε ‹ἐν› ᾶ (III), οὔτε γυνὴ οὔτε ‹κύων οὔτ›ε μυῖ‹α› εἰσήιει. (As Phylarchus says in his 17th book and as Menandros in his first, neither woman nor dog nor fly ever entered the temple of Kronos.)
35 On dogs and their inclusion or exclusion at various temples, cf. McDonough 1999.
36 It is possible that Phylarchus is speaking of the temple of Kronos in Athens. Nothing is known of the architecture of this temple because Hadrian's rebuilding obscured the foundation completely. However, Lobeck (1829, 1096) believed Phylarchus confused the temple of Kronos with the Ara Maxima of Heracles (cf. Mayer 1894, 1494; Pohlenz 1922, 1983; Wellmann 1909, 2746), which may have been constructed like a *sacellum* (cf. McDonough 1999, 468), so dogs may have been easily excluded. As McDonough (1999, 468–71) points out, however, the Ara Maxima did not have a roof, so flies (and other insects) could have easily entered.

never touched by precipitation, or Theopompus' report that those who enter the temenos on Mt. Lycaeum cast no shadow; such sensationalism can be pardoned insofar as it promotes reverence, but historiographers should not take such things too far.[37] Similarly, Phylarchus records the precise date for the fall of Troy, the seventh of Thargelion waning [FGrHist 81F74, preserved by Plutarch (Cam. 19)]. Polybius rejects this type of precision regarding events of the distant past.[38]

Fragment 49,[39] preserved in Pliny's *Historia Naturalis*, provides another example in Phylarchus of something Polybius rejects, but in this case, the habit is one that Polybius explicitly describes as Phylarchean. Phylarchus records that, when Antiochus[40] fell in battle, the Galatian who killed him, Centaretus, triumphantly mounted the dead man's horse. The horse became angry and threw itself into a precipice along with its rider, killing them both. This fragment records precisely the kind of misattribution of cause that Polybius accuses Phylarchus of habitually presenting. It is quite possible that the man who killed Antiochus mounted the horse and horse and rider subsequently died in a fall. The cause of that fall is very unlikely, however, to have been the horse's indignation at the Gaul's boastful celebration. The episode as Phylarchus records it heightens the drama of the scene by sensationally attributing the Gaul's death to his own prideful celebration – a proper peripeteia.

All of the scenes above could fall under the category of sensationalism or τερατεία as the term is usually understood. But there is perhaps another sense of the word that Polybius has in mind. The verb τερατεύεσθαι means not only "to talk marvels," but also "to gesticulate wildly," as at Aeschines 1.94: ἀποθαυμάζων οὖν περιέρχεται καὶ τερατευόμενος κατὰ τὴν ἀγορὰν εἰ ὁ αὐτὸς πεπόρνευταί τε καὶ τὰ πατρῷα κατεδήδοκεν. (In amazement, then, that the same man both prostituted himself and squandered his family estate, he went up and down the agora gesticulating wildly.) We might consider, then, that Polybius might mean something more like "verbal acrobatics."

---

[37] Plb. 16.12.9: δοτέον ἐστὶ συγγνώμην ἐνίοις τῶν συγγραφέων τερατευομένοις καὶ λογοποιοῦσι περὶ τὰ τοιαῦτα· τὸ δ' ὑπεραῖρον οὐ συγχωρητέον. (Pardon must be given to some historians who sensationalise and make up stories about these sorts of things, but one must not concede excess.)

[38] Cf. Walbank 1957–79 *ad* 4.2.3.

[39] FGrHist 81F49.

[40] Wilcken (1894, 2454) attributes this death to Antiochus I Soter. Bevan (1902, 203) to Antiochus Hierax. Aelian attributes the death of Centaretus to Antiochus' vengeful horse without mentioning Phyalrchus (*NA* 6.44).

With this sense in mind, other qualities of Phylarchus's fragments throw light on Polybius's complaints. There is, for instance, Polybius's sarcastic retort that Phylarchus referred to Mantinea as "the oldest and greatest city of all Arcadia".[41] As commentators have often pointed out, the language Polybius ascribes to Phylarchus brings to mind Homer, who includes Mantinea in the catalog of ships.[42] The fact that the formulation brings to mind the elevated language of poetry confirms that Polybius is criticising Phylarchus's diction and style as much as his reliability.

Polybius's criticism of Phylarchus's narration of the death of Agathocles also casts light on both senses of τερατεία, and furthermore illuminates his complaint that Phylarchus narrates all the utterances his subjects might possibly have made (Plb. 2.59.1–3):

> Πάλιν Ἀριστόμαχον τὸν Ἀργεῖόν φησιν, ἄνδρα τῆς ἐπιφανεστάτης οἰκίας ὑπάρχοντα καὶ τετυραννηκότα μὲν Ἀργείων, πεφυκότα δ' ἐκ τυράννων, ὑποχείριον Ἀντιγόνῳ καὶ τοῖς Ἀχαιοῖς γενόμενον εἰς Κεγχρεὰς ἀπαχθῆναι καὶ στρεβλούμενον ἀποθανεῖν, ἀδικώτατα καὶ δεινότατα παθόντα πάντων ἀνθρώπων. τηρῶν δὲ καὶ περὶ ταύτην τὴν πρᾶξιν ὁ συγγραφεὺς τὸ καθ' αὑτὸν ἰδίωμα φωνάς τινας πλάττει διὰ τῆς νυκτὸς αὐτοῦ στρεβλουμένου προσπιπτούσας τοῖς σύνεγγυς κατοικοῦσιν, ὧν τοὺς μὲν ἐκπληττομένους τὴν ἀσέβειαν, τοὺς δ' ἀπιστοῦντας, τοὺς δ' ἀγανακτοῦντας ἐπὶ τοῖς γινομένοις προστρέχειν πρὸς τὴν οἰκίαν φησίν. περὶ μὲν οὖν τῆς τοιαύτης τερατείας παρείσθω· δεδήλωται γὰρ ἀρκούντως.

> Again, he says that Aristomachus of Argos was a man from the most distinguished house – not only a tyrant but born from tyrants – and when he became the prisoner of Antigonus and the Achaeans, he was dragged off to Cenchreae and killed on the rack, suffering, of all men, most unjustly and most dreadfully. And the historian, preserving his personal idiom for this affair, too, fabricates the very cries of the man on the rack coming through the night to the ears of those living nearby. He says some neighbors were paralyzed at the impiety, others could not believe, yet others, in violent distress at the affair rushed to the house. Let this suffice, then, for sensationalism of that sort, for it is sufficiently proven.

Polybius provides a great deal of information here. Though he uses the same key vocabulary as elsewhere, the kind of sensationalism in this instance is slightly different than that in the fragments described above. Aristomachus was certainly executed at the command of Antigonus and Aratus, though Polybius does not

---

41 Plb. 2.56.6: φησί...τὴν ἀρχαιοτάτην καὶ μεγίστην πόλιν τῶν κατὰ τὴν Ἀρκαδίαν...
42 Hom. *Il.* 2.607: Μαντινέην ἐρατεινήν. Walbank 1957–79, ad loc.: "despite [the reference in Homer], the synoecism of historical Mantinea in the plain, out of five demes (Strabo, viii.337) is comparatively late.... But in any case the present passage is tendentious in Phylarchus, and ironical in Polybius." Haegemans/Kosmetatou 2005, 131 n. 32: "Mantinea is mentioned and praised by Homer."

believe he was tortured,⁴³ so Phylarchus's account is not pure fiction. The sensationalism here has more to do with some of the other elements of tragic history that Polybius has defined. In the first place, Phylarchus desires to make the reader feel his own indignation (Plb. 2.59.5): βουλόμενος αὔξειν αὐτοῦ τὴν δόξαν καὶ παραστήσασθαι τοὺς ἀκούοντας εἰς τὸ μᾶλλον αὐτῷ συναγανακτεῖν ἐφ' οἷς ἔπαθεν. (He wishes to increase (Agathocles') reputation and to bring the readers to share all the more his own indignation at the things (Agathocles) suffered.). This type of emotional manipulation is a consistent point of Polybius's attack on tragic history and, as we have seen, a common view of the nature of tragic poetry in antiquity: together, the reader and the writer experience the emotions depicted in the narrative.

In this instance, however, Polybius is more explicit about the imagined utterances that help to make historical accounts tragic in nature. His accusation is crystal clear: Phylarchus fabricates the cries that rang out through the night and he depicted the various responses of the townsfolk who lived within earshot of the rack. In dramatic terms, Phylarchus invented dialogue. The scene itself could be straight from Sophocles; in fact, in the *Hippolytus* when Theseus finds the tablet dangling from Phaedra's dead wrist, the shout he raises summons a body of citizens to the stage.⁴⁴ As a matter of fact, the depiction of the βοή is somewhat frequent in extant tragedy.⁴⁵ The scene Phylarchus constructs of the death of Agathocles exhibits tragic conventions, and both the cries of the tyrant and the reactions of the townspeople suggest the invention of the kind of dialogue appropriate to tragic productions.

Of course, vivid representation of events is not the sole province of tragic history or even of tragedy. Like Phylarchus (cf. Plb. 2.56.8) and the tragedians, rhetoricians also strive to put vivid scenes before our eyes. In a recent lucid discussion, R. Webb explores the concept of ἐνάργεια in rhetorical handbooks. She points out that for Demetrios (first century BCE), ἐνάργεια results from extreme detail (ἀκριβολογία), and particularly from a detailed description of attendant circumstances (τὰ συμβαίνοντα).⁴⁶ This detail seems, at first, enticing for the interpretation of Polybius, as he complains explicitly that it is in his overly detailed narration of attendant circumstances that Phylarchus errs, so perhaps Polybius has confused tragedy with rhetoric. Once again, however, it is not simply the

---

43 Plb. 2.60.8.
44 E. *Hipp.* 882–4.
45 cf. Barrett 1964 *ad* 884n (and addenda, 435), *ad* 902; Taplin 1978, 115; Rutherford 2012, 193 n. 62.
46 Webb 2009, 92. For a discussion of ἐνάργεια in Polybius, see Schepens 1975. For a discussion of ἐνάργεια in Greek historiography more generally, see Walker 1993.

vivid nature of the detail that makes Phylarchus's narrative tragic. Granted, when it comes to ἐνάργεια, the lines between rhetoric, tragedy, and history, are not clearly drawn.[47] Nevertheless, the author of *On the Sublime* makes a very telling distinction. For him, tragedy and rhetoric use detailed narration to two different ends: in poetry, the aim is ἔκπληξις, but in rhetoric it is ἐνάργεια.[48] As we have seen before, when the author's primary concern is to astonish his readers, the author is striving for a tragic effect.

In fragment 18, Phylarchus goes beyond using tragic conventions and simply narrates the plot of a tragedy when he describes how Asclepius restored sight to the sons of Phineus by striking them with a thunderbolt. Aeschylus wrote one play about Phineus,[49] and Sophocles wrote two.[50] Polybius explicitly rejects the inclusion of details of tragic plots in historiography, though the plot he mentions specifically is the fall of Phaethon (Plb. 2.16.13):[51]

> τἆλλα δὲ τὰ περὶ τὸν ποταμὸν τοῦτον ἱστορούμενα παρὰ τοῖς Ἕλλησι, λέγω δὴ τὰ περὶ Φαέθοντα καὶ τὴν ἐκείνου πτῶσιν, ἔτι δὲ τὰ δάκρυα τῶν αἰγείρων καὶ τοὺς μελανείμονας τοὺς περὶ τὸν ποταμὸν οἰκοῦντας, οὕς φασι τὰς ἐσθῆτας εἰσέτι νῦν φορεῖν τοιαύτας ἀπὸ τοῦ κατὰ Φαέθοντα πένθους, καὶ πᾶσαν δὴ τὴν τραγικὴν καὶ ταύτῃ προσεοικυῖαν ὕλην ἐπὶ μὲν τοῦ παρόντος ὑπερθησόμεθα διὰ τὸ μὴ λίαν καθήκειν τῷ τῆς προκατασκευῆς γένει τὴν περὶ τῶν τοιούτων ἀκριβολογίαν.

> The other stories the Greeks retail about this river, I mean about Phaethon and his fall, and then the tears of the poplars and the mourning dress of those who live by the river, whom they say still to this day dress like that in their sorrow for Phaethon, and all tragic material

---

47 See, e.g., Webb 2009, 97, 98, 100.
48 15.2: ὡς δ' ἕτερόν τι ἡ ῥητορικὴ φαντασία βούλεται καὶ ἕτερον ἡ παρὰ ποιηταῖς οὐκ ἂν λάθοι σε, οὐδ' ὅτι τῆς μὲν ἐν ποιήσει τέλος ἐστὶν ἔκπληξις, τῆς δ' ἐν λόγοις ἐνάργεια, ἀμφότεραι δ' ὅμως τό τε ⟨παθητικὸν⟩ ἐπιζητοῦσι καὶ τὸ συγκεκινημένον. (You will not fail to notice that rhetorical representation wants one thing and that representation in poetry wants another. In poetry the aim is astonishment and in arguments vividness; nevertheless, both seek ⟨an emotional response⟩ and sympathetic emotion.) Webb 2009 discusses the passage on 101.
49 Aeschylus: Radt 1985 (TrGF 258–60), 359–60. On the play and its relationship to the tetralogy of 472, cf. Sommerstein 2012, esp. 95–96, 101–2, and 104–5.
50 Sophocles: Radt 1999 (TrGF), 484–489. Sutton 1984, 106 argues that TrGF 710 (Ar. *Pl.* 635–8) represents the version Phylarchus follows. Cf. Radt *ad loc.* Arist. *Po.* 16.1455a10, if not referring to Aeschylus' play or these of Sophocles, could suggest an unattested *Phineidae*, (cf. Sutton 1984, 106–7). The subject remained a popular one for tragedies, as Accius' *Phinidae* attests. Cf. also Winnington-Ingram 1980 105–109.
51 Aeschylus and Euripides each wrote plays about Phaethon's fall: Aeschylus, *Heliades*: Radt 1985, 185–189 (TrGF 67–73a); Euripides *Phaethon*: Kannicht 2004, 798–826 (TrGF 72F771–786). On this play, cf. Diggle 1970, particularly 4–7 for the myth in Greek literature, 27–31 for Aeschylus' *Heliades*. Euripides also mentions the amber tears of Phaethon's sisters at E. *Hipp.* 737–41.

like that, I pass over for the present because minute elaboration in matters like that is absolutely unsuited in an introduction like mine.

Granted, Polybius's rejection of this kind of tragic material is a *paralipsis* and so provides him the opportunity to include the tragic material while rejecting it, but we see nothing like the elaboration that characterizes the fragment of Phylarchus.

In fact, many of Phylarchus's fragments preserve direct quotations of the historical subjects of the sort that seem to have characterised the death scene of Agathocles.[52] In fragment 40, for instance, Phylarchus relates a tale concerning Ptolemy II Philadelphus. The fragment centers on Ptolemy's debasement and in particular his claim to have found a way to become immortal. After recovering from an attack of gout, Ptolemy gazes through his window at some Egyptians having a picnic and relaxing on the banks of the Nile. The fragment records the utterance of Ptolemy himself (FGrHist 81F40): ὦ τάλας ἐγώ, τὸ μηδὲ τούτων ἕνα γενέσθαι (O wretch that I am, never to be one of these men.). The fragment contains several elements that may be fairly labeled tragic in Polybius's terms.

In the first place, it is a bit of gossip, concerned more with the wantonness of the king than with any detail that might have significant bearing on, for instance, how Ptolemy succeeded in capturing Damsascus.[53] In the second place, it is likely a fabrication, given that it appears to be something Ptolemy muttered to himself when alone, and therefore not something observed by the historian, his informants, or any of his sources. Consequently, it is one of the possible and imagined utterances that we hear Polybius single out as a feature of Phylarchus's tragic style. Additionally, it is an utterance appropriate for a character in a tragedy. The precise collocation ὦ τάλας ἐγώ appears seven times in Sophocles[54] and seven times in Euripides.[55] Exclamations of this sort are essential to tragedy, and the exclamation in Phylarchus is tragic in style according to any reasonable estimation.[56] Given that Polybius specifically mentions the attention Phylarchus pays to the tears and lamentations of the citizens of Mantineia as they are led off into slavery (Plb. 2.56.7: θρήνους ἀνδρῶν καὶ γυναικῶν), Ptolemy's tragic excla-

---

52 Others include (but this list is not exhaustive): F1, F11, F12, F21, F24, and F41. On direct speech in Phylarchus, cf. Vanhaegendoren 2010, 424–428.
53 Cf. Polyaen. 4.15.
54 *Aj.* 981, *Ant.* 1211, *Ph.* 744, *OC* 753, 847, 1338, 1401.
55 *Andromeda* FGrT 122 (Kannicht 2004, 244), *Hipp.* 875, 1090, *Ph.* 1335, 1346, 1599, *IA* 536. cf. also *Hipp.* 817–8.
56 On the centrality of exclamation in tragedy, cf. Rutherford 2012, 82.

mation becomes impossible to ignore, just as it is impossible to ignore that such an utterance is out of place in Polybius's brand of historiography.

As Rutherford has noted, in some of the most emotional passages of Herodotus and Thucydides, like Croesus's reaction to the death of Atys, or the abandonment of the Athenian camp on Sicily, both authors describe lamentations, but neither ever directly quotes a lamentation anywhere in their works.[57] This observation is particularly significant in light of Polybius's description of the betrayal and capture of Achaeus in Sardis in 213 (Plb. 8.15–21). On its surface, the episode is one that could be considered tragic. There is, for instance, Polybius's personal bias: he hates Cretans[58], and the villains in this tale are Cretans. Furthermore, there is a reversal of fortune: Achaeus passes from the verge of escape to utter destruction. There is great emotion: Antiochus III Megas is stunned into silence by his unexpected victory, and the experience is so overwhelming, that he cries. At dawn, when Antiochus' friends gather at his tent, they are amazed at the turn of events. There is torture: the Seleucids cut off Achaeus' ears, nose, tongue, lips, and hands, then cut off his head, sew it up in the skin of an ass, and crucify his body. There is a grieving widow, and in fact, this is the most telling detail. When Laodice is brought word of her husband's fate, she and the others in the citadel express their grief (Plb. 8.21.6):

> ...οἰμωγὴ καὶ θρῆνοι παράλογοι κατεῖχον τοὺς περὶ τὴν ἀκρόπολιν, οὐχ οὕτως διὰ τὴν πρὸς τὸν Ἀχαιὸν εὔνοιαν ὡς διὰ τὸ παράδοξον καὶ τελέως ἀνέλπιστον ἑκάστῳ φαίνεσθαι τὸ συμβεβηκός...
>
> ...wailing and lamentation beyond comprehension seized those in the citadel, not so much because of affection for Achaeus as because the event seemed absolutely surprising and unexpected to every person there...

The difference between Polybius's narration here, at a moment when Laodice and the citizens of Sardis realize they will be killed or captured, and Phylarchus's narration of Ptolemy's recovery from an attack of gout, illustrate perfectly the assertion that Polybius makes in his attack on his predecessor. Polybius relates the emotion; Phylarchus depicts it, going even so far as to place an actual tragic song in Ptolemy's mouth.

Another interesting example of Polybius's tendency to avoid the kind of tragic dramatization he condemns comes in the comparison of his description of a

---

[57] Rutherford 2012, 83. For a discussion of emotional scenes in Herodotus and Thucydides, see Liotsakis in this volume.
[58] Cf. Walbank 1957–79 ad 8.16.4.

skirmish between Hannibal's men and some barbarians on the banks of the Rhone and his account of Cynoscephalae (Plb. 3.43.7–8):

> ταχὺ δὲ τούτου γενομένου, καὶ τῶν ἐν τοῖς πλοίοις ἁμιλλωμένων μὲν πρὸς ἀλλήλους μετὰ κραυγῆς, διαγωνιζομένων δὲ πρὸς τὴν τοῦ ποταμοῦ βίαν, τῶν δὲ στρατοπέδων ἀμφοτέρων ἐξ ἑκατέρου τοῦ μέρους παρὰ τὰ χείλη τοῦ ποταμοῦ παρεστώτων, καὶ τῶν μὲν ἰδίων συναγωνιώντων καὶ παρακολουθούντων μετὰ κραυγῆς, τῶν δὲ κατὰ πρόσωπον βαρβάρων παιανιζόντων καὶ προκαλουμένων τὸν κίνδυνον, ἦν τὸ γινόμενον ἐκπληκτικὸν καὶ παραστατικὸν ἀγωνίας.

> And this [Hannibal's order that the boats row upstream] happened right away. And those in the boats at once vied with each other with shouts and at the same time struggled against the force of the river. And both armies were standing along the brink of the river on either side, the Carthaginian side sharing the agony of their comrades and following intently with a shout, the barbarian side in front chanting and challenging their foes to fight. The spectacle of the struggle was shocking and electrifying.

> (Plb. 18.25.1)
> Γενομένης δὲ τῆς ἐξ ἀμφοῖν συμπτώσεως μετὰ βίας καὶ κραυγῆς ὑπερβαλλούσης, ὡς ἂν ἀμφοτέρων ὁμοῦ συναλαλαζόντων, ἅμα δὲ καὶ τῶν ἐκτὸς τῆς μάχης ἐπιβοώντων τοῖς ἀγωνιζομένοις, ἦν τὸ γινόμενον ἐκπληκτικὸν καὶ παραστατικὸν ἀγωνίας.

> The engagement was met from both sides violently and with an overpowering cry. As both sides were crying aloud together, and at the same time those not engaged in battle were applauding the combatants, the spectacle of the struggle was shocking and electrifying.

Of these two descriptions, Walbank writes: "Such passages deviate from the austere standard [Polybius] demanded, and make concessions to the more sensational form of composition which P. derides." Either passage taken in isolation might well be interpreted that way. But together, they illustrate Polybius had little interest in turning a novel phrase, putting a tragic lament into the mouths of his subjects, or straining for varied expression.

My argument supports the current trend in considerations of tragic history: Polybius does not refer to any established school or tradition of historiographical writing when he coins "tragic history". Consequently, our search for the origin of tragic history in the Peripatos has been misguided. What I have added to that line of argument, however, is the idea that Polybius is using vocabulary that belongs to an established tradition of the criticism of tragedy. He understands what tragedy is, and his conception of its elements is consistent with the descriptions we find of it in much Greek literature. His attack on Phylarchus, therefore, has a firm foundation in a long tradition of Greek literary criticism. Polybius does not assert that any element that is appropriate to tragedy must be absent from history, or from the histories that he condemns, or even from his own work. Rather, he conceives of tragedy as a complex combination of several elements, and that historians should avoid indulging in that combination of those elements in their works. But in the search for tragic history, we must begin with Polybius's own language, identify the entire system of elements he defines as the constituent parts of tragedy, and then search for those elements in the authors that he condemns. When we do this, as I have shown, we find that, regardless of Polybius's political views, the assertion that Phylarchus exploited tragic elements in the narration of historical events is wholly convincing.

Bibliography

Barrett, W.S. (1964), *Euripides. Hippolytus*, Oxford.
Belfiore, E.S. (1992), *Tragic Pleasures*, Princeton.
Bevan, E.R. (1902), *The House of Seleucus*, vol. I, London.
Boncquet, J. (1982), "Polybius on the Critical Evaluation of Historians", in: *Anc. Soc.* 13–14, 277–91.
Brown, T.S. (1958), *Timaeus of Tauromeneum*, Berkeley.
Brunt, P.A. (1980), "On Historical Fragments and Epitomes", in: *CQ* 30, 477–494.
Büttner-Wobst, T. (1962–1967), *Polybii Historiae*, vols. I-V, Leipzig.
Burnet, J. (1968), *Platonis opera*, vols. I-III. Oxford.
Chronopoulos, S. / Orth, C. (eds.) (2015), *Fragmente einer Geschichte der griechischen Komödie/Fragmentary History of Greek Comedy*, Heidelberg.
Eckstein, A.M. (2013), "Polybius, Phylarchus, and Historiographical Criticism", in: *CPh* 108, 314–338.
Foulon, E. (2008), "Histoire et tragédie chez Polybe", in: *Φιλευριπίδης/Phileuripidès: Mélanges offert à François Jouan*, Nanterre, 687–701.
Gibson, B. / Harrison, T. (eds.) (2013), *Polybius and His World. Essays in Memory of F. W. Walbank*, Oxford.
Haegemans, K. / Kosmetatou, E. (2005), "Aratus and the Achaean Background of Polybius", in: G. Schepens / J. Bollansée 2005, 123–139.
Jacoby, F. (1963), *Die Fragmente der Griechischen Historiker*, C, Kommentar zu Nr. 64–105, Leiden.
Kannicht, R. (2004), *Tragicorum Graecorum Fragmenta*, vols. I-V, Göttingen.
Kassel, R. (1968), *Aristotelis de arte poetica liber*, Oxford.
Leigh, M. (1997), *Lucan. Spectacle and Engagement*, Oxford.
Lendle, O. (1992), *Einführung in die griechische Geschichtsschreibung*, Darmstadt.
Lobeck, C. (1829), *Aglaophamus*, vols. I-II, Königsberg.
Marincola, J. (2003), "Beyond Pity and Fear: The Emotions of History", in: *Anc. Soc.* 33, 285–315.
Marincola, J. (ed.) (2011), *A Companion to Greek and Roman Historiography*, Malden.
Marincola, J. (2013), "Polybius, Phylarchus, and 'Tragic History': A Reconsideration", in: B. Gibson / T. Harrison 2013, 73–90.
Mayer, M. (1894) "Kronos", in: W. H. Roscher 1894, 1452–15–73.
McCaslin, D.E. (1985), "Polybius, Phylarchus, and the Mantineian Tragedy of 223 B.C.", in: *Archaiognosia* 4, 77–102.

McDonough, C.M. (1999), "Forbidden to Enter the Ara Maxima: Dogs and Flies, or Dogflies?" in: *Mnemosyne* 52, 464–477.
Morgan, J.R. (2011), "Fiction and History: Historiography and the Novel", in: J. Marincola 2011, 553–564.
Nachstädt, W. / Sieveking, W. / Titchener, J.B. (1971), Plutarchi Moralia, Leipzig.
Olson, S.D. (2015), "Athenaeus' Aristophanes, and the Problem of Reconstructing Lost Comedies", in: S. Chronopoulos / C. Orth 2015, 35–65.
Ostwald, M. (2002), "Tragedians and Historians", in: *Scripta Classica Israelica* 21, 9–25.
Pohlenz (1922) "Kronos", in: *RE*.
Porter, S.E. (ed.) (1997), *Handbook of Classical Rhetoric in the Hellenistic Period 330 B. C. – A. D. 400*, Leiden.
Radt, S. (ed.) (1985), *Tragicorum Graecorum Fragmenta*, vol. III, Göttingen.
Radt, S. (ed.) (1999), *Tragicorum Graecorum Fragmenta*, vol. IV, Göttingen.
Rebenich, S. (1997), "Historical Prose", in: S.E. Porter 1997, 265–337.
Roscher, W.H. (1894), *Ausführliches Lexikon der griechischen und römischen Mythologie*, Bd. II, Leipzig.
Rosenbloom, D. / Davidson, J. (eds.) (2012), *Greek Drama IV. Texts, Contexts, Performance*, Oxford.
Ross, W.D. (1964), *Aristotelis politica*, Oxford.
Russell, D.A. (1964), *Longinus' On the Sublime*, Oxford.
Rutherford, R.M. (2011), "Tragedy and History", in: J. Marincola 2011, 504–514.
Rutherford, R.M. (2012), *Greek Tragic Style. Form, Language, and Interpretation*, Cambridge.
Sacks, K. (1981), *Polybius on the Writing of History*, Berkeley.
Scheller, P. (1911), *De Hellenistica historiae conscribendae arte*, Leipzig.
Schepens, G. (2005), "Polybius's Criticism of Phylarchus", in G. Schepens / J. Bollansée 2005, 141–164.
Schepens, G. (1975), "Ἔμφασις und ἐνάργεια in Polybios' Geschichtstheorie", in: *Rivista Storica dell' Antichità* 5, 185–200.
Schepens, G. / Bollansée, J. (eds.) (2005), *The Shadow of Polybius. Intertextuality as a Research Tool in Greek Historiography*. Proceedings of the International Colloquium Leuven, 21–22 September 2001, Leuven.
Schwartz, E. (1897), "Die Berichte über die Catilinarische Verschwörung", in: *Hermes* 32, 554–608.
Sommerstein, A.H. (2012), "The Persian War Tetralogy of Aeschylus", in: D. Rosenbloom / J. Davidson 2012, 95–106.
Sutton, D.F. (1984), *The Lost Sophocles*, Lanham.
Taplin, O. (1978), *Greek Tragedy in Action*, Berkeley.
Tuplin, C. (2011), "Tragedy and History", in: J. Marincola 2011, 159–170.
Vanhaegendoren, K. (2010), "Outils de dramatization chez Phylarque", in: *Dialogues d'histoire ancienne* 4, 421–438.
von Fritz, K. (1956), "Die Bedeutung des Aristoteles für Geschichtsschreibung", in: *Histoire et Historiens dans l'Antiquité*, Entretiens Hardt 4, Geneva, 83–145.
Walbank, F.W. (1957–1979), *A Historical Commentary on Polybius*, vols. I-III, Oxford.
Walbank, F.W. (1972), *Polybius*, Berkeley.
Walbank, F.W. (1985), "Φίλιππος τραγῳδούμενος: A Polybian Experiment", in: F.W. Walbank, *Selected Papers: Studies in Greek and Roman History and Historiography*, Cambridge,

210–223. = Walbank, F.W. (1938), "Φίλλιπος τραγῳδούμενος: A Polybian Experiment", in: *JHS* 58, 55–68.
Walbank, F.W. / Habicht, C. (2010), *Polybius, The Histories Books 1–2*, Cambridge.
Walker, A.D. (1993), "Enargeia and the Spectator in Greek Historiography", in: *TAPhA* 123, 353–377.
Webb, R. (2009), *Ekphrasis, Imagination, and Persuasion in Ancient Rhetorical Theory and Practice*, Surrey.
Wellman, M. (1909), "Fliege", in: *RE*.
Wilcken, (1894), "Antiochos", in: *RE*.
Winnington-Ingram, R.P. (1980), *Sophocles: An Interpretation*, Cambridge.
Zegers, N. (1959), *Wesen und Ursprung der Tragischen Geschichtsschreibung*. Cologne.

Mario Baumann
"No One Can Look at Them Without Feeling Pity": συμπάθεια and the Reader in Diodorus' *Bibliotheke*

Abstract: By analysing how Diodorus' *Bibliotheke* evokes the emotion of pity, this article explores an important aspect of the *Wirkungsästhetik* of Diodorus' universal history. The shared focus on literary emotionalism links this contribution closely to Scott Farrington's. In addition, the article highlights a marked didacticism which goes hand in hand with the pathos created by various passages of the *Bibliotheke*. This emphasis has parallels in several other contributions to this volume which discuss further examples of descriptive vividness combined with historical argument (cf. in particular the papers by Vasileios Liotsakis and Philip Waddell). On a methodological level, the article takes up narratological approaches (cf. Suzanne Adema's paper) as well as concepts from reader-response criticism to define the *Bibliotheke*'s "model reader".

This article focuses on passages of Diodorus' first pentad in which the narrator describes pitiable events and thereby moves the reader to empathise with the affected persons. The first five books of the *Bibliotheke* cover the history of the οἰκουμένη before the Trojan War and focus on the geography and ethnography of the known world. The most conspicuous instances of the evocation of pity occur in the *Bibliotheke*'s third book, more precisely in the context of a larger section about Ethiopia and the Red Sea (D.S. 3.1–48). One passage, the description of the dire working conditions in Egyptian gold mines, will serve as a model case. I will show, first, that these chapters are characterised by two closely interlinked textual dynamics, didacticism and emotionalism. Second, I will examine other passages with similar traits; they invite the reader to interact with the same didactic and emotional dynamic. Finally, I will contextualise the dual strategy of didacticism and emotionalism within a Stoic concept of reader response, thus aiming to outline the "model reader" for these sections of the *Bibliotheke*.

1 The misery of mining: gold extraction in Southern Egypt (D.S. 3.12–14)

The first text that I would like to analyse is an extended description of gold mines at the borders of Egypt. As the narrator points out, many people are forced to work there under rather horrible conditions (D.S. 3.12.1–3):[1]

> Περὶ γὰρ τὰς ἐσχατιὰς τῆς Αἰγύπτου καὶ τῆς ὁμορούσης Ἀραβίας τε καὶ Αἰθιοπίας τόπος ἐστὶν ἔχων μέταλλα πολλὰ καὶ μεγάλα χρυσοῦ, συναγομένου πολλοῦ πολλῇ κακοπαθείᾳ τε καὶ δαπάνῃ. [...] οἱ γὰρ βασιλεῖς τῆς Αἰγύπτου τοὺς ἐπὶ κακουργίᾳ καταδικασθέντας καὶ τοὺς κατὰ πόλεμον αἰχμαλωτισθέντας, ἔτι δὲ τοὺς ἀδίκοις διαβολαῖς περιπεσόντας καὶ διὰ θυμὸν εἰς φυλακὰς παραδεδομένους, ποτὲ μὲν αὐτούς, ποτὲ δὲ καὶ μετὰ πάσης συγγενείας ἀθροίσαντες παραδιδόασι πρὸς τὴν τοῦ χρυσοῦ μεταλλείαν, ἅμα μὲν τιμωρίαν λαμβάνοντες παρὰ τῶν καταγνωσθέντων, ἅμα δὲ διὰ τῶν ἐργαζομένων μεγάλας προσόδους λαμβάνοντες. οἱ δὲ παραδοθέντες, πολλοὶ μὲν τὸ πλῆθος ὄντες, πάντες δὲ πέδαις δεδεμένοι, προσκαρτεροῦσι τοῖς ἔργοις συνεχῶς καὶ μεθ' ἡμέραν καὶ δι' ὅλης τῆς νυκτός, ἀνάπαυσιν μὲν οὐδεμίαν λαμβάνοντες, δρασμοῦ δὲ παντὸς φιλοτίμως εἰργόμενοι.

> At the extremity of Egypt and in the contiguous territory of both Arabia and Ethiopia there lies a region which contains many large gold mines, where the gold is secured in great quantities with much suffering and at great expense. [...] For the kings of Egypt gather together and condemn to the mining of the gold such as have been found guilty of some crime and captives of war, as well as those who have been accused unjustly and thrown into prison because of their anger, and not only such persons but occasionally all their relatives as well, by this means not only inflicting punishment upon those found guilty but also securing at the same time great revenues from their labours. And those who have been condemned in this way – and they are a great multitude and are all bound in chains – work at their task unceasingly both by day and throughout the entire night, enjoying no respite and being carefully cut off from any means of escape.

In the subsequent sections of this chapter, the narrator describes what the different groups of mine workers are forced to do; the sufferings of one specific group are depicted as follows (D.S. 3.12.6):

> οὗτοι μὲν οὖν διὰ τὰς ἐν ταῖς διώρυξι καμπὰς καὶ σκολιότητας ἐν σκότει διατρίβοντες λύχνους ἐπὶ τῶν μετώπων πεπραγματευμένους περιφέρουσι· πολλαχῶς δὲ πρὸς τὰς τῆς πέτρας ἰδιότητας μετασχηματίζοντες τὰ σώματα καταβάλλουσιν εἰς ἔδαφος τὰ λατομούμενα θραύματα· καὶ τοῦτο ἀδιαλείπτως ἐνεργοῦσι πρὸς ἐπιστάτου βαρύτητα καὶ πληγάς.

> Now these men, working in darkness as they do because of the bending and winding of the passages, carry lamps bound on their foreheads; and since much of the time they change the position of their bodies to follow the particular character of the stone they throw the

---

[1] Here, as elsewhere in this paper, I quote Oldfather's translation of the *Bibliotheke*.

blocks, as they cut them out, on the ground; and at this task they labour without ceasing beneath the sternness and blows of an overseer.

In the next chapter, the narrator details some further steps in the process of extracting the gold. In the course of this description, the miserable fate of the workers is highlighted again (D.S. 3.13.2–3):

> προσούσης δ' ἅπασιν ἀθεραπευσίας σώματος καὶ τῆς τὴν αἰδῶ περιστελλούσης ἐσθῆτος μὴ προσούσης, οὐκ ἔστιν ὃς ἰδὼν οὐκ ἂν ἐλεήσειε τοὺς ἀκληροῦντας διὰ τὴν ὑπερβολὴν τῆς ταλαιπωρίας. οὐ γὰρ τυγχάνει συγγνώμης οὐδ' ἀνέσεως ἁπλῶς οὐκ ἄρρωστος, οὐ πεπηρωμένος, οὐ γεγηρακώς, οὐ γυναικὸς ἀσθένεια, πάντες δὲ πληγαῖς ἀναγκάζονται προσκαρτερεῖν τοῖς ἔργοις, μέχρι ἂν κακουχούμενοι τελευτήσωσιν ἐν ταῖς ἀνάγκαις. διόπερ οἱ δυστυχεῖς φοβερώτερον ἀεὶ τὸ μέλλον τοῦ παρόντος ἡγοῦνται διὰ τὴν ὑπερβολὴν τῆς τιμωρίας, ποθεινότερον δὲ τοῦ ζῆν τὸν θάνατον προσδέχονται.

> And since no opportunity is afforded any of them to care for his body and they have no garment to cover their shame, no man can look upon these unfortunate wretches without feeling pity for them because of the exceeding hardships they suffer. For no leniency or respite of any kind is given to any man who is sick, or maimed, or aged, or in the case of a woman for her weakness, but all without exception are compelled by blows to persevere in their labours, until through ill-treatment they die in the midst of their tortures. Consequently the poor unfortunates believe, because their punishment is so excessively severe, that the future will always be more terrible than the present and therefore look forward to death as more to be desired than life.

Then the narrator turns to the "complete and final working" (τὴν ὅλην συντέλειαν, D.S. 3.14.1) of the auriferous stone. After describing how the last groups of workers actually produce the gold, he concludes his account with the following words (D.S. 3.14.4–5):

> ἡ μὲν οὖν ἐργασία τοῦ χρυσοῦ περὶ τὰς ἐσχατιὰς τῆς Αἰγύπτου γινομένη μετὰ τοσούτων καὶ τηλικούτων πόνων συντελεῖται· αὐτὴ γὰρ ἡ φύσις, οἶμαι, ποιεῖ πρόδηλον ὡς ὁ χρυσὸς γένεσιν μὲν ἐπίπονον ἔχει, φυλακὴν δὲ χαλεπήν, σπουδὴν δὲ μεγίστην, χρῆσιν δὲ ἀνὰ μέσον ἡδονῆς τε καὶ λύπης.

> This working of the gold, as it is carried on at the farthermost borders of Egypt, is effected through all the extensive labours here described; for Nature herself, in my opinion, makes it clear that whereas the production of gold is laborious, the guarding of it is difficult, the zest for it is very great, and that its use is half-way between pleasure and pain.

There is hardly any need to emphasise that these chapters describe the pitiful sufferings of many human beings. The narrator himself makes this perfectly clear by explicitly stating that everyone seeing the described scene must feel pity (cf. D.S. 3.13.2).² But even without this comment, he would drive his point safely home given the plethora of words he repeatedly uses to highlight the miserable working conditions – to name but a few: ἔργα/ἐργάζομαι (e.g. D.S. 3.12.1 and 3.12.5), πόνος/ἐπίπονος (e.g. D.S. 3.13.1, 3.14.5), πληγαί (D.S. 3.12.6, 3.13.3), ἀτυχία/δυστυχής (D.S. 3.12.5, 3.13.3), and ὑπερβολή, as in ὑπερβολὴ τῆς ταλαιπωρίας (D.S. 3.13.2) and ὑπερβολὴ τῆς τιμωρίας (D.S. 3.13.3). A panorama of misfortune and hardship, it seems, unfolds before the reader's eyes.

If one asks now why the reader is presented here with such a detailed and extensive description that is focussed so narrowly on the pitiable, a twofold answer can be given. On the one hand, the whole passage enables the reader to learn from the grim fate of the mine workers. This didactic purpose is made explicit by the narrator in his conclusion to his description: nature herself, he says, shows us something through the dire conditions that surround gold mining (D.S. 3.14.5). On the other hand, the marked emotionalism of the description hints at a second textual dynamic: the pathos-laden vividness of the passage³ invites the reader of the *Bibliotheke* to give his imagination free rein, to let himself become emotionally involved by the text and to actually feel sympathy, as foreshadowed by the narrator's remark concerning the effect the scene he describes will have on the spectators.⁴

I would like to consider the didacticism of these chapters of the *Bibliotheke* first, not least of all because this is the main focus of recent scholarship. What insights can we gain from reading this description, or, to use the narrator's words again, what does nature show us with the example of the Egyptian gold mines? I propose that the narrator's depiction of Egypt and its neighbouring regions provides two "lessons": we learn something about a) the specific effects of gold on the human psyche and on human societies, and b) the distribution of natural resources throughout the inhabited world and the general effects of these distributional patterns on human life.

---

2 For a thorough study of how pity was conceived in classical antiquity see Konstan 2001; cf. also Konstan 2006, 201–218.
3 The gold mine description exhibits the quality of ἐνάργεια/*evidentia* as defined by ancient rhetorical theory (cf. Lausberg 2008, §§ 810–818; Webb 2009, 87–106).
4 This emotionalism does not make the gold mine description a piece of "tragic history". For, as Scott Farrington shows in his discussion of Polybius' attack on Phylarchus in this volume, a sound definition of "tragic history" requires more elements than the arousal of emotions, namely a plot hinging on περιπέτειαι, the depiction of wondrous events (θαυμάσια or τερατεῖαι), and the inclusion of "dramatic" utterances or even dialogue – all of which are largely absent in Diodorus' gold mine description.

Aspect a) is the "lesson" that the narrator offers most readily with his descriptions of the Egyptian gold mines: he points out that gold causes σπουδή ("zest") and a mixture of ἡδονή and λύπη ("pleasure" and "pain", D.S. 3.14.5). At first glance, these terms could be taken to refer to individual psychological effects: human individuals are affected by gold so that they feel zest for it. But in the context of the larger passage on the gold mines, the point seems to be more about social psychology: for "pleasure and pain" are not distributed evenly to those involved in the Egyptian gold business – the workers suffer (they certainly do not feel pleasure), and their suffering, it seems, is the necessary precondition for the pleasure of those who profit from the mining. In fact, according to the narrator, there is, in the end, only one man who profits from all these undertakings: the Egyptian king who collects large revenues (μεγάλας προσόδους, D.S. 3.12.2) from the miner's labours. The analysis of Bibiane Bommelaer, who has compared the descriptions of Diodorus and his source, Agatharchides of Cnidus, corroborates that this is one of the narrator's main points, arguably even the gist of the whole passage. She has convincingly shown that it is Diodorus who establishes a clear link between the king's revenues and the misery of the workers, thus drawing an original conclusion from his source.[5] It appears, then, that the statement that the use of gold is "half-way between pleasure and pain" holds true only on a general, nearly abstract level of reasoning. As soon as one starts to ask who feels pleasure and who feels pain in a society or a social structure like this mining industry – and the reader is positively invited by the narrator's description to ask this question –, the "lesson" becomes clear: very many feel pain, very few feel pleasure, and this realisation constitutes a major aspect of the didactic potential of this passage.

Aspect b) links D.S. 3.12–14 to larger parts of the rest of book 3 as well as to many passages of book 2 and book 5: Throughout these books, the narrator shows that physical conditions like climate, flora and fauna, and especially the availability of geological or biological resources, vary greatly within the οἰκουμένη, and he foregrounds the relationship between these conditions of the environment and human life and society time and again.[6] Arabia, for example, is rich in precious stones (D.S. 2.52.9) as well as in fruit-bearing trees of extraordinary fertility (D.S. 2.53.4–7), properties that the narrator explicitly states

---

[5] Cf. Bommelaer 1989, xlv–xlvii. Diodorus' source here is Agatharchides' *On the Red Sea*, book 5, which itself is lost. There is, however, an excerpt in Photius' *Bibliotheke* which is extant and – when used cautiously, as Bommelaer does – forms a sufficient basis for comparisons with Diodorus' rendering. The excerpt of Agatharchides' description of the Egyptian gold mines is found in Photius, *cod.* 250, *p.* 447b21–449a10.

[6] Cf. Trevisan 2010, 269–72, 275–77, and 285–86; De Morais Mota 2010, 95–103.

are specific to this region.⁷ The peoples living at the southern edges of the οἰκουμένη (i.e. in southern Ethiopia and/or at the southern stretches of the Red Sea) are faced with difficult environmental conditions, yet manage to make the most of the sparse resources given to them by nature – the so-called turtle-eaters, for example, not only feed on turtles but also use their shells as vessels, as ships or for housing "so that it would appear that Nature, by a single act of favour, had bestowed upon these peoples the satisfaction of many needs" (ὥστε δοκεῖν τούτοις τὴν φύσιν δεδωρῆσθαι μιᾷ χάριτι πολλὰς χρείας, D.S. 3.21.5). In Iberia, again, large silver deposits allow for mining on a nearly industrial scale. In fact, the narrator's description of the Iberian silver mines (D.S. 5.35–38) shows many similarities with the chapters on the Egyptian mines that I will discuss in detail below. All these instances enlighten the reader about the diverse natural conditions of the inhabited world and the human behaviour that is enabled or necessitated by it.⁸

It is worth noting that the reader needs to interact with the text to arrive at these conclusions that form, as I called it above, the "didactic potential" of this passage, a point that scholarship – the pertinent and helpful studies of Trevisan 2010 and De Morais Mota 2010 quoted above are cases in point – hardly pays attention to: it is more or less taken for granted that there is a didactic "message" in the *Biblioheke*'s narration without examining what a reader needs to do to get the message, to grasp and to appreciate it. In the case of the effects of gold on the human psyche, the full spectrum of what a reader can learn from the description only becomes visible when he notices the slight tension that arises between the description proper and the narrator's closing remarks and consequently engages with that tension: the reader must examine the concrete description of the workers' sufferings vis-à-vis the abstract reasoning about the intermingling of

---

7 Cf. the narrator's remark in D.S. 2.52.9 (he attributes these differences to the varying energy of the sun): διόπερ οὔτε ἡ Παρία λύγδος οὔτ' ἄλλη θαυμαζομένη πέτρα τοῖς Ἀραβίοις λίθοις ἐξισωθῆναι δύναται, ὧν λαμπροτάτη μὲν ἡ λευκότης, βαρύτατος δὲ ὁ σταθμός, ἡ δὲ λειότης ὑπερβολὴν ἑτέροις οὐκ ἀπολείπουσα. αἰτία δὲ τῆς χώρας τῆς κατὰ μέρος ἰδιότητος, καθάπερ προεῖπον, ἡ περὶ τὸν ἥλιον δύναμις [...] ("Consequently, neither white marble of Paros nor any other stone which men admire can be compared with the precious stones of Arabia, since their whiteness is most brilliant, their weight the heaviest, and their smoothness leaves no room for other stones to surpass them. And the cause of the peculiar nature of the several parts of the country is, as I have told, the influence of the sun [...]").
8 For another example of an ancient historian conveying interpretative "messages" by including geographic and ethnographic information see Vasileios Liotsakis' analysis of Th. 2.95–101 in this volume.

pleasure and pain.⁹ In the case of the distribution of natural resources in the inhabited world, the need for the reader to become active is even more marked: here, a comparison between different passages of the *Bibliotheke* is required, and the text itself suggests this approach because the narrator frequently compares different parts of the οἰκουμένη (see e.g. his comment on the extreme climates in the northern and southernmost regions in D.S. 3.34 after prompting all readers doubting his account of the wonders of Ethiopia to examine the differences in the οἰκουμένη side by side [D.S. 3.33.7]).

In a similar vein, the emotionalism of the narrator's depiction contributes to activating the reader. That aspect, too, seems to be somewhat neglected in scholarship. Apart from Bommelaer's detailed treatment in the preface to her edition, the fact that the emotionalism of passages like those examined here forms an important part of their *Wirkungsästhetik* is often mentioned without analysis.¹⁰ Even Bommelaer concludes her excellent account of "l'expression de l'émotion" in *Bibliotheke* 3 on an apolegetic note and is at pains to point out that the emotionalism contributes to the overarching aim of Diodorus' universal history:¹¹

> Le but principal de l'histoire universelle est l'instruction morale et politique qu'elle peut fournir aux hommes; […] Diodore paraît voir dans l'exposé des malheurs des hommes une occasion très favorable de mettre ses principes en pratique. […] On pourra accuser Diodore de sensiblerie […]. Mais ce qui importe, en fin de compte, c'est de rappeler que […] l'émotion n'est un simple ornement qui colorerait superficiellement l'exposé.

There is no doubt that didacticism and emotionalism are closely intertwined in the *Bibliotheke*. There might be, however, a danger in being too apologetic about the pathos of a passage like D.S. 3.12–14; namely, one might underestimate the sheer affective force of the narrator's description and downplay the genuine potential to draw the reader in, to stimulate his imagination, and to stir his emotions. Using one's imaginative and emotional capabilities should be regarded no less a mental activity than using one's intellectual abilities, and this approach

---

9 If one interprets the text in this way, there is no reason to object to the narrator's closing remark, as Bommelaer (1989, xlviii) does, that "cette clausule prend un air de banalité". What she calls "banalité" is functional in that it invites the reader to reflect on it and to "think beyond". Rather than calling it banal, then, we should see it as an instance of the *Leerstelle* so famously conceptualised by Wolfgang Iser (cf. Iser 1984, 280–355).
10 Cf. e.g. the very brief mention in Trevisan 2010, 270.
11 Bommelaer 1989, xlviii/xlix.

diminishes any need to justify the *Bibliotheke's* emotionalism because didacticism and pathos both set the reader's mind in motion.¹²

Bommelaer's analysis nevertheless provides a good starting point for examining this second textual dynamic of the gold mine description: taking Diodorus' pitiful description of the sufferings of the mine workers (D.S. 3.13.2–3, cited above) as a model case, she points out that several stylistic elements create vividness and insistence.¹³ Prominent among these are anaphora (οὐ γὰρ τυγχάνει συγγνώμης *οὐδ' ἀνέσεως ἁπλῶς οὐκ ἄρρωστος, οὐ πεπηρωμένος, οὐ γεγηρακώς, οὐ* γυναικὸς ἀσθένεια), antitheses (φοβερώτερον ἀεὶ τὸ μέλλον τοῦ παρόντος ἡγοῦνται [...], ποθεινότερον δὲ *τοῦ ζῆν τὸν θάνατον προσδέχονται*), and a vocabulary of suffering and misery (οὐκ ἔστιν ὃς ἰδὼν οὐκ ἂν *ἐλεήσειε τοὺς ἀκληροῦντας διὰ τὴν ὑπερβολὴν τῆς ταλαιπωρίας* etc.).

Beyond these stylistic means, there are at least three further literary techniques that add to the vividness of the description and help to engross the reader. First, the passage on the Egyptian gold mines is remarkable for its meticulous attention to technical details.¹⁴ An abundance of terms precisely describe tools, chemical substances or physical states, especially in the paragraphs that are dedicated to the work of the specialised τεχνῖται near the end of the whole extraction process. D.S. 3.14.1–2 provides a good example:

τὸ δὲ τελευταῖον οἱ τεχνῖται παραλαβόντες τὸν ἀληλεσμένον λίθον πρὸς τὴν ὅλην ἄγουσι συντέλειαν· ἐπὶ γὰρ πλατείας σανίδος μικρὸν ἐγκεκλιμένης τρίβουσι τὴν κατειργασμένην μάρμαρον ὕδωρ ἐπιχέοντες· εἶτα τὸ μὲν γεῶδες αὐτῆς ἐκτηκόμενον διὰ τῶν ὑγρῶν καταρρεῖ κατὰ τὴν τῆς σανίδος ἔγκλισιν, τὸ δὲ χρυσίον ἔχον ἐπὶ τοῦ ξύλου παραμένει διὰ τὸ

---

12 I draw here on the approach of Thomas Anz in his seminal book on the pleasures of reading. He stresses that a potential to afford pleasure to the reader is inherent to many different activities that a text may cause the reader to engage in (cf. Anz 1998, 29–32); among these are both the pleasure derived from "[der] stolze[n] Selbstgewißheit kritischer Kompetenz" – a pleasure that a reader may feel when he learns –, and "die Lust an der intensive Bewegung der eigenen Emotionen" (Anz 1998, 67 and 149).
13 Cf. Bommelaer 1989, xlvi with n. 5.
14 This, as well as the second technique outlined below, closely corresponds to ancient rhetorical theory. For, as Lausberg 2008, § 813 shows, the primary means of effecting ἐνάργεια/*evidentia* as discussed in ancient rhetorical treatises is "die Detaillierung des Gesamtgegenstandes", in particular "die *distributio* eines Ganzen in kleinste Vorgangs- oder Gegenstandseinzelheiten" (cf. Demetr. *Eloc.* 209; Quint. *Inst.* 8.3.63–69; see also Plett 2012, 7–13). Moreover, ancient rhetorical theory stresses that an orator only successfully "penetrates to the emotions of a hearer" (*in adfectus ... penetrat*, Quint. *Inst.* 8.3.67; cf. also 6.2.32) when he offers a detailed description. Cf. also Eugénie Fournel's analysis of Plutarch, *Caes.* 63.5 in this volume: Fournel points out that Plutarch gives more details than other historians to dramatise his description and to create pathos.

βάρος. πολλάκις δὲ τοῦτο ποιοῦντες, τὸ μὲν πρῶτον ταῖς χερσὶν ἐλαφρῶς τρίβουσι, μετὰ δὲ ταῦτα σπόγγοις ἀραιοῖς κούφως ἐπιθλίβοντες τὸ χαῦνον καὶ γεῶδες διὰ τούτων ἀναλαμβάνουσι, μέχρι ἂν ὅτου καθαρὸν γένηται τὸ ψῆγμα τοῦ χρυσοῦ.

In the last steps the skilled workmen receive the stone which has been ground to powder and take it off for its complete and final working; for they rub the marble which has been worked down upon a broad board which is slightly inclined, pouring water over it all the while; whereupon the earthy matter in it, melted away by the action of the water, runs down the inclined board, while that which contains the gold remains on the wood because of its weight. And repeating this a number of times, they first of all rub it gently with their hands, and then lightly pressing it with sponges of loose texture they remove in this way whatever is porous and earthy, until there remains only the pure gold-dust.

This level of precision helps to make the description graphic and to invite the reader to imagine what is going on in these mines.

Second, the macrostructure of the whole passage deserves mention: the three chapters present a coherent temporal succession, following all the stages of the gold extraction step by step. No stage, it seems, is left out, and every step is described in detail with a fairly constant narrative pace. The impression left by this macrostructure is one of a reckless technicality: the reader is spared no gruesome detail, every effort that must be taken by the workers to secure the gold is represented in the textual depiction as well. As the workers are not granted any respite but must continue to keep the work rhythm dictated by the technical needs of mining the gold, so the reader faces a continuous stream of descriptive elements that follow, it seems, a rhythm as relentless as the ever-constant workload of the miners.

Third, the textual presentation of the mining activities makes heavy use of focalisation:[15] since the description focuses throughout on what the different groups of workers do, we see the production of gold "through their eyes". It is not the guardians, the overseers, or the Egyptian king who provide the focal point of the description, nor is the reader presented with a detached narration that avoids any focalisation. On the contrary, the reader is continuously compelled to take up the perspective of the miners, to join them, so to speak, when they crawl through the tunnels and galleries, crush the stone, and endure the maltreatment by the guardians. All the descriptive techniques mentioned so far work towards making the reader empathise with the miners, but this third de-

---

[15] The term "focalisation" was coined by Gérard Genette (cf. Genette 1972, 206–211). For a concise overview of the theoretical implications of this concept and for a typology see Wolf 2009. Cf. also the narratological concepts of "what it's like" and "experientialty" used by Suzanne Adema for her discussion of battle exhortations in Caesar's *Bellum Gallicum* in this volume.

vice, focalisation, may be the most effective means to make the narrator's foreshadowing in D.S. 3.13.2 come true for the reader: "no one can look upon these unfortunate wretches without feeling pity for them".

To conclude my remarks on D.S. 3.12–14, I would like to stress that while the two textual dynamics that I described above may be analytically separated for the sake of an interpretation like the one proposed here, they both occur together in the concrete act of reading this description. Depending on the disposition and interests of an individual reader, he or she might at first lean more to the one side or to the other, but given the strong and explicit signals by the narrator, neither the didacticism nor the emotionalism will be lost on a reader who is even only modestly susceptible to the lures of this text. In any case, the full potential offered by the gold mine description only materialises when a reader engages with both dynamics.[16]

2 From mining to shipwreck: pitiable events in Iberia and the Red Sea (D.S. 5.35–38 and 3.40)

That these considerations are valid not only for D.S. 3.12–14 but for the *Bibliotheke* in a broader sense can be demonstrated by two other passages from the first pentad. I already mentioned that there is another detailed description of mining activities in the fifth book of the *Bibliotheke* (D.S. 5.35–38). There, the narrator gives an account of mines in Iberia that produce several precious metals, especially silver. Founded by the Phoenicians or Carthaginians, these mines were later taken over by Italians who, according to the narrator, introduced the massive scale of slave labour to Iberia. The fate of these slaves is described in words reminiscent of the account of the Egyptian gold mines (D.S. 5.38.1):

> οἱ δ' οὖν ταῖς ἐργασίαις τῶν μετάλλων ἐνδιατρίβοντες τοῖς μὲν κυρίοις ἀπίστους τοῖς πλήθεσι προσόδους περιποιοῦσιν, αὐτοὶ δὲ κατὰ γῆς ἐν τοῖς ὀρύγμασι καὶ καθ' ἡμέραν καὶ νύκτα καταξαινόμενοι τὰ σώματα, πολλοὶ μὲν ἀποθνήσκουσι διὰ τὴν ὑπερβολὴν τῆς κακοπαθείας· ἄνεσις γὰρ ἢ παῦλα τῶν ἔργων οὐκ ἔστιν αὐτοῖς, ἀλλὰ [ταῖς] τῶν ἐπιστατῶν πληγαῖς ἀναγκαζόντων ὑπομένειν τὴν δεινότητα τῶν κακῶν ἀτυχῶς προΐενται τὸ ζῆν, τινὲς δὲ ταῖς δυνάμεσι τῶν σωμάτων καὶ ταῖς τῶν ψυχῶν καρτερίαις ὑπομένοντες πολυχρόνιον ἔχουσι τὴν ταλαιπωρίαν· αἱρετώτερος γὰρ αὐτοῖς ὁ θάνατός ἐστι τοῦ ζῆν διὰ τὸ μέγεθος τῆς ταλαιπωρίας.

---

[16] Philip Waddell's discussion (in this volume) of the fall of Carthage as presented by Appian highlights a further example of pathos-oriented ecphrastic vividness combined with complex historical argument.

But to continue with the mines, the slaves who are engaged in the working of them produce for their masters revenues in sums defying belief, but they themselves wear out their bodies both by day and by night in the diggings under the earth, dying in large numbers because of the exceptional hardships they endure. For no respite or pause is granted them in their labours, but compelled beneath blows of the overseers to endure the severity of their plight, they throw away their lives in this wretched manner, although certain of them who can endure it, by virtue of their bodily strength and their persevering souls, suffer such hardships over a long period; indeed death in their eyes is more to be desired than life, because of the magnitude of the hardships they must bear.

The narrator does not explicitly state that seeing these miserable workers causes pity, but his graphic depiction is clear (and moving) enough. In addition, there is an evident didactic potential very much in the vein of the "lessons" of D.S. 3.12– 14: no Egyptian king rules these mines, but the greed (φιλοκερδία, φιλαργυρία) of the Phoenicians/Carthaginians (D.S. 5.35.4/5.38.2) and, above all, the Italians (D.S. 5.36.3) leads to the same result – many have to suffer for the profit of a few.[17]

Another striking example of the evocation of pity in the *Bibliotheke*'s first pentad occurs in D.S. 3.40. This chapter is part of an extensive description of the Red Sea in the form of a periplus. From a narratological point of view, this passage is characterised by a specific focalisation: in two movements, each from North to South, the narrator describes first the African, then the Arabian side of the Red Sea from the perspective of a seaman sailing past those shores. At one point, the narrator calls attention to a shallow and dangerous spot near the Egyptian coast and to the fate of many ships navigating there: they shipwreck. The narrator describes the fate of the crew as follows (D.S. 3.40.7–8):

οἱ δὲ τούτῳ τῷ συμπτώματι περιπεσόντες τὸ μὲν πρῶτον μετρίως ὀδύρονται πρὸς κωφὴν ἐρημίαν, οὐ παντελῶς ἀπεγνωκότες εἰς τέλος τὴν σωτηρίαν· πολλάκις γὰρ τοῖς τοιούτοις ἐπιφανεὶς ὁ τῆς πλημυρίδος κλύδων ἐξῆρεν εἰς ὕψος, καὶ τοὺς ἐσχάτως κινδυνεύοντας ὡσπερεὶ θεὸς ἐπιφανεὶς διεφύλαξεν· ὅταν δὲ ἀπὸ μὲν τῶν θεῶν ἡ προειρημένη μὴ παρακολουθήσῃ βοήθεια, τὰ δὲ τῆς τροφῆς λίπῃ, τοὺς μὲν ἀσθενεστέρους οἱ κατισχύοντες ἐκβάλλουσιν εἰς θάλατταν, ὅπως τοῖς ὀλίγοις τὰ λειπόμενα τῶν ἀναγκαίων πλείονας ἡμέρας ἀντέχῃ, πέρας δὲ πάσας τὰς ἐλπίδας ἐξαλείψαντες ἀπόλλυνται πολὺ χεῖρον τῶν προαποθανόντων· οἱ μὲν γὰρ ἐν ἀκαρεῖ χρόνῳ τὸ πνεῦμα τῇ δούσῃ φύσει πάλιν ἀπέδωκαν,

---

[17] The source of this description is probably one of the works of Poseidonius of Apameia. None of the potential sources is extant, so it is impossible to determine the relationship of Diodorus' account to his model. Laffranque (1957) has shown that amongst the extant treatments of the Iberian gold mines in classical antiquity Diodorus' is unique in focussing on the contrast between the workers and the few who profit from their labours, which is a hint that he was specifically interested in this social relationship.

οἱ δ' εἰς πολλὰς ταλαιπωρίας καταμερίσαντες τὸν θάνατον πολυχρονίους τὰς συμφορὰς ἔχοντες τῆς τοῦ βίου καταστροφῆς τυγχάνουσι. τὰ δὲ σκάφη ταῦτα τῶν ἐπιβατῶν οἰκτρῶς στερηθέντα, καθάπερ τινὰ κενοτάφια, διαμένει πολὺν χρόνον πανταχόθεν περιχωννύμενα, τοὺς δ' ἱστοὺς καὶ τὰς κεραίας μετεώρους ἔχοντα πόρρωθεν τοὺς ὁρῶντας εἰς οἶκτον καὶ συμπάθειαν ἄγει τῶν ἀπολωλότων. πρόσταγμα γάρ ἐστι βασιλέως ἐὰν τὰ τοιαῦτα συμπτώματα τοῖς πλέουσι διασημαίνειν τοὺς τὸν ὄλεθρον περιποιοῦντας τόπους.

Now the men who have suffered this mishap [*sc.* of having been ship-wrecked], at the outset bewail their lot with moderation in the face of a deaf wilderness, having as yet not entirely abandoned hope of ultimate salvation; for oftentimes the swell of the flood-tide has intervened for men in such a plight and raised the ship aloft, and suddenly appearing, as might a *deus ex machina*, has brought succour to men in the extremity of peril. But when such god-sent aid has not been vouchsafed to them and their food fails, then the strong cast the weaker into the sea in order that for the few left the remaining necessities of life may last a greater number of days. But finally, when they have blotted out of their minds all their hopes, these perish by a more miserable fate than those who had died before; for whereas the latter in a moment's time returned to Nature the spirit which she had given them, these parcelled out their death into many separate hardships before they finally, suffering long-protracted tortures, were granted the end of life. As for the ships which have been stripped of their crews in this pitiable fashion, there they remain for many years, like a group of cenotaphs, embedded on every side in a heap of sand, their masts and yard-arms still standing aloft, and they move those who behold them from afar to pity and sympathy for the men who have perished. For it is the king's command to leave in place such evidences of disasters that they may give notice to sailors of the region which works to their destruction.

Here, the reader becomes a spectator of a tragedy, as it were. This transformation is brought out well by Oldfather's pointed, but, as it seems to me, rather appropriate translation "*deus ex machina*".[18] The reader is put into the role of somebody sailing along, viewing the monuments of such past miseries. Along with the respective narrative focalisation, the passage evokes an explicitly named emotional reaction: οἶκτον καὶ συμπάθειαν (D.S. 3.40.8). The same two dynamics that I pointed out when discussing the descriptions of mines can be observed here. On the one hand, the text appeals to the emotions of the reader. As in the description of the gold mine, the elaboration and intensity of the passage – note the slow narrative pace used by the narrator when he describes how

---

18 Contrary to the gold mine description discussed above, the story of the shipwrecked sailors can actually be seen as a case of "tragic history" if one takes up the criteria established by Scott Farrington in this volume: the seamen suffer a dramatic περιπέτεια of their fortunes, the periplus of the Red Sea which forms the context of this story describes many θαυμάσια (cf. e.g. the precious stones with their "marvellous (θαυμαστήν) golden hue" described in D.S. 3.39.5), and the shipwreck narration even hints at "tragic" exclamations by the sailors (ὀδύρονται πρὸς κωφὴν ἐρημίαν, "they bewail their lot in the face of a deaf wilderness", D.S. 3.40.7). Furthermore, Polybius attributes the use of the μηχανή to tragic historians at, e.g., 3.48.8.

the crew slowly die – add to this effect. On the other hand, there is also a potential for reflection: the shipwrecks are a sign, and any passers-by who interpret them correctly learn to avoid a similar fate. The reader of the *Bibliotheke* is supposed to do something similar – he can learn from this passage as well as from the *Bibliotheke* as a whole, which aims to comprehensively collect and present the signs of the past.[19]

3 Criticism and compassion: the Stoic as model reader of the *Bibliotheke*

So much for these passages of the *Bibliotheke*. I would like to conclude my discussion by suggesting a historical – and by the same token, theoretical – contextualisation of the *Bibliotheke*'s dual strategy of didacticism and emotionalism. The context I am referring to is Stoicism, which forms an important backdrop to the *Bibliotheke*, and especially to the first pentad. This does not mean that Diodorus should be regarded as a stoic philosopher in the proper sense; rather, the role of Stoicism for Diodorus may aptly be described by the following words of Hubert Cancik: "Diodor ist kein Philosoph und kein Theologe. Aber eine 'Weltanschauung stoischer Prägung' begründet seine Universalgeschichte."[20] This *Begründung* is apparent on two levels. First of all, the proem of the *Bibliotheke* shows Stoic traits. As Luciano Canfora has shown, these traits consist mainly in the concept of the συγγένεια of mankind, the idea that the whole οἰκουμένη should be seen as one πόλις, and the pivotal role of πρόνοια for human life in general as well as for the historiographer in particular who acts as a minister (ὑπουργός) of providence (D.S. 1.1.3).[21] Moreover, many of the scientific paradigms adduced by the narrator in the *Bibliotheke*'s first books to explain physical phenomena and above all the relationship of natural conditions to human societies seem to stem from Stoic natural philosophy. A case in point is the "sun paradigm" adduced in D.S. 2.51–53 to explain the unique and marvellous char-

---

19 Diodorus' account here is once more based on Agatharchides' *On the Red Sea*, book 5. Compared to the corresponding passage in Photius' excerpt (*cod.* 250, *p.* 456b39–457a10), Diodorus' description is significantly longer (11 versus ca. 44 lines, cf. Bommelaer 1989, xlvi) and much more elaborate. The most significant difference (=addition/innovation by Diodorus?) is the comparison of the wrecks to cenotaphs and the use of the key term διασημαίνειν which are both absent in Photius' excerpt.
20 Cancik/Cancik-Lindemaier 2010, 181.
21 Cf. Canfora 1990, 317. See also Ambaglio/Landucci/Bravi 2008, 40–45 and 110–113.

acteristics of the flora and fauna of Arabia; this paradigm is probably derived from Poseidonius of Apameia.[22]

Given these points of reference, I propose to locate the *Bibliotheke*'s twofold textual dynamics of emotionalism and didacticism within Stoic concepts of reader response. In doing so, I draw on Martha C. Nussbaum's fundamental study on the Stoic views on "poetry and the passions".[23] Nussbaum identifies two such views, a "cognitive" and a "non-cognitive" one, the latter being the mainstream position held by Chrysippus and also by Seneca and Epictetus. She reconstructs this view in some detail, making use above all of Plutarch's *De audiendis poetis* to gain insight into Chrysippus' otherwise lost thoughts on the issue.[24] The gist of this position corresponds closely to what I have observed regarding the potential offered to the reader of the *Bibliotheke* in passages like the mine descriptions. For, as Nussbaum shows, central to this Stoic concept is the demand that the reader should be involved – and that means, above all, emotionally involved – with the text while still taking up an attitude of critical detachment.[25] Several techniques are recommended by the Stoics to this end, such as providing a running philosophical commentary to what one hears or reads, applying poetic statements to other similar situations (i.e. generalisation), and even employing humour and satire. Particularly relevant to the topic of this paper is the technique of generalisation. Plutarch in *De audiendis poetis* exemplifies this approach in a reference to Chrysippus (Plu. *Mor.* 34b4–34d1, transl. Babbitt):

> Τὴν δ' ἐπὶ πλέον τῶν λεγομένων χρῆσιν ὑπέδειξεν ὀρθῶς ὁ Χρύσιππος, ὅτι δεῖ μετάγειν καὶ διαβιβάζειν ἐπὶ τὰ ὁμοειδῆ τὸ χρήσιμον. [...] ὡς γὰρ φαρμάκου πρὸς ἓν ἁρμόσαντος νόσημα τὴν δύναμιν καταμαθόντες οἱ ἰατροὶ μετάγουσι καὶ χρῶνται πρὸς ἅπαν τὸ παραπλήσιον, οὕτω καὶ λόγον κοινοῦν καὶ δημοσιεύειν τὴν χρείαν δυνάμενον οὐ χρὴ περιορᾶν ἑνὶ πράγματι συνηρτημένον ἀλλὰ κινεῖν ἐπὶ πάντα τὰ ὅμοια, καὶ τοὺς νέους ἐθίζειν τὴν κοινότητα συνορᾶν καὶ μεταφέρειν ὀξέως τὸ οἰκεῖον, ἐν πολλοῖς παραδείγμασι ποιουμένους μελέτην καὶ ἄσκησιν ὀξυηκοΐας, ἵνα τοῦ Μενάνδρου λέγοντος
> μακάριος ὅστις οὐσίαν καὶ νοῦν ἔχει
> τοῦτο καὶ περὶ δόξης καὶ περὶ ἡγεμονίας καὶ περὶ λόγου δυνάμεως εἰρῆσθαι νομίζωσι [...].

Chrysippus has rightly indicated how the poet's statements can be given a wider application, saying that what is serviceable should be taken over and made to apply to like situa-

---

[22] Cf. Eck 2003, xxxviii–xl.
[23] Nussbaum 1993. The focus on the passions distinguishes her approach from the older study of De Lacy 1948.
[24] The methodological premise of this approach is that Plutarch's essay is informed by the Stoics' positions on poetry. To what degree exactly Plutarch draws on the Stoics in *De audiendis poetis* is debated; that he quotes Chrysippus and other Stoics and engages with their views, however, is evident (cf. Blank 2011; Hunter/Russell 2011, 11–15).
[25] Cf. Nussbaum 1993, 136–144.

tions. [...] For, as physicians who have learnt the efficacy of a drug adapted to one malady take it over and use it for every similar malady, so also when a statement has a general and universal value, we ought not to suffer it to be fixed upon one matter alone, but we ought to apply it to all the like, and inure the young men to see its general value, and quickly to carry over what is appropriate, and by many examples to give themselves training and practice in keen appreciation; so that when Menander says,
> Blest is the man who has both wealth and sense,

they may think of the statement as holding good also about repute and leadership and facility in speaking [...].

Nussbaum rightly emphasises the significance of the medical analogy: it shows that the attitude demanded from the listener or reader consists in "a peculiarly Stoic blend of criticism and compassion."[26]

Criticism and compassion aptly describe the stance that the passages of Diodorus' *Bibliotheke* discussed here demand from the reader. Moreover, generalisation is exactly what a reader needs to do if he intends to react to the didactic potential of these descriptions. Comparing different regions of the οἰκουμένη, which when reading the *Bibliotheke* amounts to comparing different parts of the narrator's account of the inhabited world, is a central element of, or even, as shown above, a precondition for learning from passages like the one on the Egyptian gold mines. Learning about the effects of a resource like gold on a human society involves generalisation, too, as the narrator's remark on the lesson given by nature (D.S. 3.14.5.) illustrates. At the same time, however, the reader is continuously invited to feel sympathy – not as a dynamic that overrules or contradicts criticism and learning, but on the contrary, one that interacts with, concurs with, and maybe even enables a didactic reading of the *Bibliotheke* in the first place.

It follows, then, that the reader who is conceived by this Stoic position on how to react to poetry may well be the model reader of the *Bibliotheke*[27] – a reader susceptible to the emotional as well as the intellectual charm of the book.

---

26 Nussbaum 1993, 141.
27 For the concept of the "model reader" see Eco 1979, 50–66.

Bibliography

Ambaglio, D. / Landucci, F. / Bravi, L. (2008), *Diodoro Siculo, Biblioteca storica. Commento storico. Introduzione generale*, Milan.
Anz, T. (1998), *Literatur und Lust. Glück und Unglück beim Lesen*, Munich.
Babbitt, F.C. (1927), *Plutarch's Moralia. Vol. I*, London / Cambridge.
Blank, D. (2011), "Reading Between the Lies: Plutarch and Chrysippus on the Uses of Poetry", in: *OSAP* 40, 235–264.
Bommelaer, B. (1989), *Diodore de Sicile. Bibliothèque Historique. Livre III*, Paris.
Bona, E. / Curnis, M. (eds.) (2010), *Linguaggi del Potere, Poteri del Linguaggio*, Alexandria.
Brunschwig, J. / Nussbaum, M.C. (eds.) (1993), *Passions and Perceptions. Studies in Hellenistic Philosophy of Mind. Proceedings of the Fifth Symposium Hellenisticum*, Cambridge.
Cancik, H. / Cancik-Lindemaier, H. (2010), "'Oikumenische Geschichte': Die Begründung von Universalgeschichtsschreibung bei Diodor von Sizilien", in: *Hyperboreus* 16/17, 167–182.
Canfora, L. (1990), "Le but de l'historiographie selon Diodore", in: H. Verdin / G. Schepens / E. de Keyser 1990, 313–320.
De Lacy (1948), "Stoic Views of Poetry", in: *AJPh* 69, 241–271.
De Morais Mota, C. (2010), *The Lessons of Universal History of Diodorus of Sicily's. An Educational Process of Humanity*, Saarbrücken.
Eck, B. (2003), *Diodore de Sicile. Bibliothèque Historique. Livre II*, Paris.
Eco, U. (1979), *Lector in fabula. La cooperazione interpretativa nei testi narrativi*, Milan.
Genette, G. (1972), "Discours du récit. Essai de méthode", in: id., *Figures III*, Paris, 65–282.
Hunter, R. / Russell, D. (eds.) (2011), *Plutarch. How to Study Poetry*, Cambridge.
Iser, W. (1984²), *Der Akt des Lesen. Theorie ästhetischer Wirkung*, Munich.
Konstan, D. (2001), *Pity Transformed*, London.
Konstan, D. (2006), *The Emotions of the Ancient Greeks. Studies in Aristotle and Classical Literature*, Toronto / Buffalo / London.
Laffranque, M. (1957), "Poseidonios d'Apamée et les mines d'Ibérie", in: *Pallas* 5, 17–25.
Lausberg, H. (2008⁴), *Handbuch der literarischen Rhetorik. Eine Grundlegung der Literaturwissenschaft*, Stuttgart.
Nünning, A. (ed.) (2009⁴), *Metzler Lexikon Literatur und Kulturtheorie*, Stuttgart / Weimar.
Nussbaum, M.C. (1993), "Poetry and the Passions: Two Stoic Views", in: J. Brunschwig / M.C. Nussbaum 1993, 97–149.
Oldfather, C.H. et al. (1935–1967), *Diodorus of Sicily. The Library of History*, vols. I-XII, Cambridge / London.
Plett, H.F. (2012), *Enargeia in Classical Antiquity and the Early Modern Age. The Aesthetics of Evidence*, Leiden / Boston.
Trevisan, R. (2010), "Un' eterogenea descrizione del mondo: i libri I–V della Biblioteca Storica di Diodoro Siculo", in: E. Bona / M. Curnis 2010, 265–288.
Verdin, H. / Schepens, G. / de Keyser, E. (eds.) (1990), *Purposes of History. Studies in Greek Historiography from the 4th to the 2nd Centuries B.C. Proceedings of the International Colloquium Leuven, 24–26 May 1988*, Leuven.
Webb, R. (2009), *Ekphrasis, Imagination and Persuasion in Ancient Rhetorical Theory and Practice*, Farnham, Surrey / Burlington.
Wolf, W. (2009⁴), "Fokalisierung", in: A. Nünning 2009⁴, 211–212.

Eugénie Fournel
Dream Narratives in Plutarch's *Lives:* The Place of Fiction in Biography

Abstract: This article seeks to explore the close relationship between biography and history in Plutarch's *Caesar* and *Pompey* by examining how dream narratives, however fictional and unrealistic they might seem, are deeply rooted in the historical tradition, and therefore enable the biographer to elaborate his *persona* as a historian, such as Suetonius does in the *Lives of the Twelve Caesars*. The article analyzes Plutarch's method and sources to examine how this author reconstructed historical truth by rewriting previous versions of existing dreams, or by inventing unattested dreams '*kata ta deonta*', according to Stefan Feddern's interpretation of the phrase in Thucydides' preface. Finally, the article analyzes the various narrative strategies at play in Plutarch's dream narratives, which emphasize some aspects of the protagonists' main features through inter- and intratextual literary allusions.

Historiography and biography had very different purposes and functions in Antiquity: historiographers accounted for facts, whereas biographers wrote rhetorical and subjective portraits to pass a judgement on important men, most of the time positive. Indeed, in Hellenistic times, the emerging genre of the βίος was very much influenced by *encomia* and biographical novels like Xenophon's *Cyropaedia*. Moral and ideological aims would lead biographers to distance themselves from previous historical accounts in order to emphasize some aspects of the character's (supposed) personality or actions over others. Therefore, the portraits drawn did not necessarily correspond to reality, but suited the author's will to present his character as a moral, philosophical, or political example.

Plutarch's biographies were no exception. He wrote political biographies, but was also a moralist, and his work tends to illustrate the most prominent virtues of politicians, military leaders and wise men through examples and counterexamples. Moreover, his choice to write parallel biographies in order to compare Ancient Greeks to Romans also imposed a major constraint on him and led him to emphasize, sometimes artificially, similarities over differences so that his pairs would match well together. As a consequence, he sometimes omitted facts or distorted historical truth to suit his own ideological purpose.¹

Plutarch never pretended to write history, as he asserted in the preamble to the *Life of Alexander:*

> οὔτε γὰρ ἱστορίας γράφομεν, ἀλλὰ βίους, οὔτε ταῖς ἐπιφανεστάταις πράξεσι πάντως ἔνεστι δήλωσις ἀρετῆς ἢ κακίας, ἀλλὰ πρᾶγμα βραχὺ πολλάκις καὶ ῥῆμα καὶ παιδιά τις ἔμφασιν ἤθους ἐποίησε μᾶλλον ἢ μάχαι μυριόνεκροι καὶ παρατάξεις αἱ μέγισται καὶ πολιορκίαι πόλεων, ὥσπερ οὖν οἱ ζωγράφοι τὰς ὁμοιότητας ἀπὸ τοῦ προσώπου καὶ τῶν περὶ τὴν ὄψιν εἰδῶν, οἷς ἐμφαίνεται τὸ ἦθος, ἀναλαμβάνουσιν, ἐλάχιστα τῶν λοιπῶν μερῶν φροντίζοντες, οὕτως ἡμῖν δοτέον εἰς τὰ τῆς ψυχῆς σημεῖα μᾶλλον ἐνδύεσθαι καὶ διὰ τούτων εἰδοποιεῖν τὸν ἑκάστου βίον, ἐάσαντας ἑτέροις τὰ μεγέθη καὶ τοὺς ἀγῶνας.

> For it is not histories that I am writing, but lives; and in the most illustrious deeds there is not always a manifestation of virtue or vice, but a slight thing like a phrase or a jest often makes a greater revelation of character than battles where thousands fall, or the greatest armaments, or sieges of cities. Accordingly, just as painters get the likenesses in their portraits from the face and the expression of the eyes, wherein the character shows itself, but make very little account of the other parts of the body, so I must be permitted to devote myself rather to the signs of the soul in men, and by means of these to portray the life of each, leaving to others the description of their great contests.²

The distinction between historiography and biography did not exist in classical historiographers' mind and work: Herodotus, in particular, gathered a substantial amount of biographical material in the course of his work when evoking Persian kings and Greek generals. In her analysis of Herodotus' work, Homeyer characterized these portraits as 'proto-biographies' which contributed to the elaboration of the βίος.³

Although Plutarch distances himself from historiographers, he tends nevertheless to follow the principles which he advises historiographers to apply in *On the Malice of Herodotus*: he cares very much about accounting for the truth when he knows it, and when his sources contain different versions of the same episode, he relates the version that is the most favorable to his character.⁴ His critical mind and his numerous political analyses enable us to read his biographies as forming a kind of general history of Greece and Rome.⁵ That is why Pel-

---

1 Stadter 1992, 4–5.
2 Plu. *Alex.* 1.2–3 (*Plutarch's Lives with an English Translation by Bernadotte Perrin*, Cambridge, London, 1919). See also Plb. 10.21.2–4.
3 Homeyer 1962.
4 See Plu. *On the Malice of Herodotus*, 855c–856d.
5 Pelling 2002, 132.

ling asserts that 'Plutarch is the only Greek political biographer who allows serious analysis' in the comparison between historiography and biography.[6]

On the course of his work, Plutarch relies on a large number of Greek and Roman historians: Thucydides, Herodotus, Philistus, Timaeus, Sallust, Hieronymus of Cardia, Diodorus, Dionysius of Halicarnassus, Polybius and Asinius Pollio, to name only the most important. Though he probably did not have first-hand knowledge of all these sources, he was obviously familiar with them. Whenever he could, Plutarch based his biographical work on historical sources, whether through quotation or indirect reference. It was a way for him to build his own *auctoritas* as a historical biographer, such as Suetonius does in the *Lives of the Twelve Caesars*.[7] However, Plutarch could not resort very often to autopsy in his *Lives* because most of the men he wrote about lived long before him.

A deeper analysis of Plutarch's writing process led Pelling to conclude that, for each *Life* or sequence of *Lives*, he followed one major historical source, of which he probably had a copy at hand that he could read or that a slave would read to him while he was writing; in the course of his writing, he would add material borrowed from other sources when necessary.[8] Therefore, the historical value of his biographical writings has been rehabilitated, and it is now clear that despite his ideological and moral aims, he was very concerned with accounting accurately for facts. In addition, two texts from the *Moralia*, *On the Malice of Herodotus* and *How we are to judge history*, show a real theoretical reflection on historiography.

My purpose here is to analyze how Plutarch managed to reconcile the paradoxical requirements of political biography, accounting for what he objectively believed to be the truth on the one hand, and on the other, composing and organizing his material into a coherent artistic unity with literary, philosophical and moral purposes.[9] To this end, we will focus on dream narratives, because they belong to the category of 'significant details' that have a crucial role in his biographies, according to Plutarch. Indeed, their predictive value plays an important part in putting great men's lives and careers into perspective.

Fictional dream narratives have played a major role in Greek literature since as early as Homer: we can therefore imagine that it has always been a temptation for historians to invent dreams. Indeed, no one but the dreamer can guarantee

---

6 Pelling 2002, 144.
7 See Duchêne in this volume.
8 Pelling 2002, 19–26.
9 Plutarch belongs to the tradition of political biography, whereas Hellenistic biographers mainly wrote about writers or philosophers. On this distinction, see Momigliano 1983, 65–88.

nor question the reality of a dream.[10] As the number of dream narratives in the *Lives* exceeds the limits of this study, we will concentrate on two Roman *Lives*, *Caesar* and *Pompey*, as a starting point to analyze Plutarch's approach of historical truth.[11]

We will first reflect upon Plutarch's method in order to determine which elements he had at his disposal when he was writing, and how he used them. That determination will enable us to reconsider Plutarch's attitude towards truth, and the degree of freedom he enjoyed to reconstruct some parts of it. We will then try to show how Plutarch used the symbolical and allegorical functions of dreams in order to characterize his protagonists, Caesar and Pompey, through inter- and intra-textual echoes.

1 Dreams in the *Lives:* historical truth and psychological verisimilitude

Caesar and *Pompey* are two Roman *Lives* who belong, according to Pelling,[12] to a group of six (*Antony, Caesar, Pompey, Brutus, Crassus, Cato minor*) that might have been prepared simultaneously in the 110's, as they present numerous cross-references and refer to the same historical background (i.e., the Civil wars).[13]

To document these lives, Plutarch mostly relied on Latin historical sources: evidence tends to suggest that his main source was Asinius Pollio, lieutenant and close friend of Julius Caesar, who accompanied him on several campaigns and wrote a history of the civil wars in seventeen books, of which, unfortunately, nothing remains; any textual comparison is therefore impossible.[14] Among other sources, we find Oppius, Sallust and Livy. Oppius was another of Caesar's intimates; he wrote memoirs in Latin about Caesar, of which we can find traces in Plutarch.[15] Oppius' language might have been obscure or unclear at times, and might have been the cause of approximations or errors in the *Lives*. More generally, it raises the question of Plutarch's understanding of the Latin lan-

---

10 Brenk 1975, 344.
11 Brenk (1975, 337) reports 45 detailed dream narratives in the *Lives*.
12 Pelling 2002, 1–26.
13 Pelling 2011, 36. For a detailed review of cross-references and a chronology of the group, see Pelling 1979, 80–81.
14 Pelling 1979, 84–85. For more information on Asinius Pollio and the *testimonia* of his work, see André 1949.
15 See Townend 1987, 325–342.

guage. As he confesses in his *Life of Demosthenes*, he did not have time to study Latin until late in his life, and even if he was more familiar with it when he wrote the *Lives*, he could still have encountered comprehension issues.[16]

As none of the direct sources of the *Lives* of the Republic is available to us, the only way to find whether Plutarch followed previous sources or used 'creative reconstruction'[17] is to compare his texts to the other Greek and Roman historians who wrote on the same time-period before and after him, and probably used similar materials. Therefore, we will focus on four significant dream narratives in order to analyze Plutarch's strategic choices and the intentions that underlie them.

The first important dream in *Caesar* happens just before the crossing of the Rubicon, the first turning point in Caesar's career. Plutarch is the only source to mention that Caesar had a dream the night before crossing the Rubicon:

> τέλος δὲ μετὰ θυμοῦ τινος ὥσπερ ἀφεὶς ἑαυτὸν ἐκ τοῦ λογισμοῦ πρὸς τὸ μέλλον, καὶ τοῦτο δὴ τὸ κοινὸν τοῖς εἰς τύχας ἐμβαίνουσιν ἀπόρους καὶ τόλμας προοίμιον ὑπειπὼν 'Ἀνερρίφθω κύβος,' ὥρμησε πρὸς τὴν διάβασιν, καὶ δρόμῳ τὸ λοιπὸν ἤδη χρώμενος, εἰσέπεσε πρὸ ἡμέρας εἰς τὸ Ἀρίμινον, καὶ κατέσχε. λέγεται δὲ τῇ προτέρᾳ νυκτὶ τῆς διαβάσεως ὄναρ ἰδεῖν ἔκθεσμον, ἐδόκει γὰρ αὐτὸς τῇ ἑαυτοῦ μητρὶ μίγνυσθαι τὴν ἄρρητον μεῖξιν.

> Then, finally, as if with a burst of passion, he abandoned his counsels and hurled himself forward into the path that laid before him. As he went he uttered those words that so often serve as the prelude for some incalculable risk or audacious enterprise: 'let the die be cast'. Then he moved swiftly to cross the river. He galloped the rest of the journey, and burst into Ariminum before dawn and took the city. It is said that, the night before he crossed, he dreamed a monstrous dream. It seemed to him that he was lying with his own mother – the unspeakable union.[18]

The content of this dream is similar to one that Dio and Suetonius situate in 62, during Caesar's quaestorship in Spain.[19] In both authors, this dream is associated with the theme of the *imitatio Alexandri*. This dream was considered predictive by the interpreters whom Caesar consulted: as Caesar secretly wished to surpass Alexander, the dream meant that he was destined by the gods to rule the whole earth, represented as Caesar's mother in the dream (the homology between 'earth' and 'mother' is a *topos* in Greek culture and religion).

---

16 Plu. *Dem.* 2.2.
17 Pelling 2002, 154.
18 Plu. *Caes.* 32.8–9 (Ziegler 1935), translation by Christopher Pelling (2011).
19 D.C. 37.52.2; Suet. *Diuus Iulius* 7.2. For a comparative study of all the Greek and Roman sources mentioning this episode, see Rondholz 2009.

By transferring an existing dream to a completely different context, Plutarch changes its meaning and interpretation considerably; indeed, the stimulus of the dream is completely different, and does not refer to the *imitatio Alexandri*.

It was a common technique among historiographers to use dreams to highlight climactic moments of their narratives;[20] as a consequence, dreams are particularly frequent just before a military campaign or a battle of great importance. In line with this tradition, Plutarch wished to indicate explicitly that Caesar was taking a decisive step towards the conquest of power. As no previous source mentioned a dream during the crossing of the Rubicon, he used a dream that was attested earlier in Caesar's career. Plutarch was not by nature as inclined to invent prodigies as Suetonius, who brought in a supernatural figure playing the flute to encourage Caesar to cross;[21] Plutarch might have thought that a dream was more plausible because, either in historical accounts or in epics, it often happens to generals the night before a decisive battle. Nevertheless, a slight inconsistency remains: in Plutarch's version, Caesar rode to Ariminum immediately after dinner and crossed the Rubicon before having had time to rest: we can therefore wonder when he could have had such a dream. This illogicality and the fact that he is the only source to place this dream at that moment allow the conclusion that Plutarch deliberately distorted the truth to dramatize this crucial episode; indeed, it is highly unlikely that any other source mentioned a similar version.

The second climactic moment of Caesar's career, his confrontation with Pompey at Pharsalus, is also marked by a dream. According to Plutarch, Appian and Lucan, Pompey had a dream on the night before the battle (which does not appear in Dio and Suetonius).[22] There are two versions of this dream, both of which appear in Plutarch. In *Caesar*, Pompey is sitting in his theater, applauded by the Romans:

> ὡς δ' εἰς τὴν Φαρσαλίαν ἐμβαλόντες ἀμφότεροι κατεστρατοπέδευσαν, ὁ μὲν Πομπήϊος αὖθις εἰς τὸν ἀρχαῖον ἀνεκρούετο λογισμὸν τὴν γνώμην, ἔτι καὶ φασμάτων οὐκ αἰσίων προσγενομένων καὶ καθ' ὕπνον ὄψεως· ἐδόκει γὰρ ἑαυτὸν ὁρᾶν ἐν τῷ θεάτρῳ κροτούμενον ὑπὸ Ῥωμαίων. οἱ δὲ περὶ αὐτὸν οὕτω θρασεῖς ἦσαν καὶ τὸ νίκημα ταῖς ἐλπίσι προειληφότες, ὥστε φιλονικεῖν ὑπὲρ τῆς Καίσαρος ἀρχιερωσύνης Δομίτιον καὶ Σπινθῆρα καὶ Σκηπίωνα διαμιλλωμένους ἀλλήλοις, πέμπειν δὲ πολλοὺς εἰς Ῥώμην, μισθουμένους καὶ προκαταλαμ-

---

[20] e.g. Herodotus, Xenophon, Diodorus Siculus, Tacitus, Livy, etc. Thucydides is an exception in this respect as he never uses dream narratives. For a study of the functions of dreams in ancient history, see Dodson 2009, 84–100.
[21] Suet. *Jul.* 32.2.
[22] App. *BC* 2.68–69; Luc. 7.9–28.

βάνοντας οἰκίας ὑπατεύουσι καὶ στρατηγοῦσιν ἐπιτηδείους, ὡς εὐθὺς ἄρξοντες μετὰ τὸν πόλεμον.

Both armies came to the district of Pharsalus and pitched camp. Pompey now reverted to his earlier strategy: he was influenced too by certain unfavourable omens, and also by a dream in which he had seen himself back in his theatre, applauded by the Romans. But his company were full of themselves and confident of victory, so much so that Domitius and Spinther and Scipio were already wrangling among themselves as to who should succeed Caesar as *pontifex maximus*, and there were many who sent representatives to Rome to rent and put in early bids for houses that would be suitable for consuls and praetors: so sure were they that they would take office immediately after the war.[23]

Lucan has a similar version. However, according to Appian, Pompey dreamt that he was dedicating a temple to Venus Victrix. Appian makes the meaning of the dream unambiguous by mentioning that, before the battle, Caesar vowed to dedicate a temple to Venus Victrix, and saw a supernatural light burning away on Pompey's camp.

In *Pompey*, Plutarch enriches the content of the dream by combining both versions into a single narrative;[24] this choice can seem odd at first, as the two elements seem to foreshadow opposite outcomes: Pompey, being applauded by the Romans, seems auspicious for him, whereas the reference to Venus Victrix announces Caesar's victory. Therefore, by merging two different elements, Plutarch complicates the dream, which now connects the two *Lives* and emphasizes their complementarity: as a result, he requires from his audience a parallel reading. Nevertheless, Plutarch does not associate Pompey's dedication to Caesar's vow, as Appian does. As a consequence, the meaning of the dream is more ambiguous, as Pompey's reaction suggests (τὰ μὲν ἐθάρρει, τὰ δὲ ὑπέθραττεν αὐτὸν ἡ ὄψις, 'he was encouraged by some aspects of the dream, but depressed by others').

Caesar's and Pompey's dreams call to mind the last dream of the series that Xerxes has in Herodotus' *Histories,* after he had finally resolved to campaign against Greece: Ἡ δὲ ὄψις ἦν ἥδε· ἐδόκεε ὁ Ξέρξης ἐστεφανῶσθαι ἐλαίης θαλλῷ, ἀπὸ δὲ τῆς ἐλαίης τοὺς κλάδους γῆν πᾶσαν ἐπισχεῖν, μετὰ δὲ ἀφανισθῆναι περὶ τῇ κεφαλῇ κείμενον τὸν στέφανον ('Here is the content of the vision: Xerxes was wearing a crown of olive tree, the branches covering the whole

---

23 Plu. *Caes.* 42.1–2.
24 Plu. *Pomp.* 68.2. The fact that Plutarch wrote *Pompey* at the end of the series on the end of the Roman Republic can explain that the content of the dream is more detailed, in accordance with Pelling's theory of the 'increasing knowledge' (Pelling 1979, 75–83) between the first and last *Lives* of the group. Some editors believe, thanks to *Pompey,* that there is a lacuna in *Caesar* that we have to fill, but we do not need to assume that both versions were identical.

earth; after some time, the crown which surrounded his head disappeared.').[25] As Caesar's dream, this oniric vision contains a symbol of domination over the whole earth, and it has the same binary structure with Pompey's dream, the first part portending victory and the second one, a more pessimistic outcome. This passage is an example of the influence which Herodotus had on later writers such as Plutarch, especially regarding dreams.[26] The biographer borrowed symbols and patterns which had become *topoi* in classical literature in order to enrich his own narrative and give it a deeper meaning. Indeed, as Pelling rightly asserted, 'a narrative is simply *more plausible* if it already maps on to a pattern that its audience finds familiar'[27] (we will come back to this assertion later in the discussion).

Finally, at the end of *Caesar* we encounter a dream which seems marginal in the narrative but is very important in light of our study, because we find it nowhere else in the sources on the period. Dio and Suetonius relate that after the assassination of Caesar, Heluius Cinna, a *tribunus plebis*, was torn into pieces because he was mistaken for Cornelius Cinna, a *praetor* who had spoken violently against Caesar the day before.[28] Plutarch draws the reader's attention on this character by mentioning a dream that Cinna had the night before his death:

> Κίννας δέ τις τῶν Καίσαρος ἑταίρων ἔτυχε μέν, ὥς φασι, τῆς παρῳχημένης νυκτὸς ὄψιν ἑωρακὼς ἄτοπον· ἐδόκει γὰρ ὑπὸ Καίσαρος ἐπὶ δεῖπνον καλεῖσθαι, παραιτούμενος δ' ἄγεσθαι τῆς χειρὸς ὑπ' αὐτοῦ, μὴ βουλόμενος ἀλλ' ἀντιτείνων. ὡς δ' ἤκουσεν ἐν ἀγορᾷ τὸ σῶμα καίεσθαι τοῦ Καίσαρος, ἀναστὰς ἐβάδιζεν ἐπὶ τιμῇ, καίπερ ὑφορώμενός τε τὴν ὄψιν ἅμα καὶ πυρέττων.

> But there was a certain Cinna, a friend of Caesar, who (so they say) had had a strange dream on the previous night. He dreamed that Caesar was inviting him to dinner, and he was trying to decline; but Caesar led him along by the hand, even though he was unwilling and trying to resist. When Cinna heard that Caesar's body was burning in the forum, he rose from his bed and went to pay respect, even though his dream caused him some misgiving and he was suffering from a fever.[29]

---

25 Hdt. 7.19.
26 The *Histories* contain several interesting dreams, most of which present noticeable similitudes with epic and tragic dream narratives.
27 Pelling 2013, 1.
28 Suet. *Diuus Jul.* 85.2; D.C. 44.50; Appian (App. *BC* 2.127) states that a group of veterans and supporters of Caesar threw stones at Cornelius Cinna because he was wearing the *toga praetexta* that he had publicly abandoned the day before.
29 Plu. *Caes.* 68.3.

In this case, it is most probable that Plutarch invented the dream, as far as we can tell from the preserved sources at our disposal. Indeed, if this dream was attested by the historiographical tradition, it would be surprising that neither of the three other authors mentioned it, and the fact that Appian and Dio are supposed to have used the same sources with Plutarch supports this assumption.[30] There is every probability that Plutarch enriched Cinna's story to make it more meaningful. As a matter of fact, this fictional dream subtly echoes Caesar's death, through the gesture that reminds the attentive reader of Brutus' behaviour when he was trying to make Caesar follow him to the Senate on the Ides of March: ταῦθ' ἅμα λέγων ὁ Βροῦτος ἦγε τῆς χειρὸς λαβόμενος τὸν Καίσαρα ('As Brutus spoke, he took Caesar by the hand and began to lead him out').[31]

Plutarch does not hesitate to elaborate on details to dramatize a situation: when he relates Calpurnia's dream on the night preceding the Ides of March, he gives more details than Appian, Dio, or Suetonius, who focus on the factual content of the dream. In particular, he emphasizes the sounds (the noise of the doors opening suddenly, τῷ κτύπῳ, Calpurnia's murmurs, ἀσαφεῖς δὲ φωνὰς καὶ στεναγμοὺς ἀνάρθρους).[32] He also mentions her weeping in the dream (κλαίειν). In the silence of the night, these visual and auditive perceptions create a gloomy and macabre atmosphere that provokes Caesar's distress. Plutarch mentions two versions of this dream, a 'theorematic' vision showing what will actually take place, and an allegorical version attributed to Livy, who uses the sacred symbol of the broken gable to evoke Caesar's death.[33] We can assume that Plutarch chose to develop the theorematic dream because its visual dimension could have a greater impact on the reader's mind: therefore, the dream contributes better to creating the *pathos* of the situation, whereas a symbolic dream would have implied intellectualization through the process of interpretation.[34] The narration of this dream is an example where Plutarch, like previous historiographers, quotes his sources faithfully and objectively presents the various versions of a dream so that the reader can decide by himself which version is most likely true.

As we have shown so far, Plutarch treats his sources in many different ways. Most of the time, he is respectful of the historical tradition, but also resorts to

---

[30] It is one of the most significant examples of the process that Pelling (1997, 199) calls 'creative reconstruction'; furthermore, it is not exceptional, as according to Pelling (2010, 315), two thirds of the dream narratives in the *Lives* are attested only in Plutarch.
[31] Plu. *Caes.* 64.4.
[32] Plu. *Caes.* 63.5.
[33] The distinction between 'theorematic' and 'allegorical' dreams refers to Artemidorus (*Oneirocritica*, 1.2).
[34] Brenk 1975, 339.

'creative reconstruction'[35] when needed, through various authorial choices; indeed, when it comes to dreams, he sometimes distances himself from his sources and fills the gaps or distorts the truth according to probability (τὸ εἰκός): therefore we can say that, in line with Thucydides in his speeches, Plutarch reconstructs the past κατὰ τὰ δέοντα, inventing dreams which are appropriate to the characters and circumstances he describes, and give information about their true nature.[36] As a biographer, Plutarch enjoys the license to rewrite history, to some degree, and imagine circumstances, as long as he writes things as they must have happened. In this perspective, the relevant distinction in Plutarch is not between truth and fiction, but between 'plausible' and 'implausible' invention.[37] Moreover, as dreams depend so much upon the subjectivity of the dreamer, they allow the biographer more room to enrich a situation with additional significations and implicit judgments that we will now bring to light.

2 Dreams and characterization: inter- and intratextual patterns in the *Lives*

Plutarch uses dreams to indicate climactic moments, combined with other portents and divine signs which make the gods' will manifest. In our modern perception, dreams are considered a part of a person's inner life, relevant to the study of the *psyche*, but not to the comprehension of historical events. The situation is very different in antiquity, where dreams are believed to be prophetic. It is therefore capital to understand what they forecast and how, but, within the frame of biographies like *Caesar* and *Pompey*, they are also useful for putting events into perspective, for characterizing great men more completely and for passing moral judgments on their career.

In *Caesar* and *Pompey*, Plutarch gives different accounts of the preparation of the battle in order to contrast the two generals. Pompey is presented as indecisive and weak, because he changes his mind twice before the battle: according to Plutarch, Pompey wanted to avoid battle because he feared its outcome. Ac-

---

[35] Pelling 2002, 154 about Wiseman 1981, 389.
[36] See in this volume the discussion of κατὰ τὰ δέοντα by Feddern in Thucydides' preface.
[37] Levene (2011) showed that in ancient time historiographers were given the license either to follow closely (almost word for word) a previous account of an event, or to rewrite it completely in accordance with their own conception of the historical truth. Indeed, apart from a very narrow substrate of unquestionable historical facts, the rest of what we consider as part of 'history' can vary a lot from an author to another, especially in the description of circumstances, the addition of details or the emphasis put on specific characters.

cused of cowardice and treason, he finally resolves to fight, but at the last minute, reverts to his original decision because of disturbing signs; in addition, he cannot decide on the meaning of an ambiguous dream he had. Plutarch, therefore, makes Pompey appear as a weak general, lacking authority and self-confidence and unable to make a decision. Caesar is also confronted by ambiguous portents, because the priests whom he consults regarding the outcome of the battle tell him to expect a reversal of fortune, but let him decide if it will be for good or bad, according to his own estimate of his actual situation. Nevertheless, contrary to Pompey, he never hesitates, and his conviction to win seems even strengthened by the challenge. He seems to respect the gods and the religious rituals that ensure their assistance in a battle (sacrifices, prayers), whereas Pompey omits them.

On another level, this episode proves that, for Plutarch, knowing the future does not enable anyone to avoid facing its consequences, because divine causality is inescapable: even though Pompey almost avoided facing Caesar twice, he let his army rush into battle in spite of the gods' warnings because of his indecision. The dream reinforces the tragedy of his situation by reminding him of his past popularity, a time where his authority was respected and approved by the Roman people.

Some dreams arouse confusion and hesitation, but others remedy it, as we can see in the episode of the crossing of the Rubicon. It is a bold political act on Caesar's part, because he knows very well that his decision will change the course of history, for better or worse. Caesar first hesitates to cross the river, and tries to solve his dilemma by consulting his friends. Then he abruptly decides to rush forward: this haste is surprising because it contrasts with his previous circumspection. It is only at the very end of the paragraph that Plutarch quickly mentions the dream, as if he intended to explain what helped Caesar make up his mind. If we examine closely the vocabulary used by Plutarch (ἀφείς, ὥρμησε), we notice that both words connote a sudden action.[38] Caesar's decision is therefore not pondered but irrational and impulsive. The reader is led to think that the meaning of the dream was so obvious that Caesar had no reason to hesitate anymore, as if the gods had already decided for him.

Caesar seems to interpret the dream as a prediction of success. It might prove that this typical dream, later mentioned by Artemidorus in his *Oneirocritika*, was already common in Caesar's days (ἀγαθὸν δὲ καὶ παντὶ δημαγωγῷ

---

[38] This element of haste is underlined by Rondholz (2009, 447) as a *topos* of the 'myth' of the crossing of the Rubicon by Caesar. Indeed, we find it in all the detailed versions of the episode (Plutarch, Appian, Lucan). Only Suetonius interestingly makes the opposite choice by mentioning Caesar's wanderings between Ravenna and the Rubicon.

καὶ πολιτευτῇ· σημαίνει γὰρ τὴν πατρίδα ἡ μήτηρ, '[the dream] is good also for demagogues and politicians: mother stands for motherland').[39] Such an interpretation is consistent with the original context of the dream, when Caesar was *quaestor* in Spain, because it was a sign for him that he would soon equal or even surpass Alexander the Great by conquering the whole earth. In 62, he was indeed on the threshold of a promising career. The superposition of contexts characterizes the crossing of the Rubicon as a *discrimen* which marks a turning point both in Caesar's career and in Italy's destiny: if Artemidorus' interpretation was shared by Plutarch's audience, they could then read this dream as a forecast of Caesar's conquests and domination over Italy. Indeed, if the mother represents motherland, the dream prefigures one of the consequences of the crossing of the Rubicon, Caesar seizing absolute power over Rome, his *patria*.[40]

Plutarch distances himself from this interpretation by adding a moral judgment in the dream, through the use of the words ἔκθεσμον and τὴν ἄρρητον μεῖξιν to qualify the sexual act. To his eyes, the union is 'monstrous' and not permitted because of its incestuous nature.[41] This condemnation contains an implicit reference to the *topos* of the incestuous τύραννος, of which we find an example in Herodotus. The night before Marathon, the tyrant Hippias receives the same dream than Caesar: τοῖσι δὲ βαρβάροισι κατηγέετο Ἱππίης ὁ Πεισιστράτου ἐς τὸν Μαραθῶνα, τῆς παροιχομένης νυκτὸς ὄψιν ἰδὼν τοιήνδε· ἐδόκεε ὁ Ἱππίης τῇ μητρὶ τῇ ἑωυτοῦ συνευνηθῆναι ('Hippias son of Peisistratus led the barbarians to Marathon; the previous night, he had the following vision: he dreamt that he was lying in bed with his mother').[42] In the context of the Graeco-Persian wars, Hippias, who originated from Athens, interpreted his dream in a positive way, as meaning that he would return to his fatherland, win back his power and die there afterwards. But as soon as he reaches Marathon, he loses a tooth in the sand, and understands that the dream concerned his tooth only, and not him. Hippias died shortly after, during the battle of Lemnos. This episode is an example of the tragic irony often displayed in dreams.

---

[39] Artem. 1.79. Plutarch does not say explicitly how Caesar interpreted his dream, but guides the reader's interpretation of the passage.
[40] The *patria* appears to Caesar in a more disguised way than in Lucan, but represents in both cases a divine warning about the transgression of law.
[41] The periphrasis used by Plutarch might be a sign of his embarrassment and reluctance to name the sexual act properly (Brenk 1977, 226). See also Grotanelli 1999, 150.
[42] Hdt. 6.107. The *topos* of the incestuous *tyrannos* appears in Herodotus, but also in S. *OT*, in D.L. about Periander (1.96) and in Pl. *R*. 9.574d–575a.

The similarity of Hippias' and Caesar's dreams invites us to think, though it is never explicit, that Plutarch intentionally alluded to Herodotus in order to underline Caesar's misinterpretation of the warning contained in the dream: if he acts against the laws of his fatherland, he will become a τύραννος like Hippias, and experience the same end.[43] We can therefore read it as a proleptic condemnation of Caesar's *hybris* which will lead him to death because of his unlimited *libido dominandi*.

The superimposition of these two opposite interpretations shows the complexity of this dream, which requires the reader to decode multiple layers of signification.[44] The proleptic meaning of prophetic dreams enables Plutarch to elaborate narrative strategies similar to those of Heliodorus or Achilles Tatius. Indeed, these novelists make an extensive use of symbolic dreams and play on the variety of possible interpretations in order to maintain suspense and to violate – entirely or partially – the reader's expectations.

Shadi Bartsch analyzes several examples of these strategies in *Leucippe and Clitophon* and in the *Aithiopica*.[45] For example, in the first novel, when Clitophon enters Leucippe's room at night to convince her to escape with him, her mother Pantheia has a dream:

> ἐδόκει τινὰ ληστὴν μάχαιραν ἔχοντα γυμνὴν ἄγειν ἁρπασάμενον αὐτῆς τὴν θυγατέρα καὶ καταθέμενον ὑπτίαν, μέσην ἀνατεμεῖν τῇ μαχαίρᾳ τὴν γαστέρα, κάτωθεν ἀρξάμενον ἀπὸ τῆς αἰδοῦς.

> She was being disturbed by a dream, in which she saw a bandit with a naked sword seize her daughter, drag her away, throw her down on her back and slice her in two all the way up from her stomach, making his first insertion at her modest spot.[46]

When Pantheia rushes to her daughter's room and sees Clitophon running away, she is persuaded that the dream meant he had dishonoured Leucippe. Indeed, the allegorical meaning of the vision seems clear: Clitophon is the bandit who destroyed Leucippe's reputation by having illicit intercourse with her, the opening of the belly being a metaphor of the sexual act. The reader is therefore encouraged to believe Pantheia's explanation, which seems logical, though it is clear in the narrative that Clitophon did not intend to harm Leucippe. However,

---

[43] We cannot be entirely sure that Plutarch had Herodotus in mind when he was writing this passage, but his audience was probably familiar with the herodotean text.
[44] The complexity of incestuous dreams is analyzed in detail by Grotanelli (1999), who raises the issue of the contradictory interpretations of this type of dream in the literary tradition.
[45] Bartsch 1989, 85–106.
[46] Ach. Tat., *Leucippe and Clitophon*, 2.23.5.

it is only much later in the narrative, when the reader has completely forgotten the dream episode, that it is unexpectedly reenacted: Leucippe is captured by bandits, who stage a fake human sacrifice witnessed by Clitophon, and repeat the very gesture that Pantheia saw in her dream.[47] It is not until that moment that the reader understands that the dream was also forecasting Leucippe's first *Scheintod*. Achilles Tatius, therefore, creates a strong element of surprise for the reader: though this dream seemed merely anecdotal, it announced a crucial episode; this use of dreams is very subtle because the author combines an immediate, literal fulfillment of the dream, with a truer and more metaphorical one, delayed later in the narrative.

This strategy is, to some degree, similar to what we encounter in Plutarch. In the Rubicon episode, the dream also announces a double fulfillment: Caesar will conquer power, become master of the Roman Empire and extend its geographical boundaries, but a series of acts of *hybris* starting with the crossing of the Rubicon will then turn him into a tyrant and cause his death. The dream establishes a connection between Caesar's crossing of the Rubicon and his assassination on the Ides of March, and helps to present the succession of events as a coherent sequence. This connection is even more explicit in Suetonius, who states, among the prodigies announcing Caesar's death, that 'a few days likewise before his death, he was informed that the horses, which, upon his crossing the Rubicon, he had consecrated, and turned loose to graze without a keeper, abstained entirely from eating, and shed floods of tears'.[48]

A similar intratextual pattern exists in *Pompey*. Plutarch relates the dream that Mithridates received the night before Pompey's final victory:

> καὶ δεδιὼς μὴ φθάσῃ περάσας τὸν Εὐφράτην, ἐκ μέσων νυκτῶν ἐπῆγεν ὡπλισμένην τὴν στρατιάν· καθ' ὃν χρόνον λέγεται τὸν Μιθριδάτην ὄψιν ἐν ὕπνοις ἰδεῖν τὰ μέλλοντα προδηλοῦσαν. ἐδόκει γὰρ οὐρίῳ πνεύματι πλέων τὸ Ποντικὸν πέλαγος ἤδη Βόσπορον καθορᾶν καὶ φιλοφρονεῖσθαι τοὺς συμπλέοντας, ὡς ἄν τις ἐπὶ σωτηρίᾳ σαφεῖ καὶ βεβαίῳ χαίρων· ἄφνω δὲ ἀναφανῆναι πάντων ἔρημος ἐπὶ λεπτοῦ ναυαγίου διαφερόμενος, ἐν τοιούτοις δὲ αὐτὸν ὄντα πάθεσι καὶ ψύμμασιν ἐπιστάντες ἀνέστησαν οἱ φίλοι, φράζοντες ἐπιέναι Πομπήϊον.

> Fearing lest the king should get the advantage of him by crossing the Euphrates, he put his army in battle array and led it against him at midnight. At this time Mithridates is said to have seen a vision in his sleep, revealing what should come to pass. He dreamed that he was sailing the Pontic Sea with a fair wind, and was already in sight of the Bosporus, and was greeting pleasantly his fellow-voyagers, as a man would do in his joy over a manifest and sure deliverance; but suddenly he saw himself bereft of all his companions and

---

47 Ach. Tat., *Leucippe and Clitophon*, 3.15.4–5.
48 Suet., *Diuus Jul.* 81.8.

tossed about on a small piece of wreckage. As he dreamed of such distress, his friends came to his couch and roused him with the news that Pompey was advancing to the attack.[49]

Mithridates does not have time to interpret or even think about the dream, as he is immediately called to the battlefield. Upon first reading, we could believe that the dream only forecasts Mithridates' imminent defeat; but the binary structure of the dream that we had also encountered in *Pompey* 68.2, indicates that there is more to it. On a second level, the dream offers an anticipated summary of Pompey's career. Indeed, Pompey will enjoy success and popularity until his campaign in Greece, but after his defeat at Pharsalus against Caesar, he will suddenly be reduced to utter destitution and despair. Abandoned by his men, he will be forced to sail to Egypt without escort, in the same situation as Mithridates at the end of his dream. Therefore, it is quite obvious that the dream is prophetic for both men.

Some dreams are proleptic, and others, analeptic: Cinna's dream belongs to the second category. The dream explicitly announces Cinna's death as a reenactment of Caesar's murder. Indeed, Caesar takes his friend by the hand as Decimus Brutus had done to force Caesar to come to the Senate on the Ides of March. In the *Brutus*, the parallel dream says that Caesar forced Cinna to follow him to a dark place that we can identify with Hades.[50] The retrospective connection between the two murders can either be interpreted as a way for Plutarch to suggest that Caesar, like Cinna, could not escape his death; it also means that the cause of his murder was not only his own ambition but the treason of his friends.

These dreams have in common the juxtaposition of allusions to the current situation of the dreamer and to anticipations of his future, through different kinds of signs and symbols. In this way, Plutarch suggests the reality of events and situations which are still virtual in the narrative. It creates a sort of 'alternate reality', similar to the one P. Waddell describes in Appian: after the victory over the Carthaginians at Zama, Appian accounts for the *agon* which took place in the Senate to decide whether Carthage should be destroyed or not. Indeed, by inverting the classical order of speeches in a literary *agon*, Appian leads his readers to anticipate on the future destruction of Carthage, and then deceives their expectations by mentioning the Senator's vote against Carthage's destruction.[51] The

---

49 Plu. *Pomp.* 32–4.
50 Plu. *Brut.* 20.5–6. This account is more detailed and explicit about the connection between the dream and Cinna's fever. It enables the reader to understand that it is because of his guilt at not witnessing Caesar's funerals that Cinna came to the forum in spite of his dream.
51 See Waddell in this volume.

superimposition of two opposite situations and the disappointment of the reader's expectations are common features to Appian's and Plutarch's methods.

In *Caesar* and *Pompey*, Plutarch uses similar narrative techniques to dramatize the reversal of fortune which affects the two great men. The biographer uses dreams as divine warnings, strategically situated at the beginning and end of a crucial sequence of events to create an effect of closure. By implicitly anticipating the future fate of the two generals, Plutarch produces suspense and echoes within each life and between the two lives. The origin of dreams is not explicit in the *Lives* that we have examined, but it is clear from the *Moralia* and from Plutarch's experience as a priest of Apollo, that he believed in the divine origin of dreams. Consequently, Plutarch uses dreams to connect human and divine causality in order to make sense of sequences of events. They underline climactic episodes and delineate patterns which serve as keys to understanding the *Lives*.

Even if most of Plutarch's dreams come from his sources, we notice that it is not first for their historical value that he includes them, but because of the references they call to mind, the symbols they contain, their tragic or dramatic potential, and more largely because of the whole literary and historical tradition that precedes him and includes prophetic dreams, from Homer on. Dreams also enable Plutarch to characterize better the personality of his 'great men' by opposing their behavior and responses to their dreams. His method shows a keen sense of psychology and a real knowledge of the impact that something as personal as a dream can have on one's emotions and actions. Plutarch seems to condemn impulsive and irrational responses to prophetic dreams and invites his reader to ponder wisely their meaning. He reminds his audience of the need to be aware of the gods' providence and respect it by paying attention to the signs and messages that the gods send us. Indeed, Plutarch's statement about the circumstances of Caesar's murder (παντάπασιν ἀπέφαινε δαίμονός τινος ὑφηγουμένου καὶ καλοῦντος ἐκεῖ τὴν πρᾶξιν ἔργον γεγονέναι, '[the place of the murder] made it wholly clear that it was the work of some heavenly power which was calling and guiding the action there')[52] could apply to many turning points in the *Lives*, and proves that history, according to Plutarch, depends not only on human actions but also on the gods' will. As a consequence, any attempt to escape one's destiny would be useless, even for 'great men'. Like Croesus in Herodotus, Caesar and Pompey are constantly reminded in their dreams that their fortune is transient.

---

52 Plu. *Caes.* 66.1.

The study of the complex dreams contained in *Caesar* and *Pompey* shows how Plutarch contributed to the elaboration of historical tradition regarding these two Roman generals. In this process, Plutarch relied on previous accounts which he considered truthful, but sometimes corrected them in the way which, according to him, most reflected the truth, and added dreams when he thought it was needed to complete the character's portrait or explain his behavior. Dreams belong indeed to the same category of historical 'objects' as speeches or thought: it was commonly admitted that historians could 'recreate' them, within the frame of plausibility, thanks to material consciously or unconsciously borrowed to the previous literary tradition and corresponding to their cultural patterns. Indeed, 'plausible invention' had almost the same status and strength of conviction than the attested truth. The numerous intertextual references in Plutarch illustrate this multiple-layered elaboration of an historical narrative through time, that Konstantakos explored in his paper.[53] In addition, the often ambiguous content of dreams invites the reader to involve himself into the game of interpretation, in particular through the confrontation of several biographies, and provides Plutarch with a variety of narrative strategies to create suspense, highlight connection between events and at time disappoint the reader's expectations.

Bibliography

André, J. (1949), *La Vie et l'œuvre d'Asinius Pollion*, Paris.
Bartsch, S. (1989), *Decoding the Ancient Novel. the Reader and the Role of Description in Heliodorus and Achilles Tatius*, Princeton.
Brenk, F. (1975), "The Dreams of Plutarch's *Lives*", in: *Latomus* 34, 336–349.
Brenk, F. (1977), *In Mist Apparelled. Religious Themes in Plutarch's* Moralia *and* Lives, Leiden.
Dodson, D.S. (2009), *Reading Dreams. An Audience-Critical Approach to the Dreams in the Gospel of Matthew*, London.
Grotanelli, C. (1999), "On the Mantic Meaning of Incestuous Dreams", in: D. Shulman / G. Stroumsa 1999, 143–168.
Homeyer, H. (1962), "Zu den Anfängen der griechischen Biographie", in: *Philologus* 106, 75–85.
Levene, D. (2011), "Historical Allusion and the Nature of the Historical Text", in: *Histos* 5, 1–17.
Pelling, C.B.R. (1979), "Plutarch's Method in the Roman *Lives*", in: *JHS* 99, 74–96.

---

53 See Konstantakos in this volume about the story of the murder of the Apis bull by Cambyses: Egyptians transposed, according to their own religious culture, a propagandistic Persian narrative regarding Cambyses' falsification of the sacrifice of a sacred bull. In the Egyptian version, Cambyses killed the Apis bull, a supreme sacrilege in the Egyptian religion. This narrative was then reported by Herodotus in his *Histories*.

Pelling, C.B.R. (1997), "Tragical Dreamers: Some Dreams in the Roman Historians", in: *G&R* 54, 197–213.
Pelling, C.B.R. (2002), *Plutarch and History. Eighteen Studies*, London.
Pelling, C.B.R. (2010), "'With Thousands Such Enchanting Dreams': the Dreams of the *Lives* Revisited", in: L. van der Stockt / F.B. Titchener / H.-G. Ingenkamp / A. Pérez Jiménez 2010, 315–332.
Pelling, C.B.R. (2011), *Plutarch. Caesar*, Oxford.
Pelling, C.B.R. (2013), "Intertextuality, Plausibility, and Interpretation", in: *Histos* 7, 1–20.
Rondholz, A. (2009), "The Crossing of the Rubicon. A Historiographical Study", in: *Mnemosyne* 62, 432–450.
Scardigli, B. (ed.) (1995), *Essays on Plutarch's Lives*, Oxford.
Shulman, D. / Stroumsa, G. (eds.) (1999), *Dream Cultures. Explorations in the Comparative History of Dreaming*, New York / Oxford.
Stadter, P. (ed.) (1992), *Plutarch and the Historical Tradition*, London.
Townend, G.B. (1987), "C. Oppius on Julius Caesar", in: *AJPh* 108, 325–342.
van der Stockt, L. / Titchener, F.B. / Ingenkamp, H.-G / Pérez Jiménez, A. (eds.) (2010), *Gods, Daimones, Rituals, Myths, and History of Religions in Plutarch's Works: Studies Devoted to Professor Frederick E. Brenk by the International Plutarch Society*, Utah.
Wiseman, T.P. (1981), "Practice and Theory in Roman Historiography", in: *History* 66, 375–393.

III Roman Historiography

Suzanne Adema
Encouraging Troops, Persuading Narratees: Pre-Battle Exhortations in Caesar's *Bellum Gallicum* as a Narrative Device

Abstract: In literature, representations of speech and thought do not merely function as a means of communication for characters in the story world, but also as a means of communication between the narrator and his narratees. Several contributions in this study illustrate that this holds for speeches in historiography, starting from Thucydides' famous *Methodenkapitel* (Feddern, Harris) and discussing the historiographical *topos* of paired speeches (Waddell). In this article, I focus on the pre-battle exhortations in Caesar's *Bellum Gallicum* (books 1 and 7). I take a combined linguistic and narratological approach to this type of speech and investigate their role as a recurring element in the presentation of battles in historiography. The authenticity or historicality of especially pre-battle exhortations has often been discussed. Whether they reflect reality or not, I show that pre-battle exhortations not only function to encourage troops in the story world, but also function on the level of the narrator and his narratees. An analysis of their forms and narratological functions shows that they contribute to persuading the narratees that war, and battles within war, are predictable and, to a certain extent, controllable procedures. Thus, pre-battle exhortations are put to use by the Caesarian narrator as a literary tool.

1 Introduction[1]

In real life, acts of speaking often have merely a social function and do not necessarily cause other acts, let alone set grand things in motion. In literature, how-

---

[1] This article was written as part of the NWO-project *Ancient War Narrative*, led by Prof. Dr. Caroline Kroon and Prof. Dr. Irene de Jong (VU University Amsterdam and University of Amsterdam). In '*Words of Warriors. Speech and Thought in Latin War Narratives*' (Adema forthc.), I investigate the forms, functions, and ideological interpretations of representations of speeches and thoughts in Latin war narratives, combining a quantitative linguistic approach (corpus: Caesar, *Bellum Gallicum* 1 and 7, Vergil, *Aeneid* 11 and 12, Sallust, *Bellum Iugurthinum*) with a qualitative, close-reading approach in which the linguistic form and narratological function of speeches and thoughts are analyzed and interpreted (corpus: Caesar, *Bellum Gallicum* 1 and 7, Vergil, *Aeneid* 11 and 12).

DOI 10.1515/9783110496055-011

ever, representations of speech and thought are usually more than just a means to keep a conversation going or to negotiate and establish social relationships between speakers.² Moreover, a representation of a speech or a thought tends to be an event that brings about other events, such as orders that bring about the execution of those orders or a thought or insight that brings a character to take a certain action. This means that representations of speech and thought do not merely function as a means of communication for characters in the story world, but also as a means of communication between the narrator and his narratees.

In this article, I apply the idea that speeches by characters are a communicative means for narrators to one specific and topical type of speech: the pre-battle exhortations of Caesar's *Bellum Gallicum*.³ Pre-battle exhortations in *Bellum Gallicum* do not only convey motivational messages from a general to his troops, they also seem to convey more general communicative goals of the narrator to his narratees. The narratorial choices concerning linguistic forms and narratological techniques in Caesar's pre-battle exhortations, in short, seem to contribute to the idea that wars, and battles within wars, are controllable and predictable procedures.⁴

In taking a combined discourse-linguistic and narratological approach, this article differs from most existing scholarly work on pre-battle exhortations, which tend to consider the question of the historicity of pre-battle exhortations. It has been argued, by Hansen for instance, that generals could not have given full-blown speeches before their assembled armies.⁵ Hansen states that "the whole genre [of battle exhortations] was a literary and rhetorical fiction, not a historical fact". Rather, Hansen claims, generals will have given short encouragements.⁶

---

2 Cf. Laird 2009.
3 In Greek and Latin historiography, we find examples of long and elaborate pre-battle exhortations, see Albertus 1908 for examples. Highet 1972, 82–89, in his book on speeches in the *Aeneid*, discusses exhortations in epic, as does Latacz 1977. See also the contribution of Waddell in this volume.
4 It has often been observed that the form of and thus the use of speeches and thoughts supports the communicative goals and ideologies of its narrator in many ways. The literature on Caesar's (manipulative) narrative techniques is vast. Rasmussen (1963) specifically addresses the speeches in Caesar, cf. also Tsitsiou-Chelidoni 2010. The most influential suggestions and ideas on Caesar's narrative techniques in general can be found in Rambaud 1966; Görler 1976; Richter 1977. See also Kroon 2001; Riggsby 2006; Choitz 2011.
5 Hansen 1993.
6 The question is also addressed by e.g. Keitel 1987; Pritchett 1994; Daly 2002; Zoida 2007; Yellin 2008; Anson 2010. Some of these (e.g. Daly, Pritchett) argue strongly against Hansen.

My aim is not to provide historical arguments about the length of actual pre-battle exhortations or, indeed, about their occurrence. I consider pre-battle exhortations from a more literary standpoint, investigating their role as a recurring element in the presentation of battles in historiography and epic.[7] The narrator of Caesar's *Bellum Civile*, too, presents them as recurring elements in battle or, at least, knows that they are a common part of stories about battles. In an often quoted excerpt, the narrator explicitly states that giving an exhortation speech was part of the military routine.[8]

> Example 1, Caes. *Civ.* 3.90.1
> Exercitum cum militari more ad pugnam cohortaretur, ...
>
> When, according to the custom, he was exhorting his army to battle, ...[9]

Also in the second book of the *Bellum Gallicum*, the narrator explicitly states that the exhortation of the troops (*milites cohortandi*) is one of the things that have to be done before battle, though he remarks that Caesar did not have much time for all these things.

> Example 2, Caes. *Gal.* 2.20.1
> Caesari omnia uno tempore erant agenda: vexillum proponendum, quod erat insigne, cum ad arma concurri oporteret; signum tuba dandum; ab opere revocandi milites; qui paulo longius aggeris petendi causa processerant arcessendi; acies instruenda; *milites cohortandi*; signum dandum.
>
> Caesar had everything to do at one moment – the flag to raise, as signal of a general call to arms; the trumpet-call to sound; the troops to recall from entrenching; the men to bring in who had gone somewhat farther afield in search of stuff for the ramp; the line to form; the troops to harangue; the signal to give.[10]

The narrator of the *Bellum Gallicum* thus shows that he considers exhortations part of the routine.[11] It is of course up to this narrator, *how* or even *if* he presents exhortations, as I will show in my discussion of seven battles presented in books

---

[7] On this topic, see also Grossi on Homeric influences in historiography in this volume.
[8] These Caesarian excerpts are quoted in many studies on this subject, e.g. Highet 1972; Hansen 1993; Lendon 1999. Highet 1972, 82–88 mentions several Latin authors that speak of *cohortationes* or use the verb *cohortare*, to wit Quint. 12.1.28, Cic. *Balb.* 51, Caes. *Gal.* 2.21 and 2.25, Nep. *Han.* 11.1 and Liv. 28.19.9. In Greek, terms for general's speeches are προτρεπτικός or παραίνεσις (cf. Pritchett 1994).
[9] Translation taken from A.G. Peskett, *Caesar. The civil wars.* (Loeb).
[10] Translations of the *Bellum Gallicum* are taken from Edwards 1914.
[11] See Anson 2010, 316 for a more historical elaboration on Caesar's exhortational routines.

1 and 7 of the *Bellum Gallicum*.[12] First, however, I briefly introduce the linguistic forms and narrative techniques relevant for an analysis of pre-battle exhortations in Caesar's *Bellum Gallicum*.

2 Linguistic forms of speech and thought representation in Latin war narrative

The most common linguistic forms of representations of speech and thought in Caesar's *Bellum Gallicum* are indirect speech, indirect thought, mentioned speech and mentioned thought.[13] Direct speech does occur, but is very infrequent in Caesar's *Bellum Gallicum*.[14] The distinction between speech and thought is made on the basis of the presence of an addressee in the story world. An addressee means that the utterance is a speech, whereas the absence of an addressee means that the utterance is a thought.

The difference between direct, indirect, and mentioned forms of speeches and thoughts is a syntactic difference.[15] Direct discourse is a complement of

---

[12] Zoida 2007 makes this observation about Thucydides. What Zoida observes is, in short, that Thucydides adapts both the form and the function of exhortation speeches to his needs. Implicitly, Zoida refers to the narratological functions of characterization and seed/foreshadowing, when stating that Thucydides creates battle exhortations that fulfil new functions in the structure of his work, e.g. "to look ahead (setting out the tactics that will be played out afterwards), to show the character and intelligence of a general, and lastly to elucidate the real reasons behind a victory or a defeat" (Zoida 2007, 146).

[13] Other forms of speech and thought in Latin war narrative are direct speech (e.g. Caes. *Gal.* 7.20.8–12), direct thought (e.g. Verg. *A.* 12.620–623), direct writing (e.g. Sal. *Jug.* 9.2.1), indirectly presented writing (e.g. Sal. *Jug.* 25.5.23), and mentioned writing (e.g. Caes.*Gal.*1.29.1). Furthermore, we may have to distinguish passages that have been labeled 'free indirect speech/thought'. I am not completely convinced that we should distinguish this category in Latin, because free indirect discourse in Latin cannot be syntactically defined and seems to be a matter of interpretation (Bayet 1931; Mellet 1998). Nevertheless, there are clauses for which an interpretation as free indirect discourse is possible (e.g. Verg. *A.* 11.232–233). These are results form the NWO-project '*Words of Warriors. Speech and Thought in Latin War Narratives*' (Adema forthc.).

[14] The most influential monograph on direct speech (and other forms of speech) in Caesar's *Bellum Gallicum* still is Rasmussen 1963. Cf. also Tsitsiou-Chelidoni 2010.

[15] Leaving free indirect discourse out of consideration for a moment, the tripartite division between direct, indirect, and mentioned discourse seems generally accepted as a formal division of types of representations of speech and thought, e.g. Leech/Short 1981; Fludernik 1993. The division into direct, indirect and mentioned discourse has been applied to classical texts by, for instance, De Bakker 2007 (Herodotus' *Histories*); Beck 2012 (Homer). On direct and indirect

an (implied) verb of communication in which the clauses are not presented in a subordinated form, whereas in indirect discourse the complement does consist of clauses presented in subordination to the verb of communication. Indirect discourse differs from mentioned discourse in that indirectly presented discourse is a presentation of the content in the utterance, and not a mere reference to it. Mentioned discourse is a complement of a verb of communication that does refer to the content of the speech or thought rather than presenting (or summarizing) it.

Indirect discourse is explicitly marked by means of specific syntactic constructions in Latin. The most common syntactic forms of indirect discourse in Latin are accusative and infinitive constructions (Ex. 3) or clauses in the subjunctive (Ex. 4), possibly starting with a subordinating conjunction (e.g. *ut*, *ne*).[16]

> Example 3, Caes. *Gal.* 1.22.1
> Considius equo admisso ad eum accurrit, dicit *montem quem a Labieno occupari voluerit ab hostibus teneri: id se a Gallicis armis atque insignibus cognovisse.*
>
> At this moment Considius galloped back to him, saying that the mountain he had wished Labienus to seize was in possession of the enemy: he knew it by the Gallic arms and badges.
>
> Example 4, Caes. *Gal.* 1.20.5
> Caesar eius dextram prendit; consolatus rogat *finem orandi faciat.*
>
> Caesar took him by the hand and consoled him, bidding him end his entreaty.

The form of the complement in mentioned discourse may also vary, but always merely refers to the content of the speech representation, as the anaphoric expression *ea res* in example 5 illustrates.

> Example 5, Caes. *Gal.* 1.23.2
> *Ea res* per fugitivos L. Aemilii, decurionis equitum Gallorum, hostibus **nuntiatur.**

---

speech in Herodotus and Thucydides, see Scardino (2007, 2012). Van Gils (2009) discusses the (rhetorical) use of embedded focalization in Cicero's forensic speeches. Laird (1999) (Vergil's *Aeneid*), too, distinguishes between direct, indirect and mentioned discourse, but adds several other categories (e.g. free direct discourse, free indirect discourse, mimetic indirect discourse).
16 Another form of a subordinated predicate frame representing indirect discourse is the prolative infinitive, which is a subordinated predicate frame that takes it subject from the gouverning clause (Pinkster 1990, 126). The subordinated predicate *habere* in *dilectum tota provincia habere instituit* (Caes. *Gal.* 7.1.6) is a prolative infinitive, for instance. It has the same subject as *instituit*, viz. Caesar. I regard prolative infinitives as indirect discourse and not as mentioned discourse because they are predicate frames presented in subordination and represent the content of the speech or thought representation.

> The change was reported to the enemy by some deserters from Lucius Aemilius, a troop-leader of the Gallic horse.

Ea res refers back to events presented in the preceding clauses and the narratees need to infer the content of the message that is here presented in a summarized form. This makes *ea res* mentioned discourse. Other forms of mentioned discourse are nouns (e.g. *de caede*) or indirect questions similar to *quid fieri vellet* or *quae sint dicta* (depending on e.g. *ostendit*).

Apart from using indirect and mentioned discourse, a narrator may also narrate that a speech was uttered, using a verb of communication without a complement indicating the content of the speech, as is illustrated in example 6.

> Example 6, Caes. *Gal.* 1.18.2
> Dicit liberius atque audacius.
>
> Liscus now spoke with greater freedom and boldness.

In Caesar's *Bellum Gallicum* 1 and 7, pre-battle exhortations are presented in indirect or mentioned form (see e.g. example (13) below). Example (1) and (2) above illustrate that the Caesarian narrator may also merely narrate that a battle exhortation took place. Furthermore, some battles are not preceded by a speech of the general, or the speech of the general does not really seem to be a pre-battle exhortation [see examples (11) and (12)].

As I will argue below, the choice for a specific form of pre-battle exhortation speech should be incorporated in our interpretation and analysis of the speech and its role in the context. In order to analyse the role of a speech within the episode or even within the work as a whole, I have made use of a set of several narratological concepts pertaining to representations of speech and thought.

3 Narrative techniques and speeches and thoughts in Latin war narrative

The representation of speech and thought plays a role in several narrative techniques in Latin war narratives. I approach these techniques using the theoretical frameworks of the narratologists Mieke Bal (1997) and Irene de Jong.[17] These

---

[17] E.g. Bal 1997; de Jong 2004, 2007. Several functions of speeches are described, in less technical terms, by Marincola 2007b, in his introductory chapter to speeches in classical historiography. For a similar discussion of the functions of speeches in Statius' *Thebais*, see Dominik

techniques pertain to the *time* (*tempo* and *order*) and *space* in a narrative text and to its *characters* (*characterization*, *explanation* and *experientiality* or 'what it's like').

I would like to emphasize that speech and thought representation is just one of the textual means that narrators can use for these narrative techniques. That is, a narrator can, of course, influence the tempo or order of his text in ways other than by means of speech or thought. He may, for instance, use his own voice to characterize his characters, explain their motivations or make clear what it is like for them in the story world they inhabit. Furthermore, there hardly ever exists a one-to-one relationship between a representation of speech or thought and a particular function within the larger narrative. Speeches, thoughts, and writings often combine two or more of the narrative techniques enumerated above. A speech may characterize a character and his or her relations with other characters, while also delaying the tempo of the narrative and presenting a prolepsis, for instance.[18]

Variation between different forms of speech and thought representations is an instrument for narrators to influence the tempo of their narratives.[19] Contrasting directly presented speeches with mentioned speeches, it is unproblematic to claim that direct representations lead to a slower narrative tempo than mentioned representations. Indirect discourse is somewhere in the middle and its influence on the tempo of the narrative depends on the context. Depending on the tempo of the surrounding narrative, indirect discourse can either slow down or speed up the pace of the narrative. In a fast paced episode, the insertion of indirect discourse will mean a retardation of the tempo, for instance.

In the *Bellum Gallicum,* speeches and thoughts often have functions pertaining to the tempo of the narrative. Long indirect speeches, slowing down the narrative tempo, occur in those episodes of the *Bellum Gallicum* 1 and 7 in which diplomatic efforts are emphasised, for instance (e.g. Caes. *Gal.* 1.32–47). When a conflict is still in a diplomatic stage, the most important action seems to be speech. However, when negotiations are finished or seem pointless from the start, the narrator clearly focuses on more physical actions than speech. Battle

---

1994, especially his chapter on 'Narrative strategy and the rôle of speeches'. Cf. also Pausch 2010, 5–8.

18 On characterization by means of speeches, see also the contributions of Feddern and Harris in this volume.

19 I use de Jong 2007 and Bal 1997 as my basis, applying their ideas to the excerpts of my corpus. For another example of the influence of representations of speech and thought on the tempo of a classical text, see de Bakker (2007, 39 ff.) who explicitly discusses the relation between forms of speech and thought and the tempo of the narrative in Herodotus' *Histories*.

scenes, such as the fights against Ariovistus (Caes. *Gal.* 1.48–54), contain mostly mentioned forms of speeches and thoughts and short indirect speeches. Battles, especially successful ones, seem to be presented in the *Bellum Gallicum* as rapid successions of efficient and clear-cut actions and brief forms of speech and thought representation or a complete lack thereof contribute to this presentational effect.[20]

The narratological concept order meets with that of speech and thought representation in the particular techniques of actorial analepsis and actorial prolepsis, in which characters speak or think about past or future events.[21] Closely related to prolepsis and especially relevant for thoughts in *Bellum Gallicum* are anticipations of upcoming events, foreshadowing in narratological terms.[22] A specific type of foreshadowing is the seed, which is the insertion a piece of information, the relevance of which will only later become clear.[23] Especially the thoughts and speeches of Caesar often contain seeds or foreshadow later events, suggesting that Caesar could anticipate all events of the war, especially those that were negative to Rome, such as an uprising in all of Gaul, as in example (7).

> Example 7, Caes. *Gal.* 7.43.5
> ipse maiorem Galliae motum exspectans
>
> He himself was anticipating a greater rising in Gaul.

In the *Bellum Gallicum*, the many instances of seeds and foreshadowing in indirect thought and speech contribute to a positive presentation of the main character Caesar and present war as something you can plan and anticipate.[24]

The narratological concept space covers several types of space, e.g. the space in which the story is narrated or the space that serves as a container of

---

[20] Lendon (1999, 277) observes that "Caesar's battle descriptions are not works of fiction, but attempts to reduce the chaos of reality to understandable narrative, perhaps favorable to himself and his men. For this he necessarily relies upon preconceived models for interpreting his and his army's experience of combat. He makes use of pre-existing schemes, however implicit, about how battles work".
[21] Actorial prolepsis and analepsis are opposed to narratorial prolepsis and analepsis, presented by the primary narrator, see e.g. de Jong 2007, 3–8.
[22] Hunter (1973) provides a study of Thucydides' use of this particular technique.
[23] de Jong 2007, 8. For this narratological function of speeches in Latin narrative, see e.g. Laird 2009; Pausch 2010b.
[24] Adema (forthc.).

the text.²⁵ I confine myself to that part of the narratological concept space that is concerned with the "setting of the action of a story, other localities that are referred to, e.g. in memories or dreams, and objects ('props')".²⁶ In Latin war narrative, speeches are often used to indicate the transition of one location within the story world to another. The transition from chapter 1.6 to chapter 1.7 in *Bellum Gallicum* coincides with a change of space: the narrator moves from the Helvetians to Caesar. The message presented in the first clause of chapter 1.7 functions as a textual pivot, linking these two spaces.

> Example 8, Caes. *Gal.* 1.6.4–1.7.1
> Extremum oppidum Allobrogum est proximumque Helvetiorum finibus Genava. Ex eo oppido pons ad Helvetios pertinet. Allobrogibus sese vel persuasuros, quod nondum bono animo in populum Romanum viderentur, existimabant vel vi coacturos, ut per suos fines eos ire paterentur. Omnibus rebus ad profectionem comparatis diem dicunt, qua die ad ripam Rhodani omnes conveniant. Is dies erat a.d. v. Kal. Apr. L. Pisone A. Gabinio consulibus.
>
> Caesari cum *id* nuntiatum esset, *eos per provinciam nostram iter facere conari*, maturat ab urbe proficisci, et quam maximis potest itineribus in Galliam ulteriorem contendit et ad Genavam pervenit.
>
> The last town of the Allobroges, the nearest to the borders of the Helvetii, is Geneva, from which a bridge stretches across to the Helvetii. These supposed that either they would persuade the Allobroges (deeming them not yet well disposed towards the Roman people), or would compel them perforce to suffer a passage through their borders. Having therefore provided all things for their departure, they named a day by which all should assemble upon the bank of the Rhone. The day was the 28th of March, in the consulship of Lucius Piso and Aulus Gabinius.
>
> When Caesar was informed that they were endeavouring to march through the Roman Province, he made speed to leave Rome, and hastening to Further Gaul by as rapid stages as possible, arrived near Geneva.

Since war cannot be fought without intelligence about the actions of the enemy, this is in my corpus a rather common function of, especially, mentioned speeches such as *id esset* in example (8) or a formulation like *ea res nuntiatur*. A report of events that have just happened in one location is in these cases brought by messengers or spies to another location.

---

25 *Space in Ancient Greek Literature* by Irene de Jong is a standard work for the narratological concept space in ancient Greek narrative and forms an excellent starting point for research on space in Latin narrative as well (de Jong 2012).
26 Definition taken from de Jong 2012, 1.

The characterization or portrayal of a character can be brought about in several ways in representations of speech and thought.[27] A character may explicitly present characteristics of himself or of another character in speech or thought. In the first book of the *Bellum Gallicum*, for instance, Caesar reflects extensively on the character of Dumnorix (Caes. *Gal.* 1.18.10–1.19.2). These reflections, at the same time, present the narratees of the primary narrator with information about Dumnorix. Speeches, thoughts, and (other) actions of a character can also indirectly provide information about his nature, thus painting his portrait in a more implicit way. This technique is used regularly in the *Bellum Gallicum*, for instance by means of thoughts and speeches by Caesar, which make him stand out as a thoughtful, provident, and efficient general. This was illustrated already in example (7), in which the expectation of the uprising of the whole of Gaul does not only have a proleptic function, but also functions in the more general, positive characterization of Caesar.

Representations of speech and thought may thus have a characterizing function, as part of getting to know the general nature of characters, but it may also function to explain specific actions by characters. When Caesar decides to help the Aedui solve an internal conflict, for instance, this decision is explained or perhaps even defended in a relatively long train of thought (Caes. *Gal.* 7.32.1–2). His actions need explanations because he goes through the trouble of visiting them in their own territory, thus considerably postponing his plans to find and fight Vercingetorix. Moreover, he meddles in the internal affairs of the Aedui.[28]

A final relevant narrative technique pertaining to representations of speech and thought is described by the narratological concepts 'what it's like' and 'experientiality'. These concepts concern, in cognitive narratology, the cognitive activity involved in reading narratives, focusing on the way in which "stories highlight the impact of events on the mind or minds experiencing those events within a story world", as Herman puts it.[29] Several narrative techniques may highlight the impact of events on a character, and speech and thought representation is one of these techniques. In the Latin war narratives of my corpus, this is mostly conveyed by direct speech and thought or by clusters of indirect speeches and thoughts. Examples of speeches and thoughts that convey what it is like to inhabit this particular story world are quite rare in the *Bellum Gallicum*, but in

---

[27] Characterization in Latin historiography is addressed in e.g. Kraus/Woodman 1997; Vasaly 2009 (also for further references). For characterization in Greek narratives, see e.g. de Temmerman 2014.
[28] For a more elaborate analysis and further references, see Adema 2014.
[29] Herman 2009, 137.

book 7, we get a glimpse of the emotions of the Aedui, when they regret their treason and miss Caesar's kindness.

> Example 9, Caes. *Gal.* 7.63.8
> Magno dolore Aedui ferunt se deiectos principatu, queruntur fortunae commutationem et Caesaris indulgentiam in se requirunt, neque tamen suscepto bello suum consilium ab reliquis separare audent.
>
> The Aedui were greatly distressed at their rejection from the leadership, complaining of the change in their fortune and feeling the loss of Caesar's kindness towards them; but nevertheless, having undertaken the campaign, they durst not part counsel from the rest.

The excerpt not only shows what this moment is like for the Aedui, but also functions to characterize them and Caesar, thus illustrating that there usually is not a one-to-one relationship between a speech representation and a specific narrative technique.

Influencing the tempo or order, marking a change of space, portraying characters and explaining their actions, and conveying what it's like to inhabit the story world are the most important narratological functions of speech and thought representations I have come across in my analysis of speech and thought representation in Latin war narrative.

4 Seven battles in *Bellum Gallicum* 1 and 7 and the speeches preceding them[30]

The previous sections have shown that the Caesarian narrator indeed has and makes choices on how to present utterances of characters. By discussing seven important battles in books 1 and 7, I hope to show that this also holds true for battle exhortations. Moreover, I will argue that these choices are significant and should be taken into account in our interpretation of both the speeches and the work as a whole.

Before I analysed the specific speech type of the pre-battle exhortation in terms of the narrative techniques presented above, I had several expectations and questions. I expected that the presentation of a pre-battle exhortation

---

30 I analysed the speech(es) in preceding phase of the battle against the Helvetians (Caes. *Gal.* 1.21–29), the battle against Ariovistus (Caes. *Gal.* 1.48–54), the battle at Bourges (Caes. *Gal.* 7.22–31), the battle at Gergovia (Caes. *Gal.* 7.43.4–53), the battle fought by Labienus (Caes. *Gal.* 7.57–62), a battle between the cavalries of Vercingetorix and Caesar (7.66–67), and the battle at Alesia (Caes. *Gal.* 7.68–90).

might be elaborate and, thus, retard the narrative tempo. In the light of the discussion on the historicity of pre-battle exhortations, I was curious if the highly literary device of foreshadowing the outcome of battles would occur, and what the role of exhortations in the characterization of Caesar in particular would be. Lastly, pre-battle exhortations seemed an appropriate environment to convey to narratees what war is like. In my analysis, I found that not every battle is preceded in the narrative by an exhortation speech, that speeches that do occur differ in form and length and that some speeches preceding battle are not really exhortations, upon closer inspection. The exhortations and other speeches indeed have functions pertaining to the tempo and order of events and contribute not only to the characterization of Caesar, but also to explanations of his actions.

The first important battle in the *Bellum Gallicum* is a battle against the Helvetians (Caes. *Gal.* 1.21–29). The narrative preceding this battle merely contains a reference to an exhortation speech by Caesar, in the form of the participle *cohortatus*.

> Example 10, Caes. *Gal.* 1.25.1
> Caesar primum suo, deinde omnium ex conspectu remotis equis, ut aequato omnium periculo spem fugae tolleret, *cohortatus* suos proelium commisit.
>
> Caesar first had his own horse and then those of all others sent out of sight, thus to equalise the danger and to take away hope of flight. Then after a speech to encourage his troops he joined battle.

The narrator chooses a very brief form, merely narrating *about* the speech, which suggests that he wants to maintain the fast pace of the narrative and give more emphasis to the battle itself. This is in line with what he does in other battle scenes.

We find a similar technique, for instance, in the presentation of the next important battle, the battle against Ariovistus (Caes. *Gal.* 1.48–54). In the initial phase of the conflict with Ariovistus, the narrator used many lengthy speeches in an effort to show that Caesar tried to solve the problems in Gaul through diplomacy (Caes. *Gal.* 1.32–47). The conversations between Ariovistus and Caesar make clear that Ariovistus would not listen to reason and as a result war was inevitable. Perhaps to emphasise that speech was no longer an option and to speed up the inevitable process of battle, the narrator does not include a pre-battle exhortation in his presentation of the battle itself. One of the few speechlike events that do occur in the episode is a short representation of the plaintive shouts and pleas of the German women.

Example 11, Caes. *Gal.* 1.51.3
eo mulieres imposuerunt, quae ad proelium proficiscentes milites passis manibus flentes
implorabant, *ne se in servitutem Romanis traderent.*

Upon these [wagons] they set their women, who with tears and outstretched arms entreated
the men, as they marched out to fight, not to deliver them into Roman slavery.

The German women make sure that the German fighters know what is at stake by
their pleas not to make them slaves of the Romans. Thus, their pleas may be seen
as a substitute for an exhortation speech, but it is also one of the very few instances in which the narrator of the *Bellum Gallicum* uses speech to inform his narratees what it is like to inhabit his story world.[31]

Exhortation speeches could be a chance for narrators to highlight the impact
of war and battle on soldiers and their general, but the narrator of the *Bellum
Gallicum* does not often do this. Nevertheless, the first exhortation speech in
book 7 seems to contain a glimpse of what the Gallic war was like for Roman
troops and their general. Caesar incites his men in two steps: he urges them to
reap victory in return for their great labours, *tantis laboribus,* and promises
money to those who climb the walls first.

Example 12, Caes. *Gal.* 7.27.3
Legionibusque intra vineas in occulto expeditis, cohortatus *ut aliquando pro tantis laboribus fructum victoriae perciperent,* eis *qui primi murum ascendissent praemia* proposuit militibusque signum dedit. Illi subito ex omnibus partibus evolaverunt murumque celeriter
compleverunt.

The legions made ready for action secretly under cover of the mantlets; and having urged
them to reap at length the fruit of victory in return for their great labors, he offered prizes to
those who should first mount the wall, and gave the signal to the troops. They dashed out
suddenly from all sides and speedily lined the wall.

The syntactic form of the first exhortation is indirect speech, an *ut*-clause depending on *cohortatus*. Within indirect speech, we may distinguish between
words that we can ascribe to the narrator and words in which we may recognize
the character talking. In cognitive linguistics this is called the dual voice, narratology speaks of elements focalised through a secondary narrator.[32] The elements

---

[31] The motif of pleading women is also found in e. g. Caes. *Gal.* 7.26. There, however, the pleas
of the women do not have an exhortational function, but betray a flight of their men to the Romans.
[32] The "dual voice" concept refers to the concomitant availability of the deictic centre of the
narrator and that of the character in non-direct forms of speech or thought representations.
The concomitant presence of narrator and character in non-direct representations of speech

aliquando and *tantis laboribus* seem to echo the words of the speaking character and give expressiveness and persuasiveness to this brief indirect speech, showing what this war was like for Caesar and his soldiers. The speech resembles a one-liner rather than the lengthy pre-battle exhortation speeches known from historiography. As a one-liner should be, Caesar's exhortation is effective, given that in the next sentence his men have rapidly filled the walls (*compleverunt*). The brief exhortation thus characterizes Caesar as an inspiring and persuasive general.

The next battle in book 7 is the one lost at Gergovia, which is not preceded by a typical exhortation speech in the narrative. I interpret the conspicuous absence of an exhortation of the troops as part of the strategy of the narrator to moderate the defeat at Gergovia. An exhortation such as the exhortation at Bourges (example 12) would have put much more emphasis on the fact that the Romans lost this battle.[33]

At this point in time, Caesar is presented as planning to leave Gergovia without taking the city, while he does not want to give the impression that this departure is a flight caused by fear (Caes. *Gal.* 7.43.5).[34] Therefore, he decides to perform one more, small, attack. Instead of an exhortation speech to his soldiers, we find a speech in which Caesar explains his plans to his lieutenant-generals. The actual details of Caesar's plan are left out, as that part of speech is presented as *ostendit quid fieri velit*. The narrator highlights two other parts of the speech, by presenting them indirectly. Caesar warns his lieutenant-generals to keep control over their soldiers (*monet*) and explains that the location is unsuitable for a long fight (*proponit*).

---

and thought has been acknowledged in the fields of the philosophy of language, discourse linguistics, and cognitive linguistics. These approaches offer concepts that disentangle instances of dual voice (e.g. *referential domains, mental spaces, deictic centres*). Thus, scholars working in these fields attempt to separate the words of the primary narrator-focalizer from those of embedded (narrator-)focalizers. Publications in the fields of language philosophy, discourse linguistics and cognitive linguistics concerning the representation of speech and thought are, for instance, Banfield 1973; Fludernik 1993; Fauconnier/Sweetser 1996; Vandelanotte 2009; Dancygier 2012. Their insights have been put to use for Latin in several studies, cf. Sznajder 2002, 2005; Rosén 2013; Adema (forthc.).

33 These statements, of course, concern the presentation of the events as found in the *Bellum Gallicum*. On the basis of just the *Bellum Gallicum*, we cannot and thus should not speculate about the question whether Caesar exhorted the troops right before the fight at Gergovia.

34 The presentation of the Gergovia story line is analysed in detail by Choitz 2011, who shows how the narrator presents the episode in such a way that Caesar is not responsible for the loss of this battle.

Example 12, Caes. *Gal.* 7.45.7–10
Vacua castra hostium Caesar conspicatus tectis insignibus suorum occultatisque signis militaribus raros milites, ne ex oppido animadverterentur, ex maioribus castris in minora traducit legatisque, quos singulis legionibus praefecerat, *quid fieri velit* ostendit: in primis monet *ut contineant milites, ne studio pugnandi aut spe praedae longius progrediantur; quid iniquitas loci habeat incommodi* proponit: *hoc una celeritate posse mutari; occasionis esse rem, non proeli.* His rebus expositis signum dat et ab dextra parte alio ascensu eodem tempore Aeduos mittit.

When Caesar saw that the enemy's camp was empty, covering the badges of his men and concealing the war standards, he moved soldiers from the greater to the lesser camp in small parties so as not to attract attention from the town. He showed the lieutenant-generals whom he had put in command of each legion what he wished to be done: first and foremost he instructed them to keep the troops in hand, lest in the zeal for battle or the hope of booty they might advance to far. He explained the disadvantage caused by the inequality of the ground, and said that this could be remedied by speed alone: it was a question of surprise, not of battle. After these explanations he gave the signal, and started the Aedui at the same moment by another ascent, on the right side.

The speech gives the impression that Caesar knew what he was doing and had a well-defined goal, although it remains unclear what this goal might have been.[35] The speech is not presented in one 'go', but the narrator cuts the speech up into several parts, suggesting that a longer speech was given but that only a few points are presented. Thus, the form of the speech directs attention away from Caesar's exact plans, while emphasising that he knew about two complications that could appear. In other words, the speech contains two seeds for the events in the upcoming battle.

These seeds are part of the strategy of the narrator to moderate the loss at Gergovia. Indeed, when the events unfold during the battle scene, precisely these complications occur (e. g. Caes. *Gal.* 7.47.3). Lastly, when the battle is lost, Caesar reprimands his soldiers on exactly these points (Caes. *Gal.* 7.52–53.1). The separate parts of the pre-battle speech, depending on *monet* and *proponit*, make it easier for the narratee to remember Caesar's warnings. Thus, the insertion of seeds contributes to a characterization of Caesar as an almost prescient general, at the same time also underwriting the idea that war is something you can plan. Caesar may not always win, but at least he anticipates his losses.

One battle in book 7 is fought by Labienus, and he utters an exhortation on that occasion. Labienus acts as Caesar's replacement in this episode and is por-

---

[35] As Kraner (*ad l.*) points out, the narrator leaves unsaid what exactly Caesar had in mind. Even when Caesar eventually has reached his goal, it remains unclear what this goal was (Caes. *Gal.* 7.47.1: *consecutus id, quod in animo proposuerat*).

trayed accordingly as a competent leader of the troops. By inserting this exhortation speech, for instance, the narrator shows that Labienus knows how to give a proper pre-battle exhortation.

> Example 13, Caes. Gal. 7.62.2
> Labienus milites **cohortatus**, *ut suae pristinae virtutis et tot secundissimorum proeliorum retinerent memoriam atque ipsum Caesarem, cuius saepenumero hostes superassent, praesentem adesse existimarent*, dat signum proelii.
>
> Labienus urged the troops to remember well their own courage in the past and the brilliant success of their battles, and to think that Caesar himself, under whose leadership they had often overcome the enemy, was present to see them; then he gave the signal for action.

Labienus starts with the motif that the men should remember earlier feats, but the main encouragement seems to lie in his suggestion to pretend that Caesar is there. Thus, Labienus presents Caesar as their true and most inspiring leader. Especially the expressive *saepenumero* is flattering for Caesar. The content of his exhortation, an indirect speech depending on the participle *cohortatus*, characterizes Caesar as the one person who can truly incite his troops.

Between the episode about Labienus and the battle of Alesia, a brief episode recounts a cavalry battle, preceded by a speech of Vercingetorix.[36] In general, Vercingetorix' speeches demonstrate that he is a worthy and dangerous opponent of Caesar, being a gifted leader with a certain amount of strategical insight. The narratees learn that he does not hesitate to deceive his public. The speech that Vercingetorix presents on the eve of this cavalry battle illustrates all these features. The deceitfulness of Vercingetorix is underscored when he, at the very start of his speech, exaggerates the situation on the Roman side (Kraner 1913 *ad l.*).

> Example 14, Caes. Gal. 7.66.2–3
> magno horum coacto numero, cum Caesar in Sequanos per extremos Lingonum fines iter faceret, quo facilius subsidium provinciae ferri posset, circiter milia passuum x ab Romanis trinis castris Vercingetorix consedit convocatisque ad concilium praefectis equitum *venisse tempus victoriae* **demonstrat.** *fugere in provinciam Romanos Galliaque excedere.*
>
> While Caesar was marching to the country of the Sequani across the outermost borders of the Lingones, so as to be able to lend support more easily to the Province, Vercingetorix got together a great number of these contingents and established himself in three camps about ten miles from the Romans. He called the cavalry commanders together to a council of war,

---

[36] This cavalry battle does not receive much attention in the narrative, probably to create a strong effect in the sequence of the battles of Bourges, Gergovia and Alesia, of which the first was won, the second lost and the last won again (Kraus 2010).

and stated that the hour of victory was come; that the Romans were fleeing to the Province and leaving Gaul.

In the adverbial clause starting with *cum* the narrator states that Caesar went to the territory of the Sequanians, a fact that contradicts, beforehand, Vercingetorix's claims that the Romans are fleeing to their own province.

Vercingetorix succesfully incites his cavalry (Caes. *Gal.* 7.66.7), convincing them they will defeat the Roman cavalry by means of the strategy he proposes. The speech is presented indirectly and is rather lengthy (94 words), contributing to a build-up in the narrative tension. It evokes the expectation of a difficult battle that would severely damage the Romans. The ensuing narrative of the battle itself, however, is rather brief and shows that Caesar knew of the strategy and answers the attack with an action that resembles an everyday routine (Caes. *Gal.* 7.67). The contrast between the amount of attention for Vercingetorix' speech and the ensuing narrative characterizes Vercingetorix in relation to Caesar. Vercingetorix is portrayed as a general who is excellent at encouraging his troops, but who underestimates Caesar's strategic insight and the flawless organisation of the Roman army. Eventually, it is the Gallic cavalry that flees (Caes. *Gal.* 7.68.1) and Vercingetorix has to retreat to Alesia.

The battle of Alesia is presented at the end of the seventh book of the *Bellum Gallicum*. This battle was decisive for the war, as it brought Vercingetorix to capitulate, and Caesar's exhortation speech foreshadows this upcoming climax by means of the phrase *in eo die atque hora*.

Example 15, Caes. Gal. 7.86.3
Ipse adit reliquos, cohortatur *ne labori succumbant*; *omnium superiorum dimicationum fructum in eo die atque hora* docet *consistere*.

He himself went up to the rest of the troops, and urged them not to give in to the strain, telling them that the fruit of all previous engagements depended upon that day and hour.

The emphasis on the decisiveness of a battle is, of course, topical in pre-battle exhortations, but then again, in the other exhortations in this book such an emphasis to 'now is the time' was conspicuously absent.

The length of this speech as it is represented in the narrative is a mere thirteen words. Another narrator might have given more attention to this speech, given that it is uttered at such a decisive moment. The speech could have been a nice specimen of Caesar's rhetorical abilities and a climax in the account of the battle of Alesia.[37] The narrator of *Bellum Gallicum* does not choose such a

---

37 The narrator does present a speech in direct discourse in the prelude to the battle of Alesia,

presentation, thus maintaining an even and fast tempo in his account of this battle. The speech is one event in the seemingly clear and straightforward sequence of events that presents the battle of Alesia and Caesar's victory over Vercingetorix.[38]

Despite its brevity, the speech does add to the characterization of Caesar. It shows that Caesar correctly identifies the most significant battle in this war, presenting it to his troops as the final blow they will inflict on their enemies. Thus, the pre-battle exhortation speech in this last book once more portrays Caesar as a focused, provident and competent general.

5 Conclusion

A summary of my findings on the forms and narrative functions of the pre-battle exhortations in *Bellum Gallicum* 1 and 7 is presented in table (1).
In short, the table shows that the narrator makes choices concerning the absence or occurrence of pre-battle exhortations, their form and the narratological function. The brevity of the speeches contributes to maintaining a fast narrative tempo. The narratological element of what war is like is sometimes present, but certainly not foregrounded in the speeches. Rather, the speeches seem to function in characterizing Caesar, directly or indirectly, and in foreshadowing the further course of the narrative by means of seeds. All in all, especially the seeds in these exhortation speeches contribute to the idea that war seems to be something you can plan and anticipate, if you are Caesar, at least.

I hope to have illustrated that pre-battle exhortations in the narrative of *Bellum Gallicum*, whether they reflect a historical reality or not, not only function to encourage troops in the story world, but also function on the level of the narrator and his narratees. My analysis of their forms and narratological functions illustrates that speech and thought representations, and pre-battle exhortations in particular, are a literary tool put to use in Caesar's commentaries to persuade

---

viz. the speech of Critognatus (Caes. *Gal.* 7.77.1–16). Direct speech is exceptional in Caesar. On this topic see especially Rasmussen 1963. In the case of the speech of Critognatus, the narrator seems to want to present this speech in a way that allows the narratee to come to the same conclusion as he does in his introduction to the speech (Caes. *Gal.* 7.77.1): Critognatus and other Gauls were wicked, cruel and willing to do anything, as they greatly differ from Romans with respect to *crudelitas* (Rasmussen 1963, 47; Tsitsiou-Chelidoni 2010, 142; Adema forthc.).

38 The events in the battle are almost all presented in historical presents, a presentational style that contributes to the seemingly effortlessness with which the battle is won, as Stienaers argues in his forthcoming dissertation.

Table 1 Speeches preceding battles in *Bellum Gallicum* 1 and 7

Battle	Speech	Form	Length	Functions
Against Helvetians (1.21–29)	1.25.1	Narrated	0	fast tempo
Against Ariovistus (1.48–54)	(1.51.3)	Indirect speech	6	fast tempo, what it's like
Bourges (7.22–31)	7.27.3	Indirect speech Mentioned speech	8 5	fast tempo, characterization, what it's like
Gergovia (7.43.4–53)	(7.45.7–10)	Mentioned speech Indirect speech Indirect speech	3 11 15	seed, characterization
Labienus (7.57–62)	7.62.2	Indirect speech	20	characterization
Cavalry battle (7.66–67)	7.66.3	Indirect speech	94	characterization
Alesia (7.68–90)	7.86.3	Indirect speech Indirect speech	3 10	seed, characterization

the narratees that war, and battles within war, are predictable and controllable procedures.

Bibliography

Adema, S.M. (2014), "De Defectione Haeduorum, Caesars Crisis Management", in: *Lampas* 47, 83–99.
Adema, S.M. (2015), "Deictic Centres of Referential Expressions in Indirect Speech and Thought: Caesar's *De Bello Gallico* I.1–32", in: G. Haverling 2015, 423–435.
Adema, S.M. (forthc.), *Words of Warriors. Speech and Thought Representation in Latin War Narrative*.
Albertus, J. (1908), *Die Parakletikoi in der Griechischen und Römischen Literatur*, Strassburg.
Anson, E. (2010), "The General's Pre-Battle Exhortation in Graeco-Roman Warfare", in: *G&R* 57, 304–318.
Bal, M. (1997 [1988]), *Narratology. Introduction to the Theory of Narrative*, Toronto.
Banfield, A. (1973), "Narrative Style and the Grammar of Direct and Indirect Speech", in: *Foundations of Language* 10, 1–39.
Bayet, J. (1931, 1932), "Le style indirect libre en latin", in: *Revue de philologie, de littérature et d'histoire anciennes*, 327–342 & 325 ff.
Beck, D. (2012), *Speech Presentation in Homeric Epic*, Austin.

Calboli, G. (ed.) (2005), *Latina Lingua! Proceedings of the Twelfth International Colloquium on Latin Linguistics (Bologna, 9–14 June 2003)*, Rome.
Choitz, T. (2011), "Caesars Darstellung der Schlacht von Gergovia", in: *Gymnasium* 118, 135–155.
Daly, G. (2002), *Cannae. The Experience of Battle in the Second Punic War*, London.
Dancygier, B. (2012), *The Language of Stories. A Cognitive Approach*, Cambridge.
de Bakker, M.P. (2007), *Speech and Authority in Herodotus' Histories*, Dissertation, University of Amsterdam.
de Jong, I.J.F. (ed.) (2012), *Space in Ancient Greek Literature*, Leiden.
de Jong, I.J.F. / Nünlist, R. (eds.) (2007), *Time in Ancient Greek Literature*. Leiden.
de Jong, I.J.F. / Nünlist, R. / Bowie, A. (eds.) (2004), *Narrators, Narratees, and Narratives in Ancient Greek Literature*. Leiden.
de Temmerman, K. (2014), *Crafting Characters. Heroes and Heroines in the Ancient Greek Novel*, Oxford.
Dominik, W.J. (1994), *Speech and Rhetoric in Statius' Thebaid*, Hildesheim.
Fauconnier, G. / Sweetser, E. (eds.) (1996), *Spaces, Worlds, and Grammar*, Chicago / London.
Feldherr, A. (ed.) (2009), *The Cambridge Companion to the Roman Historians*, Cambridge.
Fludernik, M. (1993), *The Fictions of Language and the Languages of Fiction. The Linguistic Representation of Speech and Consciousness*, London.
Foster, E. / Lateiner, D. (eds.) (2012), *Thucydides and Herodotus*, Oxford.
Gils, L.W.V. (2009), *Argument and Narrative. A Discourse Analysis of Ten Ciceronian Speeches*, Amsterdam.
Görler, W. (1976). "Die Veränderung des Erzählerstandpunktes in Caesars *Bellum Gallicum*", in: *Poetica* 8, 95–119.
Hansen, M.H. (1993), "The Battle Exhortation in Ancient Historiography. Fact or Fiction?", in: *Historia* 42, 161–180.
Haverling, G. (ed.) (2015), *Latin Linguistics in the Early 21st Century, Acts of the 16th International Colloquium on Latin Linguistics, Uppsala 6th – 11th June 2011*, Uppsala.
Herman, D. (2009), *Basic Elements of Narrative*, Malden / Oxford.
Highet, G. (1972), *The Speeches in Vergil's Aeneid*, Princeton.
Hunter, V.J. (1973), *Thucydides. The Artful Reporter*, Toronto.
Keitel, E. (1987), "Otho's Exhortations in Tacitus' 'Histories'", in: *G&R* 34, 73–82.
Kraner, F. / Dittenberger, W. (1913 [1961]), *C. Iulii Caesaris. Commentarii de bello Gallico*, Berlin.
Kraus, C.S. / Woodman, A.J. (1997), *Latin Historians*, Oxford.
Kraus, C.S. (2010), "Divide and Conquer. Caesar's *De Bello Gallico* 7", in: C. Kraus / J. Marincola / C. Pelling 2010, 40–59.
Kraus, C.S. / Marincola, J. / Pelling, C. (eds.) (2010), *Ancient Historiography and its Contexts. Studies in Honour of A. J. Woodman*, Oxford.
Kroon, C.H.M. (2001), "Communiceren in een dode taal. Of: Hoe Caesar geschiedenis schreef", in: *Lampas* 34, 220–241.
Laird, A. (1999), *Powers of Expression, Expressions of Power. Speech Presentation and Latin Literature*, Oxford.
Laird, A. (2009), "The Rhetoric of Roman Historiography", in: A. Feldherr 2009, 197–213.
Latacz, J. (1977), *Kampfparänese, Kampfdarstellung und Kampfwirklichkeit in der Ilias, bei Kallinos und Tyrtaios*, Munich.

Leech, G. / Short, M. (1981), *Style in Fiction. A Linguistic Introduction to English Fictional Prose*, London / New York.

Lendon, J.E. (1999), "The Rhetoric of Combat. Greek Military Theory and Roman Culture in Julius Caesar's Battle Descriptions", in: *Clas. Ant.* 18, 273–329.

Marincola, J. (ed.) (2007a), *A Companion to Greek and Roman Historiography*, Oxford.

Marincola, J. (2007b), "Speeches in Classical Historiography", in: J. Marincola 2007a, 118–132.

Mellet, S. (1998), "Imparfait et discours rapporté", in: *Oratio soluta, Oratio Numerosa. Études Luxembourgeoises d'histoire et de littérature Romaines* 1, 117–125.

Pausch, D. (ed.) (2010a), *Stimmen der Geschichte. Funktionen von Reden in der Antiken Historiographie*, New York / Berlin, 183–209.

Pausch, D. (2010b), "Der Feldherr als Redner und der Appell an den Leser: Wiederholung und Antizipation in den Reden bei Livius", in: D. Pausch 2010a, 183–209.

Pinkster, H. (1990), *Latin Syntax and Semantics*, London.

Pritchett, W.K. (1994), *Essays in Greek History*, Amsterdam.

Rambaud, M. (1966 [1953]), *L'art de la déformation historique dans les commentaires de César*, Paris.

Rasmussen, D. (1963), *Caesars Commentarii. Stil und Stilwandel am Beispiel der direkten Rede*, Göttingen.

Richter, W. (1977), *Caesar als Darsteller seiner Taten*, Heidelberg.

Riggsby, A. (2006), *Caesar in Gaul and Rome. War in Words*, Austin.

Rosén, H. (2013), "About Non-Direct Discourse: Another Look at Its Parameters in Latin", in: *Journal of Latin Linguistics* 12, 231–268.

Scardino, C. (2007), *Gestaltung und Funktion der Reden bei Herodot und Thukydides*, Berlin / New York.

Scardino, C. (2012), "Indirect Discourse in Herodotus and Thucydides", in: E. Foster / D. Lateiner 2012, 67–96.

Shalev, D. / Sawicki, L. (eds.) (2002), *Donum grammaticum. Studies in Latin and Celtic Linguistics in Honour of Hannah Rosén*, Leuven.

Sznajder, L. (2002), "La concordance des temps comme paramètre du discours indirect en Latin", in: D. Shalev / L. Sawicki 2002, 337–349.

Sznajder, L. (2005), "Stratégies de prises en charge énonciatives dans le discours indirect", in: G. Calboli 2005, 749–761.

Stienaers, D. (in prep.), *Report in Ancient War Narrative*. Dissertation, VU University of Amsterdam.

Tsitsiou-Chelidoni, C. (2010), "Macht, Rhetorik, Autorität: Zur Funktion der Reden Caesars und seiner Gegner in *De Bello Gallico*", in: D. Pausch 2010a, 125–156.

Vandelanotte, L. (2009), *Speech and Thought Representation in English. A Cognitive-Functional Approach*, Berlin / New York.

Vasaly, A. (2009), "Characterization and Complexity: Caesar, Sallust and Livy", in: A. Feldherr 2009, 245–260.

Yellin, K. (2008), *Battle Exhortation. The Rhetoric of Combat Leadership*, Columbia.

Zoida, J.C.I. (2007), "The Battle Exhortation in Ancient Rhetoric", in: *Rhetorica* 25, 141–158.

Philip Waddell
Carthago Deleta: Alternate Realities and Meta-History in Appian's *Libyca*

Abstract: Through examination of an inversion of the conventions of paired speeches in Appian's *Libyca*, this article posits Appian's narratological creation of an "alternate reality" wherein Carthage is destroyed after the Second Punic War. Appian's reliance on *ekphrasis* and emotion during both the Third Punic War and the soldiers' recasting of it recalls similar discussion by S. Farrington and M. Baumann in this volume. Using historiographic convention to signal his "alternate reality," Appian collapses time between the endings of the Second and Third Punic Wars (cf. K. Low's chapter in this volume), suggesting that the third war need never have happened, all of which is actively forgotten through the internal historiographical process (cf. V. Liotsakis's chapter in this volume) whereby Romans compose their own triumphal narratives. For another treatment of speeches in historiography, consult S. Adema's contribution to this volume.

Appian's *Roman History*, although experiencing a growth of interest, is still largely under-read due to the author's perceived lack of historical accuracy as well as rhetorical and narratological sophistication. Recently, however, scholarship has turned to Appian, and the literary merits of his work are beginning to be considered and addressed.[1] One particularly notable example of Appian's narrative historiography occurs at the end of his discussion of the Second Punic War. Through an inversion of the rhetorical set piece of paired speeches, Appian suggests an alternate reality, wherein the Third Punic War occurred primarily to correct the Senate's ill-fated decision to allow Carthage to exist. Although the destruction of Carthage was the natural and logical step following the Hannibalic War, its destruction comes to pass only after Rome's (necessarily) impious Third Punic War. The crime of this war, stressed throughout the narrative, is expiated and forgotten during Appian's meta-historical summary, which occurs before his description of Scipio's triumph.

---

[1] See, for example, Bucher 1997 and 2000, 411–58.

In order to understand how Appian exploits reader expectation to hint at a reality both alternate and delayed, it is necessary to first discuss paired speeches in general.[2]

1 The convention

In ancient historiography, both Greek and Latin, the historian could display rhetorical skill and training, as well as a sense of the dramatic, through the *topos* of paired speeches.[3] These speeches occur at two set and expected moments during the historical narrative. The first is directly before a battle, when both generals harangue their armies in preparation for the conflict. The skill of the orator in this case is aimed at enflaming the martial ardor of the troops, and the effects of the leader's rhetoric are then played out during the battle itself.[4] The other occasion for paired speeches is political debate before a deliberative body. The conflict in this latter type is decided during the speeches themselves and in the ensuing vote, rather than on the battlefield. In both types of paired speeches the result can be determined, with only rare exceptions, from the order in which the speeches are presented in the historical narrative.[5] The general rule is that the second speaker of the pair will win the ensuing conflict whether in battle or in ballots. This convention of the victorious second speech generally holds true for Greek and Roman historians from Thucydides through (at least) Tacitus.[6]

---

[2] Unattributed citations belong to Appian's *Roman History*. For the text of Appian, I use P. Viereck and A. G. Roos' Teubner edition. For translations, I use Horace White's Loeb text.
[3] The subject of speeches in ancient historical narratives, and its attendant scholarship, is vast. For a discussion of speech composition in Thucydides and Caesar, respectively, please see S. Feddern and S. Adema in this volume. Further, see Miller 1975, 45–57; Keitel 1987, 73; Woodman 1988, 14–15, 117, 147 n. 4; and Woodman/Kraus 2014, 236–38. For a general introduction to this question, see Marincola 2007b, 118–32, who discusses many of the conventions of speech in ancient historiography.
[4] For more on pre-battle speeches as narratological devices, please see Adema's discussion in this volume; for discussions of the historicity of pre-battle orations, see, e.g., Anson 2010.
[5] One notable exception occurs at Liv. 6.39–42, in which Appius' speech fails to convince the Senate. While there are certainly exceptions, the victory of the second speech vastly outweighs the contrary outcome throughout ancient historical narratives.
[6] Noteworthy examples of paired speeches in other historians include Sallust's Caesar and Cato (Sal. *Cat.* 51–52), Livy's Scipio the Elder and Hannibal at the Ticinus (Liv. 21.40–44), Hannibal and Scipio at Zama (Liv. 30.30–31), Tacitus' Calgacus and Agricola (Tac. *Ag.* 30–34), and Tacitus' Sejanus and Tiberius (Tac. *Ann.* 4.39–40).

I will now turn to Appian's subversion of this trope and offer a possible explanation for his break from historiographical convention.

2 The exception

After the battle of Zama, the victorious Romans under the command of Scipio Africanus accepted the surrender of the Carthaginian forces. According to Appian, Scipio points out that the defeated enemy doesn't deserve mercy,[7] but grants them peace with conditions, and sends messengers back to the Senate for confirmation. The terms of Scipio's treaty are not, according to Appian, in question. Rather, the debate in the Senate centers on whether the city of Carthage should be destroyed. This highly rhetorical passage shows several signs of authorial freedom in the crafting of the account. The speakers are vague in their identities: speaking on behalf of Carthage is one of Scipio's unnamed "friends," while a certain Publius Cornelius speaks for the city's destruction. In terms of history, it is notable that neither Livy nor Polybius preserve any record of this debate. Polybius instead records a debate in the Carthaginian Assembly, where Hannibal spoke on behalf of obtaining a treaty with Rome.[8] Livy focuses on Scipio's triumph and honors, showing, like Polybius, a subservient Carthage, with direct speech by Hannibal.[9] Thus, we have no other major source for this debate at Rome. It may therefore be assumed that Appian, if not entirely inventing this rhetorical *mise-en-scene*, was at least free to relate the debate as he chose. Appian's narrative freedom is critical in explaining this inversion of rhetorical *topos* through historiography and narrative effect, rather than in terms of fidelity to events.

First to speak is Scipio's anonymous friend. Much of his discourse echoes the speech made shortly before by Hasdrubal Eriphus to Scipio.[10] Although Hasdrubal blamed the fickleness of the multitude and divine misfortune, Carthage's recent guilt was acknowledged, as was its history and former power, while Rome's differences from Carthage were stressed, namely, its piety, mercy, and reputation among nations. The speech of Scipio's friend treads familiar (to the reader) ground:

---

7 *Lib.* 53/230.
8 Plb. 15.19.1–3.
9 Liv. 30.44–45.
10 *Lib.* 50–52/215–228.

οὐ περὶ τῆς Καρχηδονίων σωτηρίας ἐστὶν ἡμῖν ἡ φροντίς, ὦ ἄνδρες, ἀλλὰ περὶ τῆς Ῥωμαίων ἔς τε θεοὺς πίστεως καὶ πρὸς ἀνδρῶν εὐφημίας, μὴ Καρχηδονίων αὐτῶν ὠμότερα πράξωμεν, οἳ Καρχηδονίοις ὠμότητα ἐπικαλοῦμεν, καὶ μετριοπαθείας ἀεὶ φροντίσαντες ἐπὶ τῶν βραχυτέρων ἀμελήσωμεν ἐν τοῖς μείζοσιν· ἃ μηδὲ λαθεῖν ἔνεστι διὰ τὸ μέγεθος, ἀλλ' ἐς ἅπασαν γῆν περιελεύσεται καὶ νῦν καὶ ὕστερον, ἢν πόλιν περιώνυμον καὶ θαλασσοκράτορα ἀνέλωμεν, ἣ καὶ νήσων ἦρξε πολλῶν καὶ θαλάσσης ὅλης καὶ Λιβύης ὑπὲρ ἥμισυ ἔν τε τοῖς πρὸς ἡμᾶς αὐτοὺς ἀγῶσι πολλὰ καὶ τύχης καὶ δυνάμεως ἔργα ἐπεδείξατο. οἷς ἔτι μὲν φιλονεικοῦσιν ἐρίζειν ἔδει, πεσόντων δὲ φείδεσθαι, καθὰ καὶ τῶν ἀθλητῶν οὐδεὶς τὸν πεσόντα ἔτι τύπτει καὶ τῶν θηρίων τὰ πολλὰ φείδεται τῶν καταπεσόντων. καλὸν δ' ἐν τοῖς εὐτυχήμασι νέμεσιν θεῶν φυλάσσεσθαι καὶ ἀνθρώπων φθόνον. (*Lib*. 57/248–50)

Gentlemen, this is not so much a question of saving Carthage as of preserving our faith with the gods and our reputation among men – lest it be said that we, who charge the Carthaginians with cruelty, behave with greater cruelty than they, and while always exercising moderation in small matters neglect it in large ones, which, on account of their very magnitude, cannot even escape notice. The deed will be sounded through all the earth, now and hereafter, if we destroy this famous city, former mistress of the seas, ruler of so many islands, and of the whole expanse of water, and more than half of Africa, a city which in contests with ourselves has exhibited such wonderful success and power. While they were combative, it was necessary to contend against them; now that they have fallen, they should be spared, just as athletes refrain from striking a fallen antagonist, and as most wild beasts spare fallen bodies. It is fitting, in the hour of success, to beware of the indignation of the gods and of the envy of mankind.

In fact, Scipio's friend goes on to claim that the leniency for which he argues is not at all out of any regard for Carthage and that he, like Scipio, is aware of the Punic penchant for breaking treaties:

ἐγὼ δ' οὐκ ἐρῶ μὲν οὐδὲν ὑπὲρ Καρχηδονίων (οὐ γὰρ ἄξιον), οὐδ' ἀγνοῶ καὶ πρότερον αὐτοὺς ἄλλας συνθήκας πρὸ τῶνδε παραβῆναι· ἃ δ' ἐπὶ τοῖς τοιούτοις ποιοῦντες οἱ πατέρες ἡμῶν ἐς τόδε τύχης προῆλθον, εἰδότας ὑμᾶς ἀναμνήσω. (*Lib*. 58/253)

I will say nothing in defense of the Carthaginians; they do not deserve it. Nor do I forget that they violated other treaties before those which are now under review. But what our fathers did in like circumstances (by which means they arrived at this summit of fortune) I will recall to your minds, though you know it already.

The speaker next recalls other perfidious enemies of Rome who went unpunished, including the Italian cities that defected to Hannibal during the last war. After an appeal to pragmatism, the speech ends with the plea that the wishes of Scipio should be honored, as he is a brilliant commander and much more familiar with the situation than the Senate.

This speech is followed by that of Publius Cornelius. While Appian gives the probable and political reason for this speech (Publius is related to Cn. Cornelius Lentulus, then *consul*, and, according to Appian, hoping to succeed to Scipio's command[11]), the speech has greater significance than is at first evident. Publius argues that there is no better time than the present for the destruction of an untrustworthy, and, by Scipio and Co.'s own admission, still powerful enemy:

> τὸ μὲν συμφέρον ἐστὶ μόνον ἐν τοῖς πολέμοις, ὦ ἄνδρες, χρήσιμον· καὶ ὅσῳ δυνατὴν ἔτι καὶ νῦν ἀποφαίνουσιν οὗτοι τὴν πόλιν, φυλάξασθαι χρὴ τὴν ἀπιστίαν αὐτῆς μετὰ τῆς δυνάμεως καὶ τὴν ἰσχὺν προανελεῖν, ἐπεὶ μὴ τὴν ἀπιστίαν δυνάμεθα. οὐδεὶς δ' ἡμῖν καιρὸς ἐς τὸ λῦσαι τὸν ἀπὸ Καρχηδονίων φόβον ἐπιτηδειότερός ἐστι τοῦ παρόντος, ἐν ᾧ πάντων εἰσὶν ἀσθενεῖς καὶ ἄποροι, πρὶν αὖθις αὐτῶν ἐς ἑκάτερον αὐξῆσαι. (*Lib.* 62/273–4)
>
> In war, gentlemen, that which is expedient is alone advantageous. We are told that this city is still powerful. So much the more ought we to be on our guard against treachery joined to power, and to crush the power in time since we cannot extinguish the treachery. No time can be better chosen to free ourselves from all fear of the Carthaginians than the present, when they are weak and poor, and before they again accumulate strength and resources.

The debate has now changed focus. The question is not *whether* Carthage will be destroyed, but *when*. We should notice also that *fear* (φόβος) enters the debate for the first time. For Scipio's friend, Carthage should be managed as an advantageous possession and source of increased fame due to Rome's magnanimity. In this second speech Carthage is still a vigorous enemy that needs to be annihilated, rather than a rival that can now be trusted. This speech seems anachronistic, giving voice to thoughts that are more emblematic of the Third Punic War than the context of Carthage's defeat in 201:

> ἐγὼ δ' αὐτοὺς ἡγοῦμαι τοὺς θεοὺς ἐς τόδε τὴν Καρχηδόνα περιενεγκεῖν, ἵνα δῶσί ποτε δίκην τῆς ἀσεβείας, οἳ καὶ περὶ Σικελίαν καὶ Ἰβηρίαν καὶ Ἰταλίαν καὶ ἐν αὐτῇ τῇ Λιβύῃ καὶ πρὸς ἡμᾶς καὶ πρὸς τοὺς ἄλλους ἅπαντας αἰεὶ συνετίθεντο καὶ παρώρκουν καὶ δεινὰ καὶ σχέτλια ἔδρων. (*Lib.* 62/277)
>
> I think that the gods themselves have brought Carthage into this plight in order to punish at last for their former impiety those who in Sicily, in Spain, in Italy, and in Africa itself, in dealing with us and with all others, were always making covenants and breaking oaths, and committing outrageous and savage acts.

Here for the first time, the wrongs of Carthage are rehearsed at length, beginning with the fall of Saguntum and ending with the unlawful capture of Roman grain ships. Publius demands at the close of the speech that Carthage surrender without terms, as all peoples usually surrender, and that the Senate make the appropriate decision, which, as Publius has already intimated, is the city's destruction.

---

11 *Lib.* 62/272.

While the two speeches are persuasive, and both argue eloquently from their points and evidence, the first speech suffers (for Appian's reader) from the fact that it is largely a thematic continuance of Hasdrubal Eriphus' speech to Scipio. Here, the speaker (Scipio's unnamed friend) enlarges on the themes of Roman *clementia* and reputation, rather than encouraging respect for a conquered Carthage and the turn of fate.[12] The reader has already heard all of these arguments made more effectively and with more *pathos* – Hasdrubal, speaking for the life of his city before its conqueror, breaks down in tears as he finishes his speech.[13] Further, the closing argument of the first speech makes a lame appeal to Scipio's record and position "on the ground" in Carthage.

The speech of Publius, on the other hand, is strengthened by the fact that Carthage's offenses have not been listed and enlarged upon during the debate, but only alluded to. This litany of wrongs also recalls the beginning of the war to the reader, and the injustice attached to the *topos* of the *urbs capta* at the fall of Saguntum.[14] Through Publius' speech, Appian provides a ring-structure for the Second Punic War, and his *Libyca*, by returning the narrative to Saguntum, stressing broken promises and wrongs that must be avenged. Given the rhetorical effects of the speeches, and especially the placement of the more dynamic speech in the secondary, winning, position, Appian's reader expects the Senate to side with Publius, or, at the very least, anticipates more speeches (as in the Sicilian Expedition debates in Thucydides).[15] Neither of these expected outcomes take place. Appian instead gives the following blanket statement, immediately following the last words of Publius' speech:

> τοιαῦτα μὲν καὶ ὁ Πούπλιος εἶπεν· ἡ δὲ βουλὴ κατὰ ἄνδρα παρ' ἑκάστου ψῆφον ᾔτει, καὶ ἐς τὴν Σκιπίωνος γνώμην αἱ πλείους συνέδραμον. (*Lib.* 65/289)
>
> After Publius had spoken, the Senate took a vote on the question, and the majority agreed with Scipio.

The Senate's decision is presented without any preamble, jarringly upsetting the established *topos* in which the second speech is destined to win the debate, as well as the reader expectations that Appian has constructed. Following Publius'

---

[12] *Lib.* 50–52/215–228. Rengakos (2006, esp. 298–99) refers to Thucydides' use of this technique, which he refers to as "cross-referencing," as a means of building suspense as the reader follows the progression from similar arguments either temporally or locally, which ultimately derives from Homer and Hesiod.

[13] *Lib.* 53/229.

[14] *Lib.* 6/23.

[15] Th. 6.9–23. For a discussion of Alcibiades' use of ancestry in his speech against Nicias on this occasion, please see Harris in this volume.

speech, the reader naturally expects the Senate to vote for the destruction of Carthage. With this sudden reversal, the reader is left with an uneasy feeling that the narrative has taken a wrong turn. This reader's unease is further increased by Appian's presentation of the Punic Wars after this point in his narrative, which, as we will see, increasingly portrays the Romans, rather than their enemy, as faithless and cruel.

Appian, through his ordering of the speeches, has purposefully challenged reader expectations and created the momentary image of an alternate reality. During Publius' speech, the reader is presented not only with more persuasive arguments, but also with a rationale for Carthage's destruction.[16] Aided by Appian's Publius, the reader has embraced a narrative pattern that is then revealed to be illusory. The reader now has two realities: that of the Senate's decision, and the anticipated narrative of Carthaginian annihilation.[17] This amounts to an echo of the alternate reality of *Carthago deleta:* Carthage should have been destroyed, but somehow isn't. Appian quickly subordinates the reader's surprise and reaction by an excursus on Roman triumphs in general, and presents the spectacle of Scipio's triumph.[18] Appian, however, reactivates the alternate reality of Carthage's destruction later in the *Libyca*.

3 Collapsing realities

Following the ratification of Scipio's treaty, Masinissa exercises his new position as Roman ally to control increasingly more Carthaginian territory, provoking a Carthaginian response. After a deputation is sent from Carthage to Rome, Cato travels to Libya to reconnoiter.[19] According to Appian, he finds Carthage has rebuilt remarkably quickly after the Hannibalic War. Again, Appian describes Cato's primary emotion as "fear rather than envy."[20] Cato becomes convinced of the idea that Rome can never be safe while Carthage exists. His opinion strongly echoes that of Publius' speech, especially the insistence on fear as a motivation. The reader recalls Publius' oration as well as the alternate reality, as Cato takes up the often-repeated cry for Carthage's destruction. Suddenly, and

---

[16] See above, *Lib*. 62/277.
[17] Both O'Gorman (2006, 281–30, esp. 283) and Pagán (2006, 193–218, esp. 197–98) refer to this narrative technique, in the works of both Tacitus and Appian. O'Gorman calls this technique "virtual history" and Pagán, "sideshadowing."
[18] *Lib*. 66/292–300.
[19] *Lib*. 69/310.
[20] "οὐ ζήλου μᾶλλον φόβου" *Lib*. 69/313.

without explanation, Appian records the Senate's immediate acceptance of Cato's policy, with only Scipio Nasica opposed. The minority has become the majority, and both realities will soon collapse into the Third Punic War.

From this point in his *Libyca*, Appian reverses his depiction of the national characteristics of both Rome and Carthage. In Publius' speech (and echoing prior indications), the complaint against Carthage emphasizes its wanton and opportunistic oath-breaking. The Romans, by contrast, are depicted as true to their promises, and willing to give the Carthaginians another opportunity to save themselves through treaty. After Appian's introduction of Carthage's alternate reality, however, Romans and Carthaginians reverse these roles. Not only does the Roman Senate take Cato's view of *Carthago delenda est*, but they immediately search for a pretext to break the treaty. This language of pretext is repeated when war is actually declared:

> ἡ δὲ βουλὴ πάλαι διεγνωκυῖα πολεμῆσαι καὶ προφάσεις ἐρεσχηλοῦσα ὧδε ἀπεκρίνατο, Καρχηδονίους οὔπω Ῥωμαίοις ἱκανῶς ἀπολογήσασθαι. πάλιν οὖν ἀγωνιῶντες ἠρώτων, εἰ δοκοῦσιν ἁμαρτεῖν, τί παθόντες ἀπολύσονται τὸ ἔγκλημα. οἳ δὲ οὕτως ἔφασαν τῷ ῥήματι· "εἰ τὸ ἱκανὸν ποιήσετε Ῥωμαίοις." ζητούντων δ' ἐκείνων, ὅ τι εἴη τὸ ἱκανόν, οἳ μὲν ᾤοντο Ῥωμαίους ἐθέλειν τοῖς χρήμασιν προσεπιθεῖναι τοῖς ἐπὶ Σκιπίωνος ὡρισμένοις, οἳ δὲ Μασσανάσσῃ τῆς ἀμφιλόγου γῆς μεταστῆναι. ἀποροῦντες οὖν πάλιν ἐς Ῥώμην ἔπεμπον καὶ παρεκάλουν γνῶναι σαφῶς, ὅ τι ἐστὶν αὐτοῖς τὸ ἱκανόν. οἳ δὲ αὖθις ἔφασαν εἰδέναι Καρχηδονίους καλῶς καὶ εἰπόντες ἀπέπεμψαν. (*Lib.* 74/343–6)

> The Senate, which had previously resolved upon war and was only seeking some petty excuse, answered that the defense so far offered by the Carthaginians was not satisfactory. The latter, much disturbed, asked again, if they had done wrong, how they could atone for it. The answer was given in a word: "You must satisfy the Roman people." When they enquired amongst themselves what satisfaction meant, some thought that the Romans would like to have something added to the pecuniary fine imposed by Scipio; others that the disputed territory should be given up to Masinissa. Being therefore again at a loss what to do they sent another embassy to Rome, and asked to know exactly what satisfaction was required. The Romans replied that the Carthaginians knew perfectly well, and having given this answer dismissed them.

The inversion is complete: the now-crafty Romans deflect the now-guiltless and guileless Carthaginians with meaningless words, while Rome continues to build its forces for the planned broken treaty. Appian's narrative has proceeded full-circle. It is now Romans, as shameless treaty-breakers, who make war on peaceful and honest Carthage.

The Third Punic War, as Appian relates it, is full of repeated Carthaginian gestures of good faith towards perfidious Romans. Among these are the

Roman requests for 300 child hostages[21] and the surrender of all Carthaginian weapons and siege engines.[22] After the Carthaginians meet both of these prerequisites for peace, Censorius, the Roman commander, praises their dutiful obedience, but adds that they must also vacate the city of Carthage to the Romans for destruction.[23] Upon this, the Carthaginians begin armed resistance that, after several highly descriptive *ekphraseis*, culminates in the final destruction of Carthage. Appian paints the scene poetically, complete with conqueror's tears and appropriate quotations from Homer.[24] Carthage has finally been destroyed, and the alternate realities have collapsed into an image of Roman *imperium*.

4 Expiation through meta-history

The fall of Carthage, repeatedly referred to by Appian as "spectacle," prefigures the scene immediately following: the reaction to the news at Rome and Scipio Aemilianus' triumph. These scenes present the successful end, not only of Carthage, but of the Punic Wars. In a vivid scene, Appian describes the transports of joy expressed by the Romans:

> οἱ δ' ἐν ἄστει, ὡσαύτως τὴν ναῦν ἰδόντες καὶ τῆς νίκης περὶ δείλην ἑσπέραν πυθόμενοι, ἐς τὰς ὁδοὺς ἐξεπήδων καὶ διενυκτέρευον μετ' ἀλλήλων, ἡδόμενοι καὶ συμπλεκόμενοι ὡς ἄρτι μὲν ἐλεύθεροι φόβων γεγονότες, ἄρτι δ' ἄρχοντες ἑτέρων ἀσφαλῶς, ἄρτι δὲ βέβαιον τὴν πόλιν ἔχοντες καὶ νενικηκότες οἵαν οὔτινα πρότερον ἄλλην.
>
> ...
>
> ὧν ἐνθυμούμενοι μάλιστα ἐξίσταντο περὶ τῆς νίκης ἐς ἀπιστίαν αὐτῆς καὶ αὖθις ἀνεπυνθάνοντο ἀλλήλων, εἰ τῷ ὄντι Καρχηδὼν κατέσκαπται (*Lib.* 134/633–4, 636)

> When the people of Rome saw the ship and heard of the victory early in the evening, they poured into the streets and spent the whole night congratulating and embracing each other like people just now delivered from some great fear, just now confirmed in their supremacy, just now assured of the permanence of their own city, and winners of such a victory as they had never won before.
>
> ...
>
> Remembering these things, they were so excited over this victory that they could hardly believe it, and they asked each other over and over again whether it was really true that Carthage was destroyed.

---

21 *Lib.* 76–77/354–58.
22 *Lib.* 80/373–75.
23 *Lib.* 81/378.
24 *Lib.* 132/629–30. Scipio quotes *Il.* 6.448–49. For discussion on this passage as it applies to a Roman understanding of the fate of Rome through the falls of Carthage and Troy, please see Guelfucci 2009, 421–23.

In this passage, Appian stresses the vividness and emotion of the Romans on hearing of Scipio Aemilianus' victory. There is palpable relief mixed with joy as the Romans no longer fear destruction. Again, fear (φόβος) is brought to the foreground as part of the intense emotion which recalls Publius' speech, Cato's opinion, and Rome's preoccupation with Carthage. In this closing chapter, however, the overriding fear that prompted the war is at once mentioned and dispelled. Appian here portrays the Roman people as uncertain about the fall of Carthage. They must ask themselves "over and over again" whether this could have happened. The reader can see here the two realities – the former physical reality of a spared Carthage and the rhetorically signaled reality of a *Carthago deleta* – finally collapsing into one amid the joyful realizations of the Roman people upon the conclusion of the Third Punic War.

Immediately following this recognition that Carthage has been destroyed, the Roman people delight in describing the war to each other:

> ἐλεσχήνευόν τε δι' ὅλης νυκτός, ὅπως μὲν αὐτῶν τὰ ὅπλα περιηρέθη καὶ ὅπως αὐτίκα παρὰ δόξαν ἐτεκτήναντο ἕτερα, ὅπως δὲ τὰς ναῦς ἀφῃρέθησαν καὶ στόλον ἐπήξαντο πάλιν ἐξ ὕλης παλαιᾶς τό τε στόμα τοῦ λιμένος ὡς ἀπεκλείσθη καὶ στόμα ὡς ὠρύξαντο ἕτερον ὀλίγαις ἡμέραις. καὶ τὸ τῶν τειχῶν ὕψος αὐτοῖς διὰ στόματος ἦν καὶ τὰ τῶν λίθων μεγέθη καὶ τὸ πῦρ, ὃ πολλάκις ταῖς μηχαναῖς ἐπήνεγκαν. ὅλως τε τὸν πόλεμον ὡς ὁρῶντες ἄρτι γιγνόμενον ἀλλήλοις διετύπουν καὶ ἐς τὰς φαντασίας τῶν λεγομένων τῷ σχήματι τοῦ σώματος συνεφέροντο. καὶ τὸν Σκιπίωνα ὁρᾶν ἐδόκουν ἐπὶ κλιμάκων, ἐπὶ νεῶν, ἐν πύλαις, ἐν μάχαις, πανταχοῦ διαθέοντα. (*Lib.* 134/636–7)

> And so they conversed the whole night, telling how the arms of the Carthaginians had been taken away from them, and how at once, contrary to expectation, they supplied themselves with others: how they lost their ships and built a great fleet out of old material; how the mouth of their harbor was closed, yet they managed to open another in a few days. They talked about the height of the walls, and the size of the stones, and the fires that so often destroyed the engines. In fact they pictured to each other the whole war, as though it were just taking place under their own eyes, suiting the action to the word; they seemed to see Scipio on the ladders, on shipboard, at the gates, in the battles, and darting hither and thither.

It should be noted that the scenes that the Roman people paint for each other are the same that Appian has just taken such care to present in his *Libyca*, and thus the author is engaging in a meta-historical and intratextual synthesis of his own narrative.[25] Not only does Appian build his own summarizing ring structure by reminding the reader of the Third Punic War (and the Punic Wars more generally), but he accomplishes this in such a way that he can comment on the pleasure

---

[25] This passage has been examined in terms of metahistory by Pitcher (2012, 204–208), with emphasis on the "plupast" of the Hannibalic War told through the *enargeia* of Scipio's soldiers.

of creating historical narrative. The Roman people, in addition to their more usual role as spectators and audience, here become historians. Their narratives focus on the dramatic highpoints and the "believe-it-or-not" aspects of ancient historiography, as well as hero-narrative, all common since Herodotus. Appian here refigures his history through the Roman people's *ekphrastic* and visually dramatic miniature histories – with the implicit conceit that we, as readers of Appian's narrative, are more reliably or realistically informed by our professional historian than the Romans are by their fellow amateurs.

In this passage, Appian shows us the levels of memory that work through his text, and are vital for reforging political and historical narrative. In the Roman histories recounted by the soldiers, there is no mention of the less-savory beginnings of the war, or of Roman trickery. Appian notes that these narratives focus only on the descriptions (possibly echoing Herodotus) of *how* these events happened and what they might have looked like. Implicit in this kind of historiography is the removal of all moral judgment based on historical events. Appian's Romans are already whitewashing the history of the Punic Wars when they are scarcely over. Their stories don't dwell on the paranoia of Cato and Publius and the injustices of naked imperialism, but rather on presentations of Scipio as a comic book like character, doing everything and practically winning the battle (and war) himself. Readers in the city of Rome or those familiar with its monuments would possibly recognize the same self-aggrandizing historiography present in the Column of Trajan, wherein the emperor is likewise seen at all stages of the Dacian Wars. Through the victorious Roman historian/soldiers, Appian shows by example how historiography can change perception, guilt, and memory.

Bibliography

Anson, E. (2010), "The General's Pre-Battle Exhortation in Graeco-Roman Warfare," in: *G&R* 57, 304–18.
Beard, M. (2007), *The Roman Triumph*, Cambridge.
Bucher, G. (1997), *Prolegomena to a Commentary on Appian's* Bellum civile, *Book 2*. Diss., Brown University.
Bucher, G. (2000), "The Origins, Program, and Composition of Appian's *Roman History*," in: *TAPhA* 130, 411–58.
Bucher, G. (2005), "Fictive Elements in Appian's Pharsalus Narrative," in: *Phoenix* 59, 50–76.
Fartzoff, M. (ed.) (2009), *Reconstruire Troie. Permanence et renaissances d'une cité emblématique*, Besançon.
Gowing, A. (1990), "Appian and Cassius' Speech Before Philippi (*Bella Civilia* 4.90–100)," in: *Phoenix* 44, 158–81.

Grethlein, J. / Krebs, C. (eds.) (2012), *Time and Narrative in Ancient Historiography*, Cambridge.
Guelfucci, M. (2009), "Troie, Carthage et Rome: les larmes de Scipion," in: M. Fartzoff 2009, 407–24.
Keitel, E. (1987), "Otho's Exhortations in Tacitus' *Histories*," in: *G&R* 34, 73–82.
Marincola, J. (ed.) (2007a), *Companion to Greek and Roman Historiography*, Chichester.
Marincola, J. (2007b), "Speeches in Classical Historiography," in: J. Marincola 2007a, 118–32.
Miller, N. (1975), "Dramatic Speech in the Roman Historians," in: *G&R* 22, 45–57.
O'Gorman, E. (2006), "Alternative Empires: Tacitus's Virtual History of the Pisonian Principate," in: *Arethusa* 39, 193–218.
Pagán, V. (2006), "Shadows and Assassinations: Forms of Time in Tacitus and Appian," in: *Arethusa* 39, 193–218.
Pitcher, L. (2012), "War Stories: The Uses of the Plupast in Appian" in: J. Grethlein / C. Krebs 2012, 199–210.
Rengakos, A. (2006), "Thucydides' Narrative: The Epic and Herodotean Heritage," in: A. Rengakos / A. Tsakmakis 2006, 279–300.
Rengakos, A. / Tsakmakis, A. (eds.) (2006), *Brill's Companion to Thucydides*, Leiden.
Van der Leest, J. (1988), *Appian and the Writing of The Roman History*, Diss., University of Toronto.
Viereck, P. / Roos, A. (1962), *Appiani Historia Romana*, vol. I, Leipzig.
White, H. (1912), *Appian. Roman History*, vol. I., Cambridge.
Woodman, A. (1988), *Rhetoric in Classical Historiography*, London.
Woodman, A. / Kraus, C. (eds.) (2014), *Tacitus. Agricola*, Cambridge.

Katie Low
Histories Repeated? The Mutinies in *Annals* 1 and Tacitean Self-Allusion

Abstract: This article compares Tacitus' accounts of two insurrections: the movements of Otho and Vitellius at the end of Galba's short principate in AD 69, which are described in *Histories* 1, and the mutinies that broke out in Germany and Pannonia shortly after Tiberius' accession in AD 14, as is recounted in *Annals* 1. Like P. Duchêne's paper, it considers how a Roman author subtly constructs a particular way of looking at and retelling imperial history. It argues that Tacitus uses a variety of intertextual techniques to evoke the earlier *Histories* in his account of the mutinies in the *Annals*, and that in doing so he makes broader points about the potential for civil strife being embedded in the Julio-Claudian principate from the beginning, and the propensity for history to repeat itself. Just as V. Liotsakis' contribution does, it assesses the role of distinct episodes in a historiographical text on their own terms, in relation to each other, and in the context of a wide-ranging narrative as a whole.

1

For several decades, the notion of 'intertextuality' has been the subject of extensive debate amongst Classicists. In addition to identifying allusions to other works in ancient texts, many scholars have broached wider issues of repetition, intentionality, and authors' relationships with their predecessors and with the broader literary tradition in which they were working. Much of this scholarship has focused on Latin poetry, but recently more interest has been shown in prose, and in historiographical prose especially.[1]

Indeed, a number of special considerations apply to the study of allusion and intertextuality in historiography. It has been persuasively suggested that when writers of history allude to other authors in their work, this generates a potential contradiction between the singularity of an individual historical event and the sense that history is a continuum in which similar things happen repeatedly. Not only that, but if one historian echoes a predecessor when recounting an episode that happened before the events treated by that predecessor did, the

---

[1] Levene (2010, 82–6) offers a useful recent survey (with bibliography at 82 n. 2). Other important contributions include Fowler 1997 and Hinds 1998.

very notion of chronological order and the sequence of history is called into question. There may be times, however, when it is not clear if a historian is alluding to another historical narrative, or to a generally known body of material about an event, or just to the event itself, without any textual mediation. The idea of textual allusion in historiography is also complicated by the possibility that characters in a text who are portrayed in a manner reminiscent of persons who feature in other texts may have imitated these other persons in real life.[2]

This discussion will explore some of these thought-provoking points with reference to two sections of Tacitus' oeuvre: Book 1 of the *Histories*, in which the first few turbulent months of 69 are narrated, and the chapters in Book 1 of the *Annals* which describe the sedition that broke out amongst the legions in Pannonia and Germany in the aftermath of Augustus' death in 14.[3] It will be suggested that, in the *Annals*' account of the mutinies that occurred as Tiberius was taking power, there are verbal and thematic echoes of various episodes of military unrest in Galba's and Otho's short principates that Tacitus had already portrayed in his earlier *Histories*.[4] At this key point at the beginning of the *Annals*, the historian seems to be drawing on the expectations of a reader who is already familiar with the *Histories*, and two ostensibly rather different situations are linked by textual allusions and a broader sense of similarity. This example of self-allusion offers insights into Tacitus' views about the first century of imperial history, and about the nature of power and its transmission under the principate.[5]

---

[2] Damon 2009 and O'Gorman 2009 are of fundamental importance on these issues; see also Moles 1983 and Clauss 1997 on individual texts, and the summary at Levene 2010, 85–6.
[3] All dates are AD and all translations are my own.
[4] On the dating of the *Histories* and the *Annals*, see Potter 1991; Bowersock 1993; Rutledge 1998; Birley 2000.
[5] The term 'self-allusion' will be used to describe Tacitus' practice in what follows. There are other possibilities, such as 'self-imitation' and 'self-borrowing', but see Burbidge 2007, 9–13 on how these do not necessary denote repetition that is meaningful. Even so, the idea of 'allusion' itself can have unwelcome connotations of authorial intentionalism, and reader response must be privileged over this when determining when one text is echoing another, for 'whether we count a particular resemblance between two texts as sufficiently marked to count as an allusion is determined by the public competence of readers, not the private thoughts of writers' (Fowler 1997, 15, quoted by Burbidge 2007, 12–13).

2

First, though, a few preliminary comments about self-allusion in ancient texts are necessary. It is not unusual to find both prose and poetic authors echoing their earlier works,[6] and such echoes are subject to the same considerations as other potential instances of intertextuality: 'if someone wants to convince the interpretative community of a particular intertextual relation, they must say how the correspondence between the source- and target-texts is special, and they must do something interesting with it, make it mean.'[7] In the case of self-allusion, however, it might be objected that parallelism is to be expected in two narratives by the same author that encompass similar themes.[8] Nevertheless, although Tacitus' own intentions cannot be ascertained for certain, the notion that in *Annals* 1 he seems to be recalling *Histories* 1 can be buttressed in a number of ways. A case will be made that the numerous thematic and verbal correspondences between the two texts are 'special', and that what can be done with them is historiographically interesting.

Indeed, there is a close precedent for this study: A.J. Woodman has already shown that two passages in *Annals* 1 in the account of the Roman campaigns against German tribes that follow the mutinies (see below) also contain echoes of the *Histories*. The visit of Germanicus at *Ann.* 1.61–2 to the site in the Teutoburg forest where Varus and his legions had been massacred five years earlier is described in terms that recall Tacitus' account of Vitellius' visit at *Hist.* 2.70 to the battlefield at Cremona where his troops had fought Otho's in the year 69. Soon afterwards, the uncomfortable night passed deep in German territory by the troops under the command of Caecina Severus at *Ann.* 1.64–5 bears some verbal resemblance to the plight of Roman troops fighting Batavians as Iulius Civilis' insurgency draws to a close at *Hist.* 5.14.2–15.2.[9] Woodman, however, goes on to attribute these parallels to mere 'substantive imitation' and to Tacitus'

---

6 See Cairns 1979; Burbidge 2007, 1–14; Levene 2010, 118. Cf. Kraus 1998.
7 Fowler 1997, 20.
8 Conversely, Williams (1997, 44–5) argues that the mutinies in the *Histories* bear very little resemblance to those in the *Annals* 1, but she seems to be seeking very basic parallels.
9 Indeed, the role of Caecina himself, commander of the lower German army (*Ann.* 1.31.2), in *Annals* 1 is far more prominent than that of the two others who also receive triumphal honours for the year's campaigning at *Ann.* 1.72.1 (see *Ann.* 1.56.1 and 66.2), and it seems possible that this emphasis evokes A. Caecina Alienus, who is introduced at *Hist.* 1.53.1 as a seditious commander in upper Germany and figures so prominently in Tacitus' account of the civil wars of 69–70.

wish to provide an entertaining story.¹⁰ It will now be argued that the connection between *Histories* 1 and *Annals* 1 to be examined here is of a more dynamic and far-reaching kind.

Moreover, as will be shown in due course, the conclusions that can be drawn from the links between the two texts fit other lines of interpretation of the *Annals*, and the series of insurrections in *Histories* 1, which unfolds in rather different circumstances from the mutinies in *Annals* 1, does not therefore necessarily invite description in a similar manner. In the *Annals*, one mutiny in the provinces is followed by another along similar lines, although only in the second case do the soldiers moot the installation of a replacement emperor, Germanicus; conversely, in *Histories* 1 there are two distinct mutinies, one in Rome and one abroad, each in favour of a different aspiring *princeps*, and later an additional uprising in the city. There are also a number of other mutinous episodes found later in the *Histories*, none of which is narrated in a manner that invites comparison with the episodes described in *Annals* 1.¹¹ Accordingly it does not look as if the echoes that do resonate between the two works are the result of mere chance, or the fact that the events in each case were similar, or the use of a standard 'model' for describing military insurrections, and as a result it seems reasonable to assert that the reminiscences of *Histories* 1 in *Annals* 1 are pointed.¹²

3

A selective summary of the narrative sections on which this discussion will focus is now in order. *Annals* 1 begins in 14 with the death of Augustus (*Ann*. 1.5.4) who, after some ineffectual wrangling in the senate (*Ann*. 1.11–14), is succeeded by his middle-aged (*maturum annis* ['mature in years'], *Ann*. 1.4.3) stepson Tiberius. Once this initial phase of Book 1 is concluded, Tacitus abruptly switches the scene to Pannonia, where a mutiny is breaking out amongst the legions (*Ann*. 1.16.1). The new emperor's son Drusus is dispatched to end it, and does

---

10 Woodman 1998, with analysis of Tacitus' motives at 80–5. Morgan (1992, 22–6) is unconvinced that there is a parallelism between the two texts, but if Tacitus had wished not to echo the *Histories*, he could surely have made more of an effort to present Germanicus' actions differently.
11 Woodman (2006, 304–8) discusses the broad similarities between the two episodes in *Annals* 1; Williams 1997, 45 n. 3 lists the other mutinies in the *Histories*.
12 Cf. Joseph 2012, 115–29, who identifies a similar pattern of verbal links and thematic continuities between Tacitus' accounts of the two battles of Cremona (*Hist*. 2.39–45, 3.25–34).

so with the help of an opportune eclipse that terrifies the superstitious soldiers (*Ann.* 1.28–9). At this point, Tacitus reports the outbreak of a similar but more serious mutiny amongst the German legions (*Ann.* 1.31.1).[13] Germanicus, Tiberius' nephew and adoptive son (and heir), and the legions' commander, has more trouble quelling this, not least because their agitation extends to offering to help him usurp Tiberius (*Ann.* 1.35.3). Once the insurrection is over, he subsequently begins a campaign against some German tribes who initially offer an easy and cathartic victory (*Ann.* 1.51.1), although before this happens his decision to let the soldiers punish the most guilty mutineers themselves leads to a scene of shocking violence termed *diversa omnium, quae umquam accidere, civilium armorum facies* ('the appearance of civil war was different from all those that had ever happened') (*Ann.* 1.49.1).[14]

Histories 1, meanwhile, opens at the beginning of the year 69 in the aftermath of another accession (cf. below). Galba has been emperor since Nero's death the previous June, but his *severitas* ('severity') (*Hist.* 1.5.5) and status as an *invalidus senex* ('weak old man') (*Hist.* 1.6.1), as well as his reliance on disreputable subordinates such as Titus Vinius and Cornelius Laco (*Hist.* 1.6.1; cf. 1.7.1), make him an unpopular figure in Rome and elsewhere. In early January, concerned by reports of a legionary insurrection in upper Germany (*Hist.* 1.14.1; cf. 1.9.1 and 26.1), and wishing to secure his position, he adopts Piso Licinianus as his heir (*Hist.* 1.14–16), but the governor of Lusitania, Otho, who had hoped to be adopted himself (*Hist.* 1.21.1), now plans a coup. His efforts culminate in a praetorian movement in which Galba is killed (*Hist.* 1.41.2) and Otho hailed as emperor (*Hist.* 1.45.1). At around the same time it is reported that Vitellius, governor of lower Germany, is mounting his own bid for the throne (*Hist.* 1.50.1: a full account of Vitellius' manoeuvres in Germany, broadly contemporaneous with the events in Rome, is then given at *Hist.* 1.51–70). For the remainder of Book 1, however, Otho is shown consolidating his rule in the city, where at one point he has to deal with an uprising of his own troops (*Hist.* 1.80–4).

Clearly the accessions and mutinies of 14 and 69 turned out somewhat differently: while Galba's reign was soon over, and followed by destructive civil war and a succession of short-lived *principes*, the mutinies of 14 petered out without provoking further movements against the emperor. Tiberius survived this uncer-

---

[13] There has been much discussion of the mutinies' timing (see Sage 1982/3, 294–308 and Pettinger 2012, 186–90) but Tacitus' presentation of events rather than their actual dating will be considered here.

[14] The complex language here leaves it unclear whether what happens is being differentiated from or identified with civil war: see Goodyear 1972, 311 *ad loc.*; Ross 1973, 219; Woodman 2004, 26.

tain start and went on to outlive both Germanicus and Drusus.[15] Nevertheless, this précis draws attention to the existence of basic similarities between *Histories* 1 and *Annals* 1. Both texts include a new but ageing or aged emperor, flanked by younger and more dynamic figures, some of whom command troops in Germany, and they both depict military insurrections that involve these other figures. It will now be argued that, despite their diverging outcomes, Tacitus emphasised this suggestive parallelism by recalling elements of *Histories* 1 in *Annals* 1.

4

One prominent parallel between the two texts has, indeed, previously been noted. The first three chapters of the *Histories*, which introduce the work as a whole, are followed by a dense review of events between June 68 and January 69 (*Hist.* 1.4–11). It pays particular attention to the newly-revealed importance of armies outside Rome and their commanders for imperial transfers of power: *evulgato imperii arcano posse principem alibi quam Romae fieri* ('the secret of empire, that an emperor could be made elsewhere than at Rome, had been made public') (*Hist.* 1.4.2). This review is concluded at *Hist.* 1.11.3 with the assertion that *hic fuit rerum Romanarum status* ('this was the state of Roman affairs') at the beginning of 69: the spotlight then returns to Galba in Rome. It is striking that in *Annals* 1 the transition from the introductory account of Tiberius' accession to the troubled situation in Pannonia is phrased in notably similar terms: *hic rerum urbanarum status erat...* ('this was the state of affairs in the city...') (*Ann.* 1.16.1).[16] In this way Tacitus' earlier work seems to be called to mind at the very beginning of the *Annals*' mutinies. Moreover, the Pannonian troops are then said to have revolted *nullis novis causis, nisi quod mutatus princeps licentiam turbarum et ex civili bello spem praemiorum ostendebat* ('for no novel reasons, other than that the change of emperor raised the possibility of popular discord and hope of rewards from civil war') (ibid.). *nullis novis causis* may well look back to the late republic, or serve as a universalising comment on soldiers' propensities, but given the *hic...status* parallel and the reference to *civile bellum* the possibility is also raised that this is a knowing reference to revolts previously described by Tacitus.[17]

---

15 The former's death is described at *Ann.* 2.72.2, the latter's at 4.8.1–2 (on this passage, cf. Duchêne in this volume).
16 Goodyear 1972, 197 *ad loc.*
17 The German legions will go on to act *isdem causis* ('for the same reasons') (*Ann.* 1.31.1), which similarly has an immediate and also a potentially more general applicability.

As the mutinies of the *Annals* unfold, further aspects of the narrative look distinctly familiar to a reader of the *Histories*. An important factor in this is the way in which characters in the *Annals* recall their analogues in the *Histories*.[18] Both texts sketch out a broad dynamic between emperor, pretenders (real or imagined) and others, hinting at links between what does happen in the *Histories* and does not happen in the *Annals*. Despite their differing fates, the two fledgling emperors prove to have a certain amount in common. In *Histories* 1 Galba's unpopularity is stressed initially (see p. 257 above), and at *Hist.* 1.37.4 Otho castigates him for hiding such qualities as *saevitia* ('savagery') under *falsis nominibus* ('false names'); similarly, Tiberius is presented as a less than winning figure from the beginning of the *Annals* (most clearly at *Ann.* 1.4.3–4) and *dissimulatio* is regularly associated with him.[19] Galba's obituary at *Hist.* 1.49.2–4 also encompasses further links to Tiberius.[20]

Early in *Histories* 1, Tacitus also establishes how Galba was compared unfavourably to Nero, in terms that look forward to the contrast between Tiberius and Germanicus,[21] and in *Annals* 1 further aspects of Germanicus' character recall the portrayal of Otho and Vitellius in the *Histories*. The way in which Germanicus is at least perceived by others finds some parallels with Otho's luxuriousness (see *Hist.* 1.22.1),[22] and the latter's efforts to win the *studia militum* 'the enthusiasm of the soldiers' (*Hist.* 1.23.1) foreshadow Tiberius' fears about the favour supposedly won by Germanicus when quashing the German mutiny (*Ann.* 1.52.1; see further p. 262–3 below). Tacitus' account of Otho's subsequent success may suggest to a

---

18 This is in accordance with the 'remarkable Roman capacity for seeing one individual in terms of another' Woodman/Martin 1996, 85 *ad* 3.2.2.
19 On Tiberius' *dissimulatio* see Strocchio 2001, 33–77. Otho also charges Galba with passing off *avaritia* ('avarice') as *parsimonia* ('stinginess'). Tiberius is not as aged as Galba (cf. *Hist.* 1.6.1), but at *Ann.* 3.52.1 he is termed a *princeps antiquae parsimoniae* ('an emperor of old-fashioned stinginess') (with which cf. Galba's *antiquus rigor et nimia severitas* ['old-fashioned rigidity and excessive severity'], *Hist.* 1.18.3).
20 Cf. *alieno imperio felicior quam suo* ('more fortunate under others' rule than under his own') (*Hist.* 1.49.2) and *egregium vita famaque, quoad privatus vel in imperiis sub Augusto fuit* ('outstanding in his life and reputation, while he was a private citizen or holding commands under Augustus') (*Ann.* 6.51.3).
21 See *Hist.* 1.7.3 and *Ann.* 1.4.3–5, and with *Hist.* 1.7.2 cf. *Ann.* 1.33.2, *iuveni civile ingenium, mira comitas et diversa a Tiberii sermone vultu...* (' the young man's easygoing personality and impressive affability, different from Tiberius' way of talking and looking'): two analogous pairs, Nero/Galba and Germanicus/Tiberius (marking youth/age, popularity/unpopularity) are established.
22 Compare Otho's reported greed for *luxus...ceterasque regnorum libidines* ('luxury...and other royal pleasures') (*Hist.* 1.22.1) with Piso's words *in luxum* ('against luxury'), directed at Germanicus at *Ann.* 2.57.4. Cf. Pelling 1993, 75–6.

reader of the *Annals* that Tiberius is less unreasonable in his reaction to Germanicus' actions than the immediate situation suggests.

Furthermore, in the *Annals* not only the more subversive plans of the German mutineers but the generally greater threat posed by a German mutiny (*Germanicae legiones turbatae, quanto plures, tanto violentius,* [the German legions in an uproar, with greater violence in proportion to their greater numbers'] *Ann.* 1.31.1) are made clear from the outset of that mutiny. This has a particular significance for readers of the *Histories*, where the same region proves to be a similar trouble spot: even before Otho has deposed Galba, Vitellius' insurrection has been signalled as a threat (*Hist.* 1.9.1, 14.1 and 26.1; cf. p. 257 above). In 69, both the upper and lower German armies proclaim their allegiance to Vitellius (*Hist.* 1.52–5); in the *Annals* it is only the lower Germany army that mutinies, but fears about the upper one are nevertheless reported (*Ann.*1.36.1), as if the course of events in the *Histories* is being anachronistically recollected. The forward implications of Vitellius' actions at this juncture for Tacitus' subsequent narrative of the German legions' mutiny in *Annals* 1 are also noteworthy.[23] Vitellius, like Otho before him, is described winning the troops' favour and his supporters praise his *comitatem bonitatemque* ('friendliness and benevolence') (*Hist.* 1.52.2); his great popularity parallels that of Germanicus.[24] At *Hist.* 1.62.2 he in fact takes the title 'Germanicus',[25] and at *Hist.* 2.59.2 he also bestows the same appellation on his son, who is described as an *infans* wearing a military cloak. Readers of the *Annals* who came across the young Caligula, the *infans in castris genitus* ('baby born in the camp') who wears soldiers' boots, at *Ann.* 1.41.2 may well have remembered this.[26] These correspondences between key individuals are complemented by a succession of noteworthy verbal parallels, especially in the depiction of soldierly psychology (see Appendix 1). The actions of each set of soldiers unfold in a rather different context in each text, but these parallels serve to draw them together.

---

[23] At *Hist.* 1.8.1 and 51.3 the armies' separation from the loyal Gallic provinces is highlighted, and this is reflected at *Ann.* 1.34.4 (*Galliarum fidem extollit* ['he praised the loyalty of the Gallic provinces']).

[24] Otho is said at *Hist.* 1.13.4 to have administered Lusitania *comiter* ('in a friendly manner') (see Morgan 1993, 568–71): cf. Germanicus' *comitas* (1.33.2). For the latter's popularity, see *Ann.* 2.13.1.

[25] As well as being a Julio-Claudian *cognomen*, the title was assumed by Domitian, Nerva and Trajan (see Syme 1958, 222 on its associations)

[26] Caligula's presence also looks ahead, to his assassination, as Cassius Chaerea has already appeared at 1.32.2 (see Kraus 2009, 108). See also n. 32 below.

5

Histories 1 and *Annals* 1 are, then, united by verbal echoes, broad narrative similarities and overlap between key characters, but it remains to be seen why this is the case. Although the fact that the two texts (and, perhaps, the sources Tacitus used in each case) were describing events and characters that were in some respects comparable may not be completely irrelevant, this rather reductive explanation is unlikely to account for all the echoes of the *Histories* in the *Annals*.[27] Moreover, while it is also plausible that some of the similarities between key individuals arose from actual imitation of their predecessor Germanicus on the part of Otho and Vitellius in 69,[28] and that these men may have been independently linked in the Roman imagination, Tacitus was not obliged to play up this parallelism and it will not serve to explain the sense of a broader connection between the two texts that has been posited here. So the final section of this discussion will consider a more wide-ranging idea: that in *Annals* 1 Tacitus recalls *Histories* 1 to make a deeper point about continuity in Roman history under the principate.

An obvious difference between the two texts is that in the *Annals* Tiberius is not unseated by a disloyal commander in the north, and the German legions' unrest is contained. Nevertheless, attention is regularly drawn in the narrative to the possibility that such events could come to pass, and these alternative outcomes are associated with Germanicus in particular. The latter plays a major role not only in the account of the mutiny in Germany but also in *Annals* 1 and 2 as a whole: his campaigns against the Germans, and most notably Arminius, span the two books (*Ann.* 1.49.3–71, 2.5.2–26), and after his recall by Tiberius he is then sent on a 'grand tour' to the eastern part of the empire (*Ann.* 2.53– 61, 69–72), where he ultimately dies in Antioch.[29] Whether he is urging the emperor to allow him to carry on fighting in Germany (*Ann.* 2.26.4), or winning ad-

---

[27] Moreover, the behaviour of the main characters concerned is broadly in accordance with their actions elsewhere in each text – there is no sense that Tacitus was simply reusing characterisation from these episodes in *Histories* within the *Annals* (or vice versa) without thought for its narrative context.

[28] See p. 254 and n. 2 above on the implications of this phenomenon for historiography, and p. 260 for Vitellius' use of the *cognomen* 'Germanicus' and his public treatment of his son, which may have been intended to evoke Caligula's famous presence amongst his father's troops in Germany. Caligula's own career would hardly have boded well, but Vitellius could have been forgiven for aspiring to become not only an emperor himself, but the father of one.

[29] On his eastern voyage, see Low 2016.

mirers in Egypt with his casual bearing and crowd-pleasing actions (*Ann.* 2.59.1–2), he is a charismatic figure. Scholars have often disagreed about whether positive or negative aspects of his characterisation are more dominant, and at times he seems to display obvious flaws,[30] but a further interesting anomaly in his portrayal is that he is often seen by others as a potential replacement emperor but appears to have no ambitions whatsoever in this direction.

At the beginning of *Annals* 1 Tacitus alleges that after Augustus' death Tiberius wrote to Rome's armies abroad as if his accession was already confirmed, and was *...nusquam cunctabundus nisi cum in senatu loqueretur. causa praecipua ex formidine, ne Germanicus...habere imperium quam exspectare mallet* ('...never delaying other than when he spoke in the senate. This was mainly because of his fear that Germanicus...would prefer holding power to waiting for it') (*Ann.* 1.7.6).[31] After this initial indication (which is not explained further) that Tiberius considered Germanicus a possible usurper, the notion that the new emperor perceived him, and his wife Agrippina the Younger, as potentially disloyal regularly recurs in Books 1 and 2. Tiberius' attitude is conveyed most explicitly when Tacitus explains how he was displeased because, in checking the German mutiny, Germanicus *largiendis pecuniis et missione festinata favorem militum quaesivisset* ('by dispensing money and by accelerating discharges he had sought the soliders' favour') (*Ann.* 1.52.1),[32] and when the emperor is said to have viewed Agrippina's leading role in boosting the morale of Roman troops panicked by Arminius' successes as a further attempt to curry the soldiers' favour (*Ann.* 1.69.1–4).[33]

Moreover, Germanicus' own troops seem to be influenced by a similar belief in the possibility that he could mount a bid for the throne. In contrast with the Pannonian soldiers, who mutiny under the influence of a generalised *ex civili bello spem praemiorum* ('hope of rewards from civil war') (*Ann.* 1.16.1), the German legions are described as acting *magna spe fore ut Germanicus Caesar imperium alterius pati nequiret daretque se legionibus vi sua cuncta tracturis* ('with great hope that Germanicus Caesar would not be able to endure another's

---

30 Shotter (1968), Ross (1973) and Rutland (1987) focus on the less praiseworthy or at least more complicated aspects of his portrayal in Books 1 and 2. See more generally Pelling 1993 and Williams 2009, 117.

31 Does the *causa praecipua* account for the letters to the armies or the hesitation? The latter, assumed by Sage (1982/3, 314) and Woodman (1998b, 53–7), seems more likely, but confirming his military support would show that Tiberius had not 'crept in' *per uxorium ambitum et senili adoptione* ('by a wife's importuning and an adoption by an old man') (*Ann.* 1.7.7).

32 Note the subjunctive suggesting that this was Tiberius' interpretation.

33 For other references to Tiberius' resentment of Germanicus see *Ann.* 1.33, 1.78.2 (Germanicus' *male consulta*), 2.5.1–2, 2.26.2–5, 2.42.1, 2.43.4–6, 2.59.2; cf. 3.3.

power, and would give himself up to the legions, who would arrange everything by force') (*Ann.* 1.31.1;³⁴ at 1.31.5 they boast that *sua in manu sitam rem Romanam, suis victoriis augeri rem publicam, in suum cognomentum adscisci imperatores* ['in their hands lay Roman affairs: the state was supplemented by their victories, and emperors were enrolled with their name']).³⁵ Within the text, however, the actions of Germanicus himself do not appear to justify any of this.³⁶ Tacitus states early on that the reasons for Tiberius' resentment were *acriores quia iniquae* ('more fierce because they were unjust') (*Ann.* 1.33.1),³⁷ and in the subsequent narrative Germanicus does nothing to suggest he had any subversive plans. After he has addressed the mutinous German troops and they have offered to help him take power, he turns them down in horror (*Ann.* 1.35.3–4), and he obeys Tiberius' command to withdraw from Germany even though he understands this as a sign of the latter's resentment and mistrust of him (*...quamquam fingi ea seque per invidiam parto iam decori abstrahi intellegeret* ['although he understood that these things were fabricated and through jealousy he was being dragged away from glory he had already achieved'], *Ann.* 2.26.5).

This striking disparity between others' expectations of Germanicus and his own unimpeachable behaviour perhaps serves to characterise Tiberius and the German legions as, respectively, excessively suspicious or enthusiastic about regime change.³⁸ Nevertheless, while their attitude appears out of place in the year 14, it makes much more sense when viewed in the light of the history of the first century as a whole, as in later decades several prominent Roman commanders of large numbers of troops in the north did attempt to become emperor. In the cha-

---

34 See Ross 1973, 211; Williams 1997, 51–2.
35 Goodyear (1972, 246 *ad loc.*) notes that they probably mean the elder Drusus and Germanicus himself as commanders with *imperium*. On *sua in manu* ('in his hand') cf. *in cuius manu* ('in whose hand'), used to refer to Germanicus' command of multiple legions at *Ann.* 1.7.6, and Mucianus' advice to Vespasian at *Hist.* 2.76.2, that *imperium* is *in tua manu* ('in your hand'). The expression seems linked to the transmission of power in civil war.
36 Whether the historical Germanicus ever entertained designs of this sort is, of course, unknowable, and no source suggests that he did. Nevertheless, other historians, in contrast with Tacitus' oblique reference to Tiberius' fear of Germanicus at his accession (*Ann.* 1.7.6; see p. 262 above), make much more of this wariness as a factor in Tiberius' hesitation over taking power, a theme that is prominent in all these texts: cf. Woodman 1998b and Pettinger 2012, 157–68. See Suet., *Tib.* 25.1–2 and D.C. 57.3.1, 4.1 and 5.1, and n. 38 below.
37 See Pelling 1993, 72. *Ann.* 1.33.2 may be focalised to Germanicus but the text does not suggest he is wrong.
38 Sage 1982/3, 313–20 sees the references to Tiberius' fear of Germanicus when he became emperor as remnants of an alternative tradition that Tacitus mostly avoided using (see n. 36 above), but this hardly seems sufficient to explain the continuing references to his supposed potential as an alternative emperor.

otic years 68–70 these of course included Vitellius and Otho,[39] but also Iulius Vindex, the governor of Gallia Lugdunensis who rose up against Nero in 68, and Iulius Civilis, leader of the Batavian revolt that Tacitus describes in *Histories* 4.[40] Moreover, as governor of upper Germany in 89 Antonius Saturninus seems to have launched an unsuccessful bid for the principate.[41] All these events would have been familiar to Tacitus and his readers in the first years of the second century.[42]

So it may be argued that Tiberius and the German legions are made to represent a strictly anachronistic but profoundly insightful point of view: their fears and hopes about Germanicus are implausible in their immediate context but look forward to future situations in which such beliefs would have been rather more understandable.[43] The rebellion and civil strife that do not happen in the *Annals* look forward to subsequent turmoil – and backwards within Tacitus' oeuvre to descriptions of that turmoil in the *Histories*. Scholars have already considered in more general terms the relationship of the mutinies in the *Annals* to the later civil wars, seeing them as a proleptic foreshadowing of events at that work's end.[44] The approach adopted here extends that view and links it with the Tacitean self-imitation that has been identified in this part of the *Annals:* the combi-

---

39 The role of Germanicus, by contrast, corresponds more to that of Verginius Rufus (see *Hist.* 1.52.3–4, 2.51 and 68.4 with Shotter 1967 and Gallia 2012, 32–6.

40 On Vindex, whose rebellion would have been described at the end of the complete *Annals* (cf. *Ann.* 15.74.2), see Syme 1958, 461–3, Hainsworth 1962 and Gallia 2012, 14–21. On the Batavian revolt see *Hist.* 4.12–37, 54–79 and 5.14–26, where the text breaks off: notable recent discussions include Rutherford 2010 and Lavan 2013, 142–7. Sources also allude to other comparable events in years between 14 and 68: the alleged attempt to rebel by Gaetulicus in AD 39 (Suet., *Cl.* 9.1 and D.C. 59.22.5), and the insurrection of Scribonianus, governor of Dalmatia, against Claudius in 42 (D.C. 60.15.1–4). Finally, see D.C. 55.31.1, who reports that when in AD 7 Tiberius was contending with the Dalmatian revolt, he was suspected by Augustus of prolonging the war in order to remain with his army, and Germanicus (!) was sent out to ensure his swift return.

41 See Walser 1951, 124–5; Syme 1978; Griffin 2000, 65–6.

42 A final potential parallel may have been provided by Trajan himself, who was commander of three legions in upper Germany when Nerva adopted him as his heir, possibly under some duress: see Eck 2002, esp. 224–6 and cf. Bennett 2001, 46 and 247 n. 20.

43 In a sense, they become meta-historical 'historians' of events that have not yet happened. Cf. the discussion of Waddell, this volume, of the vignette in Appian's *Libyca* where the Roman people become 'historians' of the fall of Carthage and produce a narrative that complements Appian's own.

44 Pelling 1993, 69; cf. Kotzé 1996, as well as Malloch 2004, 200–1, Pagán 2005 and Fulkerson 2006, 172. There has been some debate over whether the narrative of the *Annals* ended in June or December 68: see Syme 1958, 265–6; Goodyear 1970, 18 n. 1; McCulloch 1984, 169–73.

nation of the regular reminiscences of *Histories* 1 in *Annals* 1 with the broader theme of Germanicus' status as a potential usurper in the north turns a depiction of an episode that probably did not present a great threat to Tiberius into a prefiguration of the violence and chaos that followed the death of his descendant Nero.[45] The potential for military sedition and for the emergence in the provinces of a challenger to the throne is implied to have been embedded within the principate from the death of Augustus onwards, and the *arcanum imperii*, that *posse principem alibi quam Romae fieri* (*Hist.* 1.4.2), is shown to have been true not only in the immediate context of 69 but from the time of Tiberius' succession of Augustus, when the first imperial dynasty came into being.[46]

This examination of self-imitation of *Annals* 1 in *Histories* 1 has shown that these two texts can be read as part of a Tacitean continuum. Both works contribute to Tacitus' wider vision of imperial history, in which similar individuals appear and similar events take place, even if their outcomes are different.[47] A number of the particular challenges and rewards of studying intertextuality in historiography have also been emphasised. The ambiguity evoked by the possibility that the characters who are presented in similar terms behaved, perhaps intentionally, in similar ways in real life has been discussed. More broadly, the recollections of episodes in Tacitus' first full-length work in his subsequently written account of earlier events blur the distinctions between present and future, possibility and reality, and indeed between chronological and historiographical priority.[48] To understand his presentation of the Julio-Claudian princi-

---

45 See also n. 14 above on the odd phrase that occurs at the end of the Germany mutiny, *diversa omnium, quae umquam accidere, civilium armorum facies* (*Ann.* 1.49.1), which feels like a wilful confusion of metaphorical and real civil war. More generally, cf. the fruitful 'virtual history' approach to Tacitus' works of O'Gorman 2006.
46 Syme 1958, 369 emphasises the importance of Tiberius' succession in this light. It is not clear if this rather pessimistic attitude to the Julio-Claudian dynasty is applicable to the principate in general and Tacitus' own time: the vexed question of whether a consistent attitude to Trajan can be discerned in the *Annals* is unlikely to be conclusively answered and is beyond the scope of this paper (for a selection of views see Syme 1958, 481–98, Rutledge 1997, Birley 200 242–4, and Sailor 2008, esp. 6–50, 250–313).
47 See the discussion of Liotsakis, this volume, of Thucydides' view of the past as having the potential to illuminate the present and 'predict' the future.
48 See Fowler 1997, 18, and O'Gorman 2009, 239 on how intertextuality tests 'our sense of what is temporally prior and invites us to consider the authority implicit in temporal priority'. In a similar vein, while Flavian propaganda is likely to have shaped the depictions of Galba, Otho and Vitellius in historiographical works (including the *Histories*), it is worth wondering whether the tradition about Germanicus and Tiberius, favourable to the former and less so to the latter, which emerged not long after their own deaths (see Hurley 1989, esp. 328–30),

pate it is necessary to read the *Annals* and the *Histories* not merely in historical order, or in the order in which they were written, but both ways.

Appendix 1

Verbal parallels in the descriptions of soldiers in *Histories* 1 and *Annals* 1

flagrantibus iam militum animis velut faces... ('with the soldiers' spirits now burning like torches...') (*Hist.* 1.24.1)	*flagrantior inde vis, plures seditioni duces* ('then their strength burned hotter, and there were more leaders for the mutiny') (*Ann.* 1.22.1)
motas iam mentes ('minds now stirred') (*Hist.* 1.26.1)	*perculsae...mentes* ('upset minds') (*Ann.* 1.28.2)
exosculari Othonis manum ('kissing Otho's hand') (*Hist.* 1.45.1)	*per speciem exosculandi inseruerunt digitos* ('they thrust his fingers [into their mouths] on the pretence of kissing them') (*Ann.* 1.34.2) [*exosculari* here links Otho and Germanicus (and its only other use in Tacitus, at *Hist.* 2.49.3, is also of the former), although the soldiers' attitude to their commander in each case is rather different]
The detailed account of Otho's efforts to solve the problem of *vacationes* (*Hist.* 1.46.3–4) may also be recalled at *A.* 1.17.4.	
infructuosam et asperam militiam ('unprofitable and harsh soldiering') (*Hist.* 1.51.2)	
nullo...pro Galba nitente ('with no one taking the side of Galba') (*Hist.* 1.55.4)	*militiam...infructuosam* ('unprofitable...soldiering') (*Ann.* 1.17.4)
lymphatis caeco pavore animis ('minds maddened with blind panic') (*Hist.* 1.82.1)	*sed Germanicus...pro Tiberio niti* ('but Germanicus...taking Tiberius' side') (*Ann.* 1.34.1)
deiecti in terram militum vultus ac plus tristitiae quam paenitentiae ('faces cast down to the ground and more sorrow than repentance') (*Hist.* 1.82.2)	*lymphati destrictis gladiis* ('the maddened men with drawn swords') (*Ann.* 1.32.1)
	deiectis in terram oculis velut paenitentia ('with eyes cast to the ground as if in repentance') (*Ann.* 1.34.1)
...optimus quisque remedium praesentis licentiae posceret, vulgus et plures seditionibus et ambitioso imperio laeti per turbas et raptus facilius ad civile bellum impellerentur ('all the best men demanded a remedy for the current	*...mutatus princeps licentiam turbarum et ex civili bello spem praemiorum ostendebat* ('the change of emperor raised the possibility of

---

could have been a secondary influence on the perceived contrasts between these later individuals. If so, the boundaries between 14 and 69 would have been further eroded.

lawlessness, the (more numerous) crowd, delighting in mutinies and an emperor who had to win favour to secure his power, were driven more easily to civil war through riots and looting') (*Hist.* 1.83.1)

popular discord and hope of rewards from civil war') (*Ann.* 1.16.1)

Bibliography

Bennett, J. (2001²), *Trajan. Optimus Princeps*, London.
Birley, A.R. (2000), "The Life and Death of Cornelius Tacitus", in: *Historia* 49, 230–47.
Bowersock, G.W. (1993), "Tacitus and the Province of Asia", in: T.J. Luce / A.J. Woodman 1993, 3–10.
Bowman, A.K. / Garnsey, P. / Rathbone, D. (eds.) (2000), *Cambridge Ancient History* XI², Cambridge.
Burbidge, J.R. (2007), *Self-Allusion in Vergil's Aeneid* (DPhil thesis), Oxford.
Cairns, F. (1979), "Self-Imitation Within a Generic Framework: Ovid, *Amores* 2.9 and 3.11 and the *renuntiatio amoris*", in: D. West / A.J. Woodman 1979, 121–41.
Clark, G. / Rajak, T. (eds.) (2002), *Philosophy and Power in the Graeco-Roman World*, Oxford.
Clauss, J.J. (1997), "'Domestici hostes': the Nausicaa in Medea, the Catiline in Hannibal", in: *MD* 39, 165–85.
Damon, C. (2009), "Déjà vu or déjà lu? History as Intertext", in: *PLLS* 14, 375–88.
Deroux, C. (ed.) (2005), *Studies in Latin Literature and Roman History* 12, Brussels.
Eck, W. (2002), "An Emperor Is Made: Senatorial Politics and Trajan's Adoption by Nerva in 97", in: G. Clark / T. Rajak 2002, 211–26.
Feldherr, A. (ed.) (2009), *The Cambridge Companion to the Roman Historians*, Cambridge.
Fowler, D. (1997), "On the Shoulders of Giants: Intertextuality and Classical Studies", in: *MD* 39, 13–34.
Fulkerson, L. (2006), "Staging a Mutiny: Competitive Roleplaying on the Rhine (*Annals* 1.31–51)", in: *Ramus* 35, 169–92.
Gallia, A.B. (2012), *Remembering the Roman Republic*, Cambridge.
Goodyear, F.R.D. (1970), *Tacitus*, Oxford.
Goodyear, F.R.D. (1972), *The Annals of Tacitus I* (Annals *1.1–54*), Cambridge.
Griffin, M.T. (2000), "The Flavians", in: A.K. Bowman / P. Garnsey / D. Rathbone 2000, 1–83.
Hainsworth, J.B. (1962), "Verginius and Vindex", in: *Historia* 11, 86–96.
Hinds, S. (1998), *Allusion and Intertext*, Cambridge.
Hurley, D.W. (1989), "Gaius Caligula in the Germanicus Tradition", in: *AJPh* 110, 316–38.
Joseph, T.A. (2012), *Tacitus the Epic Successor*, Mnemosyne Suppl. 345, Leiden.
Knox, P.E. / Foss, C. (eds.) (1998), *Style and Tradition: Studies in Honor of Wendell Clausen*, Leipzig.
Kotzé, A. (1996), "Tacitus' Account of the Pannonian Revolt (*Ann.* 1.16–30)", in: *Akroterion* 41, 124–32.
Kraus, C.S. (1998), "Repetition and Empire in the *ab urbe condita*", in: P.E. Knox / C. Foss 1998, 264–83.

Kraus, C.S. / Marincola, J. / Pelling, C.B.R. (eds.) (2010), *Ancient Historiography and Its Contexts. Studies in Honour of A. J. Woodman*, Oxford.

Lavan, M. (2013), *Slaves to Rome*, Cambridge.

Levene, D.S. (2010), *Livy on the Hannibalic War*, Oxford.

Low, K.A. (2016), "Germanicus on Tour: History, Diplomacy and the Promotion of a Dynasty", in: *CQ* 66.1, 222–38.

Luce, T.J. / Woodman, A.J. (eds.) (1993), *Tacitus and the Tacitean Tradition*, Princeton.

Malloch, S.J.V. (2004), "The End of the Rhine Mutiny in Tacitus, Suetonius and Dio", in: *CQ* 2004, 198–210.

Moles, J.L. (1983), "Virgil, Pompey and the *Histories* of Asinius Pollio", in: *CW* 76, 287–8.

McCulloch, H.Y. (1984), *Narrative Cause in the* Annals *of Tacitus*, Meisenheim.

Morgan, M.G. (1992), "The Smell of Victory: Vitellius at Bedriacum", in: *CPh* 87, 14–29.

Morgan, M.G. (1993), "The Unity of Tacitus, *Histories* 1, 12–20", in: *Athenaeum* 81, 567–86.

O'Gorman, E. (2006), "Alternative Empires: Tacitus' Virtual History of the Pisonian Principate", in: *Arethusa* 39, 281–301.

O'Gorman, E. (2009), "Intertextuality and Historiography", in: A. Feldherr 2009, 231–42.

Pagán, V.E. (2005), "The Pannonian Revolt in the *Annals* of Tacitus", in: C. Deroux 2005, 414–22.

Pelling, C.B.R. (1993), "Tacitus and Germanicus", in: T.J. Luce / A.J. Woodman 1993, 59–85.

Pettinger, A. (2012), *The Republic in Danger*, Oxford.

Potter, D.S. (1991), "The Inscriptions on the Bronze Herakles from Mesene: Vologeses IV's War with Rome and the Date of Tacitus' "Annales"", in: *ZPE* 88, 277–90.

Ross, D.O. (1973), "The Tacitean Germanicus", in: *YCS* 23, 209–27.

Rutherford, R. (2010), "Voices of Resistance", in: C.S. Kraus / J. Marincola / C.B.R. Pelling 2010, 312–30.

Rutland, L.W. (1987), "The Tacitean Germanicus: Suggestions for a Re-Evaluation", in: *RhM* 130, 153–64.

Rutledge, S. (1998), "Trajan and Tacitus' Audience: Reader Reception of *Annals* 1–2", in: *Ramus* 27, 141–59.

Sage, M.M. (1982/3), "Tacitus and the Accession of Tiberius", in: *Anc. Soc.* 13/14, 293–321.

Sailor, D. (2008), *Writing and Empire in Tacitus*, Oxford.

Shotter, D.C.A. (1967), "Tacitus and Verginius Rufus", in: *CQ* 17, 370–81.

Shotter, D.C.A. (1968), "Tacitus, Tiberius and Germanicus", in: *Historia* 17, 194–214.

Strocchio, R. (2001), *Simulatio e dissimulatio nelle opere di Tacito*, Bologna.

Syme, R. (1958), *Tacitus*, Oxford.

Syme, R. (1978), "Antonius Saturninus", in: *JRS* 68, 12–21.

Walser, G. (1951), *Rom, das Reich und die fremden Völker in der Geschichtsschreibung der frühen Kaiserzeit*, Baden-Baden.

West, D. / Woodman, A.J. (eds.) (1979), *Creative Imitation and Latin Literature*, Cambridge.

Williams, M. (1997), "Four Mutinies: Tacitus' *Annales* 1.16–30; 1.31–49 and Ammianus Marcellinus' *Res Gestae* 20.4.9–20.5.7; 24.3.1–8", in: *Phoenix* 51, 44–74.

Williams, K.F. (2009), "Tacitus' Germanicus and the Principate", in: *Latomus* 68, 117–30.

Woodman, A.J. (1998a), "Self-Imitation and the Substance of History (*Annals* 1.61–5 and *Histories* 2.70, 5.14–5)", in: id., *Tacitus Reviewed*, Oxford, 70–85 [originally published in: D. West / A.J. Woodman (eds.) (1979), *Creative Imitation in Latin Literature*, Cambridge, 143–56].

Woodman, A.J. (1998b), "Tacitus on Tiberius' Accession", in: id., *Tacitus Reviewed*, Oxford, 40–69.
Woodman, A.J. (2004), *Tacitus. The Annals*, Indianapolis.
Woodman, A.J. (2006), "Mutiny and Madness: Tacitus *Annals* 1.16–49", in: *Arethusa* 39, 303–29.
Woodman, A.J. / Martin, R. H. (1996), *The* Annals *of Tacitus: Book 3*, Cambridge.

Pauline Duchêne
Suetonius' Construction of His Historiographical *auctoritas*[1]

Abstract: This paper examines how Suetonius constructs his authorial *auctoritas* and *persona* throughout his *Lives of the XII Caesars*, in spite of the loss of his preface. It is thus quite close to Fournel's contribution on Plutarch, addressing the conceptual difference between history and biography and the attitude of ancient biographers in front of their material. The point of departure is Marincola 1997's analysis of the conditions, especially rhetorical, in which ancient historiography was written and the rehabilitation of Suetonius as a scholar. The method used is a study of all the 1st person singular occurrences, dealing with questions such as autopsy and the biographer's use of the documents at his disposal. As a consequence, themes addressed by other contributions in this volume are also taken into account: literary construction and liability (cf. Waddel); building on previous elements (cf. Low); relations with the predecessors (cf. Donelli).

When John Marincola published in 1997 his now classic *Authority and Tradition in Ancient Historiography*, he pointed out that the influence of rhetoric on the historiographical genre was not limited to the way history was told: it also determined the way the authors presented themselves.[2] Like the orators, historians had to construct a *persona*, i.e. their own character as a narrator, in order to persuade the audience of the authority of their work. As a consequence, they were obliged to mention their experience, the efforts they deployed in their preparatory researches, and their impartiality.[3]

Marincola's book examines many ancient historians, mostly Greek, but it totally ignores Suetonius, the biographer of the *Lives of the XII Caesars*.[4] In spite of

---

[1] I would like to thank both organizers of the meeting, especially S. Farrington, who read and corrected this paper very carefully. Of course, any remaining error is mine.
[2] Woodman (1988) anticipated this idea, by considering the historiographical attitude implied by the stylistic choices of particular historians.
[3] Cf. Marincola 1997, 128–175. Other means were available within the narrative itself: see, for example, Wadell on Appian in this volume.
[4] Suetonius is evoked once, p. 32 n. 158, in connection with a 4th century imitator. It is actually the whole biographical genre that is completely left out in this book, otherwise remarkable: Cornelius Nepos and Plutarch are never referred to for their biographies and Tacitus' *Life of Agricola* appears only incidentally.

DOI 10.1515/9783110496055-014

his rehabilitation, begun with Wolf Steidle,[5] this author, when he is not presented as a pure copyist lacking any kind of reflection, is still mainly considered a second or even a third rate historian. Another obstacle for studies on his authorial *persona* is the loss of his preface,[6] a section that usually contained the necessary preliminary declarations. As a consequence, even dedicated works tend to focus on Suetonius' alleged political goal,[7] his historical self[8] or his historical method.[9] But, if he had the same subject, goals and method as "regular" historians, does he also have a similar way of constructing his authorial *persona* and is the difference between history and biography as clear as it may seem?

The loss of his preface does not mean, in fact, that we have no clue about the way Suetonius wanted to appear in his work: the occurrences in the first person singular or plural all represent authorial interventions as a narrator.[10] Following Michel Rambaud's terminology,[11] the extant *Lives of the XII Caesars* do not contain a "montionless" portrait of the author's *persona*, but a dynamic one determined by the *I* or *we*. This article aims at studying these types of occurrences: what dynamic *persona* is Suetonius displaying throughout his work? We will first examine the authorial interventions linked to the narrative organization of the text, then the references to his preparatory researches and, finally, his comments on his own material.

When describing the ways Suetonius can intervene in his text, Jacques Gascou[12] describes the first "level" of interventions, those that give information

---

5 Steidle 1951.
6 The loss happened between the 6th and 9th centuries: the oldest manuscript, the *Memmianus*, at the French National Library, was written in the 9th century and begins with an ornamented letter, so the loss had already happened at that time. On the other hand, the Suidas catalogue mentions Septicius Clarus, one of Hadrian's prefects of the Pretorian Guard, as the dedicatee. The beginning of the work was therefore still available for consultation when the catalogue was made, in the 6th century. The *Lives of the XII Caesars* now begin directly upon the death of Caesar's father, when the future dictator was 16.
7 Cf. Cizek 1977. This work is a brilliant, very careful study of all the positive and negative elements in each biography, but I am quite hesitant about the argument that the whole work was a *speculum Principis* for Hadrian and aimed at promoting the emperor's reliance on the equestrian class.
8 Cf. Wallace-Hadrill 1983.
9 Cf. Gascou 1984.
10 Cf. Fry 2003.
11 Rambaud 1970.
12 Gascou 1984, 242–249. Gascou does not examine the question of the authorial *persona*, but includes a descriptive appendix dedicated to the *I* of Suetonius. He distinguishes six "levels" of interventions: 1) allusion to a previous passage; 2) explanation of an expression; 3) choice between many elements and emphasis on the most significant; 4) presentation of the narrative

about the narrative organization, as "sans doute le moins signifiant et le plus banal". This type of intervention was quite common in ancient historiography and is in fact the most frequent kind in the works of Suetonius' contemporary colleague, Tacitus.[13] They correspond to what Gérard Genette,[14] following George Blin,[15] calls the "fonction de régie", i.e., the visible organization of the narration.[16] Although Suetonius chose, for the most part, to present his material arranged by categories and not in chronological order,[17] like another contemporary biographer, Plutarch, he nevertheless also uses narrative indications to guide his reader through the text, as he does after stressing the massive influence of Claudius' wives and freedmen over all his decisions (Suet. *Cl.* 29.1):

> His, ut dixi, uxoribusque addictus, non principem [se], sed ministrum egit, compendio cuiusque horum uel etiam studio aut libidine honores exercitus impunitates supplicia largitus est, et quidem insciens plerumque et ignarus.
>
> Since he depended, as I said, upon these men and his wives, he did not behave as an emperor, but as a servant, and he generously assigned, according to the profit or even the favor or the desire of every one of them, honors, armies, tax exemptions, executions; and, most of the time, even without knowing or being conscious of it.[18]

The interpolated clause *ut dixi* brings to a close the presentation of the persons who had an influence on Claudius and alludes to the sentence[19] that began the

---

scheme; 5) allusion to the preparatory researches; 6) introduction of some reasoning or study of the validity of one peculiar tradition. As some elements seem to be part of the same category (e.g. allusions to a previous passage, choice of giving only the most significant examples and presentation of the narrative scheme are all linked to the narrative organization), I decided to gather them under only three titles: narrative interventions; preparatory researches; comments on the material.

13 Almost half of the authorial interventions in the *Histories* and the *Annals*: cf. Duchêne 2014, 30–63. All interventions are listed in the Appendix I, 414–426 (Tacitus); 426–429 (Suetonius) of this earlier work.
14 Genette 1972, 26–262.
15 Blin 1954, 222.
16 This terminology has already been used for an ancient historian, namely Dionysus of Halicarnassus, by Fromentin 2010, 262–266.
17 Cf. Plutarch's *Galba* and *Otho*, which must have been part of a series of biographies of the first emperors, like the *XII Caesars*. Plutarch respects the chronological order so strictly that there is no rupture between the only two extant biographies: Otho's early life is presented in the *Galba* and his biography *stricto sensu* begins only when he becomes emperor and Galba is dead. For a recent analysis of the Suetonian organization, see Hurley 2014.
18 All translations are my own. The ancient texts are from Henri Ailloud's (1931–1932) edition of the *Lives of the XII Caesars* for the Collection des Universités de France.
19 Cf. Suet. *Cl.* 25.15.

portrait while denying him any credit for the good decisions he made. The circular construction is thus obvious to the reader.[20]

The same passage also contains a type of narrative indication that is almost absent in Tacitus: Suetonius quite often selects his material, openly explaining to his reader that he will tell only the most representative examples of his point (Suet. *Cl.* 29.2):

> Ac ne singillatim minora quoque enumerem, reuocatas liberalitates eius, iudicia rescissa, suppositos aut etiam palam immutatos datorum officiorum codicillos: Appium Silanum consocerum suum Iuliasque, alteram Drusi, alteram Germanici filiam, crimine incerto nec defensione ulla data occidit, item Cnaeum Pompeium maioris filiae uirum et Silanum minoris sponsum.

> And so I do not have to enumerate one by one minor affairs, his donations revoked, his judgements cancelled, the forged or even openly changed letters giving charges: he had Appius Silanus, his son-in-law's father, and the two Julias, one being Drusus' daughter, the other Germanicus', executed without any formal charge or the possibility to defend themselves; he did the same to Cnaeus Pompeius, his elder daughter's husband, and Silanus, his younger daughter's fiancé.

Since every decision Claudius made was the product of his entourage's influence, the biographer will not recall them all (*ne singillatim enumerem*); he first uses general categories (*liberalitates, iudicia, codicillos*) and then gives the most shocking examples, i.e., the arbitrary executions of his close relatives.[21] The evocation of these deaths is enough to convey the whole idea to the reader: if Claudius can be talked into executing members of the imperial family, the influence of his wives and freedmen is bound to be even stronger on other matters. The narration is not detailed, but it does not need to be.

Narrative interventions emphasizing how the narration was conceived represent about a third of those Suetonius makes,[22] but they are not the majority. The vast remainder aim at depicting him as a historian, engaged in a process of finding and evaluating both sources and collected material.[23] The initial paragraphs

---

[20] Such narrative echoes were quite frequent in ancient historiography: see the article by Low on Tacitus in this volume.

[21] Actually, these executions only seem arbitrary because Suetonius gives no explanation for them. Claudius' (and his wives') strategy was in fact the elimination of every member that could threaten his or his heir's position: see Levick 1990, 56–63.

[22] They amount to 42 out of 125.

[23] This is not a peculiarity of Suetonius: Plutarch also confronts his sources, as demonstrated by Fournel's article in this volume. However, Suetonius is the only one who does it so openly and frequently everywhere in his biographies. The article by Donelli in this volume also shows that Herodotus had a similar attitude regarding Homer.

of the biographies, dealing with each emperor's ancestors, are good illustrations of Suetonius' historical skills. After presenting, for instance, Vespasian's family, he adds (Suet. *Ves.* 1.7–8):

> Non negauerim iactatum a quibusdam Petronis patrem a regione Transpadana fuisse mancipem operarum, quae ex Vmbria in Sabinos ad culturam agrorum quotannis commeare soleant ; subsedisse autem in oppido Reatino uxore ibidem ducta. Ipse ne uestigium quidem de hoc, quamuis satis curiose inquirerem, inueni.
>
> I would not deny that some people repeated that Petro's father was from the Transpadane region and worked as a contractor for the workers who are used to migrating every year from Umbria to the Sabine country for the cultivation of the fields; then he would have established himself in the fortified city of Reate, after having married there a woman. As for me, I did not find even a trace of this version, though I made researches with the utmost care.

Here, Suetonius acknowledges an alternate version of the biography of Vespasian's great-grandfather. Before this passage, he gives much detail about his grandfather and father: the first had been engaged in the Pompeian army, before leaving and working at auction sales; the second was never a soldier and worked as a tax collector in Asia.[24] At that point, the biographer refutes a competing version that presents the father as a former soldier, who was dismissed because of illness. Those details and the textual quotation of an honorific inscription in Asia are proofs of the *satis curiose* character of Suetonius' preparatory researches. They help convince the reader that Vespasian's father performed no military service and of the questionable credibility of the story that circulated about the great-grandfather. The reader is led to conclude that, since he has been so careful about what he affirms, he must tell the truth when he says one version is wrong or there is no proof of another. The assertion concerning the great-grandfather provides the climax of this persuasive strategy: the formulation of the introductory clause, *non negauerim*, with its double negation and its perfect subjunctive, gives the impression that the biographer is very reluctant and reserved; the use of *quibusdam* to indicate the source and the verb *iactari* have the same function. At the same time, he insists on his own seriousness: he personally made the researches (*ipse*), he did them with the utmost care (*satis curiose*) and he found not even a trace (*ne uestigium quidem*) of proof of this story. As a consequence, he sends the message to the reader that there is no reason to disbelieve him in any way.

---

24 Cf. Suet. *Ves.* 1.2 for the grandfather and 1.3 for the father.

This type of authorial intervention is quite representative of what we may call Suetonius' "second-degree autopsy". The biographer's date of birth is estimated to be around 70 CE,[25] so he was a contemporary, though quite young, of the last part of his work, the Flavian book. It may explain why the only example of autopsy *stricto sensu* is about Domitian (Suet. *Dom.* 12.5–6):

> Praeter ceteros Iudaicus fiscus acerbissime actus est; ad quem deferebantur, qui uel inprofessi Iudaicam uiuerent uitam uel dissimulata origine imposita genti tributa non pependissent. Interfuisse me adulescentulum memini, cum a procuratore frequentissimoque consilio inspiceretur nonagenarius senex an circumsectus esset.

> Among other measures, the Jewish tax was collected very harshly; for under it were prosecuted both those who did not declare themselves but lived like Jews and those who had concealed their origin and not paid the tributes imposed to their people. I remember I witnessed, when I was a young boy, a procurator and a very numerous assembly inspecting a 90 year old man, in order to determine whether he had been circumcised or not.

The testimony presented here aims at confirming the harshness of the perception of the *fiscus Iudaicus*. It is convincing but the presence of the author himself to the scene is not heavily stressed. Though the clause *interfuisse me* is at the beginning of the sentence, what mostly strikes the reader is the precision of *nonagenarius senex*, not the authorial certification.

Suetonius' attitude is, however, quite different when he draws on a testimony which is not his own, but comes from a contemporary he interviewed. What his father told him about Otho's suicide is a good example of his way of dealing with witnesses (Suet. *Otho* 10.1–4):

> Interfuit huic bello pater meus Suetonius Laetus, tertiae decimae legionis tribunus angusticlauius. Is mox referre crebro solebat Othonem etiam priuatum usque adeo detestatum ciuilia arma, ut memorante quodam inter epulas de Cassi Brutique exitu cohorruerit nec concursurum cum Galba fuisse, nisi confideret sine bello rem transigi posse; tunc ad despiciendam uitam exemplo manipularis militis concitatum, qui cum cladem exercitus nuntiaret nec cuiquam fidem faceret ac nunc mendaci nunc timoris, quasi fugisset ex acie, argueretur, gladio ante pedes eius incubuerit. Hoc uiso proclamasse eum aiebat non amplius se in periculum talis tamque bene meritos coniecturum.

> My father, Suetonius Tranquillus, took part in this war as an angusticlavian tribune in the XIIIth legion. After that, he was constantly repeating that, even when he was a private individual, Otho hated civil wars to the point of being horrified as someone recalled during a

---

25 He mentions being an *adolescentulus* under Domitian (cf. Suet. *Dom.* 12.6) and his *cognomen* is Tranquillus, which suggests a birth at a period of returned peace, i.e around 70 CE; but it can also stem from a family tradition, since his father's was Laetus, another adjective of mood.

dinner the end of Cassius and Brutus; that he would not have competed with Galba, had he not been certain that the affair could be carried on without a war; and that, at that moment [*scil*. after the defeat of his army at Bedriacum], he had been caused to despise life by the example of a common soldier, who, having announced the disaster, being believed by none and accused either of lying or being a coward, as if he had fled from the battle, killed himself at Otho's feet by falling on his sword. According to my father, after having seen this, Otho proclaimed that he would not keep on endangering men of this quality and merit.

This passage is quite famous, for Jacques Gascou masterfully demonstrated[26] that Suetonius' father could not have been physically present at the scene he narrated. He most probably arrived some time after the suicide and repeated what he had been told at that moment; this may explain why Tacitus' narration is very similar to Suetonius', though he had no access to the elder Suetonius.[27] The biographer does not seem to have any doubt about this testimony. On the contrary, he insists on how often his father told this story, as if the frequency increased the reliability. The verb *solere* is reinforced by the adverb *crebro* and the two imperfect indicatives, *solebat* and *aiebat*, convey an idea of repetition. Then, the two perfect subjunctives *cohorruerit* and *incubuerit* emphasize the reality of the reported consequences.[28] The whole structure of the paragraph is conceived in order to persuade the reader that he is only presented with facts here, as if the biographer had personally witnessed the scene. Suetonius' attitude is thus quite different from Thucydides': the Greek seems conscious of the difficulties of interrogating witnesses;[29] the Roman uses his father's alleged presence as a proof of his own credibility.

Suetonius can insist on his own participation, but only in a very particular case. The question of the authorship of the verses attributed to Nero is a good example of what the biographer wants to put to the forefront of his historiographical strategy (Suet. *Nero* 52.3):

Venere in manus meas pugillares libellique cum quibusdam notissimis uersibus ipsius chirographo scriptis, ut facile appareret non tralatos aut dictante aliquo exceptos, sed plane

---

[26] Cf. Gascou 1984, 297–298.
[27] Cf. Tac. *Hist*. 2.46.1–49.4.
[28] The two elements introduced by these verbs are highly questionable: since Suetonius' father lied about being at the soldier's suicide and Otho's last hours, his story about the emperor's horror of bloodshed seems to be an invention, aimed at exonerating Otho of starting another civil war. The anecdote of the soldier also appears in Tac. *Hist*. 3.54.2–3, but about Vitellius after the second battle of Bedriacum, so it appears to be a 'floating' detail, associated with the civil wars of 68–69 CE, not with a particular battle.
[29] Cf. Woodman 1988, 15–22.

quasi a cogitante atque generante exaratos; ita multa et deleta et inducta et superscripta inerant.

> I have had in my hands tablets and papers with some of his most famous verses written with his own handwriting, so that it easily appeared that they had not been transcribed or received under someone's dictation, but had been plainly drawn as if by someone reflecting and creating them; in fact, there were many deletions, additions and corrections.

Suetonius' personal consultation of Nero's writings is here the primary evidence of his argument that the emperor was the real author of the poems attributed to him: the handwriting is identified (*ipsius chirographo*), the editing is described in detail (*et deleta et inducta et superscripta*) and the conclusion is presented as obvious (*ut facile appareret* and *plane*). The biographer's attitude is very different here, compared to the passage where he relates what he personally saw under Domitian: at that moment, his actual presence at the scene was just mentioned in passing. It is true that his argument about Nero's authorship totally contradicts another tradition, denying it, of which the most famous supporter was Tacitus himself in the *Annals*.[30] But Tacitus speaks of Nero's style, not of his concrete way of writing: he thus may have not seen the documents Suetonius had access to, which explains the biographer's insistence on that point.[31] This attitude is what we would call a "second-degree autopsy": what Suetonius saw are the documents and it appears to be as trustworthy a proof for him as if he had personally seen Nero writing the poems.

These passages show the importance Suetonius placed on his preparatory research and the emphasis he wanted it to have within the narrative. His attitude may explain why the most frequent function his scientific *persona* assumes is that of commenting or explaining alternative versions. He often evaluates his

---

[30] Cf. Tac. *Ann.* 14.16.1 : *Ne tamen ludicrae tantum imperatoris artes notescerent, carminum quoque studium adfectauit, contractis quibus aliqua pangendi facultas necdum insignis erat. Hi cenati considere simul et adlatos uel ibidem repertos uersus conectere atque ipsius uerba, quoquo modo prolata, supplere; quod species ipsa carminum docet, non impetu et instinctu nec tenore uno fluens*, "So that not only the theatrical skills of the emperor would be famous, he also simulated a taste for poetry, after having gathered those who had some talent in writing, but were not already known. These men sat together after dinner, assembled the verses he had brought or found there, and made up for his words, however they had been produced; this is demonstrated by the very aspect of his poems, the style of which has neither energy, inspiration or coherence in its flow."

[31] For the material conditions of access to the archives, cf. Moatti 2003. For her, Suetonius may have been, thanks to his position at the Chancellery, the one who had the easiest access to all official and unofficial documents.

material from the narrative point of view;[32] he also expresses his surprise or stresses some particular aspect.[33] This type of intervention is quite frequent, but it is by far outnumbered by those explaining or disproving particular elements, as in the following extract about the death of Drusus I, Tiberius' brother (Suet. *Cl.* 1.8–10):

> Fuisse autem creditur non minus gloriosi quam ciuilis animi; nam ex hoste super uictorias opima quoque spolia captasse summoque saepius discrimine duces Germanorum tota acie insectatus, nec dissimulasse umquam pristinum se rei publicae statum, quandoque posset, restiturum. Vnde existimo nonnullos tradere ausos suspectum eum Augusto reuocatumque ex prouincia et, quia cunctaretur, interceptum ueneno. Quod equidem magis ne praetermitterem rettuli quam quia uerum aut ueri simile putem, cum Augustus tanto opere et uiuum dilexit ut…

> On the other hand, he was thought to be attracted by glory no less than to behave as a simple citizen; indeed, besides the victories, he also tried to take the *spolia opima* from the enemy and, quite often with very much risk, he chased the German leaders with his whole army, and he never concealed that he intended to restore one day, as soon as he could, the previous political organization of the State. This is the reason, I assume, why some authors dared to say that he was suspicious to Augustus, called back from his province and, because he hesitated, killed by poisoning. But, as for me, I reported this more in order not to omit anything than because I would think it true or likely, since Augustus loved him so much even when he was alive that…

Drusus I is one of the Roman imperial figures credited with a longing for the Republican era and the restoration of the Republic;[34] this point was used as an argument in favor of his poisoning by Augustus. If one looks at all the occurrences of verbs of thought and belief like *credere* in Tacitus and Suetonius, they happen to be used in reference to well informed sources;[35] this tendency is confirmed in the biographer's intervention *existimo nonnullos tradere ausos*, for the same research shows *tradere* is associated with written sources.[36] As a consequence,

---

32 Cf. for instance Suet. *Nero* 13.1: *Non immerito inter spectacula ab eo edita et Tiridatis in urbem introitum rettulerim*, "Among the spectacles he gave, the arrival of Tiridates in Rome, to me, would be also worth the telling."
33 Cf. for instance Suet. *Jul.* 68.7, on the loyalty of Caesar's soldiers: *Nec mirum, si quis singulorum facta respiciat, uel Cassi Scaeuae centurionis uel Gai Acti militis, ne de pluribus referam*, "This is no surprise, if one examines the actions of every one of them, either those of the centurion Cassius Scaeva or the soldier Gaius Actus, not to mention more."
34 So was his son, Germanicus (cf. Suet. *Cal.* 3.5 and Tac. *Ann.* 2.82.2), and, quite surprisingly, Otho (cf. Suet. *Otho* 12.5).
35 For a study of Suetonius' and Tacitus' vocabulary when mentioning their sources, see Duchêne 2014, 64–118.
36 Cf. Duchêne 2014, 71–75 (*credere*), 107–109 (verbs of thought), 67–71 (*tradere*).

we can assume that this story was found in books by people who were close to the inner imperial circle. This characteristic may explain why Suetonius mentions this version, in spite of not thinking it true, and the length of his refutation. The reason given is his desire not to omit anything, but he denies the story is likely and a strong demonstration of Augustus' affection for Drusus follows the extract. This sort of passage, therefore, has two functions within the narration: first, locally, it disproves the alternative story of Drusus' death, even though it was supported by written and probably well informed sources;[37] then, at a wider level, it helps to increase the reader's confidence in Suetonius' professional skills. If he mentions this alternative even to discredit it immediately after, we tend to believe him in passages like the one about Vespasian's ancestors, where he says he could find no corroborating sources, and, when he makes no comment at all, to still think he researched exhaustively. All these interventions, combined with the interventions that put his preparatory research on the stage, create a sort of 'trust capital' through which the whole narration benefits.[38]

Do these refutations have a polemical dimension? Marincola presents the use of polemic as one of the most distinctive characteristics of ancient historiography; encouraged by rhetorical teaching, it was also a way to define one's self against the practice of previous authors.[39] He recognizes, however, that Roman historians do not really fit into this frame: those he evokes are from the earlier generation (Cato the Elder, Sempronius Asellio), writing at a moment when Greek influence was still strong, and their successors are presented as more careful to appear as heirs than rivals.[40] As a consequence, is it truly possible to extend what appears to be mainly a Greek characteristic to Roman writings? Suetonius' practice helps answer this question. In the passage about Drusus I's death, he does not adopt a polemical tone: he does not name the authors referred to and the refutation does not appear in the main clause of the sentence, but in a subordinate one (*quam quia... putem*). What is developed is the demonstration of Augustus' affection, presented as rather obvious by the consecutive construction (*Augustus tanto opere et uiuum dilexit ut...*): the most important part are the arguments in favor of genuine Augustan feelings, not the expression of Suetonius' disagreement. No blame is even perceptible: the phrase *unde existimo* implies that, given Drusus' political opinions, it was almost logical to imagine that

---

[37] Belonging to the inner imperial circles does not mean not having political reasons to alter the truth and spread a malevolent version.
[38] On how this cunning strategy can be used to mislead the reader, cf. Dubuisson 2003.
[39] Marincola 1997, 218–236.
[40] Marincola 1997, 236.

Augustus might have poisoned him, in order to preserve the new regime.⁴¹ Had he been Polybius, he would not have failed to deride the alternative version for absurdity. Similarly, in the famous passage on the authorship of Nero's poems, the biographer never violently attacks those affirming the contrary: he states his point by describing the tablets and implying that the conclusion is obvious. He thus gives the impression of refuting a global tradition, which includes Tacitus without naming him, rather than of refuting Tacitus himself.⁴² The similarity between this historiographical strategy and Marincola's remarks about the Roman historians is a sign that the difference between history and biography was not as clear as it may seem when reading Plutarch's declarations at the beginning of the *Alexander*.⁴³

Even when he names the authors he disproves, Suetonius adopts a neutral tone that is quite far from being polemical. His most famous argument is about Caligula's birthplace. Lentulus Gaetulicus said he was born in Tivoli. For Pliny the Elder, it was Coblence, on the German frontier, where he found an inscription concerning Agrippina's delivery. Anonymous verses placed the emperor's birth in a legionary camp. According to Suetonius, the *acta publica* mentioned Antium, on the coast near Rome.⁴⁴ These divergences are introduced with a neutral tone, the biographer only declaring that the point is uncertain because of them.⁴⁵ But the reader quickly realizes that it is not quite true, for an argumentation with successive refutations immediately follows (Suet. *Cal.* 8.6):

> Gaetulicum refellit Plinius quasi mentitum per adulationem, ut ad laudes iuuenis gloriosique principis aliquid etiam ex urbe Herculi sacra sumeret abusumque audentius mendacio, quod ante annum fere natus Germanico filius Tiburi fuerat, appellatus et ipse Caius Caesar, de cuius amabili pueritia immaturoque obitu supra diximus.

> Gaetulicus was refuted by Pliny, on the grounds that he lied due to adulation, so, in order to praise a young prince attracted by glory, he supplied even an element from the city dedi-

---

41 Levick (1976, 65) uses the same kind of argument in favor of Augustus' planning of Agrippa Postumus' execution upon his own death.
42 Koestermann (1965), commenting the corresponding Tacitean passage, alludes to Suetonius' work and says that his remark was "*vielleicht* mit bewußter Kritik an Tacitus" (the italics are mine), which shows that the interpretation of this passage as an indirect attack to Tacitus lacks solidity. On the problem of whether Suetonius had or had not read Tacitus' *opera maiora*, *cf.* Syme 1958, appendix 77, 781–782.
43 Plu. *Alex.* 1.1–3, commented by Fournel in this volume. Power 2014 also acknowledges the difficulty of declaring once and for all that Suetonius is a biographer or a historian, in spite of the title of the volume he directed.
44 Suet. *Cal.* 8.2–5.
45 Suet. *Cal.* 8.2: *Ubi natus sit, incertum diuersitas tradentium facit*, "His birthplace is made uncertain by the divergences between those who report it."

cated to Hercules, and on the grounds that he made full use of this lie quite impudently, because, a year before, a son had been born to Germanicus at Tivoli, who was also called Gaius Caesar and whose adorable childhood and untimely death I mentioned above.

The Tivoli proposition was discredited by Pliny, who accused Gaetulicus of flattery and intentionally confusing the two sons of Germanicus who were called Gaius. The expressions Suetonius uses in this passage, *quasi mentitum per adulationem* and *abusumque audentius mendacio*, imply that Pliny's tone is likely to have been violent against Gaetulicus. On the contrary, there is no trace of aggression when the biographer disproves Pliny's Coblence proposition (Suet. *Cal.* 10.7–10):

> Plinium arguit ratio temporum. Nam qui res Augusti memoriae mandarunt, Germanicum exacto consulatu in Galliam missum consentiunt iam nato Gaio. Nec Plini opinionem inscriptio arae quicquam adiuuerit, cum Agrippina bis in ea regione filias enixa sit et qualiscumque partus sine ullo sexus discrimine puerperium uocetur, quod antiqui etiam puellas pueras, sicut et pueros puellos dictitarent. Extat et Augusti epistula, ante paucos quam obiret menses ad Agrippinam neptem ita scripta de Gaio hoc (neque enim quisquam iam alius infans nomine pari tunc supererat): "(...)" Abunde parere arbitror non potuisse ibi nasci Gaium, quo prope bimulus demum perductus ab urbe sit.

> The chronology argues against Pliny. Indeed, those who entrusted the actions of Augustus to the memory of posterity agree on the fact that Germanicus was sent to Gaul after the completion of his consulate, when Gaius had been already born. The inscription on the altar does not help on any point Pliny's conjecture, for Agrippina gave birth twice to a girl in this region and whatever type of delivery is called *puerperium*, making no distinction of sex, since the Ancients also frequently called young girls *puerae*, as they called young boys *puelli* too. A letter by Augustus also exists, that was written a few months before he died, to his grandchild Agrippina, about the Gaius we are talking about (for indeed no other child with a similar name survived at that time): "(...)" It is abundantly clear, I think, that Gaius could not have been born in Coblence, where he was brought from the city when he was not quite two months old.

Suetonius' strategy of refutation is here very far from a direct and *ad hominem* accusation. He first appeals to the chronological consensus between historians of Augustus' reign (*qui res Augusti memoriae mandarunt... consentiunt*) and, during the presentation of his own arguments, he is not the subject of the verbs, but *ratio temporum*, *inscriptio* and *lettera*. These subjects are also proofs of his grammatical erudition and great familiarity with Augustus' correspondence. Both arguments could very well be used nowadays by a modern scholar. Even when Suetonius clearly appears in the text, with the verb *existimo*, he then employs the impersonal phrases *parere* and *non potuisse ibi nasci Gaium*; the adverb *abunde*, stressed by its place at the very beginning of the sentence, presents the whole conclusion as an obvious deduction, not a personal opinion. The general narrative strategy here aims at giving the impression that Suetonius was not by any means personally involved in the refutation.

As a consequence, in this passage, as in all passages in which he disproves some particular alternative version, there is no trace of polemical intent. It is the documents that refute the erroneous conjectures, not an author trying to increase his own *auctoritas* by discrediting his predecessors. Only the anonymous verses are quickly put aside, precisely because they do not have a known author.⁴⁶ This could be a Suetonian characteristic, were it not for Tacitus, who does not employ a polemical tone either. The death of Drusus II, Tiberius' son this time, is a good example of how the historian can discredit a story he considers absurd. After having written that Drusus II was poisoned by Sejanus, he presents another version of his death, affirming that Tiberius himself gave him the poison because his counselor drove him into suspecting his son. He then comments (Tac. *Ann.* 4.11.1–3):

> Haec uulgo iactata, super id quod nullo auctore certo firmantur, prompte refutaueris. Quis enim mediocri prudentia, nedum Tiberius, tantis rebus exercitus, inaudito filio exitium offerret, idque sua manu et nullo ad paenitendum regressu? Quin potius ministrum ueneni excruciaret, auctorem exquireret, insita denique etiam in extraneos cunctatione et mora aduersum unicum et nullius ante flagitii compertum uteretur? Sed quia Seianus facinorum omnium repertor habebatur, ex nimia caritate in eum Caesaris et ceterorum in utrumque odio quamuis fabulosa et immania credebantur, atrociore semper fama erga dominantium exitus. Ordo alioqui sceleris, per Apicatam Seiani proditus, tormentis Eudemi ac Lygdi patefactus est. Neque quisquam scriptor tam infensus exstitit ut Tiberio obiectaret, cum omnia alia conquirerent intenderentque. Mihi tradendi arguendique rumoris causa fuit ut claro sub exemplo falsas auditiones depellerem peteremque ab iis quorum in manus cura nostra uenerit ⟨ne⟩ diuulgata atque incredibilia auide accepta ueris neque in miraculum corruptis antehabeant.⁴⁷

> These commonly repeated rumors, beside the fact that they are confirmed by no known author, can be promptly refuted. Indeed, would anyone have such imited intelligence, much less Tiberius, who had experience in such important matters, to offer a deadly cup to his son without listening to him and do it with his own hands and without any possibility to reverse course because of remorses? Wouldn't he rather torture the one who administered the poison, ask him who gave the order, eventually use the caution and prudence he had even for strangers in the case of his only child, who had never been convicted of any infamy before? But, because Sejanus was considered the inventor of every crime, as a consequence of Caesar's excessive affection for him and the hate everybody felt for both of them, these stories were believed, even though they were horrifying tales, the public fame being always more terrible about the end of those who rule. Besides, the planning of

---

46 Suet. *Cal.* 8.11.
47 This text is from Wuilleumier's (1975) edition of Tacitus' *Annals* IV–VI for the Collection des Universités de France. The translation is mine.

the crime was revealed through Apicata, Sejanus' wife, and made clear by the revelations under torture of Eudemus and Lygdus. And no writer appears so hostile to reproach Tiberius with this, whereas they investigated and exaggerated all the rest. My reason for reporting and refuting this rumor was to repel false hearsay with a clear example and to ask those who will have my work in their hands that they not prefer incredible rumors eagerly received to real facts that were not corrupted in order to provoke stupefaction.

This passage has much in common with those of Suetonius above. The first argument given in order to discredit the story of Tiberius, poisoning his own son is exactly the same the biographer invoked for the anonymous verses about Caligula's birthplace:[48] they have no known author, so they cannot benefit from anybody's *auctoritas*.[49] Tacitus is also very likely alluding to documents when he evokes the revelations of Sejanus' wife and two freedmen: Dio said that Apicata wrote a letter after her husband's death, trying to avenge their executed children with revelations on Drusus II's murder;[50] on the other hand, the mention of the confessions under torture of Eudimus and Lygdus may be based on a report to the Senate.[51] The historian also feels obliged to explain why he mentioned the whole tale though he considers it highly improbable: he wanted to show his reader that being shocking is no proof that a story is true, especially when simply reasoning about coherence reveals it to be very unlikely.

This is the main difference between Tacitus' and Suetonius' ways of discrediting alternate versions. The biographer uses documents in order to demonstrate that the alternate version contradicts reality: Augustus' letters prove that he liked Drusus I so much that he could not have suspected him of anything, much less have poisoned him; these same letters show that Caligula had already been born when Germanicus left Rome for the German frontier and they correspond on that

---

[48] Suet. *Cal.* 8.11: *Versiculorum quoque fidem eadem haec eleuant et eo facilius, quod sine auctore sunt,* "The reliability of the verses is also diminished by these same elements, all the more easily because they do not have an author." The diminutive *versiculi* for *versus* is also pejorative and shows from the beginning their lack of value to Suetonius' eyes.

[49] Koestermann (1965, *ad loc.*) thinks that this version comes from Agrippina II's memoirs, so the author would actually be very well known and have an *auctoritas* of her own because she was a member of the imperial family. That may be the reason why Martin / Woodman (1989, *ad loc.*) record that 'Tacitus' stated reason for the excursus is the enhancement of his historiographical credibility through the rejection of improbabilities and fantasies. This motif is as old as Hecataeus and indicates that the excursus should not be read, as it is often by modern scholars, as an example of 'source criticism'." Tacitus achieves the same goal as Suetonius, though by different means.

[50] D.C. 58.11.6.

[51] On Tacitus' main use of the *acta Senatus* in *Annals* I–VI, see Syme 1958, 278–286.

point with the *acta*.⁵² Tacitus must also have based his narrative on documents, but does not emphasize this in his text. He alludes to the content, not the container, as if the latter had not been of much interest. What is put forward, on the contrary, is the incoherence and the unlikeliness of the alternative story of Drusus II's murder: no one would kill his own son, who had not previously been guilty of anything, without at least giving him the chance to defend himself or explain his actions; this was all the more improbable as Tiberius was an expert on this sort of matters. The confusion between the hypothetical person evoked and the precise case of Tiberius is so strong in the two rhetorical questions, that grammatically it is impossible to determine whether the pronoun *quis* or the noun *Tiberius* are subject of the verbs *excruciaret*, *exquireret* and *uteretur*. A few sentences below, unlikeliness is invoked again, about the previous authors Tacitus read: they were all hostile to Tiberius and tried as much as possible to accuse him of any crime, but they did not mention a poisoning of his own son, though they likely would have, had it been believable.

As a consequence, the historian's main arguments are not documents, but coherence and likeliness. His tone is no more polemical than Suetonius', though. He does not even blame Tiberian writers for inventing horrible stories and not respecting any obligation of objectivity. Suetonius' neutrality in this respect is thus not one of his characteristics, nor a peculiarity of the genre he chose. What is unique to Suetonius are his scientific refutations. Tacitus puts forward likeliness, even when he could have insisted on documents; Suetonius puts forward documents, even when he could have stressed only unlikeliness. But saying Augustus loved Drusus I too much to poison him was apparently not enough: it had to be confirmed by letters. In this perspective, the biographer's whole scientific *persona* does not appear to be only a trick to convince the reader of his most controversial affirmations or to give *auctoritas* to information we moderns would think totally out of place, like all the names of Caesar's mistresses.⁵³ It is a constituent feature not only of what he wanted to look like, but also of his conception of what his writing and his role as an author and a narrator should be. The loss of his scholarly works is therefore a pity all the more: they would have provided us with examples of how he worked when not in the context of historiography, and allowed us to see if what we observe here derives from his habits as a scholar.⁵⁴

---

52 Cf. also Syme 1958, 782, about Suetonius and Tacitus on the authorship of Nero's verses: "documents against the stylistic criteria".
53 Suet. *Jul.* 50.1–52.6.
54 The Suidas catalogue actually shows that the majority of his works were scholarly, not historical; thus the title of Wallace-Hadrill 1983.

The way Suetonius constructs his historiographical *auctoritas* is thus more than a set of narrative actions aiming at producing certain effects: it is linked to his whole *persona*, which is built very carefully. For he apparently does not wish to appear as a narrator, guiding his reader through the narration. He is a researcher, using documents to prove or disprove, evaluating sources and versions, motivating his judgements and choices. He is so sure of his material that he almost presents it as equivalent to personally assisting at the scene; not a hint of doubt is perceptible about his father's testimony on the death of Otho and the description of the tablets inscribed with Nero's poems has the same value as seeing Nero writing, erasing and editing.

Why did he privilege this scientific dimension? His scholarly habits have already been mentioned, but motives inherent to writing historical works can also explain this peculiarity. Suetonius decided to present his material, for the most part, not chronologically, but by categories, choosing thus quite a different path than Cornelius Nepos, Tacitus in the *Life of Agricola* or Plutarch. Did he feel that the disruption of the traditional chronology needed to be accompanied by more "scientificity"? His three colleagues sometimes introduce authorial interventions in their narrative, but not as much as he does. The use of categories in order to describe someone was not totally new in Latin literature: rhetorical treatises advised them in the case of a eulogy, for instance.[55] But if Suetonius was the first to resort to them in a historiographical work, he may have thought it necessary to emphasize his thorough research even more.

Another possible reason cannot be omitted, given Rome's social organization. Politically, one's *auctoritas* was conferred by his social position, i.e. his ancestors, family, relations, fortune and the result of his previous occupations. Unlike Tacitus, Suetonius was not a senator, but a member of the equestrian order. He never took part in politics, nor had military commands; we know from the Younger Pliny that he tried his hand at the courts, but he does not seem to have been very good at it,[56] and the inscription found in Hippone mainly records administrative offices.[57] As a consequence, his personal *auctoritas* would not have been very strong, and he may have tried to counterbalance this disadvantage, with the scientific authority of his work. This would imply a difference in the way senatorial and equestrian authors wrote, which is still to be proved.[58]

---

55 Cf. for instance Cic. *De Orat.* 2.342–348.
56 Plin., *Ep.* 1.18.
57 *AE* 1953, 73.
58 For instance, Livy did not have more social titles than Suetonius and he does not display such a scientific *persona*; but it is true that he was also a member of the close imperial circle

Whatever the reasons, this choice also interrogates the distinction between ancient biography and history, at least in Rome. For Suetonius' attitude is much closer to that of a historian than to that of an author only interested in the peculiar facts of one man's life.[59] He has a real "scientific" historical method, which he uses in order to display the *persona* of a proper historian. In this perspective, Gascou's title, *Suétone historien*, does not seem that polemical anymore.[60] It would thus be very profitable if Marincola's criteria of analyzing the composition of history in Antiquity were applied to biographical texts like those of Suetonius, in order to better understand the differences between all historiographical genres.

Bibliography

Ailloud, H. (1931–1932), *Suétone. Vies des Douze Césars*, Paris.
Biraschi, A.M. / Desideri, P. / Roda, S. / Zecchini, G. (eds.) (2003), *L'uso dei documenti nella storiografia antica*, Napoli.
Blin, G. (1954), *Stendhal et les problèmes du roman*, Paris.
Cizek, E. (1977), *Structures et idéologie dans les* Vies des douze Césars *de Suétone*, Paris / Bucarest.
Dubuisson, M. (2003), "Suétone et la fausse impartialité de l'érudit", in: G. Lachenaud / D. Longrée 2003, 249–261.
Duchêne, P. (2014), *Écrire sur les premiers empereurs: l'élaboration du récit chez Tacite et Suétone* (Diss. Université Paris Ouest Nanterre).
Fromentin, V. (2010), "Les Moi de l'historien: récit et discours chez Denys d'Halicarnasse", in: *Dialogues d'histoire ancienne* suppl. 4.1, 261–277.
Fry, C. (2003), "Suétone dans son texte: du bon usage des premières personnes verbales", in: G. Lachenaud / D. Longrée 2003, 327–341.
Gascou, J. (1984), *Suétone historien*, BEFAR 255, Rome.
Genette, G. (1972), *Figures III*, Paris.
Hurley, D.W. (2014), "Suetonius' Rubric Sandwich", in: T. Power / K.R. Gibson 2014, 21–37.
Koestermann, E. (1965), *Cornelius Tacitus Annalen*, vol. II, Buch IV–VI, Heidelberg.
Lachenaud, G. / Longrée, D. (eds.) (2003), *Grecs et Romains aux prises avec l'histoire. Représentation, récits et idéologie*, Rennes.
Levick, B. (1976), *Tiberius the Politician*, London.
Levick, B. (1990), *Claudius*, London.

(whereas Suetonius was a sort of high civil servant), which may have been a compensation in itself.

59 Plu. *Alex.* 1.2 speaks of πρᾶγμα βραχύ... καὶ ῥῆμα καὶ παιδία.
60 The recent volume directed by T. Power and R.K. Gibson, though entitled *Suetonius the Biographer*, does not adress this question, except at the beginning of the introduction by T. Power, quoted in this article.

Marincola, J. (1997), *Authority and Tradition in Ancient Historiography*, Cambridge.
Martin, R.H. / Woodman, A.J. (1989), *Annals. Book IV*, Cambridge / New York.
Moatti, C. (2003), "Les archives romaines: réflexions méthodologiques" in: A.M. Biraschi / P. Desideri / S. Roda / G. Zecchini 2003, 27–43.
Power, T. / Gibson, K.R. (eds.) (2014), *Suetonius the Biographer*, Oxford.
Power, T. (2014), "The Originality of Suetonius", in: T. Power / K.R. Gibson 2014, 1–18.
Steidle, W. (1951), *Sueton und die Antike Biographie*, Munich.
Syme, R. (1958), *Tacitus*, Oxford.
Wallace-Hadrill, A. (1983), *Suetonius. The Scholar and his Caesars*, London.
Wuilleumier, P. (1975), *Tacitus. Annals IV–VI*, Paris.
Woodman, A.J. (1988), *Rhetorics in Classical Historiography*, London.

Contributors

Suzanne Adema is an Assistant Professor at the Classics departments of both the University of Amsterdam and the Vrije Universiteit Amsterdam. Her research focuses on two areas: Greek and Latin education at the secondary level and Latin linguistics, with a special interest in the structure and presentation of narrative texts. Adema wrote her dissertation on tense usage in Vergil's *Aeneid*, and is currently preparing a book on speech and thought representation in Latin war narratives.

After studying Classical Philology at Heidelberg University and Classical and German Philology at Gießen University, **Mario Baumann** worked as *Wissenschaftlicher Mitarbeiter* for the Collaborative Research Centre (CRC) 434 "Memory Cultures" at Gießen University. Since 2006 he has been *Wissenschaftlicher Mitarbeiter* at the Classics Department of Gießen University where he took his PhD in 2010 (subject of the PhD thesis: "Die schöne Paideia. Bildung und ästhetisches Programm in Philostrats *Eikones*"). At the moment he is writing his habilitation thesis on the first pentad of Diodorus Siculus' *Bibliotheke*.

Craige Champion is currently Associate Professor of Ancient History and Classics at Syracuse University. He has published widely on the politics of culture, imperialism and citizenship, and the historiography of ancient Greece and Rome. He published *Cultural Politics in Polybius's Histories* (Berkeley) in 2004. He has edited and contributed to *Roman Imperialism: Readings and Sources* (Oxford, 2004); *The Blackwell Encyclopedia of Ancient History* (Oxford, 2013); and *The Landmark Edition of the Histories of Polybius* (New York, forthcoming). Professor Champion's most recent book *The Peace of the Gods: Elite Religious Practices in the Middle Roman Republic* is forthcoming with the Princeton University Press.

Giulia Donelli is a PhD Candidate at King's College London and a Fellow of the Advanced Seminar in the Humanities 2015–2016 (Università Ca' Foscari Venezia – Venice International University). She received her Bachelor Degree in Classics from Università Cattolica del Sacro Cuore in Milan, Italy, and her Masters of Arts in Classics from King's College London. Her research interests are Herodotus and Greek Lyric Poetry: she is currently completing her Doctoral Dissertation on the subject.

Alumna of the École normale supérieure of Paris, **P. Duchêne** is now maîtresse de conférence in Latin literature at the Université Paris Ouest Nanterre and a permanent member of the ArScAn research group. Her interests are the ancient historiography of the first imperial century (especialy Tacitus and Suetonius), the Latin conception of the writing of history and, more widely, the Roman attitude to the past. She is currently adapting for publication her PhD dissertation, *Écrire sur les premiers empereurs: l'élaboration du récit chez Tacite et Suétone*.

Scott Farrington is Assistant Professor of Classical Studies at Dickinson College in Carlisle, PA. His research interests include history, tragedy, and ancient literary criticism, and he has published on conceptions of tragedy, history, and rhetoric in Polybius and Hellenisitic historiography.

Stefan Feddern studied Classics (Latin and Greek), Philosophy and Spanish at the University of Kiel (Germany) and Salamanca (Spain). He received his Ph.D. in Classics (Latin) in 2010 with an edition and commentary of the Elder Seneca's *suasoriae*. He is currently working on the ancient discourse about literary fiction, which he analyzed in his German Habilitation that he handed in at the University of Kiel (Germany) where he is Assistant Professor.

Former student of the École Normale Supérieure of Paris, **Eugénie Fournel** is currently preparing a PhD at Paris Sorbonne University on dream narratives in Greek biographical works of the Ist-IIIrd century CE (Plutarch, Lucian of Samosata, Aelius Aristides, Philostratus) under the supervision of Pr. Alain Billault. She is a member of the Antheia association which brings together young researchers in the field of classical studies.

After a master degree in Classics at the University of Milan, **Vera Grossi** took her PhD in Greek Literature and Philology at the University of Verona (2015), with a Dissertation concerning the scholiastic *corpus* and the ancient exegesis on Thucydides' *History*. Her research interests include Greek Historiography and its reception and the ancient scholarship on Greek Literature. On such topics she has published some articles in international journals and has presented her studies at international conferences.

Edward M. Harris is Emeritus Professor of Ancient History at Durham University and The University of Edinburgh. He is the author of *Aeschines and Athenian Politics* (Oxford), *Democracy and the Rule of Law in Classical Athens* (Cambridge), and *The Rule of Law in Action in Democratic Athens* (Oxford). He has translated *Demosthenes 20 – 22* and Demosthenes *23 – 26* for the series the Texas Greek Orators series. He has co-edited *The Law and the Courts in Ancient Greece* (Duckworth), *Law and Drama in Ancienty Greece* (Duckworth), and *The Ancient*

Greek Economy: Markets, Households and City-States (Cambridge). With Mirko Canevaro, he is editing *The Oxford Handbook to Ancient Greek Law.* He has published many articles on Greek Law and Greek History.

Ioannis M. Konstantakos is Associate Professor of Ancient Greek Literature at the National and Kapodistrian University of Athens. His scholarly interests include ancient comedy, ancient narrative, folklore, and the relations between Greek and Near-Eastern literatures and cultures. He has published widely on these topics. He has received scholarships from the Greek State Scholarships Foundation and the Onassis Foundation. In 2009 he was awarded the prize of the Academy of Athens for the best classical monograph published within the previous five years. In 2012 he was a finalist for the Greek state prize for critical essay.

Vasileios Liotsakis has worked as Visiting Lecturer of Ancient Greek Language and Literature at Boğaziçi University of Istanbul. He is currently working as a Wissenschaftlicher Mitarbeiter / Alexander-von-Humboldt Post-Doctoral Fellow in the University of Heidelberg. His scholarly interests are Classical historiography, the Second Sophistic, Egyptian literature and culture, and narratology. He has published articles on these topics. He is currently preparing his PhD dissertation on Thucydides' book 8 for publication, while working on his second monograph, on Arrian's *Anabasis of Alexander*.

Katie Low was awarded a doctorate in Classics from the University of Oxford that focused on the Tiberian books of Tacitus' *Annals*, with particular reference to the historian's portrayal of foreigners. She also studied at the Ecole normale supérieure in Paris and held posts at Regent's Park College, Oxford and Royal Holloway, University of London. She has research interests in early Roman imperial history and historiography and the reception of Classics in twentieth-century France, and now lives in Brussels.

Philip Waddell is Assistant Professor of Classics at the University of Arizona. He received his Ph.D. in Classical Studies from the University of Missouri in 2010, and his interests include ancient historiography in both Latin and Greek, ancient rhetoric, and post-Augustan Latin. He is currently working on his first monograph, *Tacitean Noir Narrative*, which examines Tacitus' *Annales* through the lens of modern *noir* film.

Index nominum et rerum

Abydus   163
Acanthians   94
Acarnania   87–89, 94, 154
Accius   176
Acesandrus   154
Achaeans   112 n. 30, 164, 174
Achaemenid Empire   38, 40, 42 n. 14, 51–53, 53 n. 54, 56, 57 n. 65, 61
Achaeus   178
Achilles Tatius   211–212
Actus, Gaius   279 n. 33
Aedui   228–229, 233
Aegean   82
Aelian   64 n. 85, 173 n. 40
Aerys Targaryen   37
Aeschines   110, 151
Aeschylus   38–39, 52, 101, 101 n. 5, 147, 162 n. 15, 169 n. 30, 176, 176 n. 49, 176 n. 51
Africa   193, 244–245
Agatharchides of Cnidus   187, 187 n. 5, 195 n. 19
Agathocles   174–175, 177
Agbatana   61, 61 n. 78
agon   213
Agrianians   81
Agricola   242 n. 6, 271 n. 4, 286
Agrippa Postumus   281 n. 41
Agrippina the Elder   281–282
Agrippina the Younger   262, 284 n. 49
Ahiqar, story of   62 n. 82
Ahura Mazda   54
Aias   21
akinakes (Iranian dagger)   45–46, 46 n. 23, 63
Akka   58
Akkadian   53 n. 54, 58, 60 n. 74, 62
Alcaeus   11 n. 3, 15
Alcibiades   86–87, 93–94, 135, 145–148, 146 n. 1, n. 3, n. 5, 148 n. 12, 150, 151 n. 23, 153, 246 n. 15
Alcmeonidae   147
Alesia   229 n. 30, 234–237, 234 n. 36, 235 n. 37

Alexander (Paris)   13–14
Alexander II of Epirus   171
Alexander of Macedon   23, 28–30, 40 n. 8, n. 10, 204, 210
– *imitatio Alexandri*   203–204
Alexandria   163 n. 16
Allobroges   227
alternate reality   6, 213, 241, 247–248
Amar-Sin (Sumerian ruler)   37, 59–64, 61 n. 77
Amasis   26–27, 27 n. 66, 40 n. 8, 41–43, 48, 48 n. 35
ambiguity   13, 15, 28, 28 n. 71, 265
Ambraciots   87
Amphiaraus   29 n. 82
Amphipolis   82–85, 88, 92, 94
Amphitrite   26
Amyntas   29
Anacreon   11 n. 3, 27
analepsis   82, 86, 213, 226
– actorial analepsis   226
– narratorial analepsis   226 n. 21
ancestors   56, 132, 145–154, 275, 280, 286
ancient commentators   4, 114–115
ancient scholarship   12 n. 7, 99–116
ancient scholiasts   4, 99–116
Andocides   148 n. 12, 151
Antigonus   159 n. 2, 162, 174
Antioch   261
Antiochus Hierax   173 n. 40
Antiochus III the Great   178
Antiochus I Soter   173 n. 40
Antium   281
Antonius Saturninus   264
Apameia   193 n. 17, 196
Apicata   283–284
Apis bull   3, 37–64, 215 n. 53
Apollo   47 n. 29, 84, 84 n. 41, 171, 214
– Delian Apollo   26
– Pythian Apollo   151
Appian   2, 6, 192 n. 16, 204–205, 206 n. 28, 207, 209 n. 38, 213–214, 241–251, 264 n. 43, 271 n. 3
Appius Silanus   274

appropriateness   119, 126–128, 127 n. 45, 131–132, 140, 152 n. 26
Arabia   184, 187, 188 n. 7, 193, 196
Arabian Gulf   170
Aramaic   53 n. 54, 61 n. 78
Ara Maxima of Heracles   172 n. 36
Aratus   159, 162, 174
Araxes river   78
Arcadia   174
Archidamus   112, 112 n. 30, 126, 128–130, 149
Archilochus   11 n. 3, 12 n. 8
Ariamnes   170
Ariminum   203–204
Arion of Methymna   11 n. 3, 27 n. 65
Ariovistus   226, 229 n. 30, 230, 237
Aristogeiton   19
Aristomachus of Argos   159 n. 2, 174
Ariston, Oetaean chief   171
Aristotle   102–103, 103 n. 7, n. 9, 114, 125, 131 n. 58, 132–133, 160–161, 161 n. 10, 167–169
Arminius   261–262
art   1, 5, 55 n. 58, 56, 94, 101–102, 103 n. 7, 106, 108, 108 n18, 153, 201
– artistic licence   24
– narrative art   s.v. *narrative*
plastic art   1Artabanus   78, 80
Artabazus   154
Artaxerxes III Ochos   64 n. 85
Artemidorus   207 n. 33, 209–210
Artemis Astias   172
Artemis Cindyas   172
Asclepius   176
Asia   39, 53, 64, 151, 275
Asinius Pollio   201–202, 202 n. 14
Athena   113
– Athena Polias   151
– Athena Pronoia   172
Athenaeus   170, 170 n. 31, 172
Athenagoras   149
Athens   19, 26, 76 n. 11, 87–91, 93, 107, 146, 149–151, 153, 172 n. 36, 210
– Acropolis   148, 151
– Athenian Assembly   147–153
– Athenian foreign policy   75
– Athenian greed   12 n. 4, 83–84, 83 n. 36

– Athenian Hegemony   88
Attica   90–91, 147
Attic *skolia*   19, 19 n. 31
Atys   178
auctoritas   201, 271–287
audience   5, 39–40, 52, 60, 75, 137, 150, 152, 162–163, 166, 205–206, 210, 211 n. 43, 214, 251, 271
Augustus   254, 256, 259 n. 20, 262, 264 n. 40., 265, 279–282, 281 n. 40, 284–285
Aulus Caecina Alienus   255 n. 9
Aulus Gabinius   227
αὐστηρά ἁρμονία   101, 101 n. 5
authority   3 n. 7, 3–4, 11–17, 19–21, 31, 57, 209, 265 n. 48, 271, 286
Avesta (holy canon of Zoroastrianism)   50 n. 41, 54

Babylon   54 n. 54, 58, 62, 79
Babylonia   37, 58–62
Bacchylides   20 n. 32, 23–29
Bashan   61 n. 78
Batavians   255, 264, 264 n. 40
Bedriacum   277, 277 n. 28
Behistun   51, 53 n. 54
biography   7, 51 n. 44, 105, 106 n. 13, 110, 128, 130, 199–215, 271–272, 272 n. 7, 273 n. 17, 275, 281, 287
Bocchoris   64 n. 85
Boeotians   82
Bosporus   78, 212
Bottiaeans   75, 87
Bourges   229 n. 30, 232, 234 n. 36, 237
Brasidas   82–83, 88, 91, 94, 128
Brutus (Decimus Junius Albinus)   202, 207, 213, 277
bull sacrifice (in Persian tradition)   37–64, 55 n. 57, 55 n. 58, 55 n. 59, 215 n. 53
burying alive (Persian sacrifice)   51
Buto   49 n. 35
Byzantians   170

Index nominum et rerum — 295

Caecina Severus   255, 255 n. 9
Caesar   7, 132 n. 59, 190 n. 14, 191 n. 15,
    199–215, 219–237, 242 n. 3, 242 n. 6,
    262, 271–273, 279 n. 33, 281–283, 285
– crossing of the Rubicon   203–204, 209–
    210, 212
Calgacus   242 n. 6
Caligula   260, 260 n. 26, 261 n. 28, 281,
    284
Callias   149–150
Calpurnia   207
Calypso   108–109
Camarina   149 n. 17
Cambyses   3, 28 n. 69, 37–64, 77–80, 82,
    215 n. 53
– arrogance   77
– death   37–64
– his attitude towards Egyptian religion   39,
    41, 43–44, 43 n. 18, 48, 215 n. 53
– his decree about Egyptian temples   47–
    48, 48 n. 31
– Iranian motifs in story of Cambyses   49–
    51, 51 n. 44
– killing Apis   54–64
– madness   44–45, 55 n. 59, 57, 62 n. 82
Canaanite   61 n. 78
Caria   53
Carphinas the Acarnanian   154
Carthage   6, 192 n. 16, 213, 241, 243–250,
    264 n. 43
– Assembly   243
Carthaginians   179, 192–193, 213, 243–
    245, 247, 248–250
Cassius Chaerea   260 n. 26
Cassius Scaeva   279 n. 33
Cato the Elder   132 n. 59, 247–248, 250–
    251, 280
Ceian   20
Celts   170
Cenchreae   174
Censorius   249
Centaretus the Galatian   173
Ceos   20, 26
Cephallonia   88
Cephisodotus   147
Cercine (mountain)   78
Chalcidians   75, 87, 105 n. 11

Chaonians   87
characterization   79–80, 135, 153, 153 n. 31,
    153 n. 32, 208, 222, 225, 225 n. 18, 228,
    228, n. 27, 230, 233, 236–237
Charon of Lampsacus   29 n. 75
Chios   86–88, 90, 92–93
– revolt   90, 93
choregos   147–148
chronology   13 n. 9, 42 n. 14, 101 n. 5, 103
    n. 8, 104 n. 10, 109 n. 21, 202 n. 13,
    282, 286
Chrysippus   196, 196 n. 24
Cicero   129, 129 n. 52, 132 n. 59, 222 n. 15
Cimon   26
citation   2, 125, 242 n. 2
civil wars   202, 221, 255 n. 9, 257–258, 257
    n. 14, 262, 264, 266–267, 276, 277
    n. 28
classicists   2, 253
Claudius   264 n. 40, 273–274
Clazomenae   87
Cleaenetus   147
clementia   246
Cleomedon   151
Cleomenes I   51 n. 34, 62 n. 79
Cleomenes III   159 n. 2, 162
Cleon   94, 146–147, 151–153
Cleonae   154
Clitophon   211–212
Cnossus   26
Coblence   281–282
Coes   78
coherence   74, 79, 278 n. 30, 284–285
Considius   223
continuity   18, 30–31, 73, 82, 107 n. 16, 261
contrapasso   46, 59
Corcyra   107
Corinth   21
Corinthians   87–88, 93 n. 56
Cornelius Cinna   206, 206 n. 28
Cornelius Laco   257
Cornelius Nepos   271 n. 4, 286
credibility   3–4, 7, 44, 103 n. 9, 127, 145,
    150, 172 n. 33, 275, 277, 284 n. 49
Cremona   255, 256 n. 12
Creon   38
Cretans   178

Crete 104–105
criticism 2, 13, 15, 44 n. 20, 49 n. 36, 74, 82, 86, 99, 102–103, 106, 109, 109 n. 20, 109 n. 22 120–122, 124, 126–127, 148 n. 14, 159–164, 168–170, 174, 179, 195, 197
– historical criticism 2
– linguistic criticism 2
– methodical criticism 2
– source criticism 2, 284
Critognatus 235 n. 37
Croesus 11, 23–25, 27–29, 40 n. 8, 47 n. 28, 51, 62 n. 82, 77–78, 84–85, 178, 214
– Croesus on the pyre 23, 26
cross-reference 80, 202, 202 n. 13
Crotonian embassy 171
Cynoscephalae 179
Cyrene, the nymph 171
Cyrus 24, 39 n. 5, 51–53, 56, 62, 77–80, 82, 84
Cythera 82–83

Dacian Wars 251
Dalmatia 264 n. 40
Danaids 47 n. 29
Dante 46
Daphne 171
Dardanos 29
Darius I 38, 39 n. 5, 43–44, 51–53, 77–82
– his attitude towards Cambyses 52
deliberative oratory 146, 152
Delion 82–85
Demetrius of Phalerum 104–105, 115
Democharis 154
Demophon 171
Demosthenes 110, 129–130, 145–148, 151 n. 21, 152,
Demotic Papyrus 47–48
Derrida, Jacques 5
deus ex machina 84 n. 41, 194
didacticism 6, 183, 186, 189–190, 192, 195–196
Dimoetes 171
Dio Cassius 203–204, 206–207, 284
Diodorus of Sicily 2, 6, 81 n. 27, 164 n. 18, 166 n. 21, 183–197, 201, 204 n. 20

Diodotus 94, 146, 152
Diomedes 14, 150 n. 18
Dionysia 147–148
Dionysius of Halicarnassus 3, 100–110, 115–116, 119–123, 125–128, 130, 139, 201
direct speech 177 n. 52, 222, 228, 235 n. 37, 243
dithyramb 147–148, 167 n. 25
divine 17, 20, 24–25, 27, 38–39, 43, 46–48, 55, 57–59, 132, 167, 208–210, 214, 243
Doberus 75
Doge of Venice 25
Domitian 260 n. 25, 276, 276 n. 25, 278
Domitius 205
Dorian 105 n. 11
dramatic presentation 161 n. 10
dream 7, 84 n. 41, 199–215, 227
– allegorical dream 202, 207, 207 n. 33, 211
– incestuous dream 210–211, 211 n. 44
– interpretation of dreams 204, 207, 210–211
– predictive dream 201, 203
– theorematic dream 207, 207 n. 33
Drusus I 256, 258, 263 n. 35, 279–280, 284–285
Drusus II 283–285
dual voice 231–232
Dumnorix 228

Early Dynastic Age 58
Ecbatana 61, 61 n. 78
Echembrotus of Cleonae 154
Egypt 13–14, 25, 27 n. 66, 37, 39–45, 47, 50, 52–54, 57, 63, 154, 171, 184–186, 213, 262
– Egyptian cult 54
– Egyptian Hathoric inebriation 51 n. 44
– Egyptian priests 14, 44, 63
– Egyptians 14, 41, 63, 171, 177, 215 n. 53
ekphrasis 241
ἔκπληξις 159, 161, 163, 165–166, 168–169, 176
Elaeusa 171
Elamite 53 n. 54
Elegy 11 n. 2, 12 n. 8,, 22 n. 34

Index nominum et rerum — 297

Elephantine, Papyrus of   53 n. 54
Eleusinian Mysteries   149
emotion   6, 89, 93, 113, 152, 159–161, 163–166, 168–169, 175–176, 178, 183, 186, 186 n. 4, 189–190, 192, 194–197, 214, 229, 241, 247, 250
emotional detail   159 n. 2
emotionalism   183, 186, 186 n. 4, 189–190, 192, 195–196
emotional response   3, 6, 166
emplotment   73, 73 n. 1
ἐνάργεια   175–176, 175 n. 46, 176 n. 48, 186 n. 3, 190 n. 14
encomion   199
endogamy (in Persian tradition)   50, 51 n. 44
Enmerkar   58
Ephors   149, 149 n. 15
epic poetry   3–4, 12–16, 18, 19 n. 29, 22 n. 34, 31, 99, 99 n. 1, 105, 109 n. 21, 110, 116, 163 n. 17, 166 n. 22, 167 n. 25, 204, 206 n. 26, 220 n. 23, 221
– epicizing features   12, 12 n. 8
– epic tradition   12, 16
Epictetus   196
Epidamnus   107–109
epigram   12
Epilycus   148 n. 12
Eriphyle   172
Erythrae   87
escalation   91
Eteobutadae   151
Ethiopia   41, 77, 80, 183–184, 188–189
Ethiopians   39, 77–80
etiquette of addressing the Athenian Assembly   145–153
εὐδαιμονία   78
Eudemus   284
Eumaeus   165
Euphrates   212
Euphronios, the potter   26
Euripides   30 n. 84, 146 n. 1, 169 n. 30, 176 n. 51, 177
Eurylochus of Cydonia   154
Euryptolemus   147, 147 n. 9
Eurytion   151, 153
Evander   151

expectations   5, 83, 211, 213–215, 229, 246–247., 254, 263
experientiality   225, 228
explanation by emplotment   73 n. 1

fear   87, 89–91, 93, 159, 163, 168, 232, 245, 247, 249–250, 259–260., 262–264
Fereydun   56
Festival of Athena   19
fifth-century Enlightenment   25
flashback   83, 95, 109
focalization   83, 88, 191–194, 231, 231 n. 32, 263 n. 37
– embedded focalization   222 n. 15
folktale pattern   22–31
forced labour (or: slavery)   159 n. 2, 162, 177, 183–192, 231
foreshadowing   22 n. 34, 192, 222 n. 12, 226, 230, 236, 264
fortune (mutability of)   25, 27, 160, 163, 178, 194 n. 18, 209, 214

Galba   253–254, 257–260, 265–266, 273, 276–277
Gallia Lugdunensis   264
Gallic war   231
Gaul   173, 226–228, 230, 235, 235 n. 37, 282
Gaza   61 n. 78
Gela   149 n. 17
Geneva   227
Geography   183
Gergovia   229 n. 30, 232–233, 234 n. 36, 237
Germanicus   255–266, 274, 279 n. 34, 282, 284
Germans   261
Germany   253–255, 257–258, 260–261, 263–265
Getae   81
Gibbon, Edward   6
Glaucus   150 n. 18
Gobryes   78
gold   22, 48 n. 31, 77, 80, 154, 183–188, 190–194, 197

Gorgias 31, 114, 114, n. 34, 123–124, 132, 169 n. 29
Greece 1 n. 1, 21, 39, 93, 200, 205, 213
Greeks 1, 26, 52, 75, 81, 83, 86, 113, 132, 148, 176, 199
Gutians 59
Gyges 23–24

Hadrian 172 n. 36, 272 n. 6, 272 n. 7
Hannibal 179, 242 n. 6, 243–244
haoma (Persian intoxicating drink) 50, 51 n. 42, 51 n. 44, 55 n. 58
Harmodius 19
Hasdrubal 163 n. 16
Hasdrubal Eriphus 243, 246
Hebrew Scripture 59
Hebryzelmis, king of the Odrysians 153
Hecataeus of Miletus 30, 284 n. 49
Helen Story 13–15, 31
Heliodorus 211
Heliopolis 64 n. 85
Hellen 3
Hellenistic period 24, 148 n. 12
Hellespont 81
Heluius Cinna 206
Helvetians 227, 229 n. 30, 230, 237
Hephaestus 49 n. 35
Hera 162 n. 12, 171
Heracles 38, 149
Hermaeondas 92
Hermocrates 105, 149
Hermus 22
Herodotus 2–4, 11–15, 18, 21–31, 37–54, 58, 61–64, 73–74, 76–80, 82, 84–85, 94–96, 99–100, 102–104, 107, 109–110, 159, 170, 178, 200–201, 204–206, 210–211, 214–215, 222–223, 225, 251, 274
– anecdotal narratives 23 n. 35, 59
– Scythian *logos* 79
– sources of Herodotus 2, 24, 37–38, 47, 53
Hieronymus of Cardia 201
Hipparchus 19, 27 n. 65
Hippias 210–211
Hippocratic corpus 11–12, 18–19
Hippocratic writers 30

Hippolytus 175
Hipponax 13, 23
Hippone 286
historical fiction 40, 159
historical narrative (interpretative/informative) 37, 73, 164–165, 215, 242, 251, 254
historicity 3, 172, 220, 230, 242
historiography 2–4, 6, 11, 13, 18, 22, 31, 62, 74, 81, 94, 99, 102, 123, 159–166, 170, 172, 176, 178, 199–201, 220–221, 228, 232, 241–243, 251, 253–254, 261, 265, 271, 273–274, 280, 285
– Classical historiography 4–5, 7, 74, 76
– Greek historiography 1, 9, 37–38, 73, 100, 175
– modern historiography 4
– Roman historiography 1–7, 217
– scientific historiography 3
history 1–2, 4–7, 37–38, 49, 58, 76, 86–87, 89, 94–95, 99–100, 102, 108–110, 112, 119, 126–127, 147, 151, 159, 161, 163–164, 166, 176, 179, 183, 199–202, 204, 208–209, 214, 241, 243, 251, 253–254, 263, 271–272, 281, 287
– idea of history 1
– imperial history 6, 253–254, 265
– Roman history 5, 7, 241–242, 261
– universal history 183, 189
– virtual history 247, 265
Homer 3–4, 11–18, 99–100, 104–106, 108–111, 113–116, 166, 174, 201, 214, 222, 246, 249, 274
Homeric epic 3–4, 13, 15, 19
hope 78, 86–87, 89, 91, 119, 145, 194, 229–230, 233, 236, 258, 262, 264, 267
Hoshang 56
hubris 28, 38–39, 46–47, 52, 78 n. 17, 84

iambus 11 n. 2
Iberia 188, 192, 193 n. 17
Iberians 170
Ides of March 207, 212–213
imagination 64, 186, 189, 261
imperialism 74, 82, 95, 251
Imperium 249, 262, 263 n. 35
impious and frivolous ruler motif 78

India 171
indirect speech 222, 222 n. 13, 225–226, 228, 231–232, 234, 237
indirect thought 222, 226
Indo-Iranian background 50 n. 39
Inferno 46
innovation 73–74, 86, 95, 195 n. 19
international relationships 73
intertextuality 253, 255, 265, 265 n. 48
intratextual patterns 208, 212,
Ion 166–167
Ionians 88
Ionian Sea 81
Ionian territory 53
Iran 40, 57
Iranian aristocracy 52
Iranian cult 51
irony 81, 91, 128–130, 210
Isaeus 151
Isanthes 172
Isin 58
Istrus 78
Italians 192–193
Italy 210, 245
Ithaca 108, 167
Itys 3
Iulius Civilis 255, 264
Iulius Vindex 264

Kai Kavus 56
Kai Khosrow 56, 79
Kerykes 149
key cities 87–89
Kleitor 171
Koiranus, the Milesian 171
Kouretes the Aetolian 171
Kronos 172
Ku-Baba 59

Labienus 223, 229 n. 30, 233–234, 237
LaCapra, Dominick 5
Laeaeans 81
language of proof 18–22
Laodice 178
Lapyris of Cleonae 154
Larsa 58
Lasus 11 n. 3, 27 n. 65

legend (historical, medieval) 2–3, 25, 37, 39–40, 47, 49, 59–60, 62–64, 79
Lemnos, battle of 210
Leningrad painter 24
Lentulus Gaetulicus, Cnaeus Cornelius 281
Leonidas 21
Lesbians 87–88
Leucippe 211–212
Leucippos 171
Libya 18, 247
Licymnius of Chios 23
Ligyaistades 20
Lingones 234
linguistic turn 5
Liscus 224
literary 3–7, 37–38, 44, 58, 99, 101–102, 106, 119, 135, 161, 179, 190, 199, 201, 211, 213–215, 220–221, 230, 236, 241, 253, 271
– literary emotionalism 183
– literary qualities 2, 6
literary-analytical approach 4
liturgies 54, 145–148, 151–153
Livy 1–2, 202, 204, 207, 242 n. 6, 243, 286 n. 58
λογογράφοι 119, 136–137
Lucan 204–205, 209 n. 38, 210 n. 40
Lucius Aemilius 224
Lucius Piso 227
Ludwig II of Bavaria 37
Lusitania 257, 260 n. 24
Lycaeum (mountain) 173
Lydia 23–24
Lydian cavalry 22
Lydian trilogy 24
Lydus (Joannes Laurentius) 172
Lygdus 284
lyric corpus 12, 17, 20–22, 27
lyric inheritance 11, 13
lyric poetry (ancient Greek, poets) 3, 11–12, 18–19, 21–23, 29–31, 100
Lysimachus 170

Macedonia 28, 30, 73, 75–76, 81, 87, 148
Macedonian kingdom 75
Macedonians 75, 79
Macedonian women 29

macro-structure 74, 82
mania 50, 51 n. 44
manipulation 6, 175
Mantinea 88, 159 n. 2, 162, 174
Mantineans 162
Mantitheus 151
Marathon 210
Marcellinus 100 n. 2, 105–106, 109–111, 116, 119, 128–131, 135, 139
Marduk 58–59, 61
Martin, George R.R. 37
Masinissa 247–248
Massagetae 39 n. 5, 77–80
Mastusian Sea 171
Mastusius 171
Mazdaic religion 49
Media 52 n. 46, 61
Megacles 147
Megalopolis 5, 162
Meidias 148
Meleas 92
Memphis 37, 41, 43, 45, 49–50, 63
Menandros 172 n. 34
Menelaus 14, 154
Menelaus of Pelagonia 154
Menexenus 151
mentioned speech 222, 225, 227, 237
mentioned thought 222
Mentor 154
Mermnad dynasty 24
Mesopotamia 58–63
Mesopotamian kings 58
meta-history 86, 249
metapoiēsis 19 n. 30
method 2, 6, 18–19, 40, 73, 93–95, 106, 122, 136, 138, 151, 160, 168, 199, 202, 214, 271–272, 287
Methodenkapitel 119–120, 123, 127, 136, 138–139
Methymnaeans 91
micro-structure 74, 82
Mikon 26
Miletus 87
Milon of Croton 170
Mimnermus 19, 22
mining 184, 186–188, 191–192
Minos 3, 26–28

misinterpretation 211
Mithra (Iranian deity) 37, 54–55, 57
Mithridates 212–213
Mnevis 64 n. 85
model reader 183, 195, 197
Molon 164
monody 169 n. 30
motif(s) (folktale) 11–12, 22–23, 28, 37–38, 40, 46–47, 49, 51, 55, 59–62, 64, 78, 87, 89, 91, 99, 231, 234, 284
Mount Carmel 61 n. 78
Märchen 59
Mucianus 263 n. 35
Muse 16–19, 22, 169 n. 30
Myson amphora 24
Myth (mythological figures) 3, 20, 26, 47, 50, 54–56, 60, 62–63, 137, 176, 209
Mytilenaeans 91
Mytilene 90, 92–94, 146, 152

Nabonidus 62 n. 82, 79
Nanis 23
narration by negation 81
narrative 3–4., 7, 11–12, 14–15, 22–31, 37–41, 44, 46–47, 49–51, 53–55, 58, 60–64, 73–80, 82–89, 91–95, 99, 103, 107–109, 114–116, 153, 159–162, 165–166, 169, 175–176, 194, 199, 201–207, 211–213, 215, 219, 222, 224–230, 232, 234–236, 241, 243, 246–248, 250–251, 253, 255–256, 259–261, 263–264, 271–274, 278–279, 283, 285–286
– models 73
– narrative art 2
– pace 191, 194
– patterns 11, 23 n. 36, 30
– style 3
– techniques 6, 74 n. 4, 95, 163, 214, 220 n. 4, 222, 224–229
narratology 228, 231
narrator 22 n. 34, 39, 183–189, 192–195, 197, 219–221, 224–236, 271–272, 285–286
Naucratis 154
Naupactus 88

Near East 40, 47, 55 n. 58, 58, 73–74, 78–79, 291
Nekyia 47 n. 29
nemesis 47
Neo-Assyrian 58, 62
Neo-Babylonian 58, 79
Neoclassicism 1
Neoptolemus 47 n. 29
Neorealist School 3
Nereus 16
Nero 257, 259, 259 n. 21, 264–265, 277–278, 281, 285 n. 52, 286
Nerva 260 n. 25, 264 n. 42
New Year Festival, Babylonian 59
Nicaea, elephant 171
Nicias 83, 85–87, 94, 111–112, 128, 135, 135 n. 69, 145, 147, 147 n. 8, 246 n. 15
Nile 44, 53, 177
novel 5, 60, 62 n. 82, 84 n. 39, 159, 179, 199, 211, 258
Nymphaeus 154

objectivity 1 n. 3, 6, 123, 123 n. 22, 124 n. 25, 285
Odrysian empire 75–76, 81
Odrysians 75, 81, 153
Odysseus 17, 108–109, 111 n. 28
Oedipus 38
Olympia 145
Olympic Games 146
Onesimos, the painter 26
Oppius 202
Otho 253–255, 257, 259–261, 264–266, 273 n. 17, 276–277, 279 n. 34, 286
Oxyartos 172

Pahlavi 50 n. 39
Paionians 78
Palaephatus 119, 123 n. 20, 136–139
Panathenaea 148
Pandion 3
Pandionis 147
Panhellenic Games 146
Pannonia 253–254, 256, 258, 262
Pantheia 211–212
paralipsis 177
para prosdokian pattern 62

Pasiphaë 171
pathos 183, 186, 189–190, 192, 207, 246
Patrae 89
Pausanias 26
peace of Nicias 82–83, 86
Peisistratus 210
Peloponnese 82, 90–91, 149–150
Peloponnesian League 87, 92
Peloponnesians 88–89, 112 n. 30
Peloponnesian War 76, 108–109, 132
Pelops 29 n. 75
Pentecontaetia 107–108
Pentheus 38
Perdiccas 75, 81, 87–88
Periander 27 n. 65, 210 n. 42
Pericles 76 n. 11, 126, 128–130, 147, 147 n. 7
Peripatos 136, 160–161, 179
peripeteia 160 n. 5, 163–164, 166, 173, 186 n. 4
Perseus 165
Persia 37–43, 45–46, 48–53, 56–57, 61–64, 77–78, 80, 84, 107, 147–148, 154, 200, 215
– Persian envoys 29
– Persian officials 53
– Persian tradition 29, 57
Persians 29–30, 38–39, 52, 62, 77–78, 80, 147
Persian Wars 29, 38, 132, 210
Phaedra 175
Phaedrus 167
Phaethon 176, 176 n. 51
Pharnabazos 154
Pharsalus 204–205, 213
Phayllus 171
Philip 163 n. 16
Philistus 201
Phineus 176
Phinidae (by Accius) 176 n. 50
Phoenicians 192–193
Phormion the Acarnanian 154
Photius 187 n. 5, 195 n. 19
Phylarchus 6, 99, 102, 159–163, 166–170, 172–180, 186
– sensationalism 162, 169, 171, 173–175
Picrochole 37

Pierides 16
Pindar 4, 11 n. 3, 12, 16, 16 n. 26, 20–21, 23, 29–31, 101, 106
Piso Licinianus 257
pity 162–164, 166, 168, 183, 185–186, 192–194, 285
Plataea 15–16, 21
Plataeans 111, 126
Plato 110, 166 n. 22
Pleistoanax 83, 85–87, 94
Pliny 61 n. 78, 281–282, 286
Plutarch 146, 169, 172 n. 33, 173, 190 n. 14, 196, 196 n. 24, 199–215, 271, 271 n. 4, 273, 274 n. 23, 281, 286
political biography 201, 201 n. 9
political thinkers 1 n. 1
political turmoil in Athens 76 n. 11
politics 1 n. 2, 6, 166 n. 21, 286
Polybius 5–6, 99, 102 n. 6, 159–180, 186 n. 4, 194 n. 18, 201, 243, 281
Polycrates (and the ring) 23, 25–29, 40 n. 8
Polydamas of Pharsalus 150
Polygnotus 47 n. 29
Pompey 7, 199, 202, 204–206, 208–209, 212–215
Pontic Sea 212
pontifex maximus 205
Poseidon 26
Poseidonius of Apameia 193 n. 17, 196
postmodern 5
post-structuralists 5
Potamodorus 151, 153
Potidaea 87–88, 90–92, 94, 107
praeteritio 15, 20
pre-battle exhortation 191 n. 15, 219–237
Presocratics 1
Priam 47 n. 29
Principate 6, 253–254, 261, 264–265, 265 n. 46
Procne 3
prolepsis 225–226
– actorial prolepsis 226
– narratorial prolepsis 226
propaganda 28, 28 n. 60, 40, 40 n. 10, 80 n. 25, 265 n. 48

prophecy coming true in unexpected manner motif 60–62
prose 6, 11, 13, 22 n. 34, 99–105, 109–111, 114–115, 137, 253, 255
– prose and poetry 101 n. 5, 103, 103 n. 7
Proteus 14, 162 n. 12
proto-biography 200
proxenos 149–151, 153–154
Ptah 41, 49 n. 35
Ptolemy II Philadelphus 177–178
Publius Cornelius 243–251
Punic War II 6, 241, 246
Punic War III 241, 245, 248, 250
Puzur-Nirah 59
Pylos 82–84

Rabelais 37
Ranke, Leopold von 7
rationalists 1
Ravenna 209 n. 38
reader 3–4, 60, 76, 80–81, 86, 89, 127, 139, 159, 161–163, 165–166, 168, 175–176, 183, 186–192, 194–197, 206–207, 209–215, 242–243, 246–247, 250–251, 254, 259–260, 264, 273–277, 280–281, 284–286
– reader response 183, 196, 254 n. 5
reader-response criticism 183
readership (Ancient Greek) 3, 6
reception theory 2
Red Sea 183, 188, 192–193, 194 n. 18
regularity 73
reliability 5, 15, 174, 277, 284 n. 48
religion 1 n. 2, 39, 43–44, 48–49, 54–55, 203, 215
religious narratives 29
Renaissance 5
retaliation principle 46, 46 n. 26, 59, 63
revolt episodes 87, 89, 94
rhetoric 3–5, 30–31, 99, 102–103, 106, 108–109, 116, 123–125, 127, 127 n. 45, 152, 175–176, 186 n. 3, 190 n. 14, 199, 220, 222 n. 15, 235, 241–243, 246, 250, 271, 280, 285–286
rhetorical technique 108–109
rhetorician 5, 102–103, 175
Rhodope mountain 81

Rhone, river   179, 227
Richard III   37
ring composition   81
Rome   1 n. 1, 5, 200, 205, 210, 226–227,
     241, 243–245, 247–251, 256–258, 262,
     279 n. 32, 281, 284, 286–287
– Roman Republic   1 n. 2, 205 n. 24
royal hero combating bull (in Persian monuments)   56–57

Saguntum   245–246
Salamis, battle of   21
Sallust   201–202, 219 n. 1, 242 n. 6
Salmoneus   29 n. 82
Samos   25
Sandrokottos of India   171
Sappho   11 n. 3
Saqqara   41, 43
Sardis   23, 178
Scipio Aemilianus   249–250
Scipio Africanus   243
Scribonianus   264 n. 40
Scythia   18, 39 n. 5, 78–79
Scythians   2, 77–80
Sea of Galilee   61
second-degree autopsy   276, 278
Second Letter to Ammaeus   100, 100 n. 3
Second Philippic   148
seed   222 n. 12, 226, 233, 236–237
Sejanus   242 n. 6, 283–284
Seleucids   178
Seleucus   171
self-allusion   253–267
Sempronius Asellio   280
Senate   207, 213, 241–248, 256, 262, 284
Seneca   196
Sennacherib   79
Septicius Clarus   272 n. 6
Sequanians   235
Serapeum   41–44
Sestos   147
Seuthes   78, 81
Shakespeare   37
shipwreck   171, 192–195
Siceliots   105, 105 n. 11
Sicilian Expedition   89, 112, 145, 246

Sicily   82, 86, 105, 111–112, 115, 145, 149,
     151, 178, 245–246
sideshadowing   247 n. 17
Simonides   11, 15–16, 20–21
Smerdis   51
Social War   148
Socrates   167
Solon   11, 19–20, 23, 27, 27 n. 66, 27 n. 67,
     84–85
Sophocles   121, 175–177
sources   2, 12, 24, 37–38, 41, 47–48, 53,
     61, 82, 99–100, 104, 106, 108, 116,
     120–121, 147, 159, 170, 177, 193, 199–
     203, 206–208, 214, 261, 264, 274,
     279–280, 286
space   225–227, 227 n. 25, 229, 231 n. 32
Spain   203, 210, 245
Spartan Assembly   149–150, 153
speaker   3–4, 15, 120, 124, 126–127, 131,
     134–135, 145–148, 151–153, 242–244,
     246
speeches   3–4, 93–94, 99, 110, 119–120,
     123–124, 126–136, 140, 146–149, 151–
     153, 208, 213, 215, 219–222, 224–232,
     234, 236–237, 241–242, 246–247
– forensic speech   223
– hortatory speech   7
– paired speech   6, 241–242
– speech in character   4, 134
Sphacteria   82–84
Spinther   205
Statius   224 n. 17
stereotypical episodes   73
Stesichorus   15
Sthenelaidas   149
Sthorys of Thasos   153
Stoicism (or: Stoic literary criticism)   195
Stratus   88
Strife   112 n. 30, 253, 264
stylistic characterization   135
Suetonius   7, 199, 201, 203–204, 206–207,
     209 n. 38, 212, 271–287
Sumerian mythical heroes   58
συμπάθεια   6, 183–197
supernatural   84, 84 n. 41, 204–205
Sybarites   171
symmoria   148

sympotic poetry 19, 29
Syracusans 113, 149
Syracuse 113, 145, 149
Syria 61, 61 n. 78

Table of the Sun 77
Tacitus 6, 204, 252, 242 n. 6, 247 n. 17, 253–266, 271, 273–274, 277–279, 281, 281 n. 42, 283–286
Tegea 88
Telemachus 14
Telephos 12 n. 8
tempo 225, 225 n. 19, 229–230, 236–237
Tenedians 91
Teutoburg Forest 255
Thalamae 171
Thargelion 173
Thasos 92
26th Dynasty of Egypt 42
theatrical performance 24
Theogenes of Naucratis 154
Theon 100 n. 2, 103, 103 n. 8, 103 n. 9, 108–109, 109 n. 19, 116, 131, 131 n. 57, 136 n. 70
Theopompus 173
Thermopylae, battle of 21
Theseus 26, 175
Thessaly 150
Thetis 15, 162 n. 12
Thibians 171
Third Dynasty of Ur 58–59
Thrace 75–76, 82, 84, 88 n. 47, 91–92
Thracians 75, 87–88
Throne Hall 57
Thucydides 3–6, 11, 12 n. 4, 39 n. 5, 47 n. 28, 73–95, 99–116, 119–140, 145–147, 149, 151–153, 159, 162 n. 15, 178, 178 n. 57, 199, 201, 204 n. 20, 208 n. 36, 219, 222 n. 12, 222 n. 15, 226 n. 22, 242, 242 n. 3, 246, 246 n. 12, 265 n. 47, 277
– book 8 73, 82, 86, 88, 90, 92–95
– compound verbs 92–93
– *History* 4, 99, 100 n. 2, 102, 108–110
– Melian Dialogue 103 n. 7, 125
– *scholia* in Thucydidem 4, 99–100, 105 n. 12, 106 n. 13, 110, 110 n. 24, 111–116

– Sitalces digression 75–82
– summer/winter organization 107 n. 16
– *Thucydides Mythistoricus* 1
Thyamis river 171
Thyestes 29 n. 75
Thymondas 154
Tiberius 242 n. 6, 253–254, 256–266, 279, 283–285
Ticinus 242 n. 6
Tilataeans 81
Timaeus 201
time 1, 3, 6, 12, 16, 23, 40, 42 f., 45, 48, 50, 56, 58, 62–63, 74, 76–77, 82–83, 86, 90, 92, 107, 109, 113–114, 120, 127, 137, 151, 163, 165, 169, 171, 177, 179, 184, 187, 191, 194, 197, 199, 202–204, 206–209, 212–213, 215, 221, 225, 228, 232–233, 235, 241, 245, 254, 257, 262, 265, 272–273, 275, 277, 282–283
Timocreon 20
Timosa 172
Tiridates 279 n. 32
tisis 46
Tištrya 54
Titus Vinius 257
Tivoli 281–282
Tomyris 77–78, 80
topos 30, 39 n. 5, 86, 203, 209 n. 38, 210, 210 n. 42, 219, 242–243, 246
tragedy 6, 24, 38–39, 99, 99 n. 1, 102 n. 6, 111 n. 27, 125, 133, 159–180, 194, 209
– ἔλεος 38
– tragic history 6, 160, 160 n. 5, 162–165, 169–170, 172, 175, 179–180, 186 n. 4, 194 n. 18
– tragic style 6, 159, 161, 169–170, 177
tragic irony 81, 210
Trajan 251, 260 n. 25, 264 n. 42, 265 n. 46
Treres 81
Trojans 29, 112 n. 30
Trojan War 14–15, 29, 183
Troy 14–15, 56, 114, 167, 173, 249 n. 24
Tullius Cicero, Quintus 129 n. 52

Ur 37
urbs capta 246

use of ethnographic data 74, 80, 80 n. 25, 95
Utu-hegal 59

variatio 92–93, 108, 225
Varus 255
vase painting 24, 26
Vedas, Sanskrit 50 n. 39
Venus Victrix 205
Vercingetorix 228, 229. n. 30, 234–236
Vergil 219, 222 n. 15
Verginius Rufus 264 n. 39
Verse Account of Nabonidus 79
Vespasian 263 n. 35, 275, 280
Vico, Giambattista 1
Vidēvdād 54 n. 56
Visconti, Luchino 37
Vitellius 253, 255, 257, 259–261, 264, 265 n. 48, 277 n. 28
vividness 159 n. 2, 176 n. 48, 183, 186, 190, 192 n. 16, 250
vocabulary 60 n. 74, 77, 99–101, 103, 109 n. 20, 161, 161 n. 11, 168, 169 n. 30, 174, 179, 190, 209, 279 n. 35
Vərəthraghna 54

Weidner Chronicle or *Chronicle of the Esagila* 37, 58–60, 62
White, Hayden 5, 73 n. 1
Winckelmann 1
wise advisor motif 78
Wolf, Friedrich A. 1

Xanthippus 147
xenia 150 n. 18
Xenoetas 164
Xenophanes 13
Xenophon 46 n. 24, 145–147, 149, 152, 199, 204 n. 20
Xerxes 38–39, 56, 205

Yama 50 n. 39
Yima (first man in Iranian myth) 37, 50, 50 n. 34, 56–57

Zama 213, 242 n. 6, 243
Zeus 20–21, 47 n. 29
Zoroastrian religious texts 50

Index locorum

Achilles Tatius
Leucippe and Clitophon
3.15.4–5   212 n. 47

Aelian
NA
6.44   173 n. 40
10.28   64 n. 85
11.11   64 n. 85

VH
4.8   64 n. 85

Aeschines
1.94   173
2.147   151
3.51–52
3.171–172   151 n. 22

Aeschylus
A.
1546   112 n. 28

Pers.
249–514   39
550–557   39
717–831   39
773   38, 52 n. 47
809–812   39
831   39
834–851   39
908 ff.   39
TrGF 67–73a   176 n. 51
TrGF 258–260   176 n. 49

Alcaeus
fr. 42 V   15

Andersen
The Steadfast Tin Soldier 25

Andocides
On the Mysteries
1.141   151
1.147–149   151

De Pace
3.6   148 n. 12
3.29   148 n. 12

Appian
Lib.
6/23   246 n. 14
50–52/215–228   243 n. 10, 246 n. 12
53/229   246 n. 13
53/230   243 n. 7
57/248–250   244
58/253   244
62/273–274   245
62/272   245 n. 11
62/277   245, 247 n. 16
65/289   246
66/292–300   247 n. 18
69/310   247 n. 19
69/313   247 n. 20
74/343–346   248
76–77/354–358   249 n. 21
80/373–375   249 n. 22
81/378   249 n. 23
132/629–630   249 n. 24
134/633–634, 636   249
134/636–637   250

BC
2.68–69   204 n. 22
2.127   206 n. 28

Archilochus
P. Oxy. LXIX 4708   12 n. 8

Aristophanes
Ra.
849   169 n. 30
924–926   169 n. 30

928–930	169 n. 30	6.2	54 n. 56
937	169 n. 30	7.5	54 n. 56
1154	169 n. 30	9.17 f.	50 n. 41
1173	169 n. 30	9.20	50 n. 41
1177–1248	169 n. 30	9.27	50 n. 41
1329–1363	169 n. 30	9.30 f.	50 n. 41
		32.8	56 n. 60

Pl.
635–638   176 n. 50

Yašt
2.4   54 n. 56
2.9   54 n. 56

Aristotle
Po.
1447a13–16	167 n. 25	5.21	56 n. 62
1450a7–10	169 n. 28	5.25	56 n. 62
1450b4–5	125 n. 29	5.33	56 n. 62
1451a36–38	133 n. 64	5.45	56 n. 62
1451a36–b5	123 n. 21	5.49	56 n. 62
1454a16–28	133 n. 63	6.5	54 n. 56
1454a33–36	132 n. 61	8.7	54 n. 56
1455a10	176 n. 50	8.58	54 n. 55
1460b23–26	168	9.3	56 n. 62
1462a14–17	167–168 n. 25	9.8	56 n. 61
		9.13	56 n. 62
		9.21	56 n. 62

Pol.
8.1340a12–13	167	10.1–15	54 n. 56
		10.28	54 n. 56
		10.39–52	54 n. 56

Rh.
1355b9–11	125 n. 30	10.65	54 n. 56
1358a36–b8	131 n. 58	10.86 f.	54 n. 56
1375b29–30	12 n. 7	10.112	54 n. 56
1404a–b	102	10.119	55 n. 57
		14.50	54 n. 55
		14.57 f.	50 n. 41
		19.35	54 n. 56

Artemidorus Daldianus
1.2   207 n. 33
1.79   210 n. 39

Vidēvdād
19.15   54 n. 56

Attic *skolia*
10 Fabbro = 893 *PMG* 19
12 Fabbro = 895 *PMG* 19
15–6 Fabbro = 898–9 *PMG* 19 n. 31
17–8 Fabbro = 900–901 *PMG* 19 n. 31

Bacchylides
3.23–62	23
3.57–58	28
17.117–118	28
19.37 f.	20
fr. 20b	29

Avesta
Yasna
1.3 54 n. 56
2.3   54 n. 56

Index locorum

Caesar
Civ.
3.90.1 — 221

Gal.
1.6 — 227
1.6.4–1.7.1 — 227
1.7 — 227
1.18.2 — 224
1.18.10–19.2 — 228
1.20.5 — 223
1.21–29 — 229 n. 30, 230, 237
1.22.1 — 223
1.23.2 — 223–224
1.25.1 — 230, 237
1.29.1 — 222 n. 13
1.32–47 — 225, 230
1.48–54 — 226, 229 n. 30, 230, 237
1.51.3 — 231, 237
2.20.1 — 221
2.21 — 221 n. 8
2.25 — 221 n. 8
7.1.6 — 223 n. 16
7.20.8–12 — 222 n. 13
7.22–31 — 229 n. 30, 237
7.26 — 231 n. 31
7.27.3 — 231, 237
7.32.1–2 — 228
7.43.4–53 — 229 n. 30, 237
7.43.5 — 226, 232
7.45.7–10 — 233, 237
7.47.1 — 233 n. 35
7.47.3 — 233
7.52–53.1 — 233
7.57–62 — 229 n. 30, 237
7.62.2 — 234
7.63.8 — 229
7.66–67 — 229 n. 30
7.66.2–3 — 234–235
7.66.7 — 235
7.67 — 235
7.68–90 — 229 n. 30
7.68.1 — 235
7.77.1 — 236 n. 37
7.77.1–16 — 236 n. 37
7.86.3 — 235, 237

Callinus
frr. 2–2a W² — 13 n. 9

Cicero
Att.
10.10.6 — 129 n. 49

Balb.
51 — 221 n. 8

De Orat.
2.342–348 — 286 n. 55

Colapesce — 25

Cornelius Nepos
Han.
11.1 — 221 n. 8

Ctesias
fr. 13.14 Lenfant — 46 nn. 24–25

Dante
Inferno XXVIII 142 — 46

Demetrius
Eloc.
36 — 104 n. 10
112–113 — 104–105
209 — 190 n. 14

Demosthenes
1–6 — 148
3.21 — 148
3.23–24 — 148
3.36 — 148
5.9–10 — 148
6.11 — 148
8–10 — 148
8.49 — 148
9.41 — 148 n. 13
9.74 — 148 n. 13
10.15 — 148
10.46 —
10.73 —
11.21–22 — 148 n. 13
12.22 — 148 n. 13

13–16	148	3.13.2–3	185, 190
13.12	148 n. 14	3.13.3	186
14.1	148	3.14.1–2	190–191
14.29	148 n. 13	3.14.1	185
14.30	148 n. 13	3.14.4–5	185
14.40	148 n. 13	3.14.5	186–187, 197
14.41		3.21.5	188
15.33	148 n. 13	3.33.7	189
15.35	148 n. 13	3.34	189
18.99	148	3.39.5	194 n. 18
18.258–260	151 n. 22	3.40	192–195
21	148	3.40.7	194 n. 18
21.153	148	3.40.7–8	193–194
21.156	148	3.40.8	194
21.161	148	5.35–38	188, 192–195
27.7	148	5.35.4	193
27.9–11	148	5.36.3	193
30.15–17	148	5.38.1	192–193
40.25	151	5.38.2	193

Dio Cassius

Diogenes Laertius

37.52.2	203 n. 19	1.96	210 n. 42
44.50	206 n. 28		
55.31.1	264 n. 40	**Dionysius of Halicarnassus**	
57.3.1	263 n. 36	*Amm.*	
57.4.1	263 n. 36	2.2	100 n. 3, 101 n. 4, 102
57.5.1	263n. 36		
58.11.6	284 n. 50	*Comp.*	
59.22.5	264 n. 40	21–24 101 n. 5	
60.15.1–4	264 n. 40	22	101 n. 5, 106 n. 14

Diodorus Siculus

Dem.

1.1.3	195	37–41	101
2.51–53	195	39	101–102, 106 n. 14
2.52.9	187		
2.53.4–7	187	*Pomp.*	
2.59.2	188 n. 7	3	107 n. 16
3.1–48	183		
3.12–14	184–192	*Th.*	
3.12.1	186	2	3
3.12.1–3	184	9	103 n. 9, 106, 107 n. 16, 108
3.12.2	187		
3.12.5	186	9–20	106 n. 15, 107
3.12.6	184–186	10–12	107
3.13.1	186	11	107
3.13.2	186	12	108 n. 17

13–20	107 n. 16	**Herodotus**	
20	121 n. 10, 122 n. 13	1.5	27 n. 67
23	102, 103 n. 7	1.12	11 n. 3
24	100 n. 3, 102	1.23	11 n. 3, 27 n. 65
36	126 n. 35	1.28–87	84 n. 40
41	125 n. 32	1.29–34	11 n. 3, 23
43–45	126 n. 38	1.29 ff.	27
44	127 n. 41	1.29–94	84 n. 39
45	126 n. 39	1.30–32	11
50–51	102	1.30	27 n. 66
		1.32–33	27
Euripides		1.32	23, 27
Hipp.		1.33	27
737–741	176 n. 51	1.73–74	29 n. 75
817–818	177 n. 55	1.86–87	23–25
875	177 n. 55	1.86	24–25
882–884	175 n. 44	1.118–119	29 n. 75
1090	177 n. 55	1.126.2	56
		1.201	80
IA		1.201–216	77
536	177 n. 55	1.202–203	79
		1.204.2	78
Ph.		1.205.2	78
349	30 n. 84	1.206.1	78
1335	177 n. 55	1.207	78
1346	177 n. 55	1.207.1–2	78
1599	177 n. 55	1.211	78, 80
		1.212.2	80
Supp.		1.214	80
298	30 n. 84	1.215–216	79
TrGF 122	177 n. 55	2.23	13 n. 11
TrGF 771–786	176 n. 51	2.53	13 n. 11
		2.113–20	13–14
Gorgias		2.113	13
Hel.		2.116	13 n. 11, 15
1	124 n. 26	2.117	13 n. 11
2	124 n. 24	2.118	14
fr. 6.2	125 n. 31, 132 n. 60	2.120	14
fr. 82 B 27 D.-K	114	2.135	11 n. 3
fr. 82 B 23 D.-K	169 n. 29	2.177	11 n. 3
		3.1	109 n. 19
Gyges Tragedy		3.16	39
P. Oxy. 2382 = TrGF Adespota 664	24 n. 43	3.16.5	49 nn. 34–35
		3.17–25	78
		3.24	79
		3.25	39
		3.25.3	39

3.25.6–7	78	4.83.1–2	78, 80
3.25.7	39	4.85–88	78
3.27–29	3, 28 n. 69, 37–71	4.94–96	79
3.27.1	39	4.97–98	78
3.27.3	49	4.97.1	78
3.28.1	63 n. 83	4.127.1–2	80
3.28.2f.	42	4.134–135	78
3.29.1	57	4.146	29 n. 76
3.29.1f.	63 n. 83	5.17–22	23, 28–30
3.29.2	41 n. 12	5.21.2	30
3.29.3	43–44	5.25	52
3.30–32	51	5.94	12 n. 7
3.30.1	49 n. 34	5.95	11 n. 3
3.31	50	5.102	11 n. 3
3.32.3	49 n. 34	5.113	11 n. 3
3.34.2f.	50	6.75f.	62 n. 79
3.35	50, 52	6.80	62 n. 79
3.35f.	51	6.84	51 n. 42
3.35.5	51	6.107	210 n. 42
3.37	39, 49 n. 35	6.131.2	147
3.37.2f.	63 n. 83	7.6	11 n. 3, 27 n. 65
3.38	11–12, 11 n. 3, 31	7.19	206 n. 25
3.40–43	23, 25–28	7.20.2	29 n. 79
3.40	26–27	7.43	56
3.43	26, 56	7.54.2	46
3.64	3, 28 n. 69, 37–71	7.61.1	46
3.64.3–5	61	7.114	51 n. 43
3.64.3	45	7.161	12 n. 7, 13 n. 11
3.64.4	49 n. 35	7.228	11 n. 3
3.65.7–66.1	39	9.111	29 n. 75
3.66.2	45		
3.66.3–67.1	52	**Hipponax**	
3.80–82	31	fr. 74 W^2	13
3.80.2	52	fr. 77 W^2	13
3.89.3	52	fr. 104 W^2	23
3.121	11 n. 3, 27	fr. 128 W^2	13
3.122	26, 28		
3.134–136	78	**Homer**	
4.1–142	78	*Il.*	
4.1–13	79	2.453	113
4.1.1	78	2.453–454	113 n. 31
4.16–31	79	2.607	174 n. 42
4.29	13 n. 11, 18	3.278	111
4.32	13 n. 11	4.440–443	112 n. 30
4.36–45	79	4.442	112 n. 30
4.46.2–3	80	4.450–451	114 n. 32, 115
4.59–80	79		

4.539	112	*IG* ii³ 316	154
4.539–544	112 n. 30		
6.145–211	150 n. 18	*IG* ii² 356	154
6.289–92	14–15		
6.448–449	249 n. 24	*IG* ii³ 358	154
10.401	111		
22.408–410	114 n. 33, 115	*IG* ii³ 361	154
22.409	114		
22.410	115	*IG* ii² 365	154

Od.

		IG ii³ 375	154
3.261	112 n. 28		
4.85	18	*IG* ii³ 399	154
4.227–30	14–15		
5.351–2	14–15	*IG* ii³ 413	154
11.474	111 n. 28		
19.172–173	104	*IG* ii² 1613	148
		IG ii² 2318	147

Ibycus

PMGF S151	15

Inscription of Behistun (DB)

I § 10 (1.26–35)	52 n. 46
IV § 70 (4.89–92)	53 n. 54

Inscriptions

IG i³ 97	151

Isaeus

5.40–42	151

IG ii² 17	153
IG ii² 31	153

Isocrates

7.56	146 n. 2
13.7–8	124 n. 27
16.4–38	151 n. 23
16.34	146 n. 1

IG ii² 79	153
IG ii² 110	154
IG ii² 172	154
IG ii² 181	154

Josephus
Vit.

54–57	61 n. 78

IG ii² 187	154

Licymnius of Chios

fr. 772 *PMG*	23

IG ii² 206	154
IG ii² 234	154

Longinus
On the Sublime

15.2	168, 176 n. 48

IG ii³ 294	154
IG ii² 304	154

Lucan
7.9–28	204 n. 22

Lysias
19.47	147 n. 8
26.21–22	151

Marcellinus
Vit. Thuc.
35	106, 110 n. 23
37	110–111
53	106 n. 14, 109 n. 22
56	129 n. 53
57	110 n. 22, 128 n. 47

Mimnermus
fr. 2 W^2	20
fr. 6 W^2	19
fr. 9 W^2	13 n. 9
fr. 13a W^2	
fr. 13a.1 W^2	12 n. 8, 13 n. 9
fr. 14 W^2	12 n. 8, 22

Palaephatus
1.5–9	136 n. 72
1.9–2.3	136 n. 73
2.4–6	136 n. 75
2.5–9	138 n. 81

Pausanias
4.4.2 f.	29 n. 76
1.17.3	26

Photius
Bibl.

cod. 250
447b21–449a10	187 n. 5
456b39–457a10	195 n. 19

Phylarchus (*FGrHist* 81)
F1	177 n. 52
F2	170 n. 32
F3	170
F4a	171
F6	172
F7	170
F11	177 n. 52
F12	170, 177 n. 52
F13	170
F16	171, 172 n. 33
F17	171, 172 n. 33
F18	176
F20	172
F21	177 n. 52
F23	171
F24	170 n. 31, 177 n. 52
F26	171
F27	171, 172 n. 33
F28	171, 172 n. 33
F32a	171, 172 n. 33
F32b	171, 172 n. 33
F33	172 n. 34
F34	172
F35b	171
F36	171
F40	177
F41	177 n. 52
F45	171
F49	173 n. 39
F61a,b	171
F63	171
F64a	172 n. 33
F64b	172 n. 33
F65	171
F69	171, 172 n. 33
F70	172 n. 33
F71	171, 172 n. 33
F74	173
F79a	171, 172 n. 33
F79b	171, 172 n. 33
F83	171

Pindar
O.
1.52–53	20
2.86–88	20
6.21	21 n. 33
6.73	21 n. 33
7.20–21	20–21
13.8	21 n. 33

Index locorum — 315

P.
1.94 — 23
2.86–88 — 31
4.143 — 29 n. 82
4.277–279 — 17

N.
6.8
7.17–23 — 17
9.13 — 29 n. 82
10.64 — 112 n. 28

I.
4.37–39 — 17
5.46–50 — 21
5.48 — 21
fr. 52 h S.-M — 16 n. 26
frr. 120–121 S.-M — 29
fr. 121.4 S.-M — 30
fr. 169a S.-M — 12, 31

Plato
Ion
535b1–c8 — 166–167

Phdr.
234d1–6 — 167

R.
2.381d5–7 — 162 n. 12
8.559a3–4 — 122 n. 16
9.574d–575a — 210 n. 42
10.595c1–3 — 166 n. 22
10.598d7–8 — 166 n. 22
10.605c–d — 166 n. 20
10.607a2–3 — 166 n. 22

Smp.
201b1 — 122 n. 15

Pliny
Ep.
1.18 — 286 n. 56

Nat.
5.75 — 61 n. 78

Plutarch
Alc.
11.2 — 146 n. 1

Alex.
1.1–3 — 281 n. 43
1.2–3 — 200 n. 2
1.2 — 287 n. 59

Brut.
20.5–6 — 213 n. 50

Caes.
32.8–9 — 203 n. 18
42.1–2 — 205 n. 23
63.5 — 190 n. 14, 207 n. 32
64.4 — 207 n. 31
66.1 — 214 n. 52
68.2 206 n. 29

Cam.
19 — 173

Dem.
2.2 — 203 n. 16

De virtutibus molierum
18.255a–e — 29 n. 75

Mor.
34b4–34d1 — 196–197
255a–e
348b11–c8 — 169 n. 29
355c — 64 n. 85
363c — 64 n. 85
850f–851b — 151 n. 21
855c–856d — 200 n. 4

Nic.
3.1 — 147 n. 8
11.2 — 147 n. 8
15.2 — 147 n. 8

Pomp.
32.4 — 213 n. 49
68.2 — 205 n. 24, 213

Sol.

8.5	29 n. 76
26.1	27 n. 66

Polyaenus

4.15	177 n. 53

Polybius

2.16.13	176–177
2.56–63	160 n. 8
2.56.6	174 n. 41
2.56.7	166, 177
2.56.7–8	160 n. 2
2.56.8	175
2.56.9	160 n. 7
2.56.10	162
2.56.11	163
2.56.13	163, 166
2.56.14	166 n. 19
2.58.9	159 n. 2
2.58.12	159 n. 2
2.59.1–3	174
2.59.5	175
2.60.8	175 n. 43
3.4.4–6	164
3.43.7–8	179
3.48.8	194 n. 18
4.2.3	173 n. 38
5.48.5–10	164–165
8.15.21	178
8.16.4	178 n. 58
8.21.6	178
10.21.2–4	200 n. 2
15.19.1–3	243 n. 8
15.25–33	163 n. 16
16.12.9	173 n. 37
16.7	163 n. 16
16.30–34	163 n. 16
18.25.1	179
23.10–11	163 n. 16
29.5.3	165
34.4.1–5	163 n. 17
36.5–7	6 n. 15
38.1–4	163 n. 16
38.16.7	163 n. 16
38.20	163 n. 16

Quintilian

3.8.49	132 n. 59
6.2.32	190 n. 14
8.3.63–69	190 n. 14
8.3.67	190 n. 14
12.1.28	221 n. 8

Sallust

Cat.

51–52	242 n. 6

Jug.

9.2.1	222 n. 13
25.5.23	

Sappho

fr. 16 V	15, 20

Scholia in Homerum

Il. 4.450 (1, 523, 62–65 Erbse) 114

Il. 22.410 (5, 343, 47–48 Erbse) 115

Il. 16.280 (4, 229, 74–77 Erbse) 115 n. 36

Il. 21.9b (5, 124, 62–63 Erbse) 115 n. 36

Il. 23.144 (5, 392, 36–393,42 Erbse) 115 n. 36

Scholia in Pindarum

O. 2.157–158 Drachmann 20 n. 32

Scholia in Thucydidem

1.25.4 (28.7–11)	110 n. 25
1.33.2 (35.4–6)	110 n. 25
1.89.3 (71.13–15)	110 n. 25
1.109 (82.4)	115 n. 36
2.11.4 (117.15–16)	112 n. 30
2.47.3 (140.2–7)	110 n. 25
3.3.3 (164.12–15)	110 n. 25
3.4.1 (164.25–27)	110 n. 25
3.40.8 (190.17–20)	110 n. 25
3.42.4 (191.24–26)	110 n. 25
3.59.2 (201.12–14)	111
4.64.3 (262.2–4)	105 n. 12

6.8.4 (331.10–12)	111
6.24.3 (340.25–26)	112–113
7.71.4 (401.26–29)	114
7.71.6 (402.2–4)	114–115
P. Oxy. 6.853 coll. I, 7–III, 35	109 n. 22
P. Oxy. 6.853 col. VII, 9–11	112

Simonides

frr. 10–18 W^2	12 n. 8, 15
fr. 11.15–21 W^2	15–16
fr. 13a.1 W^2	
fr. 16 W^2	21–22
fr. 261 Poltera	21
fr. 261.5–9 Poltera	21

Solon

fr. 20 W^2	19–20
fr. 28 W^2	27 n. 66
fr. 33 W^2	20

Sophocles

Aj.

981	177 n. 54

Ant.

1211	177 n. 54

OC

753	177 n. 54
847	177 n. 54
1266	121 n. 8
1338	177 n. 54
1401	177 n. 54

Ph.

744	177 n. 54
TrGF 710	176 n. 50

Stesichorus

PMGF 192	15, 20
PMGF 210	20

Strabo

8.337	174 n. 42

Suda

α 3201	64 n. 85

Suetonius

Cal.

3.5	279 n. 34
8.2–5	281 n. 44
8.2	281 n. 45
8.6	281–282
8.11	283 n. 46, 284 n. 48
10.7–10	282

Cl.

1.8–10	279
9.1	264 n. 40
25.15	273 n. 19
29.1	273
29.2	274

Dom.

12.5–6	276
12.6	276 n. 25

Jul.

7.2	203
32.2	204 n. 21
50.1–52.6	285 n. 53
68.7	279 n. 33
81.8	212 n. 48
85.2	206 n. 28

Nero

13.1	279 n. 32
52.3	277–278

Otho

10.1–4	276–277
12.5	279 n. 34

Tib.

25.1–2	263 n. 36

Ves.

1.2	275 n. 24
1.3	275 n. 24
1.7–8	275

Index locorum

Tacitus
Ag.
30–34	242 n. 6

Ann.
1.4.3–5	259 n. 21
1.4.3–4	259
1.4.3	256
1.5.4	256
1.7.6	262, 263 nn. 35–36
1.7.7	262 n. 31
1.11–14	256
1.16.1	256, 258, 262, 267
1.17.4	266
1.22.1	266
1.28.2	266
1.28–29	257
1.31.1	257, 258 n. 17, 260, 263
1.31.2	255 n. 9
1.31.5	263
1.32.1	266
1.32.2	260 n. 26
1.33	262 n. 33
1.33.1	263
1.33.2	259 n. 21, 263 n. 37
1.34.1	266
1.34.2	266
1.34.4	260 n. 23
1.35.3–4	263
1.35.3	257
1.36.1	260
1.41.2	260
1.49.1	257, 265 n. 45
1.49.3–71	261
1.51.1	257
1.52.1	259
1.56.1	255 n. 9
1.61–62	255
1.64–65	255
1.66.2	255 n. 9
1.69.1–4	262
1.72.1	255 n. 9
1.78.2	262 n. 33
2.5.1–2	262 n. 33
2.5.2–26	261
2.13.1	260 n. 24
2.26.2–5	262 n. 33
2.26.4	261
2.26.5	263
2.42.1	262 n. 33
2.43.4–6	262 n. 33
2.53–61	261
2.57.4	259 n. 22
2.59.1–2	262
2.59.2	262 n. 33
2.69–72	261
2.72.2	258 n. 15
2.82.2	279 n. 34
3.2.2	259 n. 18
3.3	262 n. 33
3.52.1	259 n. 19
4.8.1–2	258 n. 15
4.11.1–3	283–284
4.39–40	242 n. 6
6.51.3	259 n. 20
14.16.1	278 n. 30
15.74.2	264 n. 40

Hist.
1.4–11	258
1.4.2	258, 265
1.5.5	257
1.6.1	257, 259 n. 19
1.7.1	257
1.7.2	259 n. 21
1.7.3	259 n. 21
1.8.1	260 n. 23
1.9.1	257, 260
1.11.3	258
1.13.4	260 n. 24
1.14–16	257
1.14.1	257, 260
1.18.3	259 n. 19
1.21.1	257
1.22.1	259, 259 n. 22
1.23.1	259
1.24.1	266
1.26.1	257, 260, 266
1.33.2	260 n. 24
1.37.4	259
1.41.2	257
1.45.1	257, 266
1.46.3–4	266
1.49.2–4	259

1.49.2	259 n. 20	1.22.1	151
1.50.1	257	1.22.1–2	120 n. 2
1.51.2	266	1.22.1–3	123 n. 21
1.51–70	257	1.56–65	87
1.51.3	260 n. 23	1.56.2	89
1.52–55	260	1.57.1	92
1.52.2	260	1.57.4	89
1.52.3–4	264 n. 39	1.57.6	92
1.53.1	255 n. 9	1.58.1	91
1.55.4	266	1.60.1	89
1.62.2	260	1.61.3	92
1.80–84	257	1.63.1	92 n. 54
1.82.1	266	1.64.1	89
1.82.2	266	1.80–85	149
1.83.1	267	1.86	153
2.39–45	256 n. 12	1.89.1	147
2.46.1–49.4	277 n. 27	1.140–144	147
2.49.3	266	1.144	147
2.51	264 n.39	2.11	149
2.59.2	260	2.11.4	112 n. 30
2.68.4	264 n. 39	2.11.7	112
2.70	255	2.23.2	76
2.76.2	263 n. 35	2.29	3
3.25–34	256 n. 12	2.60–64	126, 147
3.54.2–3	277 n. 28	2.62	147
4.12–37	264 n. 40	2.71f.	126
4.54–79	264 n. 40	2.80–82	87
5.14–26	264 n.40	2.80.1	88
5.14.2–15.2	255	2.81.8	88
		2.83f.	89
Theon Rhetor		2.83–84	89
Prog.		2.84.2	122 n. 17
6	136 n. 70	2.87	81
10	131 n. 55	2.95–101	75–82, 188 n. 8
79.20–21	103 n. 9	2.95	75
80.8–10	103–104	2.95.1–2	81
80.12–26	103 n. 9, 109 n. 20	2.96	75, 81
81.8–10	103–104	2.96.3–4	81
86.7–20	108–109	2.97	75
		2.98	75
Thucydides		2.98.1	78
1.1	29 n. 79	2.98.4	81
1.3–4	3	2.99	75, 79
1.10.3–4		2.100	75
1.21–22	3–4	2.101	75
1.21.1	119, 136 n. 77	2.101.2–4	81
		2.101.5	78

Index locorum

2.101.5–6	78, 81	4.108.3	91
3.2–19	88	4.108.6	91
3.2.3	91–92	4.108.7	83
3.3.1	88, 90, 92	5.15–16	82–86
3.4.3	90	5.15.2	83
3.4.5	91	5.29.1	90
3.5.2	92	5.29.2	88
3.10.4	90	5.29.3	90
3.11.2	90	5.30.1	92
3.11.6	90	5.32.3	88
3.12.1	90	5.32.3–4	88
3.12.3	92	5.32.4	90
3.13.1	90, 92	5.38.3	90
3.13.7	88	5.40.1	90
3.14.2	90	5.40.3	90
3.25–51	88	5.43	150
3.33.2	90	5.44.3	90
3.36.6	152	5.45–48	150
3.37–40	152 n. 29	5.50.4	81 n. 30
3.41	146	5.57.1	92
3.44.4	152	5.61.5	90
3.53–59	111	5.85–111	125
3.55.3	122 n. 18	6.8.4	111
3.59.2	111	6.9–23	147, 246 n. 15
4.3–5.11	82–86	6.9–14	147
4.3.1	83	6.12.2	145
4.12.3	83	6.15.4	153
4.14.3	83	6.16	145
4.15	83	6.16.1–3	145
4.17	83	6.20–23	135 n. 69, 147
4.21.2	83	6.24.3	112
4.27.2	83	6.33–40	149
4.53–56	83	6.68	135 n. 69
4.55–57	84	6.72.1	149
4.59–64	149 n. 17	6.76–80	149 n. 17
4.64.3	104–105, 105 n. 11	6.89.1	150
4.65.4	83	7.11–15	135 n. 69
4.78–88	88	7.71.4	113–114
4.79.2	90–91	7.71.5	113
4.84.2	90	7.71.6	113–115
4.88.1	90	7.75.5	115 n. 35
4.102–116	88	7.86.4	147 n. 8
4.104.5	92	8.1.1	90
4.105.1	90, 92	8.1.1–4	89–90
4.106.1	90	8.1.4	90
4.108.1	88, 90	8.1–24	86–94
4.108.1–3	88	8.6.3	87

8.7	89, 91–92	**Xenophanes**	
8.8.2	91	fr. 2 D.-K	13
8.9.1	92	frr. 10–13 D.-K	13
8.10.1	91		
8.11.3	89–90	**Xenophon**	
8.12	87	*Cyr.*	
8.12.1	92	1.2.13	46 n. 24
8.15.1	88, 91	8.3.11–24	56
8.17.2	92	8.3.33 f.	56
8.17.3	92		
		HG	
Timocreon		1.2.12	146 n. 3
fr. 10 W²	20	1.4.19	147
		1.7.16–33	147
Titus Livy		6.1.4	150
6.39–42	242 n. 4	6.1.4–17	150
21.40–44	242 n. 6	6.3.3	149
28.19.9	221 n. 8	6.3.4	149
30.30.31	242 n. 6	6.4	
30.44–45	243 n. 9	7.1.12–14	147
		Vect.	
Tyrtaeus		4.14	147 n. 8
fr. 5 W²	13 n. 9		
		Weidner Chronicle	
Vergil		48–55 (reverse 6–13)	59 n. 70
A.		65–68 (reverse 23–26)	59 n. 71
11.232–233	222 n. 13	72 f. (reverse 30 f.)	60 n. 73
12.620–623	222 n. 13		

www.ingramcontent.com/pod-product-compliance
Lightning Source LLC
Chambersburg PA
CBHW031722230426
43669CB00007B/215